MRS. HILL'S
Southern Practical Cookery
AND
Receipt Book

The Hills' House on Newnan (now Hill) Street
(Courtesy Danson Family Photo Collection,
Troup County Archives, LaGrange, Georgia)

MRS. HILL'S
Southern Practical Cookery
AND
Receipt Book

by Annabella P. Hill

A facsimile of *Mrs. Hill's New Cook Book*, 1872 edition, including a comparison of the changes made from the first edition plates

With a biographical sketch of the author and historical notes and glossary on the cookery by Damon L. Fowler

THE UNIVERSITY OF SOUTH CAROLINA PRESS

©1995 University of South Carolina

Cloth edition published by the University of South Carolina Press, 1995
Paperback edition published in Columbia, South Carolina,
by the University of South Carolina Press, 2011

www.sc.edu/uscpress

Manufactured in the United States of America

18 17 16 15 14 13 12 11 10 09   10 9 8 7 6 5 4 3 2 1

The Library of Congress has cataloged the cloth edition as follows:
Hill, A. P
  [Mrs. Hills new cook book]
  Mrs. Hill's southern practical cookery and receipt book / by
Annabella P. Hill ; with a biographical sketch of the author and
historical notes and glossary on the cookery by Damon L. Fowler.
     p. cm.
  "A facsimile of Mrs. Hill's new cook book, 1872 edition, including
a comparison of the charges made from the first edition plates."
  Includes bibliographical references and index.
  ISBN 1-57003-048-0
  1. Cookery, American—Southern style. 2. Confederate States of
America—Social life and customs. I. Fowler, Damon Lee. II. Title.
III. Title: Southern practical cookery and receipt book.
TX715.2.S66H55   1995
641.5975—dc20   95-5388
                                                                    CIP

ISBN: 978-1-57003-989-8 (pbk)

*For Martha Pink,
who brought Mrs. Hill home*

CONTENTS

Acknowledgments	ix
Historical Commentary	xiii
The Facsimile of *Mrs. Hill's New Cook Book*	1
Glossary	429
Appendix I: Notes on the Edition Used	445
Appendix II: Notes on the Original Introduction and Its Author	447
Bibliography	450

ACKNOWLEDGMENTS

WE Georgians owe many thanks to the University of South Carolina Press for bringing Mrs. Hill back into print. This charming book contains a wealth of information on our culinary heritage, and I am grateful to the editors for making it generally available and for helping me restore Mrs. Hill to what I believe is her rightful place in the history of American, and especially Southern, gastronomy.

I would also like to express my deep gratitude to my friend and teacher Karen Hess, not only for her support in championing this project but for her gentle guidance and generous sharing of her vast knowledge (not to mention library) of American culinary history. All of us owe Mrs. Hess a debt of gratitude for her tireless work in her field.

Thanks are due also to Dr. Willie Greer Todd, of Guyton, Georgia, and Mr. Forrest C. Johnson III, Troup County historian, who gave generously of their time and knowledge in helping me track down Mrs. Hill's family and personal history. The Georgia Historical Society and the Atlanta Historical Society were both generous and helpful in illuminating details. The research staff at the Savannah-Chatham Public Library were ever patient in helping with the collection and never tired of showing me (over and over) how to thread the microfilm projectors.

But I am especially grateful to my friend Martha Pink, who brought Mrs. Hill to my attention and generously allowed me to keep her own fragile first edition for the interminably long time it took for me to read it, study it in detail, compare it with other books, use it in the research of my own book, and, finally, to write the notes.

MRS. HILL'S
Southern Practical Cookery
AND
Receipt Book

HISTORICAL COMMENTARY

by Damon L. Fowler

In the history of American gastronomy, *Mrs. Hill's Southern Practical Cookery and Receipt Book* by Annabella P. Hill is seldom properly appreciated. Originally published by James O'Kane of New York in 1867 as *Mrs. Hill's New Cook Book*, this remarkable book is usually treated as a product of Reconstruction—in part because of the date and place of publication and in part because of its short introduction by the Rev. Ebenezer W. Warren. Yet even though the book was very influential during the last quarter of the nineteenth century as a record of cooking practice, its proper place is beside *The Virginia House-wife* (1824), *The Kentucky Housewife* (1839), and *The Carolina Housewife* (1847) as a major record of antebellum Southern cookery. Unfortunately, Mrs. Hill is seldom given that place, and so her importance for culinary historians is often underestimated. With this facsimile edition, the University of South Carolina Press places Mrs. Hill in her proper company and, we hope, will change some of those old perceptions. But before we tackle the weighty problem of properly placing Mrs. Hill's cookbook in history, it is essential that we understand a little about its author.

She was born Annabella Powell Dawson,[1] to Major John Edmonds and Annabella Burwell Dawson, in autumn of 1810. Her parents were Virginia natives who migrated to Georgia in 1802, settling first in Washington County and later in Morgan County on a plantation situated on Indian Creek, four miles from Madison. It was here that she was born and raised. The youngest of

---

1. On the 1850 and 1860 census, "Annabella" is spelled with only one *n*. A misreading of these records is probably the reason that she has been previously misidentified as "Arabella." Her signature (which survives) and other sources confirm the correct spelling is "Annabella."

five children, she was, by her own account, petted and spoiled by the entire family.[2]

Major Dawson was wealthy, socially prominent, and active in state politics. He had already served as the state representative for Washington County and, in 1811, was elected to the legislature in Morgan County. Sadly, he was not destined to serve; only two weeks after the election, the Major was taken unexpectedly ill and died. He was only thirty-six.[3]

The five Dawson children, including young Annabella, were later sent to boarding school in Madison. Mrs. Dawson eventually remarried, but her second husband, Mr. D. W. Porter, died in 1823, and John Edmonds, Jr., being the eldest child, came home to look after the family plantation.[4]

After completing her education, Annabella met Edward Young Hill, a promising young lawyer from South Carolina who was solicitor general on the Ocmulgee circuit in Jasper County (adjacent to Morgan County). They married on December 12, 1827,[5] and settled in Monticello, where Mr. Hill was elected to the bench of the circuit court.

The marriage was a fruitful one: the Hills had eleven children. But the infant mortality rate in those days was high; four of the children died in infancy, and still another before her fifth birthday. Their surviving children were Edward Young, Jr. (1833–1862), Beatrice H. (born 1837), Mary Reese (1838–1873), John Dawson (1839–1862), Annabella Martha (1843–1853), and Charles Montgomery (born in LaGrange, 1848).[6]

---

2. A[nnabella] P[owell] Hill, *The Life and Services of Rev. John E. Dawson, D.D.* (Atlanta: J. J. Toon, 1872), 11.

3. Charles C. Dawson, *A Collection of Family Records with Biographical Sketches and Other Memoranda of Various Families and Individuals Bearing the Name Dawson, or Allied to Families of That Name* (Albany, N.Y.: Joel Munsell, 1874), 386. The material on Mrs. Hill's father, brothers, and immediate family in this book is particularly useful because most of it was provided by Mrs. Hill herself.

4. Hill, *The Life and Services of Rev. John E. Dawson, D.D.*, 14.

5. Jasper County marriage records.

6. Dawson, *A Collection of Family Records*, 390.

Judge Hill was not only developing a promising legal career; for a time he represented Jasper County in the state senate and the house of representatives. In 1845, he was elected to the superior court of the Cowetta Circuit, and the family moved to LaGrange, Georgia, the seat of Troup County. They settled in a handsome two-story, columned house on Newnan Street,[7] which Troup County historians believe they may have built. The household must have been a lively one. Besides six children, the 1850 census reveals that there were ten students boarding in their household—a boy, aged seventeen, and nine girls ranging in age from eighteen to nine. The Hills were also socially prominent and well-known in the community for their hospitality.

As the family grew, the Hills' property expanded as well. Aside from the Newnan Street house, Judge Hill maintained a plantation six miles outside town on Franklin Road and briefly shared interest in an Alabama plantation with the Rev. John Edmunds Dawson (Mrs. Hill's eldest brother) across the Chatahoochee River from Columbus. Eventually, the continuing war with the Indians and failed crops made the project unworkable, and the farm was sold.[8]

Aside from their position in the community, the Hills were active in Georgia Baptist circles and were involved in education (as is hinted by the 1850 census). This connection with education later served Mrs. Hill well in the lean years that followed the War Between the States. Meanwhile, Judge Hill continued to take an active interest in state politics. In 1849, he allowed himself to be nominated to stand as the minority Republican party's candidate for governor, and in 1850, he chaired the statewide convention at Milledgeville.[9] He was never elected gover-

---

7. Newnan Street was later renamed Hill Street in honor of Judge Hill and his son, Capt. Edward Y. Hill, Jr. See Clifford L. Smith, *History of Troup Count* (Atlanta: Foote and Davies, 1933), 279.

8. *History of the Baptist Denomination in Georgia* (Atlanta: Jas. P. Harrison for *The Christian Index*, 1881), 183.

9. Johnson, Forrest Clark III, *Histories of LaGrange and Troup County, Georgia*, vol. 3 (LaGrange: Family Tree) 335. Mrs. Hill also outlined her

nor, and his seat on the superior court appears to have been his last public office. He voluntarily retired from the court in 1853 to return to private practice. In November of 1860, he suffered what was probably a stroke while delivering an anti-secession speech at the courthouse. His condition deteriorated rapidly, and he died a few days later, on November 20. He was fifty-five.[10]

The 1860 census reveals that the Hills' nest was practically empty by the time of the Judge's death. Of their five surviving children, only John and Charles were still living at home. Little Annabella had died on June 21, 1853.[11] The two elder daughters were by then married. Edward had finished his education and become editor of the *LaGrange Reporter;* John was beginning a career as a civil engineer.[12] Judge and Mrs. Hill sold their large house on Newnan Street in 1857 and moved to smaller quarters on Greenville Road.[13]

In the spring following Judge Hill's death, Georgia seceded from the Union and was plunged into war. Despite the family's anti-secessionist sentiments, Edward, Jr., and John both enlisted in the Confederate army. Both were killed in the Virginia

---

husband's political career in the material she provided Charles Dawson (see Dawson, *A Collection of Family Records*, 389–90). I take particular pains with Judge Hill's political career because I have seen Mrs. Hill's broad knowledge of cookbooks explained away as having resulted from her living in Washington while her husband was a senator. I can find no record of his ever having been elected to the United States Senate or Congress, and surely this would have been an accomplishment that Mrs. Hill would have mentioned. I can only surmise that Judge Hill is being confused with Benjamin H. Hill, who was also from LaGrange. But Sen. Hill was in no way related to Judge and Mrs. Hill.

10. Dawson, *A Collection of Family Records*, 390.

11. A grave marker in the family plot, Hill View Cemetary, LaGrange.

12. Dawson, *A Collection of Family Records*, 391. Confirmed by the 1860 census.

13. According to F. C. Johnson, Troup County historian, who cites county deed records.

campaigns of 1862 within only three months of one another.[14] In short, Mrs. Hill's days as a housekeeper were effectively ended in the winter of 1860–61.

In the aftermath of the war, Mrs. Hill remained in LaGrange at least until the end of 1866, where she executed her last will and testament in late October. The following year, the cookbook—which appears to be her only endeavor in food writing— was published. Mrs. Hill's fortunes were, like those of most widows of the day, considerably reduced. She had been forced to sell the Greenville Road house almost as soon as the war ended (November 1865) and gave up the Franklin Road plantation in 1870.[15] Sometime between the end of 1866 and 1870 (one source says 1867),[16] she moved to Atlanta to become principal of the Orphans' School (established in 1866 by the State Lottery Board). I have not been able to confirm the exact date, and whether she had already moved to Atlanta by that time isn't clear. The first Atlanta city directory listing I have found is 1872, where she is listed as boarding with Mrs. Overby. Her youngest son, Charles, survived the war (having been too young to fight until the very end) and became a physician. He lived briefly in Atlanta[17] and eventually moved to California,[18] leaving his mother's care to his widowed sister Beatrice.

The Orphans' School occupied Mrs. Hill full-time until shortly before her death.[19] However, she did find time for at

---

14. Dawson, *A Collection of Family Records*, 391.

15. *The LaGrange Reporter*, November 3, 1865, p. 3, and November 4, 1870, p. 1.

16. Franklin Garret, *Atlanta and Environs: A Chronicle of Its People and Events* (New York: Lewis Historical Publishing, 1954), 1:753.

17. Dawson, *A Collection of Family Records*, 390.

18. Clerk of court record attached to the Last Will and Testament of Mrs. Annabella P. Hill, Fulton County Probate Court, December 1878.

19. *Sholes' Directory of the City of Atlanta, for 1877* (Atlanta: A. E. Sholes, Sunny South Publishing House, 1877), 189. A revision to Mrs. Hill's will, dated March 10, 1877, indicates that Mrs. Hill was still due an income from the Lottery Board. According Garrett (*Atlanta and Environs*, 754), the lottery was discontinued on February 24 of that year.

least one other literary effort. In 1872, she published a biography of her adored elder brother, *The Life and Services of Rev. John E. Dawson, D.D.* This effort, coupled with her professional responsibilities at the school, is probably the main reason that, unlike Mary Randolph (*The Virginia House-wife*) and Sarah Rutledge (*The Carolina Housewife*), Mrs. Hill made few changes and no real additions to her cookbook. Though the 1875 edition is listed as revised and improved, the changes were actually minimal. The same plates were used for the printing, and the copyright was not even renewed. In 1877, she retired from the school, presumably due to failing health, and she died in Atlanta on January 2, 1878. (This date is taken from the affadavit filed in probate court. An obituary in the *Christian Index* gives the date as January 28. The affidavit is handwritten and crumbling, so part of the date could be missing.)

We know little of Annabella Hill's personality and temperament beyond her writing. Speculating on her nature is, of course, of little interest to historians, but the facts do shed some light on it and suggest that her guiding maxim—"nothing is wise that is not practical"—is probably a fair assessment of her sensibilities. The real importance of these facts lies in what they help us understand about the cookbook. First, it must be noted that—though her family was well-off, with genteel Virginia roots, and she married into the small, but significant, professional class—Mrs. Hill was by no means an old-line aristocrat. Moreover, her world was that of rural, almost frontier, western Georgia. LaGrange, founded well after Mrs. Hill was born, was a young town, a wholly different world from the old, aristocratic cities and social circles that Mary Randolph and Sarah Rutledge had known. Another distinctive fact is that, as best as can be determined, Mrs. Hill never lived outside central and western Georgia. Finally, and significantly, Mrs. Hill's prime years as a housekeeper were the three decades between 1830 and 1860—the late antebellum period. Reinforcing this fact is the reality that she sold off her kitchen furniture along with the Greenville Road house in 1865.[20] All of these factors are critical

---

20. *The LaGrange Reporter*, November 3, 1865, p. 3.

HISTORICAL COMMENTARY   xix

in helping us understand the kitchen, temperament, customs, and outside influences that shaped Mrs. Hill as a cookery writer.

Now, having placed Mrs. Hill in time, let us return to her book and its place in history. Given the publication date and the tone of the Rev. Warren's short introduction to the book, there is a strong inclination to view Mrs. Hill's cookbook primarily as a Reconstruction-era document. And certainly it must be said that Mrs. Hill was an influential figure during Reconstruction: her book remained in print for three decades (I know of at least eight editions) and was widely used. Copies of it have been found in kitchens as far away as Maine. Its recipes turn up in later books such as the *Carolina Rice Cook Book* (Charleston, 1901), the *Texas Cook Book* (Houston, 1883), the *Ever Ready Cook Book* (Savannah, n.d.), the *Tested Recipe Cook Book* (Atlanta, 1895), and the *Picayune Creole Cook Book* (New Orleans, 1900). Given those facts, some have been tempted to view Mrs. Hill strictly from her role in the reconstructed South and to dismiss her old-fashioned recipes and cooking traditions as merely nostalgic longing for departed glory days. Perhaps her role as something of a bridge between two distinct eras in Southern social history may seem like the most important aspect of her book. But in the realm of culinary history, to limit Mrs. Hill in this way is to misunderstand her essential character and to overlook an important record of antebellum, and, to a lesser degree, of Georgia, cookery. There are many things that point in this direction.

First of all, it is important to realize that Mrs. Hill was of an older generation than most (if not all) of the other Reconstruction writers. She precedes Theresa Brown (1828–1899, *Theresa C. Brown's Modern Domestic Cookery*, 1871) by a full generation; Mary J. Waring (1851–1947, *The Centennial Receipt Book*, 1876) was young enough to be her granddaughter. Mrs. Hill's basic career as a housekeeper was ended before the Civil War had even begun, whereas most of the Reconstruction-era writers were only beginning theirs. In other words, far from merely trying to recall glories from bygone days, Mrs. Hill was simply writing from her own experience as a housekeeper—specifically, an antebellum housekeeper. This could not be said of the Misses Brown or Waring, nor of Mrs. Tryee (editor of *Housekeeping in Old Virginia,* 1879), nor of most of the other writers and editors of the flood of Reconstruction-era books that followed. Just as Mary Randolph's *The Virginia House-wife* is more reflective of cooking practice at the end of the eighteenth century (her heyday as a housewife), so Annabella Hill's book reflects on earlier practice—that is, from the 1830s, '40s and '50s.

Her cooking methods, which we will discuss later in more detail, bear this out: they were very old-fashioned by the standards of the 1870s and made few concessions to contemporary practice. Her roasts were still true roasts—spitted and cooked before an open fire, a practice that was already beginning to disappear with the coming of the cast-iron range. She did not, as Miss Brown did barely four years later, say that spit-roasting was the best way; she said it was the *only* way.[21] She was clear about the difference between baking and roasting meat; most Reconstruction writers (Miss Brown included) were already beginning to get these two methods hopelessly confused. And as for baking, Mrs. Hill continued to prefer her old-fashioned Dutch oven and mentioned the range oven almost as an afterthought. She made frequent use of muffin rings, as well—by the 1870s, this was very old-fashioned. That's to say nothing of her sparse use of such modern innovations as chemical leavenings (soda and baking powder), packaged gelatine (though she was partial to Cox's gelatine), and bottled condiments.

Another factor that we must consider is the length of time that would have been needed to write a book of this size. Given the devastating conditions in Georgia immediately following the war, it is inconceivable that Mrs. Hill could have begun the

---

21. Theresa C. Brown, *Theresa C. Brown's Modern Domestic Cookery* (Charleston, S.C.: Edward Perry, Printer, 1871), 32; A[nnabella]. P[owell]. Hill, *Mrs. Hill's New Cook Book* (New York: James O'Kane, 1867), 80–82. I do note that Miss Brown also advocates medium rare as opposed to Mrs. Hill, whose roasts would have been on the done side of medium. Within another generation, roasts were all cooked to death.

project any later than 1865, if that late. Even though there were recipes borrowed from other writers, as Mrs. Hill acknowledged, every one of them is rewritten in her own words, often with added observations from her own experience. This would have taken a great deal of time. And that's without considering the problem of paper: by 1863, the paper shortage throughout the Confederacy was critical, and it wasn't fully alleviated until well into the Reconstruction era.[22] The manuscript would have been a long one, and it seems doubtful that the bulk of it could have been written during the latter part of the war and the early Reconstruction. Anyone who has any experience at cookery writing knows that Mrs. Hill must have begun compiling recipes long before the book was sold and prepared for publication. Probably her own household notebook was the nucleus for the collection, fleshed out with borrowed material from what appears to have been an extensive cookbook collection. Her own preface and the Rev. Warren's introduction, which are so often used to date the book, would certainly have been written last, probably after the book was sold to O'Kane—at any rate, later than the recipes themselves.

One thing that supports this logic is that there were shortages other than paper to consider. Many commodities were in scarce supply during the war and in the years after it (at any rate until well after 1867),[23] yet Mrs. Hill made no concessions for them. There are only a few real war-era recipes such as "Confederate candles" in her book: most of her patriotically named recipes were actually old ones with new names. They offered no substitutes for scarce domestic items such as butter, wheat flour, and eggs, or imported goods such as sugar, coffee, tea, capers, and anchovies. She hardly mentioned sorghum syrup, a common substitute sweetener, and her "mock apple pie" was actually an old, prewar recipe for making a pie when apples were out of

---

22. Mary Elizabeth Massey, *Ersatz in the Confederacy: Shortages and Substitutes on the Southern Homefront* (Columbia: University of South Carolina Press, 1952), 139–46.

23. *Ersatz in the Confederacy*, 55–77.

season. It contained not only lemons, an imported commodity,[24] but also sugar, eggs, and butter—hardly a wartime recipe.

Another telling aspect of the book that must be considered is the outside influence on Mrs. Hill, that is, of other cookery writers. It is not generally appreciated how much English cooking and English cookbooks continued to influence American, and especially Southern, kitchens. Often, Mrs. Hill's fondness for English cookery writers is thought to be unusual, but actually it was not. Mrs. Webster (*The Improved Housewife*, 1838) remarked that American cookery had "mostly followed English practice," and English books continued to be quite popular in America. It was not at all uncommon for them to be reprinted in this country, sometimes under a different name and with added recipes designed to appeal to American audiences. (Mrs. Maria Eliza Rundell's popular and very influential *A New System of Domestic Cookery* [London, 1806], first published in Boston in 1807, saw numerous American editions published in Boston, New York, Philadelphia, and, significantly, Richmond. Beginning with the 1814 New York edition, according to Karen Hess, a number of distinctly American recipes were added. Mrs. Rundell was very popular in the South.)[25]

It should come as no surprise, then, that, of the authors whom Mrs. Hill mentioned by name, four were English. One of the most influential was Dr. William Kitchiner (1775–1827), author of *The Cook's Oracle*. Mrs. Hill called this book her "favorite text-book" and considered Dr. Kitchiner "the wisest and most reliable writer upon the subject of cookery I have ever read." *The Cook's Oracle* was first published in London in 1817. After 1822, there were American editions, though English copies had been (and continued to be) available. It was particularly popular with Southern households during the second quarter of the nine-

---

24. *Ersatz in the Confederacy*, 70. Citrus fruit was sporadically imported from Florida into Georgia during the war, but it was neither universally not regularly available.

25. Karen Hess, ed., *The Virginia House-wife* (Columbia: University of South Carolina Press, 1984), xx.

teenth century and continued to be of some influence after the war (Theresa Brown quoted Dr. Kitchiner frequently in *Modern Domestic Cookery*, 1871). Mrs. Hill indicated that she had used Dr. Kitchiner for more than thirty years in her kitchen, but whether hers was an English or early American edition we will probably never know.

Another writer whom Mrs. Hill referenced frequently was Alexis Soyer (1809–1858). Though French born and trained, Soyer made his reputation in London while chef at the Reform Club, and it was to an English audience that he directed his books, which included *The Gastronomic Regenerator* (1846), *The Modern Housewife, or Menagere* (1847), and *The Shilling Cookery Book* (1855). Soyer was also popular on this side of the Atlantic, especially in the South, and Mrs. Hill was not the only Southern cookery writer to quote him. An interesting thing to note about Soyer is that he and Mrs. Hill were essentially the same age, and his books were contemporary with Mrs. Hill's heyday as a housekeeper. We might not think it unusual for a housewife in Charleston, Savannah, or Richmond to have access to such current books (Miss Rutledge wrote that they were widely available in "any book shop"),[26] but that inland housewives such as Mrs. Hill should know them demonstrates to us that contemporary cookbooks were more widely circulated than is often supposed.

Not all of the European authors quoted by Mrs. Hill were English, nor were they, strictly speaking, cookery writers. Izaak Walton (1593–1683) authored *The Compleat Angler: Or, The Contemplative Man's Recreation* (1653), a book that was long considered the definitive work on fishing and was widely known. Mrs. Hannah More (1745–1833) was a popular English religious writer. There are also references to Count Rumford (Benjamin Thompson, 1753–1814), an American-born English physicist and diplomat who developed fuel-efficient iron cookstoves and to Baron Justus Von Liebig (1803–1873), a German chemist

---

26. Sarah Rutledge, *The Carolina Housewife, or House and Home*. (Charleston, S.C.: W. R. Babcock, 1847), iv.

whose studies on the chemistry of food and agriculture were published in *Chemistry and Its Application to Agriculture and Physiology* (1846). In her discussion of pineapples, Mrs. Hill quotes from "an old writer" whom she identifies only as Sturm, probably Johannes Sturm (1507–1589), a German author, educator, and classicist. The reference might be to Julius Sturm (1816–1896), a theologian and author of mostly religious poetry, though it seems unlikely since he was roughly Mrs. Hill's contemporary. The only other direct reference I have found is to an unnamed French writer on the subject of game cookery. This brings us to another important point about Mrs. Hill, who was probably the most literate of all the South's cookery writers. Obviously, this was an educated, well-read woman, interested not only in the art but also in the science of cooking. (A preoccupation with cooking as science later became an unhappy trend in American cookbooks.) Now, one might point to the Dawson family's involvement in education as an explanation, or even suggest that Annabella Hill must have traveled in order to have such a broad knowledge of books. But we know from her personal history that she never lived outside Georgia, and her traveling, such as it was, cannot have been extensive. The reality is that her education was not really unusual. Georgia (in fact, all the South) was dotted with female academies (Mrs. Hill's brother had been involved in two such institutions), and most young women of any standing at all were "finished" at boarding school, as Mrs. Hill had been. These schools provided a surprisingly well-rounded education.

Cookbooks used in the South were, of course, not limited to English, or even Southern, authors, and the ones used in Mrs. Hill's kitchen were not excepted. She credited three American writers by name, taking a recipe directly from Mary Randolph (1762–1828, *The Virginia House-wife*, 1824) and from Mrs. S. J. (Sarah Josepha) Hale (1788–1879), a prolific early nineteenth-century writer who edited Eliza Acton for American audiences and borrowed freely from Miss Acton and others in her own books—among them, *The Good Housekeeper* (1839) and *Mrs. Hale's New Cook Book* (1857). And there was at least one reference to Eliza Leslie, author of *French Domestic Cookery* (1832), *Directions for Cookery* (1837), and *Miss Leslie's New Cookery Book* (1857). Miss Leslie was one of America's best and most prolific food writers, and her works were widely used and respected in the South. Sarah Rutledge, in *The Carolina Housewife* (1847), recommended "Miss Leslie's excellent *Directions for Cookery*" to her readers for general-purpose kitchen instructions.[27] It is not unusual to find copies of Miss Leslie's several cookbooks in Southern collections. From time to time, one can detect her guiding hand in the structure and substance of Mrs. Hill's concise directions. (By the way, it is interesting, and possibly instructive, that the reference to Miss Leslie was taken from *Miss Leslie's New Cookery Book*, which came late in Mrs. Hill's career as a housewife.) There is also a minor reference to *Hints upon Cookery*, which book, and author, I have not been able to find. This might be a prefatory subtitle, as "House and Home" was of the 1855 edition of *The Carolina Housewife* and as was Mrs. Hill's "Housekeeping Made Easy"; Mrs. Hill and her contemporaries frequently referred to her book by this title. Or possibly it was a small, anonymous publication, for Mrs. Hill was generally careful about naming authors.

Many of the recipes suggest a knowledge of Sarah Rutledge's popular *The Carolina Housewife*. This influential book was widely used in Georgia, and it seems inconceivable that Mrs. Hill, with her extensive knowledge of cookery books, would not have known it. However, it was published anonymously; Miss Rutledge is not mentioned by name. Several of Mrs. Hill's recipes are virtually identical to Miss Rutledge's (see, for example, no. 134, "Rice Pillau" [p. 77] and no. 494, "Rice Waffles," [p. 224]), but such dishes were commonplace throughout South Carolina and Georgia. In that regard, it's hard to say where Miss Rutledge's direct influence ends and her record of common practice begins. At any rate, given Mrs. Hill's habit of rewriting recipes in her own words, it would be difficult to tell how much (if at

---

27. *The Carolina Housewife*, v.

all) *The Carolina Housewife* directly influenced her, even with a recipe-by-recipe comparison.

Borrowing from other cookbooks was commonplace among nineteenth-century cookery writers; in fact, outright plagiarism was not unusual. For example, Mrs. Webster (*The Improved Housewife*) lifted a number of recipes from Mary Randolph verbatim and apparently felt no scruples about not giving that lady credit. Mrs. Hill's carefulness in crediting borrowed material therefore makes her invaluable, even though she was often loose about which book she had used.

This borrowing from other cookbooks does not, however, mean that Mrs. Hill's book was lacking in personal or regional recipes. Regional lines in America, particularly the Mason-Dixon line, are not as sharply drawn as many Southerners would like to think, and cross-influences are common in all American cookery (witness Mrs. Webster's free borrowing from Mrs. Randolph). Aside from the fact that she often added her own observations, Mrs. Hill credited some thirty-two recipes to other sources by courtesy title and last initial—e.g., "Mrs. R's receipt for stewing fish." Given her conscientious practice of crediting authors by full name, it seems obvious that these were friends and neighbors—women who adhered to the old Southern custom that a lady's name did not properly appear in print. At any rate, none of the recipes credited to Mrs. R. and Mrs. H was from either Mrs. Randolph or Mrs. Hale. Moreover, Kitchiner and Soyer, though frequently mentioned, are seldom referred to by initial, and then only when they are mentioned more than once in the same passage. Mrs. Hill always gives their full names in the titles of their recipes. Perhaps the most telling thing about most of the recipes marked with initials is that they are distinctly regional. "Camp Stew—Mr. B.'s Receipt" (no. 111, p. 68), for example, is effectively the Georgia (as opposed to the Virginia) version of Brunswick stew. "Miss Matilda's Ginger Cakes" was probably a recipe from Matilda Chambliss, the Hills' white housekeeper.

No, it would be a mistake to discount Mrs. Hill as a chronicler of her own region's cookery on the basis of her borrowing from printed books. I do not mean to suggest that she was little affected by outside sources. The influence of others (especially Kitchiner) can certainly be felt in recipes other than those attributed to them by name, and several introductory passages are clearly unacknowledged quotations. However, it must be pointed out that direct attributions to others (including tables such as Soyer's roasting chart) account for less than 5 percent of the more than 950 culinary recipes.

Aside from all that, no American cook or cookery writer, regardless of region, works in a complete vacuum. Cross-influences between North and South were as common then as they are today, and the fact that Mrs. Hill was so conscientious in naming her sources actually tells us more, rather than less, about western Georgia kitchens. If nothing else, it enlightens us to the fact that even rural housewives (of a certain class) were more cosmopolitan than is generally supposed—and subject to cross-cultural influences.

Setting aside, then, the outside influences, let us look at another fascinating aspect of Mrs. Hill's culinary receipts—their many local, west-Georgia features. Mrs. Hill notes a colloquial name for peach cobbler as a "Cut and Come Again" pie (recipe no. 595, p. 252). This is a rare, archaic usage that I don't find elsewhere (in fact, she was still using "cobbler" in its more old-fashioned form, referring to a drink). She indicates that fried sweet potatoes are a breakfast dish (p. 195), a long-established practice in upstate families, and gives us a lovely recipe for sweet potato custard (no. 671, p. 276). Dressing Jerusalem artichokes as a salad (p. 179) was once an old Georgia favorite. Her seasoning combination for sausage meat—sage, cayenne, salt, and black pepper (no. 215, p. 121)—is still the standard in the region. Her basting sauce for barbeque (pp. 139 and 171) remained the usual one in Georgia until well after the turn of the century. Kid, or young goat (no. 153, p. 89), which today is seldom seen on American tables, was once not uncommon in northern and western Georgia (goat stew was one of my maternal grandmother's specialties), but as Mrs. Hill hinted, it was not as highly regarded as other meats. "Chambliss Pudding" (no. 611, p. 260) may be a recipe of the housekeeper, Matilda Chambliss, although there is a Georgia town by that name. These are only a few examples; a detailed list could go on at length without even mentioning such simple dishes as catfish stew, fried chitterlings, stewed greens, fried squash, scraffle (scrapple), and hog's head cheese. Though many of these dishes are pretty much universal in the South, their details often vary from region to region, and Mrs. Hill's recipes for these have a specifically Georgia twist. This is also true of a number of the breads, cakes, and other baked goods, but I do note that things like "Georgia Sponge Cake" (no. 713, p. 288) are actually "Georgia" in name only and vary little from the recipes for the same dish from other regions. The same is mostly true of the recipes which have been patriotically renamed for (mostly Georgia) war heroes.

Now, let us turn to the cookery itself and examine Mrs. Hill's culinary practice, kitchen, and pantry in more detail. In this regard, she stands at a pivotal point in American culinary history, for her technique and practice were of an older technology and sensibility—neither of which survived much beyond another generation.

Rural kitchens throughout the South in those days were almost invariably detached from the house. This was also true of in-town houses in small cities such as LaGrange. The heat, smoke, smells, and noise, not to mention the dangers from an open fire, were even bigger problems in the hot, humid climate of the Deep South than they were elsewhere. There were attached kitchens in urban centers such as Savannah, but they were exceptions rather than the rule. Unfortunately, few detached kitchens have survived unaltered.

Most detached kitchens were centered around an open fireplace, even those as late as Mrs. Hill's day. Cookstoves of a sort had been known in the eighteenth century, but they were not the same thing as ranges, and it was not until the advent of mass cast-iron production that the range began replacing the fireplace altogether. This displacement had already begun, at

HISTORICAL COMMENTARY   xxix

least in some places, by Mrs. Hill's time. According to Stephen Bohlin-Davis (curator of the Juliette Low birthplace), in urban centers such as Savannah, townhouses built as early as 1820 were equipped with a range from the start and may not have had an open fireplace in the kitchen at all. For a time, most were equipped with both range and hearth, much as early electric lights often had both gas and electric outlets. My own house, built in 1872, had both, but such arrangements were eventually abandoned. Of course, in rural areas, modern innovations were slow to be accepted, and there the hearth remained the center of the kitchen longer than it did elsewhere.

Most of Mrs. Hill's experience as a cook would have been in such a kitchen. There is no way of knowing this with absolute certainty: the Hill residence on Newnan Street was demolished in 1931[28] and had been occupied for nearly a century by other families. All we know for certain is that both the Newnan Street and Greenville Road houses had detached kitchens.[29] No record of these buildings' configurations or equipment in Mrs. Hill's day has survived. However, even though her list of essential equipment begins with a range, she mentions it in the recipes almost as an afterthought. Her instructions mostly dictate such older, open-hearth methods as true spit-roasting, broiling on a gridiron set over coals, baking in a Dutch oven (she even notes that the stove oven is inferior for certain kinds of cooking), and roasting potatoes in banked coals (p. 195). Few of these practices were to survive another generation. Real broiling is impossible on a wood-fired range. Though some early models did contain a brazier, such features were not common, and pan-broiling replaced true broiling until the advent of gas and electric ranges. The range of course, made the old-fashioned Dutch oven obsolete.

---

28. William H. Davidson, *Pine Logs and Greek Revival* (Alexander City, Ala.: Outlook, 1964), 106.

29. *The LaGrange Reporter*, November 3, 1865. Mrs. Hill's advertisement for the sale of the Greenville Road house indicated a detached kitchen. Photographs of the Newnan Street house survive in the Troup County Archives.

Mrs. Hill's kitchen very likely contained a "stove," but this was probably not a range. A "stove" in open-hearth days was a built-in row of stewing chambers (a sort of chafing dish affair recessed into a masonry shelf), sometimes called "stew-holes." Such stoves usually contained a drying chamber and sometimes even an oven. The confusion between "stove" and "range" arises from the latter part of the nineteenth century, when Americans began to use the two words interchangeably. That isn't to say that Mrs. Hill didn't own a range; she may have, but if so, it merely supplemented her hearth and did not replace it. So, in order to understand Mrs. Hill's culinary receipts, it is helpful to understand a few basics of open-hearth cookery.

Cooking at an open fireplace was an art unto itself and required of the cook a different level of skill than is necessary today. Though it was difficult, even dangerous, it was far from crude, and it offered much more control than modern cooks realize. Moreover, it lent certain nuances (the subtle fragrance of aromatic wood burning, for example), and there are some open-hearth methods that cannot be accomplished successfully with a modern range. For true roasting, there is no substitute for an open fire, to say nothing of broiling over live coals or of hearth roasting in ashes.

The arrangement of the kitchen hearth had changed very little in hundreds of years. For baking, those of wealthier households boasted dome-shaped brick ovens, which is the best bread-baking oven ever devised. Routine, everyday baking was done mostly in the Dutch oven, a cast-iron kettle set up on legs and equipped with a deep-rimmed lid. The oven was set over a bed of coals, and more coals were spread over the rimmed lid, creating an effective, evenly heated chamber. For simpler households, it was often the only oven. Firing and regulating the temperature of a brick or Dutch oven required an experience that befuddles most of us today, but a cook accustomed to relying on sight and feel rather than a thermostat had little trouble with it.

For other cooking, adjustable cranes and notched rods made it possible to control roasting temperatures and maintain a consistent simmer in a stewpot. For other stewing (and sometimes baking), some kitchens contained a stove, or "stew-holes," the chafing-dish type arrangement described above. Sometimes the hot stones of the hearth itself were used when the cook needed steady heat. For the most delicate cooking, such as finishing an egg-thickened sauce, there was the chafing dish, a tripod brazier that would hold a few glowing embers for gentle, even heat. The cook who did not have such a device could finish a sauce (such as melted butter) in a pan set over a kettle of simmering water. To aid the cook of even modest households, there were numerous tongs, toasting forks, waffle and wafer irons, and the salamander (see glossary, p. 438), for delicate browning.

Having established the basic workings of an open hearth, let us now look at some of Mrs. Hill's actual cooking practice in more detail. Even though the basic method of open-hearth cooking had changed little, tastes had not remained static, and Mrs. Hill reveals several distinct shifts in Southern preferences and practices.

One of the most notable of these is reflected in her lucid and detailed instructions for roasting. Of themselves, they are perfectly clear and require no further discussion. But though these directions make it clear that Mrs. Hill considered roasting to be superior to most other methods of meat cookery, they also reveal that its actual use in Southern kitchens was beginning to wane in favor of other methods, especially baking and frying. As the cast-iron range took over, the careful art of real roasting virtually disappeared. Within another generation after Mrs. Hill, it had all but vanished.

Another notable change is the degree of doneness to which meat was cooked. The early American preference was mostly for rare meat. In 1796, Amelia Simmons declared that "rare-done is the healthiest and the taste of this age."[30] This remained true into the early part of the nineteenth century. Mary Ran-

---

30. Amelia Simmons, *American Cookery* (Hartford: Hudson and Goodwin, 1796), 17.

dolph's roasts in *The Virginia House-wife* were generally rare. However, as early as Lettice Bryan's *The Kentucky Housewife*, the preference had begun to change. She directed that the juices from a roast should run clear, with no hint of "bloody juices" when it was pierced or cut.[31] Mrs. Hill invariably directed that the juices must run clear, and, while the taste for rare meat had not altogether vanished, she indicated how generally the taste had changed when she noted that "the rare appearance of meat of any kind is disgusting to persons of good taste." (p. 131).

Another change of particular note is in Mrs. Hill's use of liaisons. American cooking had continued to evolve since the days of our earliest cookery writers, such as Amelia Simmons and Mary Randolph. Both those ladies had depended mostly on the richness of the sauce to provide body, and such liaisons as they did use were melted butter, eggs, blood, or a handful of breadcrumbs—all of which were ancient, with medieval and even Roman antecedents. By Mrs. Hill's day, these liaisons were falling into disuse. During the eighteenth century, wheat flour began to be used with ever-increasing frequency—at first in a classic roux or buerre manie (butter rolled in flour). By the second quarter of the nineteenth century, flour was displacing these other liaisons altogether (even Mrs. Randolph used some flour), and late antebellum cooks were losing the art and subtlety of the old liaisons. Mrs. Hill's use of flour is judicious, but almost ubiquitous in her sauce chapter. Elsewhere, the old-fashioned cream, egg, and crumb liaisons make their appearance, and so does butter, though this last is never without a little flour rolled into it. Mrs. Hill's restraint with flour is nowhere better exemplified than in her frequent use of a typically Southern preparation known as "browning," flour toasted brown in a dry pan. The toasting breaks down the glutens in the flour, reducing its ability to thicken, yet Mrs. Hill's dose of browning was invariably smaller than is usual today. As the century progressed to its

---

31. Lettice Bryan, *The Kentucky Housewife* (Cincinnati: Shepard and Sterns, 1839), 29.

HISTORICAL COMMENTARY **xxxiii**

close, her sense of balance vanished. A sauce that Mrs. Hill thickened with one or two teaspoons of plain flour for a cup of liquid was, by the turn of the century, gooped up with as much as three tablespoons.

Another common ingredient in Mrs. Hill's sauces and gravies is catsup (see glossary, p. 431). A variety of homemade "store sauces" that carried this name were commonplace in American kitchens until the onslaught of bottled sauces and condiments. However, beginning with the introduction of commercially bottled Worcestershire sauce in the first quarter of the nineteenth century,[32] commercial sauces began to erode the old, homemade varieties. Worcestershire sauce was already widely used by Mrs. Hill's day, as her recipe for "Imitation Worcester Sauce" (no. 443, p. 203) suggests. The onslaught of bottled sauces—and the eventual dominance of sweet tomato catsup over other, more aromatic versions made from mushrooms, green walnuts, and oysters—destroyed much of the subtlety of many dishes and changed the face of American cookery forever. Homemade catsups have lingered into our century in general-purpose cookbooks but are almost invariably treated as anachronisms.

Yet of all the changes in method and seasoning, the one which has most affected the texture and flavor of American food has been the use of refined sugar. Southerners are supposed to have notorious sweet tooths, but this reputation is usually based on the frequency with which recipes for sweets appear in later Southern cookbooks, or in household diaries and letters. Most of these documents, however, outline recipes that were used only occasionally and were not a part of everyday cooking. At any rate, Southern books were no more prone to cakes, pies, ices, and other sweets than were other American ones in those days. The truth is, overall America's per capita consumption of sugar has more than quadrupled since the War Between the

---

32. According to literature produced by Lea and Perrins, the company—originally a chain of chemists' shops—formulated the original Worcestershire sauce in the early 1830s.

States, increasing most drastically around the turn of the century. Mrs. Hill was on the cusp of the trend. Her salad dressings invariably contained a small dose of sugar—though, in general, no larger than that used by Mary Randolph. Mrs. Hill was already using sugar in most tomato recipes, which practice was soon to be virtually universal, but the amount in her recipes was still sparing. This was true even of sweets: her ice cream recipes contained half the amount that is usual today. Her "glaze" for ham was a coating of breadcrumbs, not the syrupy sweet glaze that has dominated in this century. Though she mentioned sugar as an option in curing bacon and ham, it was not a part of her base recipe. Although sugar cures had long been used in England and other parts of America, they did not become as universal as they are today until the latter part of the nineteenth century. The preference for sugar appears to have been regional. In South Carolina, it was usual. (As early as 1770, Harriett Pinckney Horry included it in her formula. So did her niece, Sarah Rutledge, and Theresa Brown). It was also included in Lettice Bryan's Kentucky formula. But in Virginia it is seldom mentioned. Try to find a ham without sugar in it—or on it—today.

By the time of *Housekeeping in Old Virginia* (1879), the increased use of sugar and the number of recipes for sweets were already tipping the balance (this book contains one of the earliest Southern mentions I have found of a sugar glaze on ham). By the time of Fanny Farmer's edition of the *Boston Cooking-School Cook Book* (1896), the increase in the amount of sweetening is distinct, and sugar is in practically everything.[33] Things have only gotten worse since.

Perhaps this is a good place to move on to some of Mrs. Hill's baking methods. These also highlight the old-fashioned nature of her overall practice. For example, though volume measures eventually dominated American baking practice, Mrs. Hill continued to prefer weight measures, especially for cakes and

---

33. Karen Hess, ed., *The Virginia House-wife*, xliii.

pastry. Weight measuring was soon (and unfortunately) to be completely abandoned by American bakers in favor of less exact (and less reliable) volume measuring. Mrs. Hill did, of course, use volume measures on occasion, but mainly when the consistency of the dough determined the amount of flour. In observing her volume measures, please note that she sifted flour before measuring it. Though this is usual in modern American recipes, in older practice, the flour was not sifted first. (Mrs. Randolph, *The Virginia House-wife*, says that a quart of flour should weigh 1¼ pounds. A quart of sifted flour will come nowhere near that amount.)

Notice that baking soda was creeping into the formula for most of Mrs. Hill's cakes, including her pound cake, which was otherwise very old-fashioned. Occasionally, it was used in combination with cream of tartar (which produces, in essence, baking powder). Though she included a number of chemically leavened quickbreads ("Yeast Powder Biscuits," "Rice Loaf Bread," "Quick Waffles," and "Muffins"), she still showed a marked (and, sad to say, old-fashioned) preference for real yeast in bread.

Chemical leavens are apparently American in origin and were known to eighteenth-century cooks, though early writers such as Mrs. Randolph had scant use for them. As the nineteenth century progressed, they were utilized with increasing frequency, especially in the South, where the climate made quick rising and baking attractive. In the 1850s, commercial baking powder became available,[34] and, after the War quickbreads began to dominate the Southern dinner table. Yet during Mrs. Hill's heyday, yeast bread still dominated, and quickbreads were mainly intended for breakfast and tea. (In antebellum Georgia, tea was mostly a late supper, like the so-called high tea of England.)

An interesting sidenote is that by this time, old-fashioned,

---

34. John Egerton, *Southern Food* (New York: Alfred A. Knopf, 1987), 217.

rich fruitcake which had been the traditional wedding cake until about mid-century was already being replaced by the pretty but dull white "lady cake" that is usual today ("Bride's Cake," no. 718, p. 290). Mrs. Hill's cakes particularly mark her baking as very old-fashioned: the only layer cakes she offered were jelly cakes (nos. 716, 717, and 719, pp. 289–290). There were none of the puffy, frosting-laden layer cakes that became the rage during the 1870s and dominated Southern baking in the latter part of the century.

Most Southern women took an active hand in the baking, especially the making of the household's yeast breads, and Mrs. Hill was no exception: her breads are on a par with those of Eliza Acton, nineteenth-century England's most perceptive writer on baking. Mrs. Hill wrote, "Four things are requisite to have good bread, viz.: good flour, good yeast, good baking, and that the dough should be WELL KNEADED." Amen, Mrs. Hill.

It is of particular note that Mrs. Hill's bread formula did not include sugar. She had fortunately not succumbed to the later American habit of adding sugar to bread as a matter of routine. Only a couple of her recipes contained it, and the little sugar in her yeast would have been negligible once the fermentation was complete. Mostly, she seems to consider sugar out of place in bread. She did note that Sally Lunn can be flavored with sugar and spice but said that makes it "a sweet *cake*" (emphasis mine)—in other words, it is no longer bread. Virtually all Sally Lunns contained some sugar by the 1880s, and the dose continued to get bigger.[35]

Sugar is superfluous to breadmaking, as any serious baker knows, but it began to appear in American bread in the second half of the nineteenth century.[36] The culprit behind this phenomenon was the steel-roller mill, which began to replace stone milling around mid-century. Roll milling squeezed all the bran

---

35. John L. and Karen Hess, *The Taste of America*. 3d ed. (Columbia: University of South Carolina Press, 1989), 58–60.

36. *The Taste of America*, 56.

(and the life) out of flour, and sugar was added in an attempt to restore some of the natural sweetness that was lost. Rural Southerners, by and large, continued to rely on the old mills until very late; Mrs. Hill's flour and meal were almost certainly still stone ground and must have been of a very high quality. Would that we Georgians could still say that today.

This brings us to Mrs. Hill's pantry. That stone-milled flour was from soft wheat, as had been most American flour until steel-roller milling created a market for midwestern hard wheat, which is too hard for stone milling. But Southerners continued to prefer soft-wheat flour long after the tide had shifted, in part because its low gluten content is critical for the quickbreads and pastries which were favored in Southern kitchens, and in part because water-powered stone mills survived in our region well into the twentieth century.[37]

As to other dry goods, the sugar in Mrs. Hill's pantry would have been mostly loaf sugar (see glossary for discussion of sugar types and modern equivalents). Her spices were whole and were ground up as needed with the mortar and pestle. The mustard in her pantry was dry mustard flour; imported French and English dry mustards were of differing levels of pungence and heat. Note that Mrs. Hill had access to, and used, both. "Made mustard" meant prepared mustard sauce (see recipe, nos. 457 and 458, p. 207). Better to make your own, but bottled English or French Dijon-type would make an acceptable substitute.

One little appreciated aspect of the antebellum Southern pantry is its store of green coffee beans, reflected at the beginning of Mrs. Hill's chapter on coffee and tea. Coffee is not often viewed as a particularly Southern beverage, partly because iced tea has become our identifying beverage of choice. But coffee was once so important in antebellum households that it became

---

37. My grandparents were still having their corn (and some wheat) ground at the local water-powered mill as late as the beginning of World War II. The Kymulga Mill on Talledega Creek in Alabama stayed in operation until the 1960s.

the single most missed imported item when Union blockades closed the South's ports.[38] Mrs. Hill's opening discussion reflects a lost art in America of the blending and roasting of coffee beans at home. Her careful, reverent instructions for this are still pertinent. Including eggs in the coffee pot, by the way, was a method for clarifying the brew in the days before filters.

Mrs. Hill's salad oil (or sweet oil, as she sometimes referred to it) is olive oil. Olive oil was more common in those days than we suppose. Large quantities were imported into Savannah and Charleston, and it was advertised in the newspapers of both cities with regularity. Though it was expensive and the quality of the oil might sometimes have been in doubt, as Mrs. Hill hinted, it was available.

Let us now have a look at Mrs. Hill's larder. Here again, she took for granted that her reader would be producing most of the larder's staple of lard and dairy products, especially butter. Dairy farming was not common in the South, nor was it a highly developed art, as Mrs. Hill's notes on caring for the cow suggest. This deficiency proved to be disastrous for the South during the war, when shortages of meat and dairy products became critical.[39] A little discussed enterprise of ante- and postbellum housewives was the sale of surplus butter and cured meat. But such household diaries as that of Martha Goode Tucker, mistress of Rose Hill in Milledgeville, Georgia, leave an interesting record of this apparently thriving cottage industry. Unfortunately, the South depended too heavily on these sources, and most planters' wives were not equipped to satisfy the demands of both a fighting army and a blockaded civilian population.

Mrs. Hill's instructions for curing meat are lucid in telling us what her hams, salt pork, lard, and bacon were like. They require no discussion beyond the observation that modern cooks will be hard-pressed to find ham, bacon and lard of the same quality today. Notice that, by Mrs. Hill's day, sugar and molas-

---

38. Massey, *Ersatz in the Confederacy*, 72.
39. *Ersatz in the Confederacy*, 76.

ses were beginning to appear in the curing mixture, but were not yet usual. As mentioned earlier, sugar cures had long been used in other regions, even within the South, but there were parts of the South, including Georgia, where sugar cures were not widely used and were virtually unknown until the latter part of the nineteenth century. Notice, too, that she hinted that such practice was preferred in warmer climates. There are other distinctly regional touches in her discussion of the hog-killing and curing processes. As Mrs. Hill noted, hog-killing time in the South occurred only after prolonged cold weather was assured, since pork meat taints easily without refrigeration. Of course, this was universal practice, but prolonged cold weather begins later in the Deep South than it does elsewhere. Note her instruction that sausages should never be linked or they will have a tendency to mold at the knot. In the deep South, this was sound advice.

Mrs. Hill's instructions in the dairy are equally lucid, but for those who will be using the "culinary recipes," it is helpful to know her intentions with regard to certain dairy products. "Rich" milk was real, whole milk from which little, if any, of the top cream had been removed. Modern whole milk is actually only 4 percent butterfat and isn't a satisfactory substitution. Half-and-half, preferably not ultra-pasteurized, is perhaps not the best, but it is the closer substitution. Modern cream is only a ghost of the rich cream that Mrs. Hill would have known. Our so-called whipping cream must be a minimum of 30 percent butterfat and is seldom more than 34 percent. I find that anything less than 36 percent will not react in cooking the way intended in these recipes. Look for cream with a minimum of 36 percent butterfat—again, preferably not ultra-pasteurized.

True buttermilk is the soured liquid that is leftover from making butter. What is sold as buttermilk today is actually skim milk treated with enzyme cultures to make it sour. It is usually salted (and invariably too much so). I find that an all-natural plain yoghurt without added thickeners comes closer to the intentions of these recipes.

Let's pass on to the kitchen garden. The vegetable chapter is particularly revealing of the rural aspect of Mrs. Hill's pantry and kitchen. She begins: "Vegetables intended for dinner should be gathered early in the morning. Only a few can be kept twelve hours without detriment." What she would think of the average supermarket produce cooler today would probably not be printable. Obviously, she took for granted a predominantly rural audience; most of the recipes begin with gathering instructions and are directed toward people who grow their own vegetables. Her discussion of potato varieties is actually a recommendation of what to plant, not what to buy. There is no mention of what to look for in a market. Mrs. Hill took this for granted because most Southerners were still growing their own in those days. In Savannah, Oglethorpe's original land tracts for the settlers included a contiguous space for a kitchen garden and another plot outside the town limits.[40] Of course, in-town property eventually became too valuable to continue as garden plots, and the large lots were subdivided. But Savannahians continued to expect fresh produce, either from their own farms or from the thriving market on Ellis Square, until well into the twentieth century. Contemporary accounts tell us that this was true of most Southern cities. In smaller, more rural towns such as LaGrange, in-town lots frequently included a vegetable garden. Both the Newnan Street and Greenville Road properties were large and would have included a kitchen garden.

Refrigerated transportation was new: it had only been patented in 1868. Therefore, most of the produce available to Americans, even in urban markets, was local and, of necessity, reasonably fresh. Out-of-season vegetables were dried, packed in straw, or pickled in salt. Canning was already beginning to replace these old methods of preserving (Mrs. Hill even included a chapter on it), but she continued to give instructions

---

40. Oglethorpe's city plan allotted forty acres to all settlers, which included a sixty-by-ninety-foot in-town lot, a five-acre garden plot in the town common, and another forty-five acres for farming outside the town walls. See Mills Lane, *Savannah Revisited* (Athens: University of Georgia Press, 1969), 24.

for the old, time-honored methods of drying, salting, and so forth. These methods did not survive much beyond Mrs. Hill's generation.

The wide variety of vegetables that Mrs. Hill covered is interesting, and instructive: there are more than eighty recipes for forty-plus varieties. Note the casual and knowledgeable way she discussed such vegetables as artichokes, broccoli, and eggplant—all of which popular belief would have us believe were not eaten in America until much later. She also mentions at least four different kinds of onions, including leeks, which the same myths say Southerners did not eat. Notice, too, the care of her instructions in preparing and cooking the vegetables. Her cooking times are sometimes rather longer than would be necessary, but Mrs. Hill invariably accompanied the time with careful instructions about how to test for doneness and cautioned about preserving color and texture. Clearly, she wanted her reader to watch the pot, not the clock.

As for herbs, Mrs. Hill made frequent use of a wide variety—at least a dozen—and, most of the time, intended fresh rather than dried ones. This usually comes as a surprise to modern Southerners, who unaccountably accept the conventional wisdom that early Southerners outside Creole New Orleans made scant use of herbs, fresh or otherwise. Part of the reason for that misconception lies in the fact that the use of herbs, especially fresh ones, had waned by the early part of the twentieth century, actually beginning its decline right after the War Between the States. That this occurred at the same time that African cooks began to exit white kitchens is interesting and possibly instructive.

Mrs. Hill's medicinal receipts, most of which will be only of historical interest, I will leave to the discerning reader. A detailed discussion of them is beyond my knowledge and the scope of this book, and I have confined myself and these notes to the culinary ones. Some of the treatments and remedies will seem alarming to modern readers: such drugs as opium, morphine, and laudanum were legal in the nineteenth century, and even doctors frequently prescribed them. Well, morphine will certainly stop a stubborn cough, and laudanum and opium will keep a colicky or teething baby from crying. Though we nowadays find such remedies horrific in light of our clearer understanding of the true nature and alarming side effects of such drugs, such remedies were not, in those days, seen as out of the ordinary.

But that isn't to say that Mrs. Hill's medicine was completely unfounded. Some of her simpler remedies are still respected and used by practitioners of homeopathic medicine. Moreover, such remedies as her sulfur and milk poultice for acne and her gargle of red pepper (cayenne) tea for sore throats are not that far-fetched: sulfur and lactic acid are still used to treat acne today, and cayenne is a natural disinfectant which is also an ancient herbal remedy for chills and fever.[41] With the advent of patent medicine and prescription drugs, medicinal recipes were beginning to disappear from American cookbooks. In fact, Mrs. Hill was already recommending brand-name preparations.

Most of Mrs. Hill's formulas for soap and household cleaners were commonplace and were probably frequently used in her household. Eventually such cleaners were replaced by commercial ones, but many of them did—and still do—work, though they are hardly likely to replace packaged cleansers and modern dry cleaning. Again, I have confined myself to the culinary aspects of the book and will not attempt to discuss any of them here.

Now, before we turn to the facsimile and the actual recipes, a few closing notes are in order. In order to understand some of Mrs. Hill's directions for timing, one needs to know something of Southern dining habits during the period. Most of the South continued to observe older English practice long after it had gone out of fashion elsewhere. There were two main meals,

---

41. Sarah Garland, *The Complete Book of Herbs and Spices* (New York: Viking, 1979), 41.

breakfast and dinner. Breakfast was a large and substantial meal and was not limited to bacon, eggs, and cereal. Such things as hash, veal cutlets, grilled game birds, croquettes, broiled steak, and even shellfish are frequently mentioned breakfast dishes. Dinner, the main meal of the day, was at two or three o'clock in the afternoon. This remained standard in the South until after World War II, and there are still Southerners who refer to their midday sandwich as "dinner"; "luncheon" is something for Yankees and ladies' clubs. The day was usually rounded out by a late evening supper or tea, but these meals were light.

Of course, the most important feature of the kitchen is always the cook. This was especially true in the antebellum South, where that cook was, for virtually all upper-class households, an African. The contributions of Africans to Southern cookery are as numerous as they are undocumented; however, this influence is evidenced by a number of common elements—the use of okra, peanuts, sesame seeds, and eggplant, and such dishes as hoppin' John, *calas* (rice croquettes), okra and tomatoes, and groundnut candy are just a few suggestive elements. By Mrs. Hill's day, these elements were so thoroughly incorporated into the cuisine that they were almost taken for granted, but they point back to a strong and continuing African influence in Southern cooking. Where Mrs. Hill is concerned, it is apparent that she knew how to cook and that she put this knowledge to frequent use. However, day-to-day cooking would have been left to a servant, that is, to an African slave. Unfortunately, slaves are almost never mentioned, and we can only speculate on the influence that this cook might have had on Mrs. Hill, for we will never even know her name. The only servant whose name we know is the housekeeper, Matilda Chambliss, who was white.

As for the recipes themselves, I am sometimes asked if they really work, as if we have somehow learned something magical about cooking in the last century of which Mrs. Hill and her generation were ignorant. I am never sure whether the person asking this is arrogant or merely naive, but it's a silly question.

Of course, they work. Mrs. Hill clearly knew what she was doing, and there are times when she shows a knowledge of cookery that is lost on many modern cooks. With a minimal understanding of the workings of open-hearth cooking, almost all of the recipes can be translated easily to a modern kitchen. A few things like spit-roasting can, of course, only be imitated, and the broiled things would nowadays have to be done on a charcoal grill to produce Mrs. Hill's originally intended results. Though my own tastes make me less inclined to agree with her aversion to rare roasts and steaks, and so less apt to adhere closely to some of her cooking times, I have actually used a good many of them, and most of them are excellent. No, we have not learned something magical about cooking in the century that has passed since Mrs. Hill's death. In fact, there are many things that she knew which have been lost in our century—and concerning which we would do well to heed this wise lady and learn. And so, without further discussion, let us turn to her work.

MRS. HILL'S
NEW COOK BOOK.

THREE VALUABLE WORKS.

Well-known and Popular Hand-books of Society.

Beautifully printed and elegantly bound.

I.
The Art of Conversation,

With Directions for Self-Culture. An admirably conceived and entertaining book—sensible, instructive, and full of suggestions valuable to every one who desires to be either a good talker or listener, or who wishes to appear to advantage in good society. *⁎* Price $1.50.

II.
The Habits of Good Society.

A Handbook for Ladies and Gentlemen. With thoughts, hints, and anecdotes concerning social observances; nice points of taste and good manners; and the art of making one's self agreeable. Sound common sense, rendered fascinating by a pleasant and agreeable style. *⁎* Price $1.75.

III.
Arts of Writing, Reading, and Speaking.

An attractive work for teaching not only the beginner, but for perfecting every one in these three most desirable accomplishments. For youth, this book is both interesting and valuable; and for the adult, whether professionally or socially, it is one they cannot dispense with. *⁎* Price $1.50.

———o———

*These three books are the most perfect and complete of their kind ever published. They are made up of no dry stupid rules that everybody knows, but are fresh, sensible, good-humored, entertaining, and readable. Every person of taste should possess them, and cannot be otherwise than delighted with them. *⁎* Each will be sent by mail, free, on receipt of price, by*

G. W. Carleton, Publisher,
New York.

Housekeeping Made Easy.

MRS. HILL'S NEW COOK BOOK.

A PRACTICAL SYSTEM
FOR PRIVATE FAMILIES, IN TOWN AND COUNTRY.

WITH DIRECTIONS FOR
CARVING AND ARRANGING THE TABLE FOR DINNERS, PARTIES, etc.,

TOGETHER WITH
Many Medical and Miscellaneous Receipts extremely useful in Families.

. By MRS. A. P. HILL,
WIDOW OF HON. EDWARD Y. HILL, OF GEORGIA.

NEW YORK:
Carleton, Publisher, Madison Square.
LONDON: S. LOW, SON & CO.
M DCCC LXXII.

Entered, according to Act of Congress, in the year 1870, by

MRS. A. P. HILL,

In the Clerk's Office of the District Court of the United States, for the Southern District of New York.

INTRODUCTION.

The book which meets the wants of the times deserves a place in every household, and the writer who, in these degenerate days, contributes to the pleasures, and at the same time advances the real welfare, of the race, deserves a place in the Calendar with all the benefactors of the age. "The Southern Practical Cookery and Receipt Book" comes up to the standard here laid down.

In reading the advertisements in our daily papers, the eye frequently falls upon something like this:—"*Wanted, A good Cook.*" This is a universal want, and one that must, to some extent, be supplied. We are an eating race, and people will eat; they have been educated to eat. Indeed, hitherto we have lived by this process, and even now there appears no sign among the improvements of the age, of such a reformation as will dispense with "table comforts." Happy is that family that has this want gratified. I do not mean that we are an Epicurean race; so far from it, indeed, that there are no visible tendencies in that direction, and it is hoped none will ever appear. But man is an animal, and all animals must eat; and although it is written of him, "Thou shalt not live by bread alone," yet, a bountiful Providence has decreed seed time and harvest, bread earned by the sweat of his brow, and a table of plenty.

The forest grows timber, but it must be cut and dressed before it is prepared for the temple; the quarries furnish the stones, but the workman must hew and polish them before they are fit for the building; and so nature, cultivated, furnishes the food; but art must dress and prepare it before it is ready for the palate and digestion. We are not just now in a condition to sacrifice much to fancy or ornament; we must address ourselves to the useful and substantial. Every mother, wife, and daughter must now become a practical operator in the domestic circle. Each should be emulous to excel in neatness, industry, usefulness and economy. The days for romance have passed, if they ever existed; the night for the dreamy visions of elegance and luxury in connection with a life of indolence has suddenly given place to the day of enterprise and industry. A crisis is upon us which demands the development of the *will* and *energy* of Southern character. Its prestige in the past gives earnest of a successful future. As woman has been queen in the parlor, so, if need be, she will be queen in the kitchen; as she has performed so gracefully the duties of mistress of the establishment in the past, so she will, with a lovelier grace, perform whatever labor duty demands. She has learned that the services of a good cook, that queen of the kitchen, are essential elements in the health, the good temper, the enjoyment and peace of every family; that the art of Cooking is the parent of all other arts, and eating and drinking the highest of all animal enjoyments. The race of good cooks among us is almost extinct. What shall be done to bring back the good old times, when a knowledge of the good housewifery demanded for the health and comfort of every family was not considered too low for the attention of any lady? Labor should not be held in disrepute by any, for it is written "In the sweat of thy brow shalt thou earn bread;" and again, "Not slothful in business;" and still again, "But if any man provides not for his own, and especially for his own house (or kindred), he hath denied the faith and is worse than an infidel." The word "he" in the last quotation is generic, and stands as the representative of both sexes.

Will not the ladies, whose opinions and actions form public sentiment, lead off in a culinary reform, which will correct the errors of the past, and introduce a system of industry and economy to meet the present emergencies? Reverse the present order of things. Make idleness and indolence disreputable, and labor and usefulness honorable. Pluck from the hand of the destroyer the premium awarded to idleness and give it to industry. Teach to all classes of our people, by your uniform example, that:—

> "Labor is rest from the sorrows that greet us,
> Rest from all petty vexations that meet us,
> Rest from sin's promptings that ever entreat us,
> Rest from world's syrens that lure us to ill."

Those now entering and soon to enter upon the duties of life, should not do so with mistaken views as to the responsibilities they will have to meet, and the manner of discharging the obligations of the domestic sphere. They should not look forward as slaves to the task, or as idle pupils to the recitation. Labor promotes health, and health fosters contentment. So, to be both healthy and happy, we should be both usefully and profitably employed.

I am most happy to be able to state that the reform here recommended has already begun, and is progressing most encouragingly. Our women have the will and intelligence; the practical development of the resources at their command is all that is necessary to insure success. The appearance of the "Southern Practical Cookery and Receipt Book" at this crisis augurs a new and brighter era in the culinary art. It is a book admirably adapted to the times and the people—the production of a eminently practical mind, one whose long experience and acknowledged celebrity among her friends as a cateress entitles her opinions, as contained in the following pages, to be held as oracular. The style of the book is graceful and easy, and is free from the monotony that usually characterizes the elucidation of subjects so analogous to each other.

Our authoress has proved herself to be mistress in literature, as well as queen in the kitchen. Her versatility of talent qualifies her for the position which her sense of duty urged her, against her inclination, to assume; namely, to assist all who may desire knowledge and improvement in the important art of cooking.

The instructions here presented are the result of a life of experience, observation, and reading. No untried theory is offered, nor have we here a system too luxurious for the poor, or too economical for the rich. The wants, tastes, and abilities of all are consulted, so that the poor may luxuriate on delicious soups every day made from the savings which a wasteful housekeeper would consider utterly worthless. If our Southern women are going to meet the present crisis as they have all the trials of the past (and none can doubt but they will), they will find this book a companion of invaluable service, and a constant adviser, whose opinions may be trusted as entirely reliable. Adopt the system here presented, and you will soon find your husband delighted with the improvement in your style of living, and it will not be long before he will compliment you on the economy of your new regulations. If, then, the system improves the style of living, and at the same time curtails the expenses of the table, none will doubt the wisdom of the authoress, the adaptation of this improvement to the necessities of the times, and its real value to every household.

If Byron was not mistaken in the subjoined lines, the ladies will find that a feast to the palate is the most successful appeal they can make to the hearts of the sterner sex. I do not endorse his views, but leave the reader to accept or reject, to prove or disprove by experience, as she may choose; assuring her that no gentleman was ever offended by being invited to a good dinner, or thought less of his hostess for displaying good taste in the preparation and arrangement of the viands of which he was to partake.

> Of all appeals—although
> I grant the power of pathos and of gold,
> Of beauty, flattery, threats, a shilling—no
> Method's more sure at moments to take hold
> Of the best feelings of mankind, which grow
> More tender as we every day behold,
> Than that all-softening, overpowering knell,
> The tocsin of the soul—the dinner bell."

But I must not close without a word to the sterner sex; and yet, why say a word to men in introducing a cook-book? Whoever knew one to take such a work in his hands, much less to read a page of its contents? Well, if I can get the ear and interest of the women, I shall not fear that the "lords of creation" will long remain in ignorance of the suggestions here offered. I therefore feel encouraged to say a word for their benefit.

I say for *their benefit;* for so it will prove if they will reduce my suggestions to practice. When you come from your business, wearied and worn, you want a good, wholesome, healthy, and palatable meal. This is a reasonable want; it may and ought to be gratified; and it can and will be, provided you will furnish the apparatus and facilities. You would not require a mechanic to build you a house without the necessary materials, nor should you expect the mistress of your house to perform her duties well unless you furnish her with the requisite conveniences. Our enterprising lady friends are deterred from entering upon the work which now so urgently invokes their personal attention. The task is a Herculean one: double the labor necessary for the end desired is to be accomplished, on account of the almost total absence of convenient utensils and the other et cæteras which make up a complete and cosey establishment. Nothing is inviting, everything is repulsive; nothing to facilitate, everything to hinder. Look around your premises and see if a reformation is not greatly needed. You sought insurance from fire in the magnificent distance which exists between the houses which make up the family group. Your kitchen is set quite a distance in the rear of your dwelling; the smoke-house off in another direction quite as far; while the well may be a remove so great that one would think that the only exercise to be enjoyed by the family was in going after water. And as for a storehouse, *that* is voted a superfluity. Now the consequence of this horrid and unsightly arrangement is, that the labor necessary to gather materials for a meal is more fatiguing than its preparation. If you cannot do otherwise, burn that kitchen and smoke-house where they stand. Your dwelling will be in no danger from the conflagration. Unite your kitchen with your dwelling, and furnish with a stove, etc. Inclose your pump under the same roof; have your pantry large enough to hold your supply of provisions, and let all your arrangements be labor-saving. When thus arranged, take the mistress of your household into your kitchen, and let her examine its contents closely, to see if all necessary articles are furnished; then, if she is satisfied, you have done your duty, and are entitled to the thanks of a gratified and happy wife, who will greet you with her smiles and reward you with her economy. Are you alarmed at the trouble and expense necessary for the arrangement of all these conveniences? You should not be; they will contribute largely to the pleasure, ease, and health of your family. Try it, and see if I be a false prophet.

E. W. WARREN.

Macon.

DEDICATION

To young and inexperienced Southern housekeepers I desire to dedicate this work. In its preparation I have been influenced mainly by the consideration that in this peculiar crisis of our domestic as well as national affairs, counsel is needed—wise and timely counsel, which not only gives warning of dangers ahead, but, in language clear and unmistakable, teaches how they may be avoided. Thousands of young women are taking upon themselves the responsibilities of housekeepers, a position for which their inexperience and ignorance of household affairs renders them wholly unfitted. Formerly "mother" or "mother's cook," or one whom the considerate mother had trained to fill this important office in the daughter's *ménage*, was, with many, the only authority considered necessary in the conduct of culinary operations. Now, however, things are changed. "Mother," even if within accessible distance, is too much occupied with the accumulated cares of her own establishment to be able to devote much time and attention to a separate one; while "mother's cook" and "trained servants" are remembered as among the good spirits that ministered to the luxury and ease of by-gone days.

Youth and inexperience are lamentable drawbacks which cannot be set aside by the brave hearts that would overcome the trials that assail them in the outset of their domestic career; and they must content themselves to "begin at the beginning;" to learn the rudiments of the science first, and by the exercise of common sense and a laudable ambition they may hope to become (through experience) thorough good housekeepers. It is with the earnest hope of benefiting this class that I have yielded to the importunities of many friends and consented to place in their hands the results of an experience of thirty years, trusting

DEDICATION.

that it may prove to many an unerring guide through the labyrinth of domestic duties.

The rules that I give are collected from experience and other "reliable" sources, and if faithfully and attentively practised will insure success. To experienced housekeepers, the directions may seem *tediously minute*. I have examined a great many Cookery books. In a majority of them too much is taken for granted, and much of the very information that a *novice* most needs is omitted, as facts with which every one is familiar. In preparing this Receipt Book, a vivid recollection of my own utter ignorance of household affairs at the time that I assumed the duties of mistress of a family, suggested the idea of taking but one thing for granted, viz.: that the majority of those for whom this book is principally intended know as little as I did, and stand as greatly in need of the aid and instruction that I would gladly have received. That these will be found in the pages of this book I sincerely believe, and although devoid of the vanity of supposing that my contemporaries in age can profit by the directions herein contained, I should confess to defeat and disappointment, should they fail to supply that absence of practical knowledge which is the source of so many failures and disappointments to those who are just taking the initiatory steps in housekeeping.

Mrs. A. P. Hill

GENERAL REMARKS.

"Whatever is worth doing at all is worth doing well."

That the duties of the cook may be properly performed, there must be suitable apparatus to work with. All other trades require nice tools suited to the business to be done, and why should not the claims of this important functionary be admitted? In many kitchens—perhaps the majority—an insufficient number of utensils is furnished, and those without any regard to adaptation, with the unreasonable expectation that, whatever the variety to be served up, all shall be performed in a skillful manner. A liberal supply of cooking utensils is good economy; it saves both time and labor. It is *wise* management to curtail expenses in fitting up the parlor, in order to spend in fitting up the kitchen. An old English writer upon the subject has humanely observed: "There is real enjoyment in a well-cooked meal; and as the practice of cooking is attended with so many discouraging difficulties, so many disgusting and disagreeable circumstances, we ought to have some regard for those who encounter them to procure us pleasure, and to reward their services by rendering their situation in every way as comfortable and agreeable as possible.'

For the benefit of inexperienced housekeepers, I subjoin a list of articles for the kitchen—some as necessary, others only convenient. I open the list with

A well-furnished stove, or range, if preferred.
Apple corer and peeler.
Baking pans—Tin and earthen, different sizes.
Bowls—Different sizes; coarse ware.
Biscuit cutter.
Biscuit-board—Of very thick poplar plank, set upon legs, and a well fitting cover of plank fixed with hinges.
Bread grater.
Bread toaster.
Bread blankets—To be kept for no other purpose but to wrap around the vessel in which light bread is put to rise in the winter.
Bread jars—With covers to keep remains of bread.
Basting ladle.
Basting pan.

KITCHEN UTENSILS, ETC.

Brooms.
Brushes.
Bottle cleaner.
Cake pans with tubes in the centre—Different shapes.
Cheese toaster.
Colanders—Two.
Covers for dishes.
Carving-knife.
Cork-screw.
Chaffing dish.
Candlestick.
Candle moulds.
Candle box.
Coffee-mill.
Coffee-pot.
Coffee roaster.
Canisters—For coffee, tea, spices.
Chocolate grater.
Chocolate boiler.
Cups—One dozen, without handles, for baking custard.
Dishes—Of different sizes; coarse ware.
Dippers.
Double kettle.
Dish-pans — For washing and rinsing dishes.
Dripping-pan.
Egg-beater,
Flour-sifter, tray, and chest for holding flour.
Flour dredging boxes; one for white flour, one for browned flour.
Fish-kettle.
Fish-knife.
Faucets.
Forks—Large and small.
Fluid-can and lamp.
Floor-cloths.
Gridirons—Large one for oysters and barbecues; smaller size for ordinary broiling.
Grindstone—Small, for sharpening knives.
Graters—Large and small.
Hand-basin.
Hammer.
Ice-cream freezer.
Ice-box and blanket.
Iron spoons—Large and small.
Iron mortar.
Iron ladle.
Iron ovens—Different sizes.
Jelly moulds.
Jelly bags—Of flannel.
Jars—Of different sizes, for soda, cream of tartar, etc.
Jagging-iron.
Knife-box.
Knife and saw for cutting out fresh meat; a knife on one side of the blade, a saw upon the other; very useful.
Larding-needles.
Lantern.
Lemon-squeezer.
Lamp-cleaner.
Mop—For scouring.
Meat-board.
Meat-mallet—Of wood.
Meat-tongs.

Marble slab—For rolling pastry.
Marble rolling-pin.
Marble mortar.
Meal chest and sifter.
Measures—bushel, peck, gallon, quart, pint, gill.
Mats—For tables.
Oyster knives.
Oyster tongs.
Oyster buckets.
Omelette frying-pan.
Pie plates—Different sizes; tin is best.
Pudding-pans.
Pudding boilers and bags.
Patty-pans—Different sizes.
Paste cutter.
Paste moulds.
Pepper-box.
Plate-warmer.
Preserving-kettle.
Porcelain stew-pan, with covers.
Plane—For shaving dried beef.
Reflectors—Of tin.
Rings—For muffins.
Refrigerator.
Rolling-pins—Two, a large and small one.
Skimmers—One perforated.
Strainers—One for straining gravies.
Sieve—For sifting spice, pepper, etc.
Sugar sifter—Very fine hair sifter for sifting corn meal for custards, etc.
Spits—Two or three sizes, one small for birds.
Skewers—Different sizes.
Soup-kettle—For boiling soup meat.
Soup-ladle.
Soup-strainer.
Scales and weights.
Shovel and tongs.
Salad spoons and forks—Wooden.
Steamer—For cooking potatoes.
Two tables, besides a covered biscuit-board and meat-block. One table to be used when preparing meals, the other to hold the dishes when taking up the meals. The latter should be covered with a coarse, clean table-cloth, or supplied with coarse dish mats.
Two towel-racks; one for holding the towel intended for wiping dishes; one for the hands. Small towels should have loops, and be suspended from hooks.
Trivets—Of different sizes.
Toasting-fork.
Waffle-irons.
Wafer-irons—these should be very shallow.
Wood box.
Water buckets.
Wooden boxes, with covers—For holding rice, tapioca, starch, etc.
Wooden bowls.
Wire covers—For dishes.
Water-bath—For sauce-pans.
Wire safe—A hanging wire safe for cold meat is a convenience. Every kitchen should, if possible, be supplied with a cheap clock, and kept in time with the

dining-room clock. Keep in a drawer of the safe plenty of foolscap paper, twine, scissors, tape. Have plenty of crash towels. Meat cloths should be frequently boiled in ley. The kitchen should have a good supply of soap. Save the ashes; if good, they are needed to make soap; if weak, they will improve the garden. A few should be thrown occasionally into the hen-house and coops.

FOR THE DAIRY.

A churn; stoneware is best. Covered jars to hold cream. Pans for holding milk; these are best shallow and broad. Always use unglazed jars for sour cream and buttermilk. Milk strainer. Milk pails or buckets; these are best made of tin. A pan for holding the water to wash the udders. Coarse towels for wiping them. A wooden bucket for water. Milk skimmer with short handle. A wire safe for holding milk. Milk and butter readily imbibe unpleasant odors, and should never be kept in the same safe, or near meats, cheese, etc. To be good, they should be kept separate, and everything about them be perfectly clean. A butter paddle of wood. Butter moulds for stamping. Butter dishes. Plenty of towels and milk cloths, which should be washed and scalded whenever used. Besides a milk strainer, my plan is to tie over the milk pail a thin muslin cloth, the ends extending several inches below the strings, so that there will be no danger of the cloth slipping from under the string. It should not be stretched tight across the pail, but hang loosely. Pour the milk into the pail through this cloth; it will not only strain the milk but protect it from dust. To "make assurance doubly sure," however, I restrain into the pans.

LAUNDRY.

Three flat-irons for each person—Fluters' iron. A padded board upon which to rub the heated iron. A padded holder made of woolen or silk. A cloth to wipe off any particles of dust. An iron ring to set the iron upon. A board under the ring to prevent its scorching the sheet. A waxed cloth to rub the iron when smoked. A bag of indigo. A bottle of ox gall; salt this a little an keep to prevent colors from fading. A tablespoonful to three gallons of suds is a good proportion. A bottle of white gum Arabic dissolved. A tablespoonful of this added to a pint of starch gives a beautiful polish to shirt bosoms. A solid ironing table; a good thick blanket to cover it; over this a sheet. There should be enough of these to change and always kept clean. They should be, when used, securely and neatly pinned at the corners. A padded board for ironing shirt bosoms; one long and tapering for ironing dress skirts. Several dozen clothes pins, which are useful to prevent the clothes falling from the lines; they are made of wood split half way through the centre. As many good clothes lines as are required; they should be taken in as soon as the drying is completed; clothes baskets for clean and soiled clothes. Tubs, large and small. Pails. A large boiler, copper or brass is best; iron rusts easily. A clothes bag to boil clothes in. A large wooden paddle to stir and remove the articles boiled. A wash-board. One or two dippers. Soap-stand. A small closet is indispensable to have these things taken care of. The washwoman should be held each week to strict account for their safe keeping. When not in use keep under lock and key. A plentiful supply of good soap; receipts for making will be found in the body of this book. Never waste soap suds: apply them to the garden beds, or to the roots of grape vines and fruit trees. "Nature is a wise economist, who takes care that nothing be lost. She knows how to turn everything to account. Insects serve as food to large animals, and those are useful to man in one way and another. If they do not afford him food, they are useful for clothing or arms, and means of defence; and some, which are not useful for the above purposes, procure him useful medicine. Even the dust, putrid and corrupted matter, are all made use of by her, either for food for certain insects or manure for earth." In our arrangements and management we should learn from nature's plans and operations. It is wise to follow the laws she has prescribed, and to imitate her example.

MRS. HILL'S
NEW COOK BOOK

SOUPS.

"*The Cardinal Virtues of Cookery—Cleanliness—Frugality—Nourishment and Palatableness.*"

To make the best soups, use lean, juicy, fresh-killed meat; beef, veal, mutton, kid, lamb, or venison. Proportion the water to the meat in preparing the broth. To one pound of meat, add three pints of water, and reduce it by boiling to one quart. Place the soup-pot over a slow fire, which will make the water hot without causing it to boil, for at least half an hour. *Gentle stewing is best.* If the meat used is a leg or shin of beef, crack the bone in several places. To this, any trimmings of poultry may be added; a few slices of lean ham, if a large quantity of soup is to be made. The vessel in which soup is made, should have a close, well-fitting cover, which should be carefully kept in its place during the whole process. This will not only preserve much of the nutritive part of the juices of the meat, by preventing evaporation, but prevent smoke getting in, which would spoil the flavor of the broth. As the water begins to boil, a quantity of scum will rise to the top, which must be frequently and carefully removed. When the water looks clear, the vegetables and salt may be put in. This will cause more scum to rise, which must also be removed. After this is done, place the pot, *carefully covered*, where it will boil gently. It will require from three to four hours to prepare soup properly, unless the broth has been made the previous day. When convenient, it is a good plan to boil the broth the day before it is to be used; when it cools, the fat can be more easily removed, and if a variety of dishes is to be prepared, this arrangement will lessen the labor of the cook. The broth will keep perfectly well, but must not stand in a metallic vessel. Keep some spare broth in case your soup boils too thick. If this is not done, and more fluid is required, use *boiling* water. Cold water will injure the quality of the soup. When wine is used, it should never be put in more than ten or fifteen minutes before sending to the table. Spices and pepper should be tied in a thin muslin cloth, so as to be easily taken out. All bones, gristle, and pieces of fat should be carefully removed before serving. As much of the meat as is needed, should be cut in small pieces and put in the tureen before the soup is taken up. The broth being well prepared, the difference in soups depends mainly upon the seasoning. Says this old English writer, from whom I have already quoted: "The art of composing a rich soup is, so to proportion the several ingredients one to another, that no particular taste be stronger than the rest; but to produce such a fine, harmonious relish, that the whole is delightful."

The vegetables mostly used in soups are tomatoes, turnips, onions, carrots, celery, asparagus, peas, ochra, corn, butter-beans, cabbage and Irish potatoes. The two latter should always be parboiled before adding to the soup. The flavor of the former is too strong when put in raw, and the water in which the latter is boiled is thought injurious. The herbs used in soups for flavoring, are principally thyme, parsley, summer and winter savory, sage and sweet basil. The spices are cloves, mace and allspice; black and cayenne pepper are also used. The articles used for thickening are, flour, rice, arrow-root, bread crumbs, maccaroni, vermicelli and pearl barley. The water in which any kind of fresh meat or poultry is boiled, may be converted into some kind of soup.

The predominant meat or vegetable gives name to the soup and any attentive housekeeper can soon learn to make a judicious combination of materials.

SOUPS.

Meats for soup should always be put in cold water to boil.

"To understand the economy of household affairs is not only essential to a woman's proper and pleasant performance of the duties of a wife and mother, but is indispensable to the comfort, respectability, and general welfare of all families, whatever be their circumstances."

---

1 *Brown Soup.*—A leg or shank of beef is best for this; other meats may be used, however, if more convenient. Break the bone in several places; wash it carefully, put it in the soup-pot, and cover well with cold water. Set the vessel where the water will heat, but not boil, for half an hour. As the scum rises to the top, it should be skimmed off carefully, until all of it is removed. Add to a gallon of broth, half a pint of turnips, peeled and sliced; the same of carrots and tomatoes. Before putting in the tomatoes, skin and cut them in slices, and stir to them an even teaspoonful of brown sugar; add a teacup of onions, the same of cabbage, shred fine and parboiled; also of Irish potatoes. Brown three tablespoonfuls of flour in a skillet, taking care to stir it well that it may not burn, as the least particle of scorched flour will injure the taste of the soup; make a thin paste of this with water; stir this paste into the soup half an hour before sending it to the table. This thickening should be thoroughly incorporated with the soup; salt and pepper to taste; cut a portion of the meat from the bone in very small pieces, and add to the soup. Put the carrots to boil first, as they require longer time to cook than the other vegetables, or else grate them. The latter is the best way of using them.

---

2. *Mock Turtle Soup.*—Take the head of a calf or kid, and two feet of the calf that have been carefully cleaned. It is best to boil these the day before they are to be used. If this has not been done, very early in the morning put them in the soup-pot and cover with cold water. (Before this is done, however, the upper and lower jaws should be separated, and the brains re-

moved.) Let the water heat slowly, and skim carefully, as directed above. Should the water become too much reduced, add boiling water as may be needed. When the meat is done, and no more, take it up, pick it from the bones, and chop fine. Strain the liquor through a fine colander; return the liquor and *part* of the meat to the pot. Tie in a thin muslin cloth a few grains of allspice, bruised slightly, and a dozen cloves; drop this in the soup-kettle, and add one nutmeg grated; this is spice enough for half a gallon of soup; then salt and pepper to taste. Stir frequently, to prevent the meat at the bottom of the pot from burning. Fifteen minutes before sending it to the table, add a large wine-glass of Madeira wine to each quart of soup, and half a gill of good catsup. To each gallon add two tablespoonfuls of lemon juice, the peel of one pared thin and cut in small pieces. After simmering ten minutes in the soup, remove the lemon peel. This soup should be thickened with flour; one tablespoonful of batter, made with water and browned flour, to each gallon of soup, added half an hour before the soup is done. A few sprigs of sweet basil is an improvement. The yolks of eight hard-boiled eggs, sliced, should be put into the soup after it is poured into the tureen. Forced-meat balls may also be added. This soup is equally good, and with less trouble, made of a shank of veal or beef. Pig's head may also be used. A little butter, and cooked Irish potatoes added to the remaining meat, laid in good pie-crust, makes good mock-turtle pie.

---

3. *Oyster Soup.*—One quart of sweet milk; one quart of oysters. Boil the *juice* of the oysters and the milk together. This must only boil up twice; very little cooking is necessary. To this quantity add a tablespoonful of butter, or less, if preferred; salt and pepper to taste. About ten minutes before taking the soup up, stir in a half pint of crackers, or light bread, rolled fine; then add the oysters. Much boiling hardens the oysters. Nothing improves the soup so much as celery, a few heads cut up and boiled with the milk; or flavor with a few

bruised seed tied up in a muslin cloth, and boiled until the flavor is imparted, and then removed. When it is not convenient to use crackers or bread crumbs, stir two teaspoonfuls of flour into the butter before adding it; or use arrow-root instead of wheat flour.

---

4. *Gumbo.*—Fry a young chicken; after it gets cold, take out the bones. In another vessel fry one pint of young, tender, cut up ochra and two onions. Put all in a well-cleaned soup-kettle; an iron stew-pan lined with tin or porcelain is best. Add one quart of water; stew gently until done; and season with pepper and salt. Another way of preparing Gumbo, is: Cut up a fowl as if to fry; break the bones; lay it in a pot with a little lard or fresh butter. Brown it a little. When browned, pour a gallon of water on it; add a slice of lean bacon, one onion cut in slices, a pint of tomatoes skinned, two pints of young pods of ochra cut up, and a few sprigs of parsley. Cover closely, removing the cover to skim off all impurities that may rise to the top. Set the soup-kettle where the water will simmer gently at least four hours. Half an hour before the soup is put in the tureen, add a thickening, by mixing a heaping tablespoonful of sassafras leaves, dried and pounded fine, with a little soup. Stir this well into the soup. Serve with a separate dish of rice.

Gather the leaf-buds of the sassafras early in the spring; dry, pound, sift, and bottle them. Miss Leslie recommends stirring the soup with a sassafras stick, when the powdered leaves cannot be procured. The sassafras taste is very disagreable to some persons, therefore should be omitted when this is the case.

---

5. *Vegetable Soup—Maigre.*—To a quarter of a pound of fresh butter, boiling hot, add two onions chopped fine; let them stew. When they are soft, add two heads of celery, teacup each of corn, butter, beans, cabbage, tomatoes, and peas. Stir them well with the butter and onions. Have ready a kettle of boiling water; pour over the vegetables a pint at a time until

as much as is needed is added. Boil until the vegetables are done. Salt and pepper to taste. Lay slices of toast at the bottom of the tureen, and pour on the soup.

---

6. *Asparagus Soup.*—Boil the asparagus with any kind of fresh meat or fowl, or the broth in which they have been boiled. To a quart of this liquor add a heaping teaspoonful of flour stirred into a teacup of cream, added just before serving. A hundred points of asparagus will answer for three pints of broth; cut them into pieces two inches long; boil half an hour; salt and pepper to taste.

---

7. *Corn Soup.*—To a small hock bone of ham, or slice of good ham, add one quart of water. As soon as it boils, skim it well until the liquor is clear; add one large teacup and a half of grated corn, one quart of sweet milk, and a tablespoonful of butter, into which has been rubbed a heaping teaspoonful of flour; salt and pepper to taste.

---

8. *Green Pea Soup.*—The pods of peas make an excellent soup after the peas are shelled out. Boil the hulls and peas in separate vessels. Strain the water in which the hulls were boiled through a colander. Return the liquor to the pot and make the soup by any of the foregoing receipts, and add the peas a quarter of an hour before serving; add crackers in the bottom of the tureen. Instead of boiling the pea-hulls in water alone, add a little fresh meat or a slice of ham; butter may be added with a small quantity of flour rubbed into it if liked.

---

9. *Potato Soup.*—Take eight large, or a dozen small, mealy Irish potatoes; peel and cut them in slices, and boil in three pints of water until they can be mashed. Take them up; rub through a colander. Into a large tablespoonful of butter rub one tablespoonful of flour, and add to the soup; let this boil half an hour. More water may be added, if necessary. Just before

serving, add a tumbler of hot rich cream. The soup must not boil after the cream is added. This may be made richer by adding any kind of fresh meat to the water; then, after boiling, strain the broth from the meat.

---

10. *Ochra Soup.*—Make a broth of fowls or fresh meat; veal is best. To a gallon of this add three dozen young, tender pods of ochra; cut up thin; boil gently and slowly three hours, stirring occasionally. Remove the meat, and season with salt and pepper. Rice and tomatoes may, if liked, be added in small quantities. This should make three quarts of soup.

---

11. *Tomato Soup.*—To a gallon of broth made of any kind of fresh meat liked (veal is best) or poultry, add six dozen medium sized tomatoes, which have been cut up, but not skinned; stir to the tomatoes a tablespoonful of good brown sugar, to soften their extreme acid taste. Put them to stew gently and steadily in a well-covered soup-kettle. Salt to taste. Boil two hours; then strain the soup through a colander; return it to the kettle. To a large tablespoonful of nice, sweet butter, rub in a tablespoonful of flour. Put this to the soup; let it simmer ten or fifteen minutes. When the flavor of onions is not disliked, one or two may be used, shred fine, or a few heads of eschalots, and put to boil at the same time the tomatoes are. The flavor of the onions must be so delicate as to be scarcely recognized. Persons differ as regards thickening. The cook must ascertain the taste of those to be served, and add or diminish as may be proper.

---

12. *Chicken Soup.*—Cut up a grown chicken as for frying; boil gently in three quarts of water, and remove all scum carefully. To half a gallon of soup add half a pint of rice, a few sprigs of chopped parsley; pepper and salt to taste. Boil until the chicken is done. Add half a pint of sweet milk and one tablespoonful of arrow-root, stirred into a spoonful of butter. If for a sick person, omit the butter. The meat may be used in the soup

if preferred, but picked carefully from the bones; if not used in the soup, make it into salad or hash. Old fowls, when in good condition, are best for soup. Never put bones or gristle in the soup tureen. Corn starch, or wheat flour, will answer for thickening.

---

13. *Curry Soup.*—Cover four pounds of beef, veal, or mutton, with one gallon of water. Boil gently until reduced to three quarts; skim *carefully;* add twelve corns of black pepper, one nutmeg, and half a teaspoonful of cinnamon. After boiling one hour and a half, strain it. While it is boiling, fry, of a nice brown, in butter and lard mixed, or in good sweet lard alone, four thin slices of beef, veal, or mutton, and four onions. When they are done, pour the broth on them; put it on the fire; remove any scum that rises, and let it simmer half an hour. Mix two teaspoonfuls of curry powder, the same of flour, with a little cold water, and a teaspoonful of salt; add this to the soup, and let it simmer gently. Add boiling water if there is less than three quarts of soup when done. Serve the meat in a separate dish, with a rich tomato sauce. This soup may be made without the curry powder, seasoning high with pepper.

---

14. *Pigeon Soup.*—Take six pigeons, partridges, or other birds; clean nicely and cut up. Put the gizzards, necks, and livers, with the other parts of the birds, into half a gallon of cold water. Boil until done. Take up the pigeons; pick all the meat from the bones; strain the broth through a sieve; return it to the pot, and thicken with half a pint of bread crumbs. Season with mace, allspice, and cloves; put the last in whole; salt and pepper. Add the meat, which must be picked up very fine. After the soup is in the tureen, add four hard-boiled eggs grated. A dozen berries of allspice, eight of cloves, is sufficient

---

15. *Rabbit Soup.*—Cut up two rabbits as for frying; put this with a knuckle of veal or beef, or a slice or two of bacon

into the soup-kettle; cover with four quarts of water; boil gently until half reduced, and skim carefully until the broth is clear. Fry two sliced onions a light brown color; stir into the onion a tablespoonful of flour until it browns, and add (stirring until well incorporated) to the soup; season with a bunch, each, of parsley, thyme, and sweet basil, six cloves, one dozen grains of whole allspice, a few blades of mace, pepper and salt; toast thin slices of light bread and lay in the bottom of the tureen; pour on the soup and serve hot, after first removing the meat from the soup. Squirrels are good used in the same way; for the same quantity of water four squirrels will be necessary if they are young.

16.—*Chicken and Oyster Soup.*—(*A superior receipt.*) Cut up a full-grown fowl as for frying. Clean the giblets nicely, and put all in the soup-kettle with just enough water to cover them; let it simmer gently; remove all the scum. When the chicken is tender, take it up, strain the liquor and return it to the kettle. Add a quart of sweet milk to a quart of broth; if there should not be as much broth as is needed, pour in sufficient boiling water; Add a quart of oysters with their juice, and two or three blades of mace. A tablespoonful of butter, one of arrow-root, wheat flour rubbed into the butter, and one gill of hot cream; stew gently five minutes. Cream must always be boiled before being put into soup or gravy. Use the chicken for salad.

17. *Rich Chicken Soup.*—Take four quarts of water, four pounds of veal or beef; stew gently, skim and strain the broth; after it has boiled two hours, cut up a full-grown young fowl; put into the broth after returning it to the soup-kettle; season with salt and parsley. Let it simmer one hour; take out the chicken; beat the whites and yolks of four eggs and mix thoroughly with the soup just before serving. Be careful to stir one way; serve the meat separately as a stew or hash, using rich gravy made of part of the skimmings of the soup-kettle, seasoned

to taste; pick the chicken from the bones, return it to the soup until hot, pour into the tureen and serve.

---

18. *Mrs. H.'s Receipt for making Turtle Soup.*—Cut off the head; hang up the turtle; let it bleed freely; cut off the fins, and separate the upper and lower shells carefully; keep the knife close to the upper shell to avoid breaking the gall bladder. Cut up the turtle; put shells and all into the stew-pan after the shells have been carefully cleaned. Let them boil five minutes, plunge the turtle in cold water and scald again five minutes; again plunge it in cold water; save all the green fat from the in testines and other parts; cut as much off the turtle as is needed for soup, using the fins, entrails, heart, and liver; put them to boil in a gallon of water, in a closely-covered soup-kettle; when done, take off the meat and return the bones to the kettle; simmer gently; they will add something to the strength of the stock. In a quarter of an hour strain this broth from the bones, cut up the meat fine, put all in the kettle, seasoning with four tablepoonfuls of green eschalot, two tablespoonfuls each of parsley, thyme. marjoram and sweet basil, two lemons cut up, with the seeds removed, one dozen allspice, one dozen cloves, one nutmeg beaten fine, half a teaspoonful of curry powder; pepper and salt to taste; let this simmer gently one hour. Make a rich brown broth in another vessel, by boiling together two pounds of beef and one pound of ham two quarts of water; fry, until a light brown, four large onions cut up in three-quarters of a pound of butter; add this (stirring in slowly) to the brown broth; add the same quantity of spice used with the turtle. Make a paste of one large tablespoonful of flour and water sufficient to form the paste; add this quantity as thickening for each gallon of soup; boil this one hour; strain this broth on to the turtle; stir all well and boil half an hour, stirring frequently, to prevent the meat from sticking to the bottom of the soup-kettle; should more seasoning be required, add it before boiling the last half hour. A quarter of an hour before the

soup is done, add the green fat, and a half pint of Madeira wine, to three quarts of soup, added hot.

Prepare the stock for this soup the day before it is wanted.

---

19. *Another Turtle Soup, less complicated.*—Boil the turtle very tender, remove all bones, cut the meat into small pieces; season with a tablespoonful each of marjoram, sweet basil, thyme and parsley ; pepper and salt to taste ; one nutmeg beaten fine ; a dozen cloves; the same of allspice. Tie these in thin muslin, and remove it before sending the soup to the table ; stir a large tablespoonful of browned flour into a quarter of a pound of fresh butter ; add this to the soup ; pour over five quarts of boiling water ; reduce by boiling to three quarts; boil gently. A quarter of an hour before it is done, add the green fat; and to three quarts of soup, half a pint of wine, a lemon sliced thin, the seeds removed, add force-meat balls ; after simmering five minutes, take out the lemon peel. This is for a small turtle; if not fat, a slice of good ham may be added, and removed before serving.

---

20. *Beef Soup.*—Cover the bottom of the soup-kettle with a pound of lean ham ; three pounds of lean juicy beef sliced and laid over the ham ; strew over this, half a pint of onions chopped fine ; cover with just water enough to extract the juices without burning. This should stew very gently for half an hour ; add three quarts of boiling water ; boil slowly ; remove the grease and scum ; when the broth looks clear, add any vegetables that may be liked. To each quart, add a tablespoonful of bread crumbs. When the vegetables are done, strain them from the soup ; return them to the kettle, and add maccaroni or vermicelli, two ounces to each quart; break in small pieces and scal in hot water before putting it to the soup; boil ten minutes; use catsup and avoid over-seasoning. In making brown soups, always stew the meat in very little water, until of a brown color. A lamb, kid, or pigs-head makes the soup well.

---

21. *Dried Pea Soup*.—Remove carefully all unsound peas wash and soak them an hour or two, as may be convenient. To one quart of dried peas put four quarts of water; a small piece of lean ham; cut up one large turnip, and one head of celery; add to the peas; boil until the broth is reduced one half; mash all through a colander; return the soup to the kettle; add another head of celery and an onion chopped fine; season with cayenne pepper and salt to taste; boil half an hour; toast slices of light bread, and lay in the bottom of the tureen; pour the soup over it; celery, vinegar, or the extract may be used if there is no fresh celery to be had. Brown peas are used for giving a richer color.

---

22. *Ox Tail Soup*.—This part of the beef is generally little esteemed, but few things make better soup, on account of the gelatinous matter contained in it. Break the bone in several places; put it to boil, with one or two of the feet, well cleaned, or half of the cheek; finish by the "beef soup" receipt, or any of the foregoing liked.

---

23. *Portable Soup*—is made by boiling very slowly a shin of beef (crack the bones), ox tails, feet, the cheeks, or any scraps of fresh meat which are not choice, to which game or old fowls of any description may be added; good bones; the skinny, gristly parts of meat; one or two hock bones of ham. Cover them with cold water enough to keep the meat from burning; cover the stew-pan; set it on the stove, where the meat will stew very gradually; when of a rich brown color, pour over the meat boiling water enough to cover the meat, and two or three inches over. Now put any vegetables or spices liked; parsley and a few onions cut up are very good (some persons prefer garlic to onions); replace the cover upon the stew-pan; boil slowly and steadily until the meat is done. Strain the broth; use the meat to pot or hash; keep the liquor in an earthen vessel until cold; skim off all the fat and save it to add to gravies or soups. Put the broth back in the stew-pan; boil it briskly putting in salt to taste, and plenty of black and cayenne pepper; the stew-pan must remain uncovered, and the liquor watched constantly at this stage of the boiling, to prevent its burning. Drop a little upon a cold plate; when it begins to jelly, pour it into shallow dishes and set it away to cool. When dry, pack the cakes away in tin canisters; it is best to cut the pieces small; put a piece of letter paper between each layer of the jelly cakes; if there is any appearance of mould, wipe it off carefully with a dry cloth; if it cannot be removed with a cloth, use a little warm water, and expose them to the sun occasionally. With this portable broth, gravies and soups may be made with very little trouble, using to each pint of boiling water, four square inches of the jelly, an inch thick; and when the soup is made, add vegetables and seasoning as is necessary.

Grated carrots will give a fine yellow color; bruised spinach will make it green. This is sometimes used to deepen the color of pea soup. Tomatoes, burnt sugar, onions browned by frying, a slice or two of loaf bread, toasted very brown; either of these will answer to give a brown color, stewed with the soup. White stock is made by the same rule, only the meat must not be browned. Vegetables should not be used which will affect the color of the stock. Veal and poultry are the best meats for this. Celery, turnips, corn, and white onions are the most suitable vegetables, and mace the only spice; black pepper should not be used, the white or Jamaica is best; and the thickening for the soup should be wet up with milk.

Glazing is done by melting as much of this jelly as is necessary, and brushing over the meat with it two or three times. Use a wooden or silver spoon in making this stock.

---

24. *To Clarify Soup.*—Add to the broth, while cold, the whites of two eggs (for half a gallon) whipped to a froth. Stir it into the broth well; simmer gently, without stirring until the

liquid looks clear; then begin to skim until the impurities are removed. Soups are seldom clarified, except for white soups. (Arrow-root is a nice article for thickening white soups.) Always wet the cloth through which the soup is to be strained, in cold water; this hardens the fat, and more entirely separates it from the liquor when it is desirable to remove the fat.

In making brown soups, broil or fry the meat first in the bottom of the soup-kettle; then pour over it cold water. Made in this way, the soup is richer and of a better color; or stew it in very little water until brown; then pour over it the water necessary to make the soup. A good proportion of wine is a tumblerful (or half a pint) to three quarts of soup; use *good Madeira*. Wine and catsup should not be added until a few minutes before serving the soup.

FISH

25. *To fry Fish.*—Use for this purpose a frying-pan, spider, or iron oven. If the frying-pan is preferred, half fill the vessel with lard; but if a larger and deeper vessel is used, have lard enough to cover the fish. The lard should be sweet and clean, and free from salt, as rancid lard imparts a disagreeable taste, and salt will prevent the article from browning. It is important to know when the lard is hot enough. If not hot enough, the fish will be pale and sodden. A good and easy way to ascertain this is to throw a small piece of bread into the vessel. If it fries crisp, the lard is ready; if the bread burns, it is too hot. As soon as the fish is done, remove it to a soft cloth before the fire; turn once. This will absorb the grease; the grease otherwise would settle upon the lower pieces. Fish, to be in perfection, must be fresh. To ascertain this, examine the gills and eyes; the former should be of a bright red, the latter bright and lively, and the flesh firm. The least taint about fish renders them worthless. Pond fish have an earthy, muddy taste. To extract this, soak them in salt and water.

"Any person who has seen the process of evaporation going on at the Salt Works, knows that the salt falls to the bottom. Just so it is in the pan where your mackerel lies soaking; and as it lies with the *skin* side down, the salt will fall to the skin, and there remain; when, if the flesh side were down, the salt falls to the bottom of the pan, and the fish comes out fresh."—*Southern Cultivator*.

---

26. *To fry Shad.*—Clean them thoroughly; cut in slices of proper size to help at the table. Wipe each piece dry. Beat one or two eggs well together, and with an egg-brush put the egg

evenly over the fish; or the pieces may be dipped in the egg. Be sure that every part is covered by the beaten egg. Roll them in bread crumbs. Shake off the loose crumbs, and fry in hot lard. Fry the thick parts a few minutes before putting in the thin. Have plenty of lard to cover the fish. Do not put it in until the lard boils, or it will not be firm and crisp. If there are eggs or roe, fry them. Shad and other fish may be rolled in corn meal, sifted fine, or in flour, before being fried. Either way is good. This receipt will answer for frying any kind of fish. Very small fresh water fish may be cooked whole, and simply rolled in Indian meal, or fried plain.

Trout, black-fish, mullet, whiting, perch, sturgeon, and drum, are all excellent cooked by either of the above receipts. Large fish should be cut into steaks or fillets.

---

27. *To fry Fillets of Fish.*—Cut them in slices half an inch thick; fry them plain, or in thin batter, or roll in Indian meal. Whole fish may be fried or boiled in plenty of boiling lard; when done, skin them, and serve immediately in a hot dish; use piquant sauce.

---

28. *To broil Fish.*—If salt, take it from the brine; wash it in two waters; lay it in plenty of water (the inside down) to cover it well, to which add half a teacup of vinegar. If the fish is hard and dry, instead of the vinegar add a tablespoonful of soda; change the water, if very salt. When sufficiently fresh to cook, remove it from the water. Wipe all fish, whether salt or fresh, very dry before broiling. Have the gridiron prepared, by rubbing the bars bright; grease them with suet or lard, without the least smoke or blaze about it. When the gridiron is hot, place the fish, skin side down, upon it, and turn it once. The dish in which the fish is to be served should be hot, and the moment it is done send, without delay, to the table. A cold fish, served upon a cold dish, upon a cold day, is an unattractive dish, when, with the proper attention and suitable accompaniments. it might

be made the reverse. Drawn butter, with lemon juice, or any of the flavored vinegars preferred, should constitute the sauce, Caviare, Worcester sauce, any of the catsups liked, should be. at

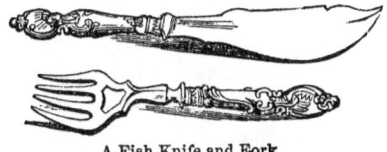

A Fish Knife and Fork.

hand, for the benefit of those who prefer extempore seasoning of that kind to the drawn butter.

---

29. *To Broil Salt Mackerel.*—When it has soaked sufficiently, remove it from the water; always taste one of the fins to ascertain if fresh enough. Hang it to drain a short time; wipe the inside dry; rub between the bars of the gridiron with beef suet, or a little nice lard. Be careful not to use much grease, or it will drip upon the coals and give a disagreeable taste to the fish. Let the gridiron be hot, but not enough so to scorch. Lay the fish open, skin side down; turn it once. When done, place over it a hot dish; invert the gridiron; pour a small wineglass of boiling water over the fish. Let this remain five minutes; pour off the water; butter it well; garnish with hard-boiled eggs, sliced, or use egg sauce, or season extempore with caviare, lemon juice, or any of the flavored vinegars preferred. Broil other salt fish in the same way.

---

30. *To Broil Fresh Fish.*—Clean them well; if large, cut a long slit down the back bone on the inside, so that the fish will lie open without being split in two; dry it with a cloth; sprinkle some salt over the fish, and let it lie until there is *just time* to cook it; for, to be eaten in perfection, it should go from the gridiron to the mouth. Have a clear brisk fire, without the least smoke. The gridiron being prepared as for the mackerel, place the skin side down; when brown, turn it carefully, sprin

kling a little flour on the inside, to prevent its sticking. When done, place a hot dish over the fish, and invert the gridiron; pour over melted butter; garnish with parsley and lemon; scraped horseradish is a good accompaniment. This receipt will answer for broiling any fresh fish. An excellent way for cooking fresh fish, is by *semi-broiling*. Place three or four muffin rings, or a small trivet, in the bottom of a stove baking-pan; pour in a wineglass of water; butter the fish well; season with pepper and salt; place the pan in the oven of the stove; baste the fish frequently, and turn once. The fish should be split open as in former receipts. If the fish is large, cut it in pieces; roll in meal or flour, and lay the slices in the pan with a little water; turn frequently, and baste often. The rings or skewers will not be needed when the fish is sliced.

---

31. *Another method of Broiling fresh Fish.*—Take a fresh fish; cut out the entrails, and without removing the scales, wash it clean; dry it with a cloth; put inside a seasoning of butter, pepper, and salt; wrap it in a wet sheet of foolscap paper, or several if necessary; cover it up in hot ashes. When the fish is done—strip the skin off and it is ready for the table. Send drawn butter to the table in a boat, to which add caviare, or any kind of catsup preferred, or serve with lemon juice stirred into drawn butter. The dish upon which the fish is placed should be hot.

Says Izak Walton: "Lying in water long, and washing the blood out of the fish after the intestines are removed, abates much of their sweetness."

---

32. *Mrs. Hale's Receipt for Broiling Shad.*—Empty and wash the fish with care. Do not open it more than necessary to do this; fill it with force-meat and its own roe. Oysters are good when in season; sew it up; fasten with fine skewers securely; wrap it in thickly buttered paper; broil gently over solid coals for one hour without the least smoke.

33. *Izak Walton's Receipt for Broiling Fresh Fish.*—"When you have scaled him, and cut off his tail and fins, and washed him very clean, then chine, or slit him thro' the middle as a salt fish is usually cut; then give him three or four *scotches* across the back with your knife; broil him—no smoke must rise from the coals, all the time he is broiling; baste him with good sweet butter, and a little salt in the butter; add a little thyme or parsley to the butter. Remember to wash the fish's throat clean; do not wash him after he is opened. It is said that though some fish be light and easy of digestion, they are of all the animal tribes, the most disposed to putrefaction. Acid sauces and pickles, by resisting putrefaction, are a proper addition to fish."

---

34. *To broil Smoked Fish.*—Wash it well in cold water; wipe it dry; broil on a hot gridiron, turning two or three times, when *thoroughly hot*; pour on it melted butter; pepper well; garnish with parsley and lemon. A good breakfast dish. It is a good plan to let fresh fish lie several hours in the seasoning, before broiling; each slice, if the fish is large, may be seasoned with butter, pepper salt, a little minced onion, or eschalot; wrap in buttered paper separately and broil; turn out of the paper and serve with sauce.

---

35. *To Boil Fish.*—Scale and clean the fish; cut open no more than is necessary to clean the inside well. Remove carefully all the black blood that attaches to the back bone; lay the fish, if fresh, in salt and water twenty minutes, before cooking. This is a better plan than to add salt to the water in the kettle. A small piece of saltpetre (one-fourth of an ounce to a gallon of water) put into the fish-kettle will make the fish firmer; use water enough to cover the fish and no more; cover with a close-fitting lid; simmer slowly; skim as long as there is any dross on the top. This is important, if you wish the fish to look white. To ascertain when the fish is done, try if the thickest part can be separated from the bone; in doing this be careful to disturb the fish as little as possible. When done, remove from the water *immediately;* every moment it remains will injure its condition. Should the fish be done before wanted, wrap around it a napkin wrung out in hot water. Suspend the strainer (if a fish-kettle is used) over boiling water, placed across the kettle; the water must not touch it. Just before serving, immerse it for a moment in the boiling water over which it was suspended. When a fish-kettle is not used, a piece of flat perforated tin, having a small handle at each end, will answer in place of the strainer. The fish should be boiled in a vessel just large enough to hold it without cramping, with a close, well-fitting cover. Serve with melted butter; this is always made thicker than for meats, as it is diluted with catsups or lemon juice. Whole fish are put to boil in warm water; fillets in hot water.

---

36. *Another way to boil Fish.*—After being well scaled and cleaned, wrap separately, if there are more than one, in cloths of several folds. Place the fish in the kettle; salt the water—a teasponful of salt to a pound of fish. Simmer gently; the time required for cooking depends upon the thickness of the fish, and, like meat, the fish requires more time in cold than warm weather. It seldom requires more than thirty or forty minutes; when the fish will separate from the bone, *it is done;* when it *falls* from the bone it is *overdone.* Send to the table in a hot dish with rich egg and butter sauce.

---

37. *A piece of boiled Salmon*—It is usual to cut a slice each of

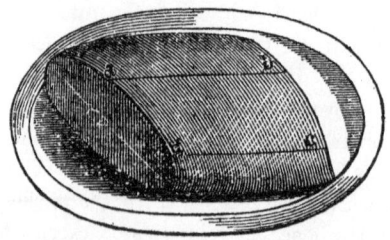

fat and lean and serve to each person. The abdomen is the fat

FISH.

test and must be cut from *d* to *c*; the upper side, or back, cut from *a* to *b*.

---

38. *To Stew Fish.*—Into one quart of hot water or broth cut up a large onion, half a teaspoonful of black pepper beaten fine. Boil these together until the onion is done. Lay the fish, *properly cleaned* and dusted with flour, in the fish-kettle or vessel in which it is to be cooked. Strain this broth to it; season with salt; simmer gently; skim off any impurities that may rise. When the fish is done (one of moderate size will require twenty minutes) pour off the gravy into a stew-pan; rub into a tablespoonful of butter a dessert spoonful of flour; add this to the gravy. Let this stew gently, stirring frequently, only five minutes; take the fish up, place it in a hot dish and strain the gravy over it. Wine or catsup may be added to the gravy if liked.

---

39. *To Stew Catfish, Eels, Perch, etc.*—After cleaning well, place the fish in the kettle; strew over two large onions, cut up fine; pepper and salt to taste; cover with warm water; set the kettle where it will simmer gently. Cut up very fine, four or five large sprigs of parsley; add this to the fish. Pour into the stew-pan one pint of sweet cream or rich sweet milk; add to this a teacup of butter into which has been rubbed a tablespoonful of flour; place it on the fire for five minutes, shaking the pan frequently. Take up the fish and pour the gravy over it.

---

40. *Mrs. R.'s Receipt for Stewing Fish.*—Scale and clean the fish well; wipe dry and dredge with flour. Fry them in lard until half done and of a light brown color. Put them in a stew-pan; cover with boiling water. To half a pint of water add half a pint of wine or catsup; a tablespoonful of lemon pickle cut up fine, cayenne pepper to taste; a large onion cut up, half a dozen cloves, a stick of horseradish. Cover the pan close; simmer gently until the fish is done. To ascertain this, draw a fin and taste it. Take the fish up in a hot dish; thicken the gravy with

flour rubbed into butter. Stew this a little and strain over the fish; send part of the gravy to the table in a tureen; garnish with pickled mushrooms or scraped horseradish.

---

41. *To Bake Fish.*—Clean nicely; keep on the head and fins; sprinkle lightly with salt; stuff with a rich force-meat and sew the sides together; wind tape around to prevent the parts from tearing. Place on the bottom of the oven in which the fish is to be baked, two or four skewers, crossed; muffin-rings will answer, or a trivet. This will slightly elevate the fish and prevent its sticking or burning. Place the fish upon the skewers; pour into the oven a teacup of water. Bake in a moderate oven; baste frequently, with lard at first, and then with its own drippings. Do not attempt to turn the fish; an hour will bake a large fish if the fire is well managed; bake slowly; thicken the gravy with a little flour; if not rich enough, add butter and season with wine, caviare or any of the catsups or made sauces. A gill of wine will season a pint of gravy; spices may be used if liked; pepper and salt to taste. If the stove is used for baking, place the fish in a deep pan or brown stone dish; first cover it all over with the yolk of an egg; roll in fine bread crumbs, and put over this small pieces of butter; pour into the stove-pan a little water, the quantity must depend upon the size of the fish; bake slowly and baste frequently; caviare should be put upon the table to eat with the fish. A good stuffing for baked fish is, sliced light bread covered thick with butter, into which has been stirred well, pepper, one or two teaspoonfuls of French mustard; saturate the bread with Sherry wine, trim off the hard crust; cut the bread in proper slices for laying inside of the fish. Omit the wine if not liked, and substitute tomato or mushroom catsup.

---

42. *To Cook Salt Cod.*—Soak the piece intended for use in plenty of tepid water, adding to each gallon of water a teacup of vinegar. If the fish is very hard and dry, use a tablespoonful of saleratus or carbonate of soda to a gallon of water. Taste one

of the flakes to ascertain when it is sufficiently fresh. Too much soaking will render the fish insipid. To cook it, set it where it will heat gradually and simmer very gently. Boiling will make the fish hard and tough. Pick it, when done, in flakes; remove the skin, and pour over a rich egg and butter sauce.

---

43. *Codfish and Potatoes.*—After the fish is done, pick it from the bones as fine as possible. Have ready as much cooked Irish potatoes as you have fish; mash them fine with a little sweet cream, two or three hard-boiled eggs, chopped fine, and a little finely minced onion, if the flavor is liked. To one pound of the mixture add a wineglass of Madeira wine, and half a grated nutmeg; salt and pepper to taste; two tablespoonfuls of melted butter. Should the mixture be too stiff to form into cakes, moisten with a little more cream; fry in lard. Very little cooking is necessary. Or make this into a large oval cake; put it in a baking-dish; brush it over with melted butter; strew over fine bread crumbs; set it in the stove just long enough to brown. Send rich sauce in a boat to be eaten with this, when baked. If fried, no sauce is needed.

Codfish is good baked after being boiled, and dressed with a rich sauce of cream, butter, and hard-boiled eggs; rub a little flour into the butter. Parsley shred fine may be used, if liked.

---

44. *Cod Sounds and Tongues.*—Cod sounds are the soft parts about the jowl of the fish, which are taken out, salted and barrelled. If pickled, soak them all night in warm water; scrape off the skin; boil them in milk and water until tender; when done, drain them, and pour over hot egg and butter sauce.

---

45. *Fish Cutlets.*—Cut a large fish in slices a quarter of an inch thick; roll them in fine Indian meal, and fry in boiling lard; or dip them in beaten egg, and roll in fine bread crumbs; fry; garnish with parsley, and use any of the fish sauces. Cutlets

may also be stewed and seasoned with parsley, thyme, onion, pepper, and salt. Very few minutes will be required to cook them. Serve with any good pickle.

---

46. *To Souse Fish.*—Boil the fish until done; add a little salt. Take equal quantities of the water it was boiled in and good vinegar. Season highly with pepper, cloves, allspice, and mace; boil the spices in the water until their strength is extracted. Cut off tne head and tail of the fish; cut the rest in pieces; pack close in a stone jar and pour over the vinegar. It must stand a day or two before using. Keep the jar, well covered, in a cool place. Should more vinegar be needed, add it cold.

---

47. *To Pot Shad and other Fish.*—Wash the fish; lay it several hours in salt and water; cut it in slices to fit the jar in which it is to be potted. Prepare the spices by mixing three tablespoonfuls of salt, two of pepper, two of cinnamon, one of allspice, one of cloves and mace. This will be sufficient to season five pounds of fish. Put in the jar a layer of fish, one of spices, sprinkled over evenly; sprinkle a little flour over; strew over bits of butter; then another layer of fish and seasoning, and so on until the fish is all in; pack down closely; fill the jar with vinegar and water, half of each; cover the jar with a coarse crust made of flour and water, pressed close to the jar, that no steam may escape; bake in a moderate oven six hours; do not remove it from the jar until cold; slice cold for supper or luncheon; serve with lemon.

---

48. *Croquettes of Fish.*—Mince cooked fish very fine; remove ll bones very carefully; use three parts of bread crumbs; season highly with pepper, salt and mace to taste; add one egg, a little milk and flour; work the mixture together; form it into small cakes; roll them in beaten eggs, then in fine bread crumbs, and fry in hot lard. Make a gravy of the head, tail, and fins; boil and strain; rub a tablespoonful of butter into an even tablespoon

ful of flour; add this to the gravy. Send to the table in a gravy boat; garnish with sliced lemon.

---

49. *Salmon and Lobster Salad.*—If the salmon salad is made of the fish preserved in cans, drain it from the oil; mince the meat fine; cut up fine, without bruising, a third as much lettuce or celery. For a box of salmon boil four eggs hard; lay them in cold water a few minutes; then shell them, and separate the whites from the yolks; lay the whites aside; mash the yolks smooth with two tablespoonfuls of sweet olive oil or melted butter, or a teacup of sweet, rich cream; the oil makes the smoothest and best paste. Strain this through a coarse sieve. Dissolve in a teacup of vinegar one teaspoonful of loaf sugar, one teaspoonful of salt, two of fine mustard; pepper to taste; mix this with the paste, and toss lightly over the meat with a silver fork. Ornament the dish in which it is served with the green leaves of the celery, or with curled parsley and the whites of the eggs cut into rings. Lobster salad is prepared in the same way. Take the nicest parts of the lobster.

---

50. *Fricassee Fish and Tomatoes.*—If the fish is large, cut it in pieces; roll these in flour; season with salt and pepper; fry about half done, and of a light brown color; take the fish up and set it aside. Scald and skin six large tomatoes, more if they are small; cut up a good-sized onion fine; mix with the tomatoes; fry these in butter, stirring them to prevent their scorching; pour over the tomatoes enough boiling water to make sauce for the fish; add a wineglass of wine, if liked; put the fish in the stew-pan; simmer in the gravy until done. Spices may be used, if liked.

---

51. *To Hash Fish.*—Take any kind of cooked fish (salt mackerel is very good prepared in this way); mince the meat fine and season with pepper; have a third as much Irish potatoes cooked and mashed, as there is fish; cut up fine three hard-boiled eggs; stir this mixture together; into a stew-pan put a tumbler of boil

ing water, a large tablespoonful of butter; stir the fish into the stew-pan, and allow it to simmer until thoroughly hot; serve in a hot, covered dish. This is a nice breakfast dish, and should not be prepared until the last moment. Cold fish may also be made into a pillau; remove all bones; cook the rice, and add the fish pulled into flakes, just long enough to become hot; season high with cayenne pepper. Some persons like mace. This may be used or not, as may be preferred.

52. *Chowder.*—Cover the bottom of the pot in which the chowder is to be cooked with slices of pickled pork, or, if preferred, use a large tablespoonful of lard. Take any kind of firm fish (cod and bass are thought best); lay them over the pork or in the lard. If pork is used, first fry it slightly; if lard, make it boiling hot. Strew over the fish a layer of chopped onions, one of split crackers, pepper and salt; spices are used, if liked, but are not necessary; another layer of fish, onions, crackers, and seasoning, until all the fish is in; dredge with flour; just cover the fish with water; stew gently; half an hour will cook one of moderate size. Take up the chowder; thicken the gravy by adding a tablespoonful of flour to a teacup of butter; add this to the gravy; stew two minutes; add wine or catsup if liked. Oyster or clam chowder may be made in the same way.

53. *Eels.*—*Dr. Kitchiner's Receipt for Stewing Eels.*—Kill them by piercing the spinal marrow, close to the back part of the skull, with a sharp-pointed skewer. If done in the right place, all motion will instantly cease. There is certainly less torture by this method than to cut and skin them alive. Rub them with salt until the slime is cleansed from them; wash them in several waters; divide them in pieces about four inches long; lay the pieces in a stew-pan. If a large eel, pour on it a quart of cold water, two onions, and let it stew twenty minutes; strain the gravy into a small stew-pan; make it thick as cream with flour; add a seasoning of pepper, salt, Port wine, and mushroom catsup;

pour this over the eel; stew two minutes, and send to the table hot.

---

54. *To Fry Eels.*—Skin them; wash well; season with pepper and salt; roll each piece in fine Indian meal; fry in boiling lard; or egg them, and roll in bread crumbs, and fry. For sauce, use melted butter, sharpened with lemon juice.

---

55. *To Broil Eels.*—Skin and wash them; dry them, after cutting in pieces; sprinkle salt and pepper upon them. Put them in an oven with a wineglass of water, a large spoonful of butter; *baste with this frequently.* Just before serving, strew over bread crumbs, a little chopped parsley, salt and pepper; put on the oven lid heated with coals, and brown a light color.

---

56. *Another Way to Broil Eels.*—Skin, clean, and slice them; sprinkle over them salt and pepper, and a little finely pulverized sage; broil upon a hot gridiron; chop three or four sprigs of parsley into a teacup of butter and one tablespoonful of boiling milk. Put in a stew-pan; let it boil up twice, and serve with the eels. They cannot be served too hot; garnish with lemon.

---

57. *Lobster.*—Have ready a pot of boiling water; salt the water, a tablespoonful to one gallon; tie the claws of the lobster, and put him in the pot of boiling water head foremost. Says Mrs. Hale: "Many people are shocked at the apparent cruelty of killing them in this way, but death takes place immediately, and life cannot be taken away without pain." This is certainly taking a very philosophic view of the subject, and if lobsters could reason, would no doubt be consolatory as they take the awful plunge. Boil briskly for half an hour; take them from the water and let them drain; cut off the head and small claws, they are never used; crack the shell slightly; remove the meat carefully, and serve hot with drawn butter, lemon juice, or either of the flavored vinegars; they require a *piquant* sauce.

Lobsters may be served in a variety of ways—boiled, made into salad, lobster pie, or lobster soup—and may be prepared by any of the fish receipts. The male lobster is best for boiling, and is known by the tail being narrower and the flesh firmer than the female. The hen is preferred for salad and sauces, on account of the coral. It gives a beautiful red color to sauces. The lobster seems rather an extraordinary creature, having some decided peculiarities. It has the power of reproducing horns and claws "Its flesh is in its tail and feet, and its stomach is in its head." There is a vein running in the back of the head called "ladies' finger," which is said to be poisonous; hence the importance of removing the head. The coral must not be boiled: this would spoil the beautiful red color which makes it valuable for ornamenting sauces. Beat the coral with butter in a marble mortar; rub it through a sieve, and either stir it to the sauce or mix it with the lobster, merely putting it on the fire a few minutes to *heat*.

---

58. *Mrs. K.'s Receipts for Cooking Shrimps, Crabs and Terrapins.*—*Shrimp Patties.*—Chop or grind one soup-plate of peeled shrimps; moisten with water one tumblerful of grated light bread, first removing the crust; mix well with the shrimps until a smooth paste is formed; add a *heaped-up* tablespoonful of butter, a teaspoonful of mixed mustard, salt, cayenne, and black pepper to taste, and half a grated nutmeg; make into small cakes and fry in butter or lard, a light brown color.

---

59. *Shrimp Pie.*—To two quarts of peeled shrimps add two tablespoonfuls of butter, half a pint of tomato catsup, half a tumbler of vinegar; season high with black and cayenne pepper; salt to taste; put into an earthen dish; strew grated biscuit, or light bread crumbs very thickly over the top; bake slowly half an hour. This may be varied by using Irish potatoes boiled and mashed, in place of the bread crumbs; or use a layer of shrimps, then macaroni, previously soaked in hot sweet milk.

---

60. *To Pickle Shrimps.*—Peel the shrimps; put them in an unglazed jar; first a layer of shrimps, then one of mixed spices, pepper and salt, until all the shrimps are in. Pour in a little water and boil them. When done and cold, cover with good vinegar. They will be fit for use in twenty-four hours, and if closely covered will keep several weeks.

---

61. *Shrimp Sauce.*—Skin a tumbler of shrimps; boil the skins in a tumbler of water; strain the water from them on a tumbler two-thirds full of butter, into which has been rubbed a heaped teaspoonful of flour; simmer a few minutes; add the shrimps chopped fine; let them stew until done. Very little cooking is necessary. Salt, pepper and catsup to taste. A good fish sauce.

---

62. *Terrapins.*—Boil three terrapins until the bones can be easily removed; chop the meat very fine; add two tablespoonfuls of butter, one pint of tomato catsup, half a pint of Sherry or Madeira wine, one tablespoonful of mixed mustard, two onions boiled and chopped fine; salt, black and red pepper to taste; allspice and nutmeg may be used if liked; stir the mixture well; scrape and clean two of the backs; line them with puff-paste; fill with the mixture; cover over with bread crumbs, and bake until a light brown.

---

63. *Crabs in the Back.*—Boil the crabs; pick the meat from the bones. To two dozen crabs, add four tablespoonfuls of fresh olive oil, one tablespoonful of mixed mustard; season high with black and red pepper; clean the backs well, and fill as many as may be needed with the mixture; cover with bread crumbs and bits of butter, and bake. Crabs are boiled alive as the lobster, and "the vein upon the back" must also be removed. They require more cooking than the lobster. They may be stewed, and are considered good cold, minced very fine and used as a stuffing to the large sweet bell pepper, or may be served cold, well seasoned and garnished with lemon and celery.

---

64. *Saunderson's Receipt for Cooking Terrapins.*—Put them into a pot of boiling water; let them remain until dead; take them up; remove the outer skin and toe nails; wash the terrapins in warm water; boil in water enough to cover them until tender, adding salt to taste to the water while boiling; take off the shells; remove the sand-bag and gall without breaking; add any juice which may have run out while cutting up, *but no water*; salt and pepper to taste; a quarter of a pound of fresh butter to each terrapin; rub into the butter a tablespoonful of flour for thickening. Put these into a stew-pan, and stir well while the butter is melting; add four tablespoonfuls of rich sweet cream; stir this in well; add enough good Madeira wine to give a delicate vinous taste to the whole; stir frequently and thoroughly, and serve very hot.

---

65. *Clams*—Are hard and soft-shelled. They may be cooked in a variety of ways, using the receipts for lobster, oyster and fish. They are used for pies, soup, fritters, salad, chowder, etc

To stew them, wash the clams, wipe the shells, and put them in a kettle, with the edges downwards; cover with water; boil over a brisk fire half an hour; turn out of the shells; put into a stew-pan, a large heaped tablespoonful of butter, into which has been rubbed an even tablespoonful of flour; half a tumbler of sweet milk; pepper and salt to taste. Lay the clams in, and simmer gently a few minutes; use more butter and milk, according to the quantity of clams.

---

66. *Oysters.*—Wash the shells clean and wipe them dry with a coarse towel; place them in the stove oven, or put a large gridiron upon a bed of solid coals and lay them upon this, or they may be placed immediately upon the coals. As soon as the shells are hot and open slightly, take them up with oyster-tongs; pro-

tect the hand with a thick napkin, and carefully open the shell so as to preserve the delicious juice; season with a little butter, pepper, salt, and vinegar if liked. Says Dr. Kitchiner: "Those who wish to enjoy this delicious bivalve in perfection, must eat it the moment it is opened, with its own gravy in the under shell; if not eaten *absolutely alive* its spirit and flavor are lost." Oyster-tongs for taking up the shells, oyster-knives for forcing them open, buckets to receive the empty shells, and thick napkins to protect the hands, are usually furnished with the oysters.

---

67. *To Stew Oysters.*—Strain the liquor so as to remove every fragment of shell. Mix in equal proportions sweet milk and the oyster liquor. Add to a quart of the liquor a teacup of finely pulverized bread or cracker crumbs; season with salt and pepper; a tablespoonful of butter. Stew this gently, stirring frequently, a quarter of an hour, then add the oysters; stew half an hour, or less time if preferred, and serve hot. Wine and spices are sometimes used as seasoning; use Sherry or Champagne, and mace is the best spice for oysters.

---

68. *Oysters a-la-blaze.*—Place a chafing-dish upon the table with the lamp burning; pour in the oyster liquor; season with butter, salt, and pepper; when hot add the oysters; cover with the chafing-dish cover, and stew fifteen minutes; beat two eggs in a bowl; remove the dish cover and pour the eggs in, stirring rapidly; serve from the chafing-dish immediately. *Another way.*—Put the oysters and butter to stew first, and when the oysters begin to lose their slimy appearance add sweet cream and their liquor in equal proportions; a few bread crumbs. When ready to boil, serve.

---

69. *To Fry Oysters.*—Scald them well in their own liquor; *wipe them dry;* make a thin batter and drop the oysters into it; take up each oyster in a spoonful of batter and fry in boiling lard; when of a light brown color, they are done. Lay a soft

napkin in a flat dish and serve the oysters upon this; they will be too greasy if not served upon a napkin, particularly those that lie at the bottom of the dish.

Another way to fry them is to dip them in the yolk of an egg and afterwards roll them in bread crumbs or corn meal and fry in hot lard; always wipe each oyster dry before dipping it in bread crumbs or egg. If gravy is liked, pour a little of the oyster liquor into the frying-pan; let it boil up just a minute, and serve in a sauce-boat. Never pour gravy over anything fried in batter, it gives it a sodden appearance. The largest should be used for frying.

---

70. *To Broil Oysters.*—Wipe them dry; dip each one in the beaten yolk of an egg; roll in very fine bread or cracker crumbs, first seasoning them with salt and pepper. Have ready pieces of well-buttered foolscap paper cut large enough to roll each oyster in a separate piece; twist the ends of the paper securely and lay them upon a gridiron, sufficiently elevated to secure them from scorching until hot. Have ready the dish upon which they are to be served hot with a tablespoonful of butter; turn upon it the oysters, roll them in the butter and serve immediately; use an extempore seasoning of caviare, lemon-juice, or celery vinegar, as may be preferred.

---

71. *To Scallop Oysters.*—Grease scallop shells or an earthen baking-dish; put in a layer of bread crumbs, pepper and salt and thin slices of butter; then a layer of oysters; repeat this until the oysters are in, using a layer of bread crumbs last with bits of butter over; season with wine and spices, or celery vinegar. Scallops are also good made with layers of Irish potatoes mashed and highly seasoned, a layer of each, beginning and ending with potatoes; lay over a few bits of butter, add oyster liquor enough to moisten the mixture, and bake a few minutes. Tomatoes are good used in this way; use very little liquor.

FISH.

72. *Oyster Patties.*—Scald together a pint of oyster liquor, three blades of mace, six cloves, and the same of allspice; put into a stew-pan a large tablespoonful of fresh butter. Season a pint of oysters with salt and pepper to taste; add them to the butter, set the stew-pan on the stove; as the butter melts, stir them carefully; when the butter is hot, but not boiling, pour the oyster liquor in; stir all together and let it stew fifteen minutes; set this aside in an earthen vessel. Have patty pans lined with puff paste: bake them a light brown color; just before serving, fill these with the oysters. They should be eaten immediately, as the gravy, by soaking in, will render the pastry heavy.

73. *Oyster Chowder.*—Butter a deep earthen dish; soak in sweet milk, as many crackers or slices of light bread as will be needed; cover the bottom of the dish with these (large square crackers are best); strew over these bits of butter; then put in a thick layer of oysters; season with pepper and salt, a little chopped celery or parsley if liked; then crackers, butter, oysters, and seasoning until the dish is full, always having the crackers on top with bits of butter over. Pour in enough oyster liquor and sweet milk mixed in equal proportions to half fill the dish; this had better be put in before adding the last layer of soaked crackers; bake three-quarters of an hour; this may be turned out; serve with pickle. Clam chowder is made in the same way.

74. *To Pickle Oysters.*—For this purpose use large oysters; pick out all pieces of shell; put them in a clean pot, and to every half gallon of the liquor put a half teaspoonful of red pepper, one of black, and a grated nutmeg, two tablespoonfuls of salt; add as much vinegar as liquor; simmer them five minutes. Take them up upon large flat dishes with a perforated skimmer. Let the liquor stew a few minutes longer. When the oysters are cold put them into cans or unglazed jars and pour over the liquor. To be eaten cold. Garnish the dish with celery, parsley, or lemons, as may be preferred.

75. *To Feed Oysters.*—Mix salt with clean water in the proportion of a pint of salt to two gallons of water; change it in twenty-four hours. They are good as long as they keep firmly closed; when they are lightly closed or at all gape, suspect their condition, and have nothing to do with them.

---

76. *To Keep Fish Fresh.*—After cleaning the fish, spread over t a mixture of one teaspoonful of finely pulverized black pepper, one of fine salt, the same of brown sugar; wipe the fish perfectly dry to prevent its moulding; spread this mixture over evenly, and set it in a cool place. This quantity will be sufficient for a large shad, and will preserve it two days, if put on immediately.

---

77. *To Cook Frogs.*—Only the hind legs of the large green kind are used; skin them; season with salt and pepper, and broil or fry them; the meat is beautifully white; the taste delicate.

---

78. *Mock Oysters.*—Take brains from the heads of hogs, as whole as possible; remove the skin and throw them into salt and water; let them remain in this two hours; then boil them, until done, in sweet milk; take them up in an earthen bowl or dish, and pour over weak vinegar to cover them; prepare sufficient vinegar to cover them, by adding to it cloves, allspice, and cinnamon to taste; season well with pepper, using part red pepper; scald this vinegar; pour off the weak vinegar; cover with the spiced vinegar. Eat cold, or stewed with crackers as oysters.

MEATS.

"There is death in the pot."

"Cookery, properly considered," writes a distinguished physician, "is an art, and one of the highest and most useful of the arts, based on chemical science, and closely related to physiology and hygiene. It is not well understood among us, and, with the greatest abundance and variety of the raw material for good living with which any nation was ever blessed, we continue to live worse than any civilized people on the face of the earth. If there is 'death in the pot' (and who can doubt it who has an extensive acquaintance with the cooking of the country?) it is through our own mixing and marring that it has generated there. It has resulted from our unscientific manipulations. In the preparation of food three grand objects ought to be kept in view: first, to retain all its nutritive and other valuable dietetic qualities; second, to make it healthful; third, to make it pleasant to the eye and agreeable to the taste."

---

79. *Boiling Meat.*—Salt meat, meat for soup, and large fish, should be put to boil in cold water. Should poultry or fresh meat, not intended for soup, be put to boil in cold or boiling water? This is a "vexed question." Says Professor Liebig: "If a piece of fresh meat be put into cold water, and this heated to boiling, and boiled until '*done*,' it will become harder, and have less taste than if the same piece had been thrown into water already boiling. In the first case, the matters grateful to the smell and taste go into the extract, viz.: the soup; in the second, the albumen of the meat coagulates from the surface inward, and envelopes the interior with a layer, which is *impermeable* to water. In the latter case, the soup will be indifferent, the meat

delicious." Opposed to this is the authority of Dr. Kitchiner. He directs that fresh meat be put in *cold water*. "Let the water heat gradually, according to the thickness of the article. For instance, a leg of mutton of ten pounds weight, should be placed upon a moderate fire, which will gradually make the water hot, without causing it to boil, for about forty minutes; if the water boils much sooner, the meat will be hardened, and shrink up as if scorched; by keeping the water a certain time heating without boiling, the fibres of the meat are dilated, and it yields a quantity of scum, which must be taken off as soon as it rises."

I consider Dr. Kitchiner the wisest and most reliable writer upon the subject of cookery I have ever read. For over thirty years his "Cook's Oracle" has been my favorite text-book, and I gratefully acknowledge my obligations to him. But, while I regard it as a kind of heresy to differ from the Doctor in any of his opinions, and have seldom found it to my advantage to do so, yet I must, in the point at issue, assert, as the result of my experience, that a *middle course* is best, securing sufficiently all the advantages. The water *should* be *hot* but *not boiling*. To immerse the meat at once in boiling water, contracts the outer skin so rapidly as to toughen the skin, and the meat parts with few of its impurities. When hot water is used, raise it slowly to the boiling point. Gentle stewing and boiling is always best. Cover the article to be boiled with water. A good proportion is a quart of water to a pound of meat. While it is necessary, the meat should be covered with water during the whole process; it must not have more than is necessary. "The less water, provided the meat be covered with it, the more savoury will be the meat, and the better will be the broth." The vessel in which the meat is placed should be well adapted to the size of the meat—not so large as to require too much water, nor so small as to cramp the article to be cooked. It should have a well-fitting cover, and be kept on during the process, removing it occasionally (always dust it first) to skim the liquor.

Attend well to the skimming, and remove carefully all impurities as fast as they rise. It is important to have this well attended to, or the meat will not make a good appearance. Should the water become two much reduced before the meat is done, replenish with boiling water; always keep a kettle of hot water to meet this and other demands. When boiling fresh meat, it is a good plan to place on the bottom of the pot, skewers crossed, muffin-rings, a trivet, or plate inverted (either of these will answer), so as to elevate it a few inches, and render the meat less liable to scorch. The pot should never boil over; thereby excellent broth is lost, which a frugal good cook will always convert into a savory soup. Says Dr. Kitchiner: "It is a waste of fuel to put it under a boiling pot. If a vessel containing water, be placed over a steady fire, the water will grow continually hotter, until it reaches the limit of boiling, after which the regular accessions of heat are wholly spent in converting it into steam." Count Rumford, in one of his essays, says: "It is natural to suppose that many of the finer and more volatile parts of food, those which are best calculated to act on the organs of taste, must be carried off with the steam, when the boiling is violent." A perfect knowledge of the time required for cooking meat, as it depends upon so many circumstances, can only be acquired by practice and close observation. If proper attention is paid to the fire, and the *pot really boils*, twenty-five minutes to the pound will be sufficient, counting from the appearance of the first bubble, for salt meat; twenty minutes for fresh. Salt meat requires more time than fresh; and more time is required in cold than warm weather.

Should meat freeze, thaw it before cooking, by immersing i in cold water, or it will be tough.

Never let meat or poultry remain in the broth after it is done It should be served as soon as ready for the table, or it will become sodden.

---

80. *To Boil a Ham.*—Although there are very few Southern kitchens in which the pot is not made to boil every day, yet in

the fewest number is it well done. The process is simple enough, and the failures are the result of irregularity and inat-

Carve—Cut in the line B, C.

tention The cook, as a general thing, places her pot over a fierce fire, which starts the water boiling with a gallop. The scum rises to the top, and is permitted to remain. Other business engages her attention. The pot for awhile is forgotten, and when at length it is remembered, and looked into, the liquor is found too much reduced. This is replenished with cold water, the fire is stirred, and the boiling goes on through the same process.

With this kind of management, is it strange that even our favorite every-day dish of boiled ham, is seldom put upon the table well cooked?

After washing and scraping the ham well, place it in a vessel that will hold it without cramping, and cover every part of it, and three inches over, with cold water; boil slowly and steadily. A ham weighing ten pounds will require four hours. They are seldom boiled long enough. Be sure the pot boils; skim frequently; keep the pot well covered; avoid piercing the meat; this makes unsightly marks and lets out the juices. When done, lay the ham, before skinning, in a stove-pan, and set it in the oven; half an hour's baking will improve it. After the ham is taken up, cabbage, greens, beans, etc., may be boiled in the broth. It is not proper to boil cabbage, or any kind of greens, with the ham, as they impart a disagreeable taste to the meat. An old salt ham should be soaked several hours before boiling. After being skinned, hams may be ornamented in different ways.

Brush over the top with the beaten yolks of eggs; sift over fine cracker or bread crumbs evenly; bake half an hour in a moderate oven, or cover with a thin coat of Irish potatoes, rubbed through a colander. Set it for a few minutes in the oven. When to be used for party occasions, and it is desired to make them *particularly fine*, the skin may be permitted to remain; cut this in diamond shapes with a sharp knife, leaving the skin on alternately; fill the skinned shapes with grated yolks of hard-boiled eggs, or grated carrots or beets; trim the dish with celery tops. Another way: Skin the ham; lay it off in diamond shapes with cloves, sticking the stems into the meat; fill alternately with the grated yolks and whites of hard-boiled eggs; be careful not to mix them; garnish the dish with green sprigs of parsley. They are very pretty ornamented with flowers cut from vegetables; make red roses of beets; yellow of carrots; white with turnips; use curled parsley or mustard for leaves; wrap the knuckle with fringed letter paper.

81. *Miss F.'s Receipt for Preparing Whole Hams for Parties.*—Boil them very done, and skin them; when cold, cut through the ham in slices to the bone; but do not cut the slices from the bone. Between each slice, put thin slices of pickle, and detach the slices as needed. The ham dressed by either of these receipts will show to better advantage by being slightly elevated above the dish; garnish with celery tops or something green.

These last receipts are entirely for ornament. If "good wine needs no bush" a well-cured, well-boiled ham *needs* no ornament to secure general appreciation. White cabbage, beans, peas, Irish and sweet potatoes are good accompaniments. Save the essence or gravy of the ham for the soup kettle.

82. *To Know when Hams are Sound.*—Stick a sharp knife to the bone in the thickest part of the ham, and also run it around the knuckle. If there is any taint, you can detect it by smelling and examining the knife.

83. *To Glaze a Ham.*—Brush over the ham (using a feather or brush) with the yolk of an egg; cover thickly with bread crumbs. Go over it with thick cream; put it in the stove or oven to brown; put the glaze on half an inch thick; if necessary go over the second time.

---

84. *To Boil a Leg of Pork.*—Pork requires longer boiling than any other meat. If it has been salted six or eight days, soak it an hour before cooking; scrape and wash it carefully; singe off any hairs with a piece of burning paper or corn shuck. Avoid making incisions about the knuckle; this lets out the juice. Put it to boil with the water *warm* only; boil slowly and steadily, skimming carefully; keep the cover on; this will not only keep out the smoke, but retain much of the nutritive properties of the meat; should the least dross remain upon the meat when done, scrape it again. It should go to the table white, clean, and thoroughly done, and yet not boiled until the meat drops from the bone. This is good cold, or slightly broiled and buttered. A peas pudding, from time immemorial, has been considered the proper accompaniment for this dish; boiled turnips, dressed with butter and cream, are also excellent; when cold, nothing can be better than chow or French mustard as an accompaniment.

85.. *To Boil a Leg of Mutton.*—The mutton should be fat; unless it is, I would advise its being cooked some other way; very few things are more insipid than poor boiled mutton. It should be killed the evening before it is to be cooked. For roasting it may be kept longer; but for boiling, if kept, the meat will be dark. To prevent it being discolored by the action of the air, tie it in a bag, and suspend it until needed. Put it in a large stew-pan or boiler; cover with water merely warm; boil steadily; skim well, and keep it well covered. Some persons boil in a well-floured cloth, tying it at the ends; this is superfluous if the water is kept well skimmed; put in salt when the meat is half done. A leg weighing ten pounds will require three hours steady simmering; take it up as soon as done; serve with caper or egg sauce; or make a rich gravy of some of the broth; add Sherry wine and tomato catsup to taste; butter, if needed.

86. *To Boil a Loin of Mutton.*—Skin the loin; remove all bone; crack the bones; put them with the skin in a stew-pan, and cover with cold water; cut up fine three sprigs of parsley, the same of thyme, and one large onion; put them into the stew-pan with the bones; pepper and salt to taste; let this stew gently until all the gravy is extracted from the bones and skin. Put the mutton on in a vessel large enough to hold it, having a well-fitting cover; pour upon it a pint of warm water, half a pint of good tomato catsup; cover it, and let it boil gently three hours, turning it over *frequently*. Just before the mutton is done, strain over it the gravy from the bones; let all stew together five minutes. Some persons prefer wine to the catsup; when used, take a tumblerful of good Madeira wine; scald two blades of mace, half a dozen cloves, a dozen grains of allspice in it, and add to the mutton half an hour before it is done, and use a tumblerful more of water when it is first put to boil. Lamb may be boiled by either of these receipts, but is not good boiled, unless very fat and well grown.

87. *To Boil a Loin of Veal.*—Take ten pounds of the best part of the loin; bind the flap around with broad tape; place it in the kettle, and manage as directed for mutton; take it up as soon as done or the meat will lose its freshness and firmness. Being an insipid meat, a highly-seasoned gravy is necessary; oyster sauce may be used, also onion or tomato sauce. The loin is generally esteemed the best part of the calf. Veal should be kept suspended in a bag, and wiped very dry. It taints very easily. Though often boiled, it is better roasted or stewed.

88. *To Boil a Calf's Head.*—After being well cleaned, it is best to keep the skin on; it will require an hour longer in cooking when

the skin is retained. The head should be fat. Cut apart the upper and lower jaws; remove the eyes; they are never used. Take out the bone containing the teeth, also the nose and ears; cut out the tongue; remove the brains; put the head and tongue to boil in enough warm water to cover them; tie the brains in a cloth; boil all until tender; vegetables may be boiled with the head, if liked—onions, carrots, parsley, and thyme; serve the head upon one dish; upon another place the tongue and brains, or make sauce of the brains; take a pint of the broth, put it in a stew-pan; add a tablespoonful of parsley chopped fine; salt and cayenne pepper to taste; let these stew a quarter of an hour; add a large tablespoonful of butter, into which has been rubbed a dessert-spoonful of flour; stew this five minutes, and serve with the head; use the remainder of the broth for soup. It is the basis of mock turtle soup. Season the brains with sage, if the flavor is liked; garnish with lemon.

---

89. *Beef Bouilli.*—Take five or six pounds of good, tender beef from the rump, brisket, or long ribs; the rump or round is best. Put a trivet or muffin-rings on the bottom of a deep stew pan or pot; cover with warm water two inches deep; boil rather briskly until the water is clear; skim closely; then put in three or four large turnips sliced, two carrots grated, two onions cut up fine, a tablespoonful each of parsley and thyme, chopped fine. Let the pot stand where the water will simmer gently and steadily until the meat is tender; take up the meat; put as much of the broth into a stew-pan as is needed for gravy; rub to a large tablespoonful of butter a heaped teaspoonful of flour; put this into the stew-pan; stew five minutes; add to the gravy a good seasoning of tomato or mushroom catsup; lay the vegetables around the meat; use the broth for soup, after taking out enough for gravy; a dish of turnips may be served with this.

---

90. *To Boil Corned Beef.*—Soak the beef over night in plenty of water to cover it well. At nine o'clock next morning, wash the

piece well, put it in the pot and cover with cold water; boil slowly; skim frequently. If it is to be served cold, let it remain in the pot until it becomes so.

To prepare it for luncheon or as a supper dish, remove all the bones when thoroughly done, pick the meat as for salad and pack in a deep dish, putting in alternately fat and lean. Skim the liquor, removing all fat; boil this broth until reduced one half; pour into the dish as much of it as may be needed to fill all the spaces left in packing the meat; lay over this a flat cover that will just fit it, place a heavy weight upon this. It is best to prepare this dish in cold weather, or put upon ice the dish it was prepared in. Serve it upon a plate or round dish, and garnish with green sprigs of parsley, or celery; serve with it chow, picillilla or any good pickle. French mustard is excellent eaten with it.

91. *To Boil a Salt Tongue.*—Soak it over night in plenty of water. Put it to boil in sufficient cold water to cover it; while boiling, if it is too salt, change the water; it requires long boiling. Ascertain when it is done by running a small skewer in; skin it carefully, remove the rough part of the root, and garnish the dish with parsley. Slice round. This is eaten hot as a dinner dish, or cold for supper. Smoked tongue is prepared in the same way. Be sure they are boiled until tender; a fresh tongue must be first boiled and then dipped in beaten egg, rolled in bread crumbs and baked in a pan. Pour in a tumbler of the broth it was boiled in; baste well with butter; half an hour will be sufficient time for it to bake. Season the gravy with any good catsup.

92 *To Boil Cow-heel.*—After being well cleaned boil them until the bones can be removed easily; skin them and serve with parsley and onion sauce.

Clean the feet by immersing them in boiling water; let them remain long enough to loosen the horny part; run a knife around and under the horn; force it off, scrape and wash well. This is an economical dish, nutritive and agreeable, when well prepared it is good fried, after being boiled, or stewed and dressed with cream and butter; cut it in pieces of convenient size for serving.

---

93. *To Boil Tripe.*—As soon as possible after the animal is killed, have the stomach emptied and well washed in cold water; sprinkle lime or ashes over the inside, fold it carefully and lay it in a jar or small tub; cover it with tepid water for six hours; scrape off all the dark part. When all this is removed, wash in several waters and again lay the tripe away for a day and night in weak salt water (use another jar than the one first used, or scald that well and sun it). Boil the tripe (putting to it cold water) until a straw can be easily run through it and the edges look transparent; skim closely, and when the tripe is tender, take it up and cut it in uniform slices of convenient size for serving; pour over milk, or milk and water, to cover it, and keep it closely covered; should the milk turn a little sour it will not injure the tripe, as it is usual to add vinegar in cooking it. It should not be kept long; either fry, stew, or make into a pillau or hash. When made into hash, use onion freely and cover over with pickle.

---

94. *To Boil a Turkey.*—Truss it with the legs drawn in; skewer the wings; remove the skewers before serving. For boiling, select a fowl of *fair skin*; after cleaning it well, if young and the weather is cold, sprinkle a little salt on the inside, and either

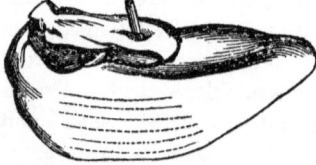

put it in a bag and suspend it or wrap it carefully in a clean cloth and turn it over after it has lain four or five hours; neither poultry nor fresh meat for boiling can be kept so long as for roasting; the meat will not look white.

When the hour for putting it in the pot arrives, stuff it with a rich stuffing previously prepared in the following manner: half a pound of bread crumbs, large heaped tablespoonful of butter, the soft part of twenty or thirty oysters (according to the size of the turkey); season with pepper and salt; mix these intimately and carefully. For variety, I sometimes season with mace or nutmeg and a few cloves. After stuffing the fowl well, but not too full—a little room should be left for the force-meat to swell—cut off the neck bone; put in a little stuffing, enough to give the craw a plump look; draw over the skin tightly and tie securely; dredge the fowl well with flour; place a trivet or muffin-rings in the bottom of the vessel; lay the turkey upon them and cover with warm water. Place the pot where it will boil gently and equally; skim closely until the water is very clear. Replenish if necessary with boiling water. A large turkey will require two hours and a half steady boiling; keep it well covered through the process. Serve with oyster sauce, or any kind of rich white sauce.

Poultry for boiling should be very fat; when the fowl is old, rub the inside with soda instead of salt as soon as it is killed; wash it off before cooking.

---

95. *To Boil Ducks or Chickens.*—Kill them over night; wrap them closely with cloths. If a little old, rub the inside with soda; early next morning lay the fowls in a deep pan and cover with milk and water, or water only, if it is not convenient to use milk. Boil by the directions for boiling a turkey, and use stuffing or not as may be liked. A good stuffing may be made of mashed Irish potato, seasoned with a little onion, butter, salt and pepper, moistened with a little sweet milk, or filled with oysters, chopped. Boil until tender; the time will depend upon the age of the fowl; half an hour is generally sufficient; but never send them to table *underdone.* Serve with parsley and butter sauce, egg or onion sauce, tomato or oyster sauce, as may be preferred. A double kettle answers admirably for boiling them; unless fowls are fat, never boil them.

---

96. *A Delicate Way to Cook Fowls, Rabbit, Veal, or Lamb.*—Keep the meat until tender. Cut it in pieces proper for serving, if meat, or unjoint if a fowl. In the bottom of a double kettle or

unglazed stone jar, put a layer of meat or whatever is to be cooked; strew over one tumblerful of white onion cut small. Chop fine a tablespoonful of parsley and thyme mixed; salt and pepper to taste. Pour over, if a jar is used, a pint of tepid water, and tie over a bladder or very thick piece of cloth folded several times so that the steam will not escape. (If the double kettle is used the water and cloth are unnecessary.) Place the jar into a pot of water that will come within five or six inches of the top, just as near the top as possible without the water getting into the jar; let the pot boil until the meat is done, but not overdone. Strain the gravy into a stew-pan; thicken sufficiently with flour; stew five minutes and pour over the meat. Wine and spices may be used for invalids, omitting the onion.

---

97. *To Blanquette Chicken.*—Prepare the chicken (which should be young and fat) as for boiling; dredge it well with flour; make a rich crust (potato is best); roll out a sheet large enough to envelop the fowl; it should be as thin as pie crust. Wrap this around the fowl, carefully closing it on the back; roll a thin napkin around this. Boil until tender; three-quarters of an hour will be sufficient for a young pullet. Kill the fowl over night; serve with egg and butter sauce poured over; rice must always accompany it.

---

98 *Mrs. P.'s Receipt for Boiling Chickens or Ducks.*—Truss them whole; fill the inside with oysters. Put them into a double kettle; boil until tender; pour the gravy, when the fowl is done, into a stew-pan; rub a teaspoonful of flour into a light tablespoonful of butter; add this to the gravy; let it simmer five minutes. Take three hard-boiled eggs chopped fine; just before serving the fowl, add these to the gravy and a teacup half full of hot cream Pour this over the chicken.

---

99. *Another very Excellent Way to Cook Grown Fowls.*—Boil the fowl until tender; first keeping it long enough after it is killed to

MEATS. 63

be ripe for cooking. Pull it to pieces, taking out all the bones; put it in a stew-pan with a tumblerful of the broth it was boiled in, a tablespoonful of butter with a dessert-spoonful of flour rubbed in, salt to taste; season high with Cayenne pepper. Stir in this a raw well-beaten yolk of an egg, a wineglass or two of Madeira wine with a teaspoonful of loaf sugar, powdered and stirred in the wine; add this to the gravy, or use the same quantity of tomato catsup.

Chickens may also be dressed in this way, and a tumbler of mushrooms cut up and stewed in the gravy.

---

100. *Scraffle.*—Boil a fresh-killed hog's head tender. This is made in the winter during what we at the South call "hog-killing." Take it up and remove all the bones; chop the meat very fine and season it with salt, pepper, and sage, as sausage meat; strain the liquor; wipe out the pot nicely; return the broth to the pot; there should be about a quart of this. Put the meat back and stir into the broth fine corn meal until the mass is the consistence of soft mush; let this simmer half an hour, stirring frequently; pour the mixture into pans three or four inches deep. When cold slice in thin slices, roll in corn meal or flour, and fry in boiling lard, a light brown. This keeps as well as souse; it should be well protected from dust and air.

---

101. *Souse.*—The feet and ears of the hog are best for this, though the upper part of the head is often used, removing the fat where there is too much. To prepare the feet, scald them well; scrape off the hair. Some persons roll them in hot ashes; I prefer the boiling water, as the other plan frequently scorches the skin, and souse should be very white. Scrape them, removing the horny part; when all are well cleaned, lay them to soak a day and night. Put them to boil in plenty of cold water; skim the pot well; simmer them gently. When the bones can be removed easily, take them up, and as soon as they can be handled, pick the meat from the bones; season the mass highly with salt, pepper, and vinegar;

pack it in pans, and lay over each a clean cloth dipped in vinegar; dip the cloth in vinegar every day, and it may be kept for some time in that way, or it may be packed in jars and covered with half vinegar and water.

The feet are excellent split in two, put in a jar, and covered with half vinegar and half the broth they were boiled in, putting a little salt in the broth. Never use salt about the souse, until it is done and removed from the pot; the broth will make good jelly; salt would spoil it for that purpose. The feet should be fried in boiling lard, first rolling them in fine corn-meal, bread or cracker crumbs, or dip them in thin batter. They may be put in spiced vinegar and eaten cold.

---

102. *Hog's Head Cheese.*—Split the head apart—the upper portion only is used; scrape it well. The brains must first be removed; cut off the nostrils and throw them away; cut off the ears; clean and scrape them well; they are to be boiled with the head, the tongue and feet. When entirely done, take them from the broth; remove all bones; grind or chop the meat, tongue, and ears together. Pick the meat from the feet carefully; season with salt, pepper, mace, allspice, and a few cloves to taste; place a cloth in the bottom of a pan, large enough to cover the cheese; pack the meat in; cover it well with the cloth; lay a tin plate on top, and a weight upon that. When cold, remove the cheese to a plate; garnish with lemon and green sprigs of parsley. Eat for supper or luncheon, with French mustard or pickles. If this is to be kept long, put it in spiced vinegar. The vinegar should not be strong, and should be changed occasionally.

---

103. *Calf's Head Cheese.*—After cleaning the head well, take out the eyes; cut off the nose. Boil all that remains in plenty of water, until the bones will come out easily. Two heels boiled with it will be an improvement. Chop the meat fine; season highly with any kind of spices liked, red and black pepper; salt to taste. Put a cloth in the bottom of a colander;

pack in the meat; cover well with the cloth; press with a heavy weight. Eat cold.

---

104. *Stewing Meat.*—This process does not differ materially from boiling. It is slow boiling, or simmering with very little water. When the meat is somewhat old or tough, a little vinegar may be used. "It acts by softening the fibres, and so renders the meat more tender and digestible."

It is an economical way of cooking, since the liquor is used with the meat, and nothing of consequence is lost. The same receipts which have been giving for boiling, will answer for stewing, using much less water. It is important that every kitchen be furnished with stew-pans of different sizes. They should be lined with tin or porcelain, and have well-fitting covers. Always use a stew-pan adapted to the size of the article to be cooked. Before being placed upon the fire, put in enough water to prevent the tin from melting; carelessness upon this point will cause the tin to melt; or, if the stew-pan is lined with porcelain, it will crack if put upon the fire without water. As soon as there is no further use for the stew-pans, the cook should immediately wash them in hot soap-suds until clear of grease; wipe them perfectly dry, and rub over the inside dry meal bran. Managed in this way, they will last a long time.

---

105. *Beef a-la-daube.*—A round is best for this; lard it well. This is done in this way: Get a larding-needle, which is a piece of steel from six to nine inches long, pointed at one end, and four slits at the other. Cut thin slips of pork or bacon, two or three inches long, and a quarter of an inch square; insert these, one piece at a time, for daubing; run the needle through the meat, leaving out half an inch on the top-side. It should be done evenly and closely. For larding, run the needle, starting with the sharp point, through the skin horizontally, leaving half an inch of the meat out at each end. Inserting fat meat in this way greatly improves the quality of meat not

satisfactorily fat. The meat being now ready for the oven, put upon the bottom a trivet or muffin-rings to elevate it. Lay it upon them; cut pieces of the beef from the shank, or any coarse part; lay all around the daube; sprinkle the top with pepper and salt, and lay over slices of bacon or pork, and strips of suet or fat of the beef; chop two or three onions; strew this over the beef; cover the meat with warm water; throw in a few sprigs of parsley, thyme, and sweet basil; shred fine a few stalks of celery; add this; stew gently, skimming occasionally until the meat is done. Take it up; strain the gravy, and let it get cold. Remove the cake of grease that will harden on the top. Save this for the soup-kettle. Put three pints of this broth in a well-lined stew-pan; beat the whites of three eggs to a froth; stir these well to the broth. After it commences boiling, it should not be stirred again; let it boil until the gravy looks clear; remove the scum carefully; strain it, but do not squeeze the cloth. When cool pour over the beef.

---

106. *To Stew a Shin of Beef.—Dr. Kitchiner's Way.*—The Doctor advises "the mistress of the house" to call this dish "ragout beef;" this, says he, will insure its being eaten with "unanimous applause, when the homely appellation of 'shin of beef stewed,' would give your genteel eater the lockjaw." Whatever objection may be urged against the name of this savoury dish, there can be none to the receipt.

Saw the bone in one or two pieces; put it in a stew-pan and just cover it with water. When it simmers, begin the skimming, and when the water looks clear, add a bundle of sweet herbs, viz., parsley, thyme and sweet marjoram; a large onion cut up; four heads of celery, or less if the flavor is not liked; one dozen berries of black pepper; the same of allspice. Stew very gently until the meat is tender. This will take about three hours, unless the meat is very young and tender. Take three carrots, peeled and sliced; the same of turnips; a dozen small silver-skinned onions; boil them until tender. The carrots should be put to cook first, as they require twice as long to cook as the other vegetables. As soon as they are done, take them up and drain them dry. Take up the beef when tender; put it upon the dish on which it is to be served. Thicken three tumblers of the broth with three even tablespoonfuls of flour (make it into a paste with a teacup of the broth), and stir into the gravy; stew this five minutes; season with salt, pepper and catsup, or Port wine if preferred. Send the gravy to the table in a sauce-boat. Lay the vegetables *hot* around the beef. A leg of mutton, or loin of veal, is good prepared in this way. After the vegetables are taken up, return them to the stew-pan, until hot. They may be served upon a separate dish, if preferred.

---

107. *Veal or Mutton Stew.*—Cut young, tender meat in thin slices. Put into a stew-pan a layer of raw Irish potatoes, peeled and sliced, a little onion if liked, a layer of meat. Season highly with red and black pepper, salt to taste; put over this, slices of cold boiled ham; over this, bits of butter, then another layer of meat, seasoning, etc., potatoes last; cover with water; stew gently until done. Thicken the gravy; season with catsup.

---

108. *Veal with Curry Powder.*—Stew two pounds of veal; strew over it two medium-sized onions. Rub together a large tablespoonful of butter, a tablespoonful of curry powder, the same of flour. Add this to two tumblers of the broth. Put this in a small stew-pan; stew five minutes, pour in a tumbler of hot cream. When the meat has stewed slowly until tender, take it up in the dish it is to be served in; send to the table hot; serve the gravy in a sauce-boat. Chicken and turtle are excellent cooked in this way. Less curry powder may be used where high seasoning is not liked.

---

109. *Beef Steak Stewed, or Steamed.*—Cut the steak in pieces of uniform size, that all may be equally done, and rather thicker than for frying. If the meat is not very young and tender, beat it slight-

ly. In the bottom of the stew-pan put a tablespoonful of lard; when this is boiling hot, lay in the steak, and fry it a light brown color. Cut up two onions, and fry at the same time with the meat. Season highly with red and black pepper, salt to taste; pour over boiling water to cover the meat, and stew gently until tender. An hour will probably be required, but this will depend upon the age of the animal, the time it has been kept, and the weather. To make the gravy: Into a small stew-pan put a large tablespoonful of butter, into which has been rubbed a tablespoonful of flour; as soon as this is hot, pour in gradually two tumblerfuls of the broth it was stewed in. Let this stew until the gravy is of the proper consistence; season with mushroom or walnut catsup; pour over the steak, and serve hot. This can be better prepared by stewing in a double kettle, putting the meat in the inner kettle.

---

110. *Delmonico Stew.*—Cut cold cooked fresh meat of any kind, into small thin slices; put them into a chafing dish or stew-pan, with a little hot water. Season with mace, pepper and salt to taste; use part Cayenne pepper. Should there be any cold gravy left, use this, and butter enough to make the stew rich. Put all in the chafing dish, cover it and let the meat simmer ten or fifteen minutes. Cut up a lemon; remove the seed; add this to the stew. Grate the yolks of two hard-boiled eggs; mix with it two teaspoonfuls of good English mustard; this should be put in a small bowl. Pour the gravy to this slowly, making it to a smooth paste. Put this over the meat; remove it from the fire, and serve immediately.

---

111. *Camp Stew—Mr. B.'s Receipt.*—Prepare one or more chickens, and twice as many squirrels, as for frying. Into the bottom of a pot, or deep stew-pan, lay slices of pickled pork or bacon, cutting off the rind and rancid parts, if bacon is used. Put a layer of chicken, one of Irish potatoes peeled and sliced, two large onions cut up fine, butter-beans, corn, and tomatoes; red

and black pepper and salt to taste; a layer of game, then of pork. Finish with a layer of vegetables; cover with water, and, putting on a well-fitting cover, set the vessel where the mixture will simmer gently and steadily four hours.

---

112. *Mutton Stew—Mrs. B.'s Receipt.*—Use any scraps of meat that are not suitable for making cutlets or chops. Stew with a little onion and parsley; season highly with red and black pepper. Boil two eggs hard; mash the yolks fine, or grate them. Stir them to a small tablespoonful of butter, or enough to make the gravy rich; add this to the gravy, and if thickening is needed, use brown flour.

---

113. *Hotch Potch.*—This is made of any kind of fresh meat, or game. To two pounds, add a quart of green peas, a tumblerful each of green corn, asparagus, and young sa~~hes cut fine, a tumblerful of grated carrot; tie together fo~~~~five sprigs of parsley, thyme, and sweet basil; stew until t~~ meat is tender. There should be very little gravy to this when done; should there be too much, leave the cover off until it is sufficiently reduced; add butter enough to make the mass rich. Take the bunch of sweet herbs out before serving. This is sometimes used as a soup, adding more water.

---

114. *Olio.*—Take two pounds of tender, juicy beef, one of veal or mutton, a whole duck, chicken or guinea fowl, a half pound of pickled pork; let this soak an hour before using it. Put it in a small pot, and add a few sprigs of parsley, two or three onions sliced, Cayenne and black pepper, and salt to taste; cover with cold water; stew gently, and skim as may be necessary, to remove all dross. After the meat has stewed two hours, or less time if the meat is very tender, add three or four pleasant acid apples chopped fine; a pint of skinned tomatoes cut up fine, and into which a dessert-spoonful of sugar has been stirred; two medium-sized squashes cut up; a pint of shelled Lima beans, the

same of green corn grated, and Irish potatoes sliced and cut thin; one or two heads of celery; stew until the vegetables are tender; stir in a large tablespoonful of fresh butter. When "*done*" lay the meat and vegetables on a dish, the fowl upon that, and serve hot. Send the gravy in a sauce-boat.

---

115. *Pepper-pot.*—Clean four calf's feet and two pounds of tripe; boil them tender; cut up the tripe in small pieces, pick the bones from the feet; return the tripe and meat to the pot, pour over the broth after skimming off the fat; add two white skinned onions sliced, half a dozen of Irish potatoes peeled and sliced, a teaspoonful each of parsley, thyme, and marjoram; stew until the vegetables are tender; season highly with black and Cayenne pepper, and salt to taste. Make a rich gravy of part of the broth, a spoonful of butter into which has been rubbed a dessert-spoonful of flour, and a tumblerful of hot cream. Serve hot.

---

116. *To Dress Cold, Underdone Beef.*—Cut it in slices an inch thick; season them well with pepper and salt; dredge with flour; fry in hot lard, a light brown; take them out of the lard, and lay the pieces in a stew-pan; pour over half a tumblerful of hot water. Rub a teaspoonful of flour into a tablespoonful of butter; put this into the stew-pan. Stew, with the cover on, a quarter of an hour; season the gravy with any kind of catsup preferred; pour over the meat. Serve hot.

---

117. *Minced Veal, Beef, or Mutton.*—Into a tablespoonful of butter (heaped) rub an even tablespoonful of flour; put this into a stew-pan, place this upon the fire and stir constantly until the butter browns a light color; should the butter burn, it will be unfit for use. Cut an onion into the butter, and pour in a teacup of boiling water. Cut tender beef steak, veal cutlets, or mutton chops; season them with pepper and salt, roll them in flour; lay them in a stew-pan and stew gently until tender. A quarter of an hour

will be sufficient to cook a pound of young, tender meat, if it is kept steadily simmering, keeping the stew-pan covered; a few sprigs of parsley cut up fine and added with the onion is very good.

---

118. *Ragout of a Breast of Veal.*—Separate the joints of the brisket; unless this is done before being cooked, it is difficult to carve; saw through the large bone, but not through the meat; saw off the sharp ends of the ribs, trim the piece neatly; bake it half done; take all the trimmings and a little of the suet; boil these, and while the meat is baking make a quart of rich gravy. Put the meat, with any gravy that may be in the pan, into a stew-pan that will hold it easily; pour over the quart of gravy made of the trimmings. Season with a teaspoonful of curry powder stirred into an even tablespoonful of flour; season with salt; stew until tender. If the stew is not rich enough, add butter, and should the gravy stew down too much, add sufficient boiling water to make the gravy.

---

119. *Stewed Sweetbread (Veal).*—Remove the veins and skin, wash them well and lay in warm water. Half an hour before they are served, parboil them five or six minutes; take them up and drop them in cold water, until you can pour into a fire-proof dish a tumblerful of the broth they were parboiled in. Roll the sweetbreads in flour; season highly with red and black pepper, and salt to taste; put them in the fire-proof dish, lay over bits of butter. Set the dish in the stove oven and stew a quarter of an hour. Oysters added to the sweetbreads is an improvement.

---

120. *To Stew Calf's Head.*—Manage as for boiling, using less water; season highly with any good catsup. It may be curried by adding curry powder to the flour used in thickening the gravy. Kid's head is excellent stewed.

---

121. *To Stew Pig's Head, Harslet, and Feet.*—Split the up-

per part of the head from the jowl. Take out the brains; cut off the ears; clean all nicely and put to stew, seasoning with pepper, salt, a dozen sage leaves, and two onions cut up fine. When tender, serve the jowl in a dish; garnish with green parsley, and have a rich butter and parsley gravy to serve with it. Take the upper part of the head, remove all the bones, and cut the meat in small pieces; split the feet in half and take out the large bones; cut the harslet in small pieces. Strain the broth, pour a pint into a stew-pan; add a tablespoonful of butter with a dessert-spoonful of flour rubbed into it; set the stew-pan upon the stove; mince a tablespoonful of parsley fine and add with the butter. When the butter melts, return the meat to the stew-pan or pot and let it gently simmer a quarter of an hour. Wash the brains while the meat is simmering; mash them with the back of a spoon and make to them, with two eggs, milk, and flour, salt to taste, a thin batter; fry this as a pancake, cut in diamond shapes; lay over the stew with sprigs of green parsley.

---

122. *To Stew Fresh Pork with Potatoes.*—Cut the spare-rib into chops, or separate the chine bone; put them into a small covered pot or deep stew-pan; just cover them with warm water; simmer gently; season with pepper and salt, and sage if liked. When tender, add, for a large spare-rib, a tablespoonful of butter with a dessert spoonful of flour for thickening. Slice sweet potatoes and put to stew when the meat is not quite half done; unless the meat is old, half an hour will cook the stew, twenty minutes the potatoes; put a layer of pork, then one of potatoes. Pork is very good stewed with green peas. Stewed apples make a good sauce for this dish.

---

123. *To Make Hash.*—Meats that have been once done, only require to be warmed over. To cook them again renders them tough and insipid. Cut up the vegetables to be used for seasoning—onions, potatoes, tomatoes, etc., as may be preferred. Put the butter, flour, salt, pepper, and vegetables (or spices if prefer

red as seasoning) into the stew-pan with all the cold gravy that may have been saved; essence of ham answers a good purpose; a few inches of portable soup is very good if there should not be sufficiency of gravy; a teacup of boiling water for a pound of meat; very little water should be used. Cover the stew-pan and let this stew gently a quarter of an hour, shaking the stew-pan frequently. Have the meat minced fine, removing all bones and gristle; add to the gravy, stirring it in well. Let it remain until the meat is thoroughly hot, and serve. Use catsup upon the plate for extempore dressing. Very little cooking is necessary and very little gravy. When there is stuffing, a small quantity may be used.

124. *Irish Potato Hash.*—This is excellent made of equal quantities of Irish potatoes peeled, sliced thin, and put to stew in very little water; when they are half done, add as much cold pickled beef, minced very fine, or cold boiled salt mackerel (a little onion and parsley may be put in with the Irish potatoes if liked); a large tablespoonful of butter; pepper and salt to taste. Serve hot. This should be just moist. Mash the potatoes and mix them well with the meat.

125. *Mrs. H.'s Receipt for Beef Hash.*—Two tumblers of hot water, a large tablespoonful of butter, three tablespoonfuls of grated cheese, the same of fine bread crumbs; season highly with Cayenne pepper; add three tumblers of beef minced. Serve as soon as hot. Stir all well together.

A very accomplished housekeeper furnishes me with several receipts by which dishes, savoury and economical, may be prepared.

126. *Mrs. J.'s Receipt for Scotch Hash.*—Mince corned beef as fine as possible, also a good portion of onion chopped fine; season highly with Cayenne pepper; add a tablespoonful of butter; add boiling water, not quite enough to cover the meat; let this be-

come very hot. Beat two eggs well in a common sized pie-pan; stir the meat to the eggs and put it in the stove-oven until a light brown crust is formed. A few minutes will form the crust, if the oven is as hot as it should be. Serve immediately. A good breakfast dish.

---

127. *Chicken Oyster.—Mrs. J.*—Pull a cold fowl of any kind into small pieces. Mix equal portions of sweet milk and water; a tablespoonful of butter with a teaspoonful heaped with flour stirred into it; any gravy that may remain, and a little stuffing; let this stew gently ten minutes. Add enough of vinegar to give a pleasant, acid taste, and two or three crackers or hard biscuit broken into small pieces. Put in the fowl, and as soon as this is hot, serve. Veal, lamb, or venison, are good prepared in this way.

---

128. *Mrs. J.'s Baked Hash Receipt.*—Take cold round beef, or good mutton, and mince it fine; season with a little minced onion, pepper, and salt. Chop up green pickle (onion is best), add a little of the vinegar. Put into a deep dish a layer of meat, then one of pickle sliced thin, one of bread crumbs, over that butter or gravy. Repeat this until all is in, putting bread crumbs and butter last; let it bake a few moments until a nice crust is formed, and serve hot. Should there be but little gravy, moisten with a little sweet milk and water, mixed in equal proportions; very little is necessary.

---

129. *Poultry or Birds Stewed with Onions.*—Prepare the fowls as for boiling; rub over well with flour, and shake off any that does not adhere. Put three tumblers of water into a stew-pan, let it warm; lay in the poultry; cover the vessel; let it simmer gently. Skim off all impurities; cut up two tumblerfuls of white onion in cold water; let it soak a quarter of an hour, then add it to the stew, with salt and pepper to taste. Turn the fowls over occasionally; avoid piercing them with a fork or sharp instru

MEATS.   75

m*nt; these holes let out the juices and look badly. Wild fowls require to be cooked less than domestic; much cooking destroys the "game taste." Many persons prefer the flesh should be considerably underdone.

---

130. *Chicken and Oysters.*—Truss a young fowl as for boiling; clean the inside well, removing all clotted blood. Chop as many oysters fine as will fill it; close the apron well with a few stitches. Stew in a double kettle, or put it in an unglazed jar; cover it well, and, putting it in a kettle of boiling water, keep it boiling an hour and a half, or until tender. Serve with a sauce made of the gravy from the stew, a little of the oyster liquor, butter and flour to make it rich enough and of proper consistence.

The plate represents the fowl with the skewers still inserted; remove them before sending to the table.

---

131. *Stewed Turkey—A French Receipt.*—Keep a large fat turkey several days after being killed. When ripe for cooking, stuff it; upon the bottom of a large stew-pan that will hold the fowl without cramping it, put a trivet to elevate it a few inches. Rub over the turkey a coat of flour, shake off all that does not stick; lay it upon the trivet; cover over the breast with slices of pickled pork or bacon. Cut up two or three calf's feet, lay these around it. Season highly with pepper, chopped onions, mace or nutmeg, a few cloves, or a stick of cinnamon broken up. Mix together a pint of cold water, the same of Sherry wine; pour to the turkey; cover well with a well-fitting cover; keep a wet towel or cloth over and around the edges of the cover; wet it as often as is required to keep it from becoming dry. Stew slowly five hours; turn the turkey when half done. For sauce, strain the gravy; send it to the table in a sauce-boat.

---

132. *To Fricassee Chickens* (*White*).—Carve into joints as for

frying, and if the fowl is large, bone it. Kill the fowl several hours before cooking; and after cutting it up, wash it well in tepid water, and pour over it boiling sweet milk, or milk and water mixed in equal proportions; let it soak in this until it is time to put it to stew. Half an hour before dinner, if the fowl is young and tender, put it to stew in water enough to just cover it. Let it stew gently, keeping the pot covered; skim off all scum as it rises; when half done, season with salt and white pepper. Add dumplings made in this way: Mash a tumblerful of Irish potatoes (more if liked); moisten it with a tablespoonful of sweet milk or water; rub it through a sieve or colander. It must be entirely free from lumps. Use neither lard nor water, but work in a tumbler even full of flour, or until a soft dough is formed; a teaspoonful of salt. Flour the board well and roll this half an inch thick; cut in strips and stew with the chicken ten minutes; at the same time add a large tablespoonful of butter with a teaspoonful of flour rubbed into it. Serve the stew in a covered dish, and stir to the gravy half a tumbler of hot cream; send the gravy to the table in a sauce-boat. Rice, potatoes, and tomatoes are all good accompaniments. For variety, drop-dumplings may be used. Scald a pint of milk; make a paste by stirring sufficient cold milk to a tumblerful of sifted flour. When the pint of milk boils, stir in the paste, stirring constantly until bubbles begin to form over the top; pour it into a bowl and let it remain undisturbed until cold. Beat two eggs well; beat these to the batter and add more flour until a stiff batter is made; salt to taste; drop, by spoonfuls, into the stew; eight or ten minutes will cook them sufficiently. Mace is sometimes used for seasoning this dish.

Turtle is excellent cooked in this way: A tablespoonful and a half of curry powder stirred into a tablespoonful of flour, and added to each pound of meat, omitting the dumplings, will make a good dish of curry chicken, and will give variety to the every day bill of fare.

In making a white stew, nothing should be used that will discolor the meat; hence white pepper is better than black. (The broth must be skimmed carefully, and the stew-pan kept well covered, to prevent smoke from getting in.) Although it might be as savoury to the appetite, yet the eye would not be so well pleased. It has been well said that food should be so prepared, and served, as to present such an agreeable appearance to the eye that the palate may be prepossessed in its favor at first sight. Rice, in a separate dish, should always be served with this.

---

133. *To Ragout Chicken.*—Prepare the fowl as for broiling; lay in a shallow oven, or stove-pan; pour to it a teacup of warm water; cover with an oven lid or tin cover, closely. When thoroughly hot, begin to baste it with butter. Let it stew gently half an hour, basting frequently. Put a little fire upon the lid, and brown it a few minutes before serving. Toast enough light bread to cover the bottom of the dish; dip each piece in hot milk, or water. Serve the chicken upon this; add a tablespoonful of butter, into which has been stirred a teaspoonful of flour, to the gravy. Let this stew a few minutes; pour over the chicken. Serve immediately, or the toast will become sodden. Fowls are excellent cooked in this way with onions and tomatoes, or tomatoes alone, peeled and cut fine, omitting the toast. Season with salt and butter.

---

134. *Rice Pillau.*—Carve the fowl into joints, as for frying; put it into a stew-pan, with a few slices of pickled pork, or fresh pig cut in thin slices. Season highly with red and black pepper; salt to taste. Cover the fowl with water. Let it stew gently; skim until the water looks clear. Have ready a pint of rice washed and soaked. Stir this slowly to the stew. Fifteen minutes will complete the cooking after the rice is added. When the rice is nearly done, should there be too much gravy, leave off the cover until it is sufficiently reduced. This dish should only be moist. No gravy is required; make it rich with butter.

The fowl, if a full-grown one, is sometimes left whole. The rice is first put into the dish, and the chicken laid upon the top

Tongues, both beef and hog, are good used in this way before being smoked. Birds are as good in pillau as chicken

---

135. *Tomato Pillau.*—Cut up the fowl; fry it in a large tablespoonful of lard; fry with it an onion. Peel a pint of tomatoes, cut them up fine, season with pepper and salt, and a teaspoonful of sugar. When the onion and chicken are of a light brown color, take them up and put them into a stew-pan; add the tomatoes, and pour over boiling water to cover the fowl. Have ready a pint of rice, well washed. Stir this to the chicken, mixing all thoroughly; simmer gently until tender. Add a large tablespoonful of butter. This should not have gravy. Green corn may be grated and used.

---

136. *Sausage Pillau.*—This is made as the rice pillau, using sausages that have been stuffed, but *not smoked*. The smoke taste is imparted to the rice. Parboil liver and kidneys, and use them for pillau. They, as also the sausages, should be cut in small pieces.

---

137. *To Stew Birds.*—Take pigeons, partridges, or any large birds; truss them as for baking; dredge them well with flour. Stuff with bread, cut an inch thick, and well buttered; dip the bread in wine, and, breaking it in small pieces, put a little in each bird, allowing room for it to swell. Lay them in a deep earthen dish, breast-side down; cover them with slices of cold ham, or bacon cut very thin; pour in water enough to cover them. Put the dish in an oven or stove, and stew gently, basting frequently. Use a lid or cover; when nearly done, remove the bacon; turn the birds; put a little fire upon the lid and let them brown slightly, or, if in the stove, remove the cover. Serve upon dry toast. If they are young, from twenty to twenty-five minutes will be time enough to cook them. Use very little seasoning. Nothing should be permitted to overcome the fine "*game-taste*" so much admired by lovers of good eating.

MEATS. 79

138. *To Semi-Stew Birds.*—Prepare them as for broiling; heat the gridiron, and lay the birds flat upon it, the inside down first. When half done, and of a good brown color (but they must not be scorched), take them from the gridiron, and lay in a stew pan; pour over a tumbler of hot water; season with pepper and salt. Rub a teaspoonful of flour into a tablespoonful of butter; put this in slices over the birds. Cover the dish, and set it in the stove. When tender, serve with tomato sauce.

---

139. *Beef Tongue and Mushrooms.*—Soak a pickled tongue; lard it across. Season highly with pepper, salt, and spices; onion and parsley cut up fine. Lay it in a stew-pan, cover with water, and put over it slices of bacon or pork. Stew gently until tender. Fry a pint of button mushrooms in butter (be particular to prevent the butter from burning). Take the tongue up, and put the mushrooms in the stew-pan, and stew five or six minutes; pour over the tongue. Serve hot.

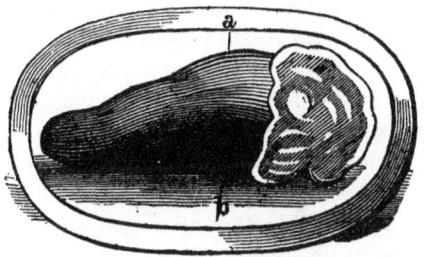

To carve : Cut across in the line *a b.* The best slices are in the middle. At the tip end the meat is dry.

---

140. *To Stew Cold Fowl.*—Wild duck is excellent prepared in this way : Cut up the fowl and remove the large bones. Put into a stew-pan, for each fowl of the size of a common duck, a tablespoonful of mustard, mixed to a paste with vinegar. Season highly with red and black pepper; add a piece of butter as large as a large hen's egg. Put this on the fire; stir it well, and,

as soon as it melts, stir in a half tumbler of Sherry or Madeira wine—or catsup if preferred. If the meat is tender, serve as soon as hot. Should it be tough, make more gravy, using a little hot water, and stew until tender.

---

141. *Roasting Meat.*—This style of dressing meat is less practised in the common every-day cooking than it should be. It is certainly of all others the most elegant. To even approximate perfection in the art, *practice* is absolutely necessary. Although there are a variety of contrivances for roasting, very many families are unprovided with any kind of apparatus for conducting the business. A very cheap and simple arrangement, and which will answer the purpose as well as more costly and complicated machinery, is to roast by the string. Procure a piece of iron or steel eighteen inches long, with a hinge in the middle, to fold it out of the way when not in use. It should be strong enough to meet any demands made upon it; at one end there should be a plate of iron three inches long and two wide, with screws inserted to fasten it to the mantel-piece. This should be done securely. At the other end a twirling hook, or common ring and hook; take a twine or twisted woollen string long enough to bring the articles to be cooked before the full influence of the fire. A hook should be securely fastened to each end of this string; catch one hook to the twirling hook, the other insert in the meat. Run a skewer through the feet of poultry and catch one hook to the skewer. If the roast is a piece of beef, veal, etc., when it is half done turn it. If it be necessary to expose one part to the fire more than the rest, prop it with a paddle or board, resting one end of the paddle against a smoothing-iron (or a brick will answer) placed directly behind the roast, and at just sufficient distance to rest the broad part of the paddle against the roast. A sharp stick must not

be used, as the least puncture will let out the juices. This plan is for a permanent arrangement. For temporary use, a wooden peg driven over the fire-place will answer. (I shall be glad to see the roaster substituted for that most popular of all kitchen utensils, the *frying-pan*.) A tin screen will greatly increase the heat, and thus save fuel. It should be so placed as to guard the roast from currents of air. The most convenient pattern I know is one made of tin three feet wide, one and a half feet deep, with a shelf in it. It may be put upon rollers. This will also answer for a plate-warmer.

General Directions for Managing a Roast.—The meat after being killed should be kept until tender. It is the practice of many cooks to use meat and fowls immediately after being killed, and parboil the article to make it tender. This extracts the juices, makes the meat insipid, and altogether fails to accomplish the object intended. The fire must be proportioned to the size of the thing to be roasted. "The fire that will roast the noble sirloin, will parch up a lighter joint." It should extend several inches at each end longer than the roast, or the ends will not be done. The thickest end of the meat must be most exposed to the fire; when a reflector or tin roaster is used, slant it so as to throw the thickest part nearest the fire. The spit should be kept bright. Be careful, when using it, never to run it through the nicest parts of the joint; every hole made by the spit is "a tap to let the juices out." It must be well balanced, so as to hang evenly; when assistance is needed to accomplish this, use leaden weights. This is important, for unless the motion is regular, the parts will not be equally exposed. The roast must not be put at first too close to the fire, never nearer than eighteen inches; if a large joint, let it heat gradually. Birds or small roasts may be put nearer, from twelve to fifteen inches. Should the meat scorch when first exposed, the heat could not penetrate; near the bone the meat would remain underdone, and, besides, would acquire a disagreeable taste, and lose the light, rich, brown color which a roast should always have.

Baste frequently, and begin as soon as the meat is warm, use sweet lard for most articles. Dr. Kitchiner says, nothing bastes roast pig so well, or makes it so crisp, as good fresh sweet oil. Good butter may be used, particularly for birds and game, and gives a more delicate flavor to pig than lard. Press the lard or butter into a silver or wooden spoon; baste with this at first, and then with the drippings. Put a pan under the roast to catch the gravy and pour into it a tumbler of hot water, slightly salted, for a large joint; less water for a small one or for game. Take up the drippings occasionally, leaving only a little in the pan; managed in this way, it will not be so strong or oily as when left until the roast is done; it is best to cover the fat with a well-greased sheet of foolscap paper or a thin sheet of dough made of any kind of dark flour and water. The latter is only used in a roaster or reflector, and may cover the whole joint. When roasting by the string, use the paper; when the meat is fully half done, remove the paper or dough. Stir up the fire; baste the meat; dredge well with flour, and let it brown a rich color. All the sweeping necessary must be done before the roast is put down. Slow roasting is all-important. When the smoke draws towards the fire, and the dripping of the clear gravy begins, it is a sure sign that the roast is nearly done.

"A diligent attention to time; the distance of the meat from, and the judicious management of, the fire, and *frequent bastings*, are the principal rules to be observed."

---

142. *M. Soyer's Time-Table for Roasting.*—Ten pounds of beef, eighteen inches from the fire, two to two and a half hours.

Six pounds of beef fourteen inches from the fire, one hour and a half.

Eight pounds of beef, eighteen inches from the fire, stuffed, two hours.

Eight pounds of beef, eighteen inches from the fire, without stuffing, one hour and a half.

Four pounds of chump-loin or kidneys, one hour and a quarter.

Six pounds of breast, fourteen inches from the fire, one hour.

Calf's heart stuffed and tied in paper, three quarters of an hour.

Eight pounds, leg of mutton, eighteen inches from the fire, one hour and a half. The same for a saddle of mutton.

Five pounds of leg of lamb, fifteen inches from the fire, one hour.

Six pounds, leg of pork, with the skin on, eighteen inches from the fire, two hours.

Lamb and pork should always be well done.

A large turkey, weighing fourteen pounds, eighteen inches from the fire, three hours.

A full-grown goose, young and tender, an hour and a half.

A grown tender chicken or duck, one hour.

A green goose (which is a goose four months old), one hour.

Wild fowls require less time than domestic.

Wild duck, from a quarter to half an hour, according to size and age.

Pheasants half an hour.

Grouse three-quarters of an hour.

Woodcocks, twenty minutes.

Partridges, half an hour.

Serve on toast. Baste constantly; have a good fire.

Ducks have frequently a fishy taste; this may be corrected by putting in the dripping-pan, onion, salt, and half a tumbler of hot water; baste with this ten minutes; then remove this, and baste with butter. It is said putting a carrot inside of the fowl will remove the fishy taste. I have not tested this; it is worth a trial. After cleaning wild fowls, hang them so that they will not touch. Different kinds should never be packed away together; a good plan is to hang them in their feathers. They may be kept in cold weather several days. I do not agree, however, with the French writer who directs that the fowl be "suspended by one of its long tail feathers, and falling from it is the criterion of its ripeness and readiness for the spit."

The wild flavor is injured by much cooking.

143. *Roast Beef.*—The sirloin, round, and ribs of the fore quarter, are best for roasting. Let the meat hang after it is killed until tender. The length of time it will require for this, will depend upon the weather, age of the animal, etc. Manage the piece to be cooked, by the rules given for roasting. Baste as soon as the meat is hot, with good sweet lard, then with its own drippings. If the meat is not sufficiently fat, insert very narrow strips of bacon, with an instrument called a larding-needle, all over it, and just under the surface. Half an hour before the meat is done, take off any covering (if any has been used); baste over the surface quickly with fresh butter; this, when used just before finishing the roast, raises a finer froth than lard. Dredge with flour as the gravy begins to drop. Let the roasting continue, until a rich brown color. The meat is not sufficiently done so long as the drippings look bloody. The juice of the meat is prepared for gravy. Strain the gravy. This is sometimes too rich; remove part of it when this is the case, and reserve it for the soup-kettle, or to aid other gravies. Serve upon a hot dish. The roast will do the cook no credit if sent to the table upon a cold dish, and eaten upon a cold plate, which will convert the gravy into a kind of jellied tallow. Chou, mustard, pickles, and any acid jelly, are good accompaniments. Cranberries are also good.

---

144. *Roast Veal.*—The shoulder, loin, and fillet are the best pieces for roasting. Keep it until tender. Veal does not keep so well as beef, and must be wiped dry every day, and hung up. Never lay it down upon wood; this keeps it damp, and it will soon spoil. Veal is the best meat for soup. The loin is considered the choicest piece for roasting. Regulate the fire as for the beef; rub over with soft butter just before putting it on the spit. It is less juicy than beef, and requires more frequent basting. Always saw through the bone of the loin, but not the skin, for the convenience of carving. Protect the fat with well-greased paper; sprinkle over a little salt, and dredge with flour. Just before it is done, remove the paper; baste well with the drippings, or with butter; dredge with flour, and let tne roast hang until of a good color, and the clear gravy begins to drip. Serve upon a hot dish. If the gravy is not sufficiently rich, add butter; if too thin, pour it into a stew-pan, rub a little flour to the butter, and let the gravy stew three or four minutes. Serve in a sauce-boat.

145. *Roast Fillet of Veal.*—Remove the leg bone with a sharp knife; fill the space with a rich stuffing, seasoned highly with pepper, onion, and parsley; salt to taste. Draw the sides together; wrap the flap around; skewer this firmly, and to prevent the skewers giving way, wrap the whole joint with tape, beginning at the hock, or small end. It requires great care, and some skill, to prepare this for the spit, so that when served it will present a good appearance. When first put down, baste as soon as the meat is hot, with salt and water, then with a tablespoonful of good sweet lard—rancid lard must not be used. Conduct the process as for roast loin of veal. A shoulder of veal may also be stuffed, and roasted in the same way. For gravy, use the drippings prepared as for the fillet.

146. *Roast Leg of Mutton.*—Keep it hung as long as it can be kept without tainting. Skewer it, and put it on the spit, so that it will hang evenly; turn it often; baste as soon as hot, and continue this very frequently. Protect the fat with paper. Put half a tumbler of hot water into the dripping-pan; as the gravy drops into this, after using lard or butter, baste with it. Heat gradually; the drippings strained, and slightly thickened with brown flour, will make the best gravy. Currant jelly, or some kind of acid jelly, should accompany this. Grated horseradish is also very good served with it. Always keep browned flour on hand, in a dredging-box. When browning it be careful to stir constantly. If it burns, it is unfit for use.

147. *To Roast a Saddle of Mutton.*—The two loins without separating is a saddle, and is carved in this way: Cut from the

tail to the end on each side of the back bone, from *a* to *b*, continuing downward to the edge *c*, until it becomes too fat. The

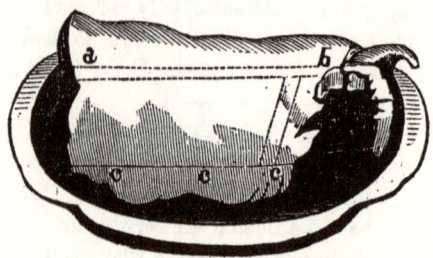

slices should be thin, and if too long divide them. The fat will be found on the sides. The upper part is generally lean. Give a part of the fat to each person.

It may be roasted by the directions given for roasting. Protect the fat with greased paper. The strings it is tied on with should be greased; twisted woollen is best. The flaps should be cut off; leave very little of the tail and chump end. This piece requires close trimming, which if the butcher does not do, the cook must. Serve with the gravy which runs down. If you wish to thicken the gravy, set a stew-pan over a slow fire; put two teaspoonfuls of fresh butter into it, and dredge in a teaspoonful of flour; stir this well until it browns—but it must not scorch; add the gravy very slowly, stirring it constantly; if too rich, skim off the grease as it rises. Let it simmer a quarter of an hour, or until as thick as cream. Strain it into the sauce-boat. The peel of a lemon boiled with the gravy, gives this a fine flavor, adding the juice after it is taken from the fire; or it may be flavored with wine, spices, currant jelly, or any kind of good catsup, using these in sufficient quantities to "delight the palate without disordering the stomach." Tomatoes and Irish potatoes may be served with the roast.

---

148. *Shoulder of Mutton.*—This may be roasted as the leg, and served with onion sauce. Place it on the dish with the skin

side down, as represented in the accompanying plate, and, in carving, take the first cut from *b* to *c;* cut a few slices each

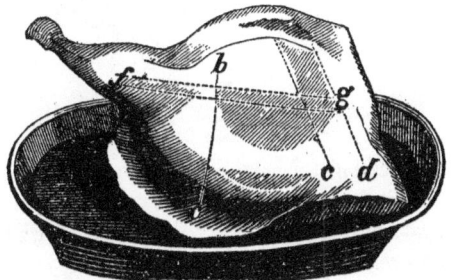

side, then on each side of the ridge of the shoulder-blade, in the direction of the dotted lines, *c d*. The tenderest part lies under the blade bone, and is called the oyster-cut. The underside has many choice slices. The best fat lies in the direction *c.* When carved on the outside, or skin-side, slice from the knuckle to the broad end, in the direction *f g*. Roast must always be served upon a hot dish. A good gravy may be made, by stirring half a teaspoonful of salt to half a tumbler of boiling water; pour this gradually over every part of the meat, after it is put in the dish, mixing with the juice that flows. When cut, it gives moisture and a pleasant taste to the meat. A separate tureen of gravy should also be served.

149. *Lamb.*—The hind quarter is best roasted. When the lamb is small, roast the fore and hind quarters together without dividing them. Lamb should never be sent to the table underdone; it requires less time in roasting than mutton, and frequent basting. Serve with mint sauce. The proper vegetables to accompany it are, green peas, asparagus, and Irish potatoes. Serve the gravy in a tureen; if liked put in the bottom of the tureen a tablespoonful of acid jelly; pour the gravy over hot, stirring briskly until the jelly is mixed with the gravy; or season the gravy with Port or Madeira wine.

150. *A Haunch of Venison.*—This being a dry meat requires

a great deal of basting. I have been informed by old hunters that on this account it is best to roast it very soon after being killed. Protect the fat with oiled paper, keep the string well greased to prevent its scorching; a twisted woollen string is less liable to burn than a cotton one. Twelve pounds will require three hours before a solid, brisk fire. Currant jelly may be served in the gravy or sent to table as an accompaniment; any acid jelly will answer; crab apple or grape jelly is very good. Wine may be added to the gravy if liked. To carve this joint, the dish should be so placed upon the table that the knuckle will be farthest from the person carving. It looks well to wrap the knuckle with fringed paper as in the plate; some of the best fat lies under, and if it should be necessary to use this, lift the joint by the part of the knuckle wrapped in paper. Cut a deep gash (but do not take out a slice) from *a* to *b*, slanting the knife a little, then take the slices from *a* to *d;* cut them of moderate thickness and put upon each plate a slice of the fat. A haunch of mutton is carved in the same way.

---

151. *Leg of Pork.*—This may be stuffed or not as preferred;
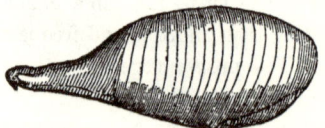
if stuffed, cut a slit near the knuckle, run the knife between the meat and bone, loosening it carefully. Make a rich stuffing, season it with pepper, salt, onion, and sage; insert as much of the stuffing as possible, or the bone may be entirely removed and the space filled with stuffing. Take a few stitches to prevent the stuffing from falling out; wrap a

tape around the joint to keep it in proper shape. Nothing bastes it so well as good olive oil; it must not be the least rancid. Should there be a prejudice against this, use fresh butter; this gives the meat a more delicate flavor than lard. Fresh pork requires longer cooking than any other fresh meat, and is disgusting to the eye and palate if not *thoroughly done*. A leg weighing six pounds will require at least two hours before a brisk solid fire. For the convenience of carving, it is well to have the skin scored before roasting, in thin strips half an inch apart, by merely passing a sharp knife through the skin. Be careful and never put the roast too near the fire at first, or it will blister. Boiled Irish potatoes, peas, and boiled onions, are the vegetables usually served with this meat. Apple sauce is a good accompaniment, and when it is not stuffed, send to the table along with the roast a sauce-boat of onion and sage sauce.

---

152. *Sparerib.*—The sparerib of a full-grown hog is better roasted than cooked in any other way. Baste it well.

---

153. *Kid.*—This animal is in its greatest perfection at five months old. The meat is delicate and juicy, and deserves to be more popular. Roast as you would lamb; serve with the same accompaniments and sauce. The head is excellent stewed or baked, and also makes fine soup. This meat is good eaten cold with French mustard.

---

154. *A Roasted Rabbit—Whole Except the Head.*—This is

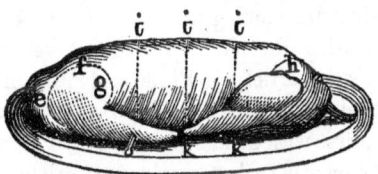

best stuffed. While roasting baste frequently with butter; dredge it with flour and manage as with any other roast. The head and liver may be boiled; split the head, take out the brains, mash them with the liver, and add to the gravy. Wine and jelly are by some persons liked in the gravy. If a little thickening is needed to the gravy; set the dripping-pan upon the stove and make the gravy to taste.

To carve: Take off the shoulders first, as indicated by the line *e, f, g*. Divide the back through, as by the dotted lines *i, k*; take off the legs at *h*. The loin and legs are the prime pieces.

Keep the rabbit in weak salt and water at least twelve hours if the weather will admit.

---

155. *Roast Turkey*.—Truss the fowl by skewering the legs;

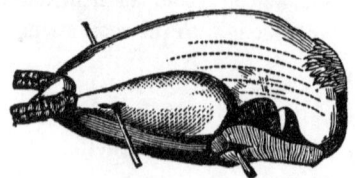

they are never drawn into the body as in boiling. Remove the skewers before sending the turkey to the table. A turkey for roasting or baking may be kept longer than for boiling. After cleaning it well, wipe it dry, and without any or very little salt, let it hang several days. When ready for the spit, fill it with a rich stuffing. The stuffing must never be crammed—allow some room for swelling; cut off the neck bone; stuff the craw and tie the skin securely. Close the slit in the abdomen with a few stitches to prevent the stuffing from falling out; break the breast bone without tearing the skin. Dredge it well with flour, and shake off any loose particles. Place it eighteen inches from the fire, which should be brisk and solid. Begin to baste as soon as the fowl is hot, first with good sweet lard, and then with its drippings; baste frequently; when nearly done, baste with a spoonful of fresh butter; dredge well and smoothly with flour; place the roast nearer the fire until it is of a light brown color and the clear

MEATS.

gravy begins to drip. It should then be immediately sent to the table upon a hot dish under a dish cover. For gravy—boil the liver and gizzard, cut them up fine; put the dripping-pan upon the stove, or upon a trivet over the fire, if a stove is not used. Sprinkle in a little flour; stir it in smoothly; add the giblets cut up, and three or four hard-boiled eggs cut in half; serve in a tureen. A dish of rice boiled dry must accompany the turkey; cranberry jam or any good acid jelly. Make the gravy just before the roast is ready for the table.

To carve: Take off the wings. Slip the knife between the leg and body and cut to the bone, then with the fork turn the leg back, the joint will give way. Cut slices on each side of the breast bone. The white meat lies there and is usually preferred. The legs, unless needed, are generally set aside to be "devilled." The side bones and bishop are favorites, and should be separated from the carcass; this is done by cutting through the ribs on each side from one end to the other. The back is then laid upward and the knife passed firmly across it, near the middle, while the fork lifts up the other end. Then separate the side bone as in the plate; the joints run as indicated by the dotted lines. The thigh and drum-stick are separated at the joint.

---

156. *A Goose.*—After keeping it several days until ripe for the spit, wash it well, and wipe dry; dredge it well with flour; stuff it with a rich stuffing, seasoned with onion and sage. In a separate chapter, I have given several excellent receipts for making stuffings. The plate represents a goose, or large fowl, ready to be roasted by the string, the lines indicating the manner in which the breast should be carved. Roast it as you would a turkey. Serve with apple sauce.

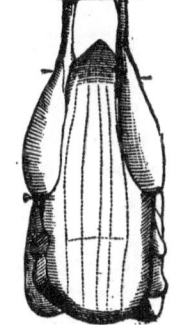

---

157. *A Green Goose.*—A green goose is a

goose not over four months old. It is not usual to stuff them and they require less time to roast than a grown fowl. When trussed, the legs are drawn into the body, as in a boiled fowl.

---

158. *Ducks*—Are sometimes roasted without stuffing. When 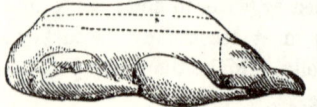 stuffing is used, well mashed boiled Irish potatoes, highly seasoned, make a good stuffing. Wild ducks are never stuffed. There is very little flesh upon the breast of these fowls, consequently they must not be allowed to remain upon the spit a moment after clear gravy appears, or they soon become dry and insipid. Some persons prefer them a little underdone. Always stew the giblets; mince them when done, and add to the gravy. When a little thickening is needed to the gravy, set the dripping-pan upon the fire, and sprinkle with a little brown flour. Onion and apple sauce are served with goose, wild and domestic ducks.

The carving knife for poultry must be smaller than for joints, and always kept sharp and bright.

---

159. *Wild Fowls*—Are usually trussed with the head on, as 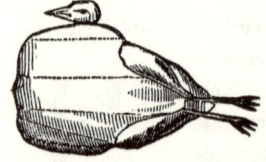 in the plate, turned under the wing; run a bird skewer through the thighs, and tie the legs. Pheasants, woodcocks, or snipes, are all trussed, and served in the same way upon toast. Baste well with butter; pour part of the gravy upon the toast; send the remainder in a sauce-boat. Woodcocks and plovers are excellent picked and not drawn, wrapped in thick brown paper, and roasted on the hearth in hot ashes.

---

160. *To Bake Meat.*—M. Alexis Soyer, a talented French *chef-de-cuisine* pronounces this mode of cooking "a semi-barbarian method of spoiling meat." As it is usually done, I

fully agree with him in this opinion; but, by care and attention, baking may be made to nearly approach, though it can never equal, the superior excellence of roasting. A deep iron oven answers the purpose better than the stove. When an iron oven is used, the meat should be elevated a few inches, to prevent its sticking or scorching. A small trivet should be kept for this purpose; skewers crossed will answer, or a few muffin-rings. The principal rules to be observed are, *bake* slowly and *steadily*; *baste frequently*.

It is a convenient, easy way of cooking, and as economical as any. A learned writer upon the subject gives this estimate of the loss of weight which takes place in cooking animal food, by the three ways of baking, boiling, and roasting:

280 lbs. of beef lost in boiling 73 lbs. 14 oz.; about 26¼ in 100 lbs.

190 lbs. of beef lost in roasting, 61 lbs. 2 oz.; weight lost, 32 per cent.

90 lbs. of beef lost by baking 27 lbs.; weight lost, 30 per cent. So that, in point of economy, baking has somewhat the advantage.

In turning, or taking up the meat, never pierce it with a pointed instrument. Keep the juice within the meat, and do not have to look for it in the gravy, leaving the meat hard, dry, and insipid.

---

161. *To Bake a Round of Beef.*—Keep the meat until tender; to hang it is best. Never parboil to make it tender. I enter my protest against this stupid management. If not sufficiently fat, lard it well, by inserting very narrow strips of bacon just under the skin. A larding-needle is necessary to do this. Pour a pint of tepid water into the vessel in which the meat is to be baked. Have a steady, moderate fire. *Slow baking is all-important.* Begin to baste as soon as the meat is warm, and continue at least every quarter of an hour. Use lard at first, then its own drippings To prevent a crust forming too soon, and to keep the

skin moist, lay over it thick slices of suet, pork, or cold ham. Over this lay a thin dough, made of flour and water. (This is recommended for thick joints, that require a long time in baking.) Remove this half an hour before the meat is done; baste well; sprinkle over a little salt, if any is required; pepper it well; dredge well with flour, and finish off by browning the meat a light color.

For gravy: Sprinkle a little brown flour into the gravy; stir it in until well mixed, and to a pint of gravy, pour half a tumbler of boiling water; let this boil up once; strain it into a tureen, and send to the table *unseasoned*. The flavor of the meat is preferred for the gravy. Should there be too much grease, skim off as much as may be necessary, and save it for soup.

---

162. *The Round.*—The round may also be stuffed. Remove the bone; fill the cavity with a rich stuffing; skewer it well; bind it around with tape; bake by the above directions. If you wish meat *juicy*, baste frequently. Remove the tape and skewers before sending to the table. Pickles, horseradish sauce, acid jelly, Irish potatoes, celery, rice, are all good accompaniments.

To carve: Cut off the first slice evenly, around the

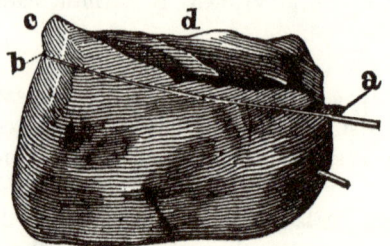

whole joint, from *a* to *b*. Do not serve this, unless an outside piece is preferred. The soft fat lies on the back, below the letter *d*. The solid fat should be cut in thin horizontal slices, at the point *e*. Each person should be asked the kind they prefer, and

MEATS.

be served with it. When the round is stuffed, it may be necessary to allow the skewer to remain. A silver one will, in this case, look more elegant.

---

163. *Dr. Kitchiner's Receipt for Baking a Round of Beef.*—Keep it lightly salted—a week if the weather will admit—less time if there is danger of its spoiling. When ready for baking, wash and wipe it dry. Put it in a brown earthenware dish, large enough to hold it. Pour in a pint of cold water. Cover it with two or three thicknesses of greased foolscap paper. Never cover anything that is baked with brown paper; the pitch and tar that is in brown paper will give the meat a bad taste. Baste frequently over the paper. Bake slowly four or five hours, in a moderate oven. Grated horseradish is a good accompaniment.

---

164. *Beef a-la-mode.*—Remove the bone from a round weighing ten or twelve pounds; keep it until tender. The day before it is to be cooked, spread over it a mixture of two teaspoonfuls of salt, two of fine black pepper, one of pulverized saltpetre. One teaspoonful of cinnamon, the same of ginger, mace, allspice, cloves, and coriander seed, all beat together and sifted, then moistened with vinegar and spread over the meat. Ten o'clock next morning, fill the space from which the bone was taken with a rich stuffing, seasoned highly with thyme, parsley and onion. Roll the piece a good circular shape, and bind tightly with a broad tape; lard it well with narrow strips of fat bacon. Put a small trivet in the bottom of a pot, or deep oven; pour in a pint of warm water; place the meat upon the trivet; put it to baking, and as soon as it warms, begin to baste with good sweet lard; rancid, strong lard should never be used for basting, it spoils everything it touches. Continue the basting with the gravy. Half an hour before the meat is done, baste and dredge with flour; bake a light brown color. Thicken the gravy very little with brown flour; pour in half a teacup of boiling water; let it boil up once, and pour into the gravy-boat. If too greasy, remove the super-

fluous grease. This is excellent cold, and will keep well. It will require at least four hours' baking.

---

165. *A Brisket of Beef.*—Joint the bone, by sawing through it without cutting the outside skin. This is done for the convenience of carving. It may be stuffed with oysters, or any rich stuffing, first removing the small bones, and supplying their places with stuffing; manage by the foregoing directions for baking. The heart and liver are excellent stuffed and baked. Remove the ventricle from the heart; clean well, and slightly parboil it, and also the liver; then stuff them. To make a good stuffing, take equal quantities of the kidney, suet and bread crumbs. Chop the suet fine; season highly with parsley, pepper, red and black; salt to taste; ginger and lemon peel if liked; work it up with a raw egg. Send the gravy to the table just as it comes from the meat, unseasoned, in a hot tureen.

---

166. *Mock Goose.*—Cut two large tender steaks from the round. Lay one in the bottom of a baking-pan. Cover it over with lard; sprinkle over this bread crumbs, or dredge thickly with flour. Season with salt, sage pulverized, and pepper. Lay on the other steak; pin them together with bird skewers, or slip a broad tape around, to prevent displacement. Spread a thin coat of lard over this; put on the bread crumbs, or flour as at first, without the seasoning. Pour a tumbler of water in the pan, and bake slowly. If baked in a stove, lay a tin plate or cover over until it is nearly done. Baste occasionally. Veal steak is best.

---

167. *A Sirloin of Beef.*—Keep this a few days, until tender. When ripe for baking, wash it and wipe dry. Put it to bake in a deep iron oven, having a trivet upon the bottom to elevate it. Pour in a pint of warm water; bake slowly, having most of the fire at the bottom of the oven. If baked in the stove, cover the meat all over the top with a crust of coarse flour, made up

with water. Baste frequently with sweet lard at first, then with the gravy; allow twenty minutes to the pound for baking, if the meat is thick. About a quarter of an hour before it is done, baste well; dredge it with flour, and bake a light brown color. If the meat is very fat, and the gravy too rich, pour off a part; save it for soup, or hash gravy. To make the gravy, dredge in a tablespoonful of flour; pour in half a tumbler of boiling water; let this boil up once, then strain into a tureen. The dish and tureen should be hot.

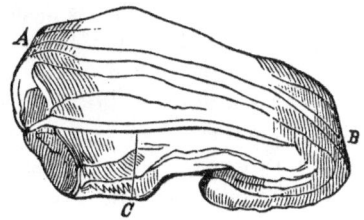

To carve: Cut long slices from *a* to *b*. There are nice tender slices indicated by the line running to *c*. Send a slice of the fat upon each plate. The inside of the sirloin makes tender steak.

---

168. *Ribs of Beef Boned and Stuffed.*—Take the first three long ribs; keep them several days slightly salted; remove the bones; lay the meat out flat; pepper it over well, and lay over a rich stuffing, made of a quarter of a pound of suet, or butter cut fine, the same quantity of bread crumbs, a tablespoonful of parsley shred fine, the same of thyme and sweet basil, (if liked), a tablespoonful of onion minced; salt to taste; pour over half a tumbler of hot water. Let this set until the bread crumbs are saturated with the water; then beat in two eggs, and pour the mixture into a hot frying-pan, into which has been melted a teaspoonful of lard. Stir the batter until it is of the consistency of mush. After spreading the stuffing over the meat, roll it a good shape; wrap it with tape; insert a skewer, and bake it as the sirloin. Begin to carve from the thinnest end. This is good

pressed and eaten cold. When one part of the meat is thinner than the other, cover the thin part with greased paper, and baste over it frequently, or the thin part will be overdone when the thickest is only sufficiently so. Fifteen or twenty minutes to the pound (depending upon the size and weather) will be sufficient time to bake.

---

169. *Spiced Beef.*—Make a brine with half a pound of salt, the same of sugar, half an ounce of saltpetre, a tablespoonful of allspice, whole grains; measure and bruise them; half as many cloves; a tablespoonful of black pepper ground course; half a teaspoonful of red pepper pulverized. Boil these in three tumblers of water. Take a piece of the round weighing eight pounds; pour this spiced water over it; turn it once or twice a day for ten days. Then salt it sufficiently, and put it to bake in a deep earthen dish; pour the brine over it; cover with a dough made of course flour and water. Lay pieces of suet over the meat thick, before putting on the sheet of dough. Bake slowly, and let the meat become cold in the pan. To be eaten cold with pickle and French mustard. This keeps well. Fresh beef tongues are good prepared in the same way.

---

170. *Mrs. Randolph's Receipt for Hunter's Beef.*—Select a fat round weighing twenty-five pounds. Take three ounces of saltpetre, one ounce of cloves, half an ounce of allspice, one large nutmeg, one quart of salt, a tumblerful of syrup. Beat the spices, salt, and saltpetre together; pour over the syrup; rub it well on both sides with this mixture (first take out the bone); sprinkle some of it on the bottom of a tub that will just hold the beef. Lay it in and strew the remainder over the top. Turn it, and rub the mixture on well, every day for two weeks, or as long as it can be kept without tainting. At the end of this time, wash the meat; fill the hole from which the bone was taken with suet; roll it tight, and bind with tape to keep it round and compact. Lay the meat in a pan of convenient size; cover the pan with a crust

of coarse flour and water, rolled thin. Five hours will be required to bake.

---

171. *Steak a-la-mode.*—Cut the steak in thin slices; pound slightly. It should be kept until tender. Lay the slices in an earthen dish, and between each layer put a seasoning of a mixture of bread crumbs, half a teaspoonful each of mace, cloves, allspice, ginger, and red pepper; salt to taste; a tumbler of tomato catsup; a tablespoonful of butter. Bake half an hour in a moderate oven. Veal, pork, mutton, and venison are good prepared in this way. When spices are not relished with meat, always omit them and use any seasoning preferred.

---

172. *To Bake a Fillet of Veal.*—Hang it until tender, wiping it every day with a dry cloth. Meat should not be laid upon wood, as this keeps it damp. When ready for baking, separate the fillet or thigh from the loin and shank. Take out the bone with a sharp knife; fill the space with a rich force-meat of bread crumbs, chopped onion, parsley, and a tablespoonful of butter; salt and pepper to taste; beat in two eggs and fry the mixture, stirring constantly, ten minutes. Wrap the flap around. After being stuffed and wrapped it should look as before the bone was removed. Wrap tape around and insert a skewer as in the plate; put it in the oven with something under to elevate it an inch at least; pour in a pint of warm water. Bake slowly and

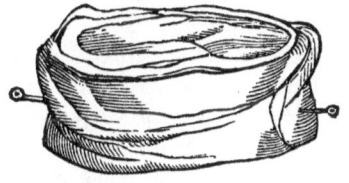

baste frequently. If the gravy is not rich enough, rub an even tablespoonful of flour into a tablespoonful of butter and add to the gravy. Tomato catsup with the gravy is an improvement;

to two tumblers of gravy add half a tumbler of catsup, or stew a few tomatoes and a little spice with the gravy.

To carve: A fillet resembles a round of beef and is carved in the same way. Cut off the top outside piece, then cut round, thin slices. Send some of the stuffing upon each plate. Serve with pickle, catsup, or French mustard.

---

173. *Veal a-la-mode.*—Prepare this two days before cooking. Cut half a pound of bacon in thin strips, removing the skin and any rancid parts. Let them be two inches long and a quarter of an inch thick; with a sharp knife make deep incisions all over the meat very near each other. Prepare a seasoning of a quarter of a pound of kidney suet, one tablespoonful each of thyme, parsley chopped fine, four tablespoonfuls of onion minced very fine, a quarter of an ounce each of mace, cloves, and allspice, and one nutmeg, beaten together and sifted; mix with the onion and parsley. Season high with red and black pepper mixed, a tablespoon even full of salt. Put a little of this seasoning into each incision, then roll each slice of bacon in it, and press them down in-into the slits or incisions; also cover the top of the meat with the seasoning. Lay it in a deep earthen pan large enough to hold it without cramping; cover it close and keep it two days after it is prepared in this way. When ready for baking, pour a tumbler of warm water in the dish, and bake four hours, if the piece weighs ten pounds; baste well with good sweet lard. This is excellent cold; should be prepared in cool weather.

---

174. *To Bake a Calf's Head.*—After boiling it remove the bones (cut out the tongue and serve upon a separate dish); cut the pieces in slices of uniform size. Lay them in a fire-proof dish. Grate a tumblerful of bread crumbs, mix with them a tablespoonful of powdered sage, the same of parsley shred fine, and a quarter of a teaspoonful of Cayenne pepper. Beat up the yolk of an egg, put this smoothly all over the meat; then sprinkle over thick the bread-crumb mixture; put it in the stove and

when it begins to brown, begin immediately to baste over it with melted butter; a very few minutes will be required to bake it. Serve with a piquant sauce, made by seasoning a pint of the broth the meat was boiled in with mace, pepper, wine, or catsup; or stew mushrooms in the gravy. The brains may be mashed and added to the gravy. Celery vinegar seasons the gravy well. The person who directs in such matters in each family should give especial instructions as to the sauce to be used with each dish, adding the ingredients to suit the taste of those who are to be served. In many families there is but one style of gravy or sauce, or at best two, and this never varies. Where a supply of flavored vinegars and catsups are kept on hand, nothing is easier than to give a pleasing variety. To have the same unvarying sauce, gravy, or stuffing, denotes, as Dr. Kitchiner expresses it, "poverty of invention." Lamb and kid's head are good prepared in this way; also calf's feet and turtle fins.

---

175. *To Bake Sweetbreads.*—Lay them in water an hour before using; parboil them. Cut slits over them and lay in strips of pork or bacon. Put the sweetbreads in a shallow fire-proof dish; pour in a tumbler of the water they were boiled in; a tablespoonful of butter with an even tablespoonful of flour rubbed in. Salt and pepper to taste. Baste well, and serve as soon as done. A pint of oysters added to the gravy will improve it.

---

176. *To Bake a Fresh Beef Tongue.*—Parboil it in very little water, just enough to cover it, two hours. Take it up, cover it over with the yolk of an egg; then sift over a thick coat of fine bread crumbs; lay it in a pan; pour in a tumblerful of the broth it was boiled in; bake, basting well with butter.

---

177. *Veal Cake.*—Take any kind of veal free from bone or gristle; chop it fine. It may be cooked or uncooked, but it is best uncooked. Season highly with pepper, salt, parsley, and

onion; use part red pepper. Mix these well with the meat; work in an even tablespoonful of butter. Mince very fine four hard-boiled eggs and a teacup of bread crumbs; work all together, binding the whole with three eggs, the whites and yolks beaten together a few minutes; shape this into a large ball or cake. Grease a fire-proof dish well with butter; lay the cake in; sprinkle over the top very fine bread crumbs; lay over bits of butter and bake an hour and a half in a moderate oven if the meat is raw, or less time if the meat is already done.

For gravy: As soon as the meat is removed from the bones, put them (and break them if necessary), with any skin or scraps of meat that would not answer for the cake, into a stew-pan; pour over water to cover them well, and simmer steadily until the cake is nearly ready for the table; strain the liquor; return it to the stew-pan, and thicken with a tablespoonful of flour rubbed into a tablespoonful of butter, for a pint of gravy. Season with catsup. Send to table in a gravy-boat.

---

178. *To Bake Mutton.*—Keep it as long as it can be done safely. If not fat, lard it with strips of bacon. As with all other joints, bake slowly and baste well. Attention and good judgment are necessary to know when to take the meat up; it will very soon become dry and hard if suffered to remain in a hot oven after it is done. Serve with a sauce made in this way: Strain the gravy into a stew-pan, stir it over the fire a few minutes; add a glass of Madeira wine, and a large tablespoonful of acid jelly, currant or grape is best; serve in a tureen. As the wine and jelly may not be liked by some persons, send a sauce-boat of gravy made without them, slightly thickened with browned flour.

---

179. *Mutton to Imitate Venison.*—Take the breast, or best part of a neck of mutton. Rub it over well with a mixture of half an ounce of allspice and the same of black and red pepper mixed. Rub with this and turn once a day for two days; when ready to bake, wash off the spice; put it in a pan or oven, lay over it slices

MEATS. 103

of cold ham taken from the fat part; over this lay a thin sheet of dough made of flour and water; pour in a tumbler of hot water. Bake with a brisk solid fire; baste with its own gravy. When nearly done remove the crust; baste well; dredge with flour; brown a light color. Eat hot or cold. This is excellent.

---

180. *To Bake Lamb or Kid.*—Follow the directions given for baking mutton. It requires less time to bake lamb or kid than mutton. When half done, season well with salt and pepper; wait ten minutes; baste well, and dredge with flour; bake a light color. If properly basted, the meat will be delightfully juicy. The fore quarter and loin are sometimes baked together when the animal is small. Joint the large bone to make the carving easy. This is also good barbecued. A hind quarter is excellent stuffed; remove the bone and fill the cavity with a rich force-meat. Thicken the gravy slightly with a paste made of flour (browned flour is best) and water; stir this into the gravy, and stew a few minutes. Should there be unnecessary grease, take it off. With a proper fire, one hour will bake a joint weighing five pounds. Mint sauce must always be served as an accompaniment. Send the gravy in a tureen. Green peas, lettuce, potatoes, are suitable vegetables to be served with lamb.

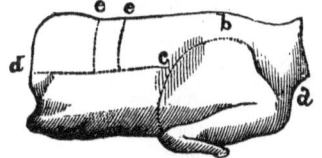

To carve: Divide the shoulder from the breast and ribs, by passing the knife under the knuckle, in the direction *a b c*. Leave part of the meat on the ribs. Lay this upon a separate dish; cut in the direction of *c* to *e*. The ribs are now separated from the gristly part, and may be divided as indicated by the dotted lines *e e* or *d*.

---

181. *To Bake a Fresh Venison Ham.*—If not very fat, cut incisions lengthwise on the top; into these insert narrow strips of pickled pork or fat bacon; press them in below the surface; run a sharp narrow-bladed knife between the shank bone and

meat, and insert rich stuffing; tie it around the shank to secure the stuffing from falling out. Spread a coat of butter over the whole surface of the meat; lay over it a thin crust of flour and water, put it to bake in a pan; pour in a tumbler of water. When half done, season with salt and pepper; remove the crust; baste well; dredge well with flour, and let it bake until a light brown. Carve it as in the directions given for roasting a haunch of venison, and serve with the same accompaniments.

---

182. *Mock Venison.*—Cut the meat from a good round of veal; trim the skin off carefully; grind the meat; season with spices to taste; pepper highly; add a third bread crumbs; two or three eggs to bind the whole together. Give the meat a good shape; wrap it well in the skin; bind it with broad tape; bake it; serve hot with gravy, or press and eat cold; will keep several days in cold weather; remove the tape.

---

183. *To Bake a Pig.*—All meats are better for being kept several hours after being killed, except pig. Dr. Kitchiner says, "it loses part of its goodness every hour after being killed; if not fresh, no art can make the crackling crisp." If intended to be baked whole, it should not exceed a month old, and should be fat and plump. Kill it early in the morning, if for dinner. Immerse it in hot water (but not boiling) a few minutes; then scrape off the hair, repeating the process until every part is white and clean; force off the horny part attached to the feet. Cut off the feet at the first joint; do this carefully, with a sharp knife. They are often very carelessly chopped off, leaving the bone projecting beyond the meat. Mrs. Hale gives excellent directions for thoroughly cleaning a pig: "Take the wax out of the ears; the dirt from the nostrils, by using a small skewer (or piece of wire) covered with a bit of thin rag, which you must wipe often upon a coarse towel or dish-rag; take out the eyes with a sharp knife or fork; clean the tongue, gums and lips, by scraping with a sharp knife; wipe them; be careful not to cut them;

run your hand up the throat; take out all the clotted blood and loose pieces found there, and lastly cleanse the other end of the pig, by putting a skewer covered with a cloth through from the inside; wipe the inside clean with a damp cloth; make a slit in the abdomen, and take out the entrails; wash it in two or three waters; wipe it dry, and wrap it immediately in a cloth to protect it from the air. Prepare the stuffing of bread crumbs, moistened with water, seasoned with onion and sage; a tablespoonful of butter; pepper and salt to taste; mash the bread smooth; beat into it two eggs, and put the mixture to fry until as thick as mush; then with a spoon, and while hot, put it inside the pig; a few stitches will prevent the stuffing from falling out; the thread must be removed before sending it to the table. If to be baked in a brick oven or stove, lay it in a large pan that will hold it comfortably; if in an iron oven, put a trivet upon the bottom; pour in a pint of warm water, and brush it all over with sweet olive oil, or good fresh butter. Besides my own experience, I have the very high authority of Dr. K—— for saying that nothing answers for basting pig so well as salad oil. Says he, "rub a little sweet oil on the skin with a brush or goose feather; this makes the crackling crisper and browner than basting it with its own drippings, and is the best way to prevent its blistering." The crackling or skin must be nicely crisped and delicately browned, without being either blistered or burned. After oiling it, baste with salt and water twice; then with salad oil or fresh butter. Stew the harslet; chop fine and season with pepper and parsley; serve in a separate dish; thicken the gravy slightly with a paste made of flour and water. If too rich, pour off part of the grease. Send to the table in a tureen. Apple sauce is a good accompaniment; also grated horseradish, or mustard pickle.

When done, take off the head; cut it in two; part the whole body; put the brains in the gravy; lay the pig in the dish, back to back. The ears should, while baking, be covered with oiled paper, or they will become too hard before the rest of the pig is done. Cut them from the head, and lay upon the dish as may be preferred. The head may also be placed as in the plate, or as one may fancy. Lay the stuffing around and under the pig, or upon a separate dish; put some of this upon each plate.

---

184. *Baked Pork and Beans.*—Wash a quart of good white beans early in the morning; put them in a kettle with sufficient water to cover them; place the kettle upon the fire, and when the water becomes boiling hot—but it should not boil—pour the water and beans into a colander, until the water drains from them. Put them again into the kettle, and cover with cold water, adding a piece of soda, or saleratus, as large as a bean. Scald and again drain the water from them, and put the beans in cold water. Soak a pound of pickled pork of the lean part of the middling, in water enough to cover it, three hours. Put the pork and beans to stew in separate kettles. Half an hour before the beans are done, put them in a deep earthen pan, clear of the water they were boiled in. Take up the pork; score it across in gashes or slits, a quarter of an inch apart. Season it highly with pepper, and put it down in the dish of beans, until only the rind is visible; pour in a pint of warm water, and bake until the beans are soft and the meat entirely done. The water in which they were boiled makes a wholesome soup.

---

185. *To Bake Turkey.*—Prepare the fowl as for roasting. A very deep oven will be required for a large gobbler. If the fowl is old, directly it is killed put it in a large jar or tub and cover it entirely with cold water; let it remain twelve hours completely immersed. Then remove the feathers. I never suffer a fowl to be beheaded and thrown upon the ground to flutter until life is extinct, but before the head is taken off, have the feet tied firmly with a small cord, half a yard long; then decapitate. Tie the other end of the cord to a board, fastened at each end to a post, (a *fowl* gallows);

the fowl should swing until dead; managed in this way, the meat is whiter and there are no bruises; stuff with a rich force-meat. I ometimes spice the force-meat; for variety, add sausage meat to the batter used in making the stuffing. When put to bake, elevate the turkey a little; it will be less liable to burn than if laid upon the bottom of the oven. Lay slices of pickled pork or fat bacon, taking off the rind and any rancid part, over the breast thick and tuck a piece under each wing; pour in a pint of warm water. Cover the vessel with a well-fitting cover and bake slowly, putting most of the fire under the oven until ready to brown it. If baked in a stove, put over a cover of dough, made of flour and water; remove it when the turkey is nearly done. Baste very frequently, with sweet lard at first, then with the gravy. In turning or taking it up, be careful not to puncture it with a fork or other sharp instrument; this makes unsightly gashes and lets out the juice. Half an hour before the turkey is done, put the giblets to stew; boil four or five eggs hard; cut up the giblets when done; slice the eggs, and put them with the gravy into a tureen. Serve the turkey upon a hot dish. Rice boiled dry should be sent to the table with it, and cranberries or stewed apples.

---

186. *Goose.*—Rub the goose, the night before it is to be cooked, with a mixture of pulverized sage, salt and pepper—equal proportions of sage and pepper, and as much again of salt. When ready for baking, wash it well and wipe dry; stuff it with the following preparation: one tea-cup of bread crumbs, one of well-mashed Irish potatoes, two tablesponfuls of onion shred very fine, two teaspoonfuls of sage, rubbed fine and sifted if dry, chopped fine if green; salt and pepper to taste; beat in two eggs; add a tablespoonful of butter, and fry a few minutes, stirring constantly; put this hot into the goose. If the flavor of sage is not relished, use less or omit it altogether. Put it to bake in a pan or oven; baste well. Stew the liver and gizzard in very little water; slice them and add to the gravy, or keep them whole, and lay upon the dish. The liver is considered a great delicacy. Thicken the

gravy slightly with flour. Carve as the roast goose. Onion sauce or apple sauce are the proper sauces.

187. *Ducks.*—Two are necessary if the family numbers half a dozen. Clean them well the evening before they are wanted. Singe off any hairs that may remain after being picked; season the stuffing highly with onions and sage. Rub the ducks over with butter. Put them to bake; when warm begin to baste. If young and tender, an hour will be sufficient time to bake them. Mince the giblets and add to the gravy. Onions, stewed cranberries, apple sauce, and rice—all, or either of them, should be sent to the table with the ducks.

Wild ducks are seldom stuffed, and require less baking than the domestic.

188. *Partridge.*—To carve: Divide in half lengthwise. Pigeon the same way.

189. *Large Fowls, Chickens, Guinea Fowls, Capons—How to Fatten and Bake.*—Fowls should be cooped several days before being killed, and supplied regularly with fresh water and an abundance of nutritive food. Nothing is better for them than corn meal, made into dough with boiling water. To feed them once a day with rice, just scalded well until the grains begin to swell, fattens them rapidly and improves the quality of the meat. Never prepare more dough or rice than can be used before it sours; when it becomes so it is injurious, and fowls will not fatten upon it. Their coops should be kept clean and dry; a good plan is to build fattening-coops, by driving four posts into the ground,

the size you wish the coop; fill up the space between with narrow strips of plank, far enough apart to allow the fowls to feed by thrusting their heads through the bars of their prison. Cover the roof with boards, making them project over the body of the coop far enough to protect the troughs placed close to the coop The troughs should be shallow and narrow, kept clean, frequently replenished with fresh water; there should also be troughs for holding food. The advantages of this way of feeding are so obvious they need not be pointed out. A handful of dry grains of corn and wheat may occasionally be thrown to them. All this should receive regular attention; ample compensation will be found in the rich, delicate flavor of the flesh, so different from half-starved poultry suffered to run at large, and when needed, run down, caught, killed and put upon the table in a marvellously short time. One should have the stomach of an anaconda to digest such meat. I give no directions for cooking fowls managed in this way, since no skill or art of the cook can make them "salubrious or savory."

A young pullet, capon, or guinea fowl just come to its growth, "fat, plump and rosy," is always acceptable to the majority of palates. Kill them over night; swing the fowl immediately after killing. Bake by the directions given for baking fowls. Rice, pickles and Irish potatoes are good accompaniments.

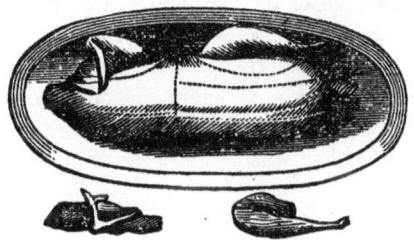

To carve: Fix the fork in the breast; take off the wings, then the legs, then the merry-thought. In the plate the fowl is represented as turned upon the side; this is done to show how it is carved on the back. Separate the breast from the back by cutting through the tender ribs on each side. Carve the back by the lines.

It is usual to truss wild fowls with their heads on, to distinguish them from domestic; remove the intestines carefully, and skin the feet.

---

190. *Pompey's Head—Mrs. B.'s Receipt.*—Three pounds of tender beef or mutton, a quarter of a pound of lard, and three onions, minced fine. Season highly with red and black pepper, and sage; chop the meat fine; mix the seasoning with it thoroughly; form it into a large ball. Make a circular hole half through the centre of the ball; dredge it well with flour; put it in a pan to bake, baste it well with butter; sprinkle again with flour; continue to baste until done. Serve upon a flat dish.

☞ In nearly all first-class cookery books it is usual to devote a chapter to directions in the art and mystery of carving. Observation and conversation have taught me that very little attention is given to this chapter, ladies deeming it entirely a masculine accomplishment. This is an error; though they may seldom be called upon to handle the carver, yet an emergency may arise, and it is well to be prepared to act with grace and confidence; besides, a knowledge of this art will enable mothers to teach their sons, sisters their younger brothers. I have therefore purposely so connected these receipts for cooking meats, etc., with the rules for dissecting, that a knowledge of one could not be acquired without at the same gaining some information as to the other. Practice and experience must perfect the work.

"Cleanliness should be the first lesson in the kitchen."

191. *To Fry Meat.*—The frying-pan is decidedly the most popular of the kitchen utensils. It is a convenient, expeditious way of cooking, requiring less fire than any other mode. Some persons condemn it as "a *pernicious* way of preparing meat;"

giving as a reason that "the influence of heat on fatty substances effects chemical changes whereby they are rendered more difficult of digestion; hence those culinary operations in which oil is subjected to high temperatures are objectionable."

Frying, however skillfully performed, can never be a delicate way of cooking meat, or one suited to the stomachs of children or persons of weak digestive powers. Monsieur Soyer says that "the usual complaint of food being too greasy prepared by frying, is totally remedied by frying the meat in a small quantity of lard, oil, or butter, which has attained a *proper degree of heat*, and, he adds, the objection to this mode of cooking lies in the manner it is performed, the usual practice of cooks being, "to lay the article in cold fat, and letting it soak while melting." Dr. Kitchiner defines good frying to be "boiling in fat." Some things are best cooked in this way, others in very little fat—a process between frying and broiling, which M. Soyer calls *semi-frying* or *sauteeing*. This is particularly suitable for cooking meats partly dry or underdone. It is important to know the precise time for putting the meat in the fat; throw in a piece of bread just as the lard ceases hissing; if it browns a light color, the fat is just right; if the bread burns, the fat is too hot. For frying a large quantity of steaks or cutlets, a shallow oven or spider will answer better than the frying-pan. Watch the vessel carefully while the frying is going on; turn the meat frequently; be careful not to pierce it and let out the juice. Meat-tongs are best for turning, but where it is not convenient to use these, stick the fork in the fat, or slip a broad-bladed knife under, and turn in that way. Take up the meat the moment it is done, before a hard crust forms; cover it in a hot dish. Nothing is so good for frying as nice lard. Butter scorches too easily.

"The world is full of duties for willing hands."

192. *M. Soyer's Receipt for Semi-frying Round Beef Steak.*— Cut the steak three-quarters of an inch thick; saw through the bone, if it is taken from the rump. It should weigh a pound,

and be fat and tender; roll the steak in flour or meal; shake off any particles that will not adhere. Put a frying-pan upon the fire or stove, with a tablespoonful of lard in it (the spoon should not be heaped); when sufficiently hot, lay in the steak; in two minutes, turn it. Repeat this until it is done, never leaving the steak after it begins to fry, until it has been in the pan twelve minutes. Should the fat become too hot, lessen the fire; remove the pan until it cools sufficiently; the gravy must not be allowed to scorch When the steak is half done, season with a teaspoonful of salt, half a teaspoonful of pepper, putting half on one side; then turn it, after frying two minutes, and season the other side. Feel with the finger, and when the meat is firm under the pressure, it is done. Lay it immediately upon a hot dish, and pour over melted butter, or gravy may be made in the pan by pouring in a small teacup of boiling water when the steak is nearly done, after seasoning it. Persons who like onion or eschalot with steak, can fry the onion cut up fine in the frying-pan, allowing a quarter of a pound of onion to a pound of steak. The seasoning may also be varied by rubbing mustard, a little of any flavored vinegar preferred, or curry powder, into the butter before melting.

---

193. *Beef Steak.*—The tenderest are to be found on the sirloin. The tenderloin is delicious, but good steaks may be taken from the round. Some prefer the seventh and eighth ribs, because the fat and lean are better mixed. If the weather is cold enough to admit its being kept several days, it will be better than to seek to make the meat tender as soon as killed, by beating or pounding. As soon as possible, put the steak in a clean bag; tie it tight, and if in fly season, roll the bag in a paste of lime and water, to stop all the interstices through which the green fly could deposit its eggs. Some persons carelessly leave the steak exposed for hours, giving the fly time to scatter eggs over it, and in this condition it is bagged or set away for use. The sequel may be guessed. Hang the bag in a cool place; use no salt about the meat as long as it can be kept without

tainting. Cut the pieces when about to cook them, of uniform size. Should one part be thicker than the rest, equalize the size by beating the thickest part. Should there be too much fat, trim it down. Roll each piece in flour or meal; shake slightly, and lay in a pan of boiling lard. There should be fat enough to cover the steak. When brown on one side, turn it, and as soon as the whole is a light brown, take it up on a hot dish. Into the lard necessary to fry a pound of steak, dredge or sprinkle a small tablespoonful of flour; stir this in smoothly, pressing out all lumps; pour in half a tumbler of boiling water; let this boil up once; pour it over the steak. Onions may be fried in the gravy, after the steak is taken up; the white silver skin are the most delicate. Fried apples are a good accompaniment; also horseradish sauce.

---

194. *Mrs. F.'s Daubed Beef.*—Have a round of beef, weighing ten pounds, prepared as for roasting. Cut a dozen long thin slices of fat bacon; remove the skin, and should there be any rancid part, remove that. Lay them in a seasoning of salt, pepper and vinegar. Spread the meat out after cutting out the bone. Make deep incisions in the flesh, but do not cut through to the skin. Press the slices of bacon into the incisions; roll the meat compactly; wrap it well with broad tape, and insert two skewers. Cover the top and bottom with sliced onion, and set the round away until next morning. Remove the onions, but reserve them, and also any vinegar seasoning that may be left. Put into an oven that will just hold the meat, a pound of good sweet lard. When hot, lay the beef in and fry it slowly, turning it twice. Be careful and do not puncture it with a fork. When it is a light brown color, take it up; put it into a deep stew-pan, or pot that will hold it without cramping. Put skewers, muffin-rings, or an inverted plate under the meat, to prevent its resting upon the bottom of the vessel; flour the meat well; put it in the pot, and pour over boiling water enough to cover it. The vessel must be well covered with a close-fitting cover; simmer gently

one hour; turn 't; pour in the vinegar seasoning in which the bacon lay over night; put the onions in with three sliced carrots, a bunch of parsley, thyme, and sweet basil; a dozen cloves; the same of allspice; three large pieces of mace; a tablespoonful of butter. Cover the oven, and simmer gently another hour. Take the meat up on a hot dish. Make of the broth as much gravy as is needed; the remainder may be converted into good soup, by adding a little thickening, catsup and wine.

---

195. *Beef Liver.*—Wash it well; remove the veins; parboil it an hour before it is to be cooked. Pour the liver and water into a vessel, let it set until nearly cold; slice it in pieces an inch thick; season them with salt and pepper. Cut half a dozen slices of fat bacon; remove the skin; put them with a tablespoonful of lard into the frying-pan; when the lard is hot, roll the slices of liver in flour, shake them slightly and put them to fry; turn frequently. Take the bacon up when crisp; they will be ready to take up before the liver. Take the liver up when done; dredge a little flour into the pan; pour in a small teacup of boiling water; let all boil up until the gravy thickens sufficiently, and pour into a sauce-boat. It should not be poured over the liver. Serve the liver and bacon together upon the same dish. Calf and hog's liver are better than beef, and may be prepared in the same way. Butter may be used for making gravy, if preferred to the lard.

---

196. *Beef Kidney*—Should be parboiled; cut in small pieces, seasoned highly with pepper and salt, and fried as the liver. Serve with tomato sauce.

---

197. *Sweetbreads.*—Parboil them five minutes; take them up and drop them in cold water. When ready to fry, remove all skin, roll them in flour; season with pepper and salt, and fry a light brown. They should be taken up immediately, or they will be too rich. Strain the gravy; sprinkle a little flour in the pan; stir it well; pour in a wineglass of boiling water; just as this boils

up, pour in a wineglass of good Madeira wine, or catsup if preferred.

---

198. *Tripe Fried.*—Cut it in slices, after being boiled done; dip each piece in thin batter and fry in hot lard; take them up clear of grease. Very few minutes will be required to cook it sufficiently, and if suffered to remain too long the tripe will be hard and tough. It may be fried without the batter; put a tablespoonful of lard into a frying-pan; shred an onion fine, and as soon as the lard is hot, put the onion and tripe in; fry until a light brown. Serve without gravy; make a sauce and send in a tureen; for the sauce, use a tumblerful of melted butter, a tablespoonful of chopped pickle (onion is best), the same of lemon juice, or strong vinegar. Let this simmer five minutes; send to the table hot. In frying, lay the rough side down first.

---

199. *Cow-heel.*—After being well cleaned, boil them until the bones can be removed easily. Cut each heel in four parts; dip them first in beaten egg, then roll in bread crumbs or corn meal, and fry in hot lard until a golden color; very little cooking is necessary; or fry them plain until slightly brown. French mustard is good eaten with them, or any of the store sauces. Season extempore.

---

200. *Veal Cutlets.*—Cut them half an inch thick from the fillet or thick part of the thigh; if not quite tender, beat slightly with a wooden meat-mallet, not enough to cut through the meat; flour them; shake off any flour that does not adhere, and fry in hot lard, turning frequently, or they may be dipped in egg, then rolled in fine bread crumbs, and fried. For gravy: Pour off the fat (use it for greasing the griddle); put a tablespoonful of butter in the pan; stir in a heaped tablespoonful of flour until it browns; pour in half a tumbler of boiling water. Season with catsup of any kind liked, and pour over the cutlets. Serve upon a hot dish.

201. *Veal Cutlets with Oysters.*—Empty into a bowl a pint of oysters with their liquor; grate a tumbler not quite full of bread or cracker crumbs; add that to the oysters. Season with pepper and salt; let this stand until you can prepare half a dozen thin tender cutlets. Put a pint of lard into the frying-pan; when boiling hot, roll the cutlets in flour and drop them into the boiling lard. Watch them carefully, turning often; they must not be permitted to scorch; when half done, pour off half of the lard and add the oysters. Take them up when the oysters begin to shrink. Serve in a hot covered dish. Send the gravy in a tureen; a little flour may be added to the gravy if it is not thick enough.

---

202. *Veal Cutlets with Tomatoes.*—Scald and skin half a dozen large tomatoes; more if they are small. Cut up fine and add to the tomatoes a medium-sized white onion, a dessert-spoonful of brown sugar; salt and pepper to taste; stir them to the tomatoes. Put into a stew-pan a tumbler of hot water, the tomatoes, two tablespoonfuls of fine bread or cracker crumbs, and a tablespoonful of butter. Let these simmer gently, covered while the cutlets are being fried. As soon as the cutlets are done, put them in a hot covered dish; pour over them the tomatoes from the stew-pan.

---

203. *Veal Cutlets Curried.*—Cut a pound of veal into slices two inches square. It should be kept until tender. Beat up two eggs; have a plate of fine bread crumbs; dip each cutlet first in the egg, then roll in the bread crumbs, pressing the bread on with the back of a spoon. If they are not well covered, dip again in the eggs and bread crumbs. Have a frying-pan ready with half a pound of boiling lard; fry a light brown color. Before putting the cutlets to fry, put into a stew-pan an onion and tart apple cut up, one tablespoonful of butter. Let these stew, stirring constantly until of a golden color. Now put the cutlets to fry; turn them. Mix upon a plate two teaspoonfuls of flour, the same of curry powder; make this into a paste with sweet milk. Pour into the stew-pan a tumbler and a half of sweet milk; stir it well with the butter. Be careful that the butter does not burn; pour in the milk as soon as the onion is of the right color. When it begins to boil, stir in the paste of flour and curry powder. Take up the cutlets, as soon as done, on a hot dish; pour over the gravy. A dish of boiled rice should accompany this.

---

204. *Another Way to Use the Curry Powder.*—Omit the egg and bread crumbs; rub the curry powder upon the cutlets, and fry; leave the powder out in making the sauce, as that rubbed upon the cutlets will be sufficient. Mutton cutlets are good prepared in the same way.

---

205. *Mutton Chops.*—After the chine is split open and the mutton quartered, cut the chops from the best end of the neck and loin which attaches to the fore quarter—the scraggy part that joins the head is fit only for soup or stews. Cut them of the same size, about two inches long. It is usual to leave one bone to a chop. Beat the thick part of the bone until it is all thick alike; with a sharp knife scrape the meat from the end of the bone half an inch; round the bone. Great care should be taken to give each chop a good shape. If they are too fat, remove part of it. Roll in flour and fry in hot lard. When half done, season the upper side with salt and pepper; turn them frequently, and as soon as done serve immediately. "From the frying-pan to the mouth" is the proper way. Let the dish be hot upon which they are served. From ten to fifteen minutes will be required to cook them, depending upon the size of the chops and age of the animal, and the time the meat has been kept. For gravy: Pour off the fat they were fried in, and for a pound of chops put in the pan a large tablespoonful of butter; set this on the fire, and stir in an even tablespoonful of flour until it has a rich brown color; pour in a tumbler of boiling water; stew until the sauce is as thick as rich cream. Season with any kind of catsup liked, and pour over the chops; or it is good without the catsup.

---

206. *Mutton Chops—Another Way.*—Cut and prepare them as directed in the foregoing receipt; fry them half done; make a thin batter of flour, eggs, sweet milk, pepper and salt; dip the chops in, and fry a light brown color. Serve with horseradish or tomato sauce. Meats fried in batter should never have the gravy poured upon it.

---

207. *Mutton Collops*—Are cut from the best end of the neck. Let there be a bone to each collop three inches long; flatten the large part of the bone (the chine end), so that they will be of uniform size; fry them a light brown color. Into a stew-pan that will hold the collops (a pound at least) pour a quart of boiling water, one tumblerful of onion shred fine, pepper and salt to taste; let them simmer ten minutes; add the meat. Put on the cover, and stew gently until the meat is tender; remove any scum that may collect upon the top. Into the gravy-kettle or a small stew-pan, put a large tablespoonful of butter; set this upon the fire. When the butter begins to melt, stir in a dessert-spoonful of flour; pour the gravy from the collops into the butter slowly, stirring constantly until it boils and begins to thicken. Lay the meat in a hot dish and pour over the gravy. Lamb, beef, veal, kid and venison are all good prepared in this way. Season upon the plate with catsup. This is an excellent way of cooking when the meat is a little tough.

---

208. *A Receipt for Keeping Collops.*—Chop raw, tender meat, into small pieces; season well with salt and pepper; pack in small jars, and pour over clarified butter. Tie an oilcloth over the jar to exclude the air, or use an earthen self-sealing can. To cook: Fry slightly, and then stew until tender, seasoning with onion or anything liked. The difference between a chop and collop is, that collops are partly fried and then stewed.

---

209. *Lamb Steaks or Cutlets.*—These are cut from the hind quarter, without bone, and may be cooked as mutton steaks, by frying them plain or dipping them in egg, then rolling in bread crumbs or corn meal. They require less cooking than mutton steak.

---

210. *Lamb's Fry and Pluck.*—The small bowels, sweetbreads and kernels compose the fry; the lights, liver and heart make the pluck. Clean and soak them well, cutting open the intestines with sharp scissors. When clean, cut them into small pieces, roll in flour, and fry a golden color. Put all into a stew-pan, cover them with boiling water, and stew until tender. Season with red and black pepper, salt to taste, onions and tomatoes.

---

211. *Venison Steaks.*—Cut the steaks from the haunch or saddle, half an inch thick; fry in half lard and butter. Never leave them a moment after putting them in the pan, but turn constantly. Season with salt and pepper when half done; a very few minutes will be required to cook them, but they should be thoroughly done. Take up the steak into a hot covered dish; dredge a little flour into the gravy, stir it in smoothly; pour in half a tumbler of boiling water; let it boil up once, then immediately pour in a wine-glass of good Madeira wine; pour over the steak. If preferred, mushroom or tomato catsup may be used in place of the wine. Serve with cranberry jam or any pleasant acid jelly.

---

212. *Pork Chops.*—Quarter the animal, remove the chine bone, cut the blade bone from the ribs (chops are taken from the fore quarter); cut the ribs into pieces two or three inches long, one bone to a chop; if very fat, remove a part of it. Sprinkle a a little finely pulverized sage over each piece; fry a light brown; serve without gravy. Fried apples, tomato sauce, or dried apple sauce are good accompaniments.

---

213. *Pork Steaks.*—The tenderloin makes the best steak. Cut them a quarter of an inch thick; fry in boiling lard, turning constantly; serve hot. Make gravy by dredging in a little flour,

pouring in a small quantity of boiling water; let it boil up once, and pour over the steak. Serve with them tomato or onion sauce. Steaks may be cut from the hind quarter or chine.

---

214. *Hog's or Pig's Feet.*—Clean them nicely; let them soak a day and night, changing the water once; scrape them well, and boil until the bones can be easily removed. Take out the largest bone when the feet are large; split them in half lengthwise. Make a thin batter of sweet milk, eggs, flour, salt and pepper, and for two eggs a teaspoonful of yeast powder. Dip the feet in this, and fry in boiling lard a light brown color. The feet being already done, the batter requires very little cooking. Take each piece up with a perforated skimmer. Lay a clean napkin upon a flat dish, and put the feet upon the napkin; it will absorb the surplus grease. Serve without gravy; season upon the plate with French mustard, vinegar, or pickles. They are excellent rolled in corn meal and fried. To keep hog's feet in winter, after they are boiled pack them in jars and pour over half the broth they were boiled in, skimming off all grease, and half good apple vinegar; scald the vinegar every three or four days, and, if liked, spice it with mace, ginger, cloves, and allspice.

The feet are good picked up while hot, carefully removing all bones. Season highly with pepper; add vinegar and salt to taste. Put the meat in pans; press it down; when cold, slice, dip in egg, roll in corn meal and fry only until the meal browns slightly; or it may be fried plain in very little lard; the meat will fall to pieces, but tastes well. Garnish the dish in which it is served with parsley.

---

215. *Sausages.*—If in skins, first scald them in boiling water; let them remain in the water *five* minutes. Put a tablespoonful of lard into a frying-pan and when it is hot (but not boiling), prick the sausages and fry slowly, turning them frequently; keep the pan covered with a tin plate. The manner in which sausages

MEATS. 121

are usually fried renders them hard and indigestible; they will not be, if these simple directions are followed.

When sausage meat is fried in cakes, form the meat into round thin cakes; roll them in flour; put them to fry in warm lard, enough to half cover them. Put a cover on the vessel they are fried in; cook slowly, turning twice. They are generally cooked too rapidly—the outside only becomes done, the inner part is raw. When the sausage meat is very rich, less lard may be used; some is necessary to prevent a hard crust from forming.

---

216. *To Prepare Sausage Meat.*—Grind, *very fine*, lean and fat pork in the proportion of two of lean to one of fat. Never use leaf fat; if more fat is needed than is afforded by the trimmings of the chines and joints, cut it from the thick part of the middling. Take out all the skins and stringy pieces of meat. Season it well, by adding to every eight pounds of meat three tablespoonfuls of black pepper finely pulverized, five tablespoonfuls of salt, six of sage, dried, beaten fine and sifted (measure it after being sifted), two of Cayenne pepper; make a very strong tea of this, using only half a tumbler of boiling water; strain this. Mix the seasoning intimately and thoroughly with the meat. The taste of persons differs so much in all matters pertaining to the kind and quantity of seasoning, that much must be left to the discretion of the housewife, or the person best acquainted with the different tastes of the family. While some ignore pepper and the different spices as highly injurious to the tender coats of the stomach, others require such a tremendous quantity of *Cayenne*, spice, brandy, the *combustibles generally*, that, as has been well observed, "only a fire-proof palate lined with asbestos can endure."

Stuff the meat in well-prepared skins; hang them, spreading them considerably. *Never link them*, they are apt to mold and sour where the links are formed. In damp weather wipe them and smoke slightly; turn occasionally. They may be kept through the spring by packing in jars, and pouring over sufficient thick re-boiled molasses, or melted lard, to exclude the air (the lard is best). The jars should be kept well covered, and not set upon a ground floor; there would be danger of their acquiring an earthy taste. The meat may be kept without being stuffed, by packing it in small jars; strain over the top melted lard an inch thick. It is best to use the contents of the jar as soon as may be after it is opened.

---

217. *To Clean the Skins.*—Empty the small intestines; turn and wash them well, first in tepid, then cold water. Put them to soak at least twelve hours, changing the water. Lay them on a smooth board or table and scrape off the inner skin. Be careful and tear them as little as possible. As they are being scraped blow them up by inserting a reed in one end; when an air hole is discovered, cut the intestines. Casings for sausages may be made by scraping the fat very clean from the thin membrane that lines the leaf fat. Sew them into bags and stuff them. Smoke slightly. They keep well. When fresh they are usually cut in slices and fried or broiled. When they become hard, boil them and dress with butter and hard-boiled eggs sliced. Garnish the dish with green sprigs of parsley. They are good boiled and sliced cold for luncheon; served with pickle. When sausage meat is stuffed in large casings they rejoice in the euphonious appellation of "Tom Thumb."

---

218. *Chitterlings.*—Take the intestines and maws selected for chitterlings (and take those only which are in good condition); cut them open with a sharp knife. Hog chitterlings are best—indeed the only kind in general use. Turn and wash them in several waters; scrape them; lay them to soak in weak salt and water two days, changing the water and washing them well; when changed, in fresh cold water. Boil them until tender; pack them in a jar. Pour over weak vinegar to cover them; renew the vinegar as may be necessary. Cut them in pieces if large; roll in corn meal or bread crumbs, and fry until hot in boiling lard, or dip them in thin batter and fry until the batter is a golden color; very little cooking is required. This is a popular dish, very rich; but should

be attended to by a very neat, careful person, and not suffered to lie a moment that can be avoided after being taken from the animal until they are cleaned and in soak. The water should be changed often and the vessel in which they are put to soak washed clean each time of changing. Seasoned like oysters, they make a good mock oyster.

---

219. *Liver Pudding.*—This is best made of calf's or hog's liver; other kinds are used, however. Boil together a pound of hog's liver, half a pound of the thin part of the middling or breast of pork. When tender, mince them together fine, or it will be easier to pass the meat through a sausage grinder; remove all skins and stringy parts; season highly with onions shred fine, red and black pepper; salt to taste. They may be stuffed or fried in cakes; roll the cakes in flour and fry as sausages. They may be kept some time in cold weather by first frying the cakes and then packing in small stone jars, with melted lard poured over to cover them. When used, set the jar in hot water to soften the mass. Pour off the surplus fat and take out the cakes; re-fry them slightly.

---

220. *Liver Cakes.*—Parboil calf's liver; chop it fine with a third of the thin part of the breast of pork; season with any spices liked, Cayenne and salt. To a pound of meat add a teacup of fine bread crumbs, a teaspoonful of butter and two eggs; work it up well; roll the meat in small balls, flour them and fry in hot lard. These are good in soup, and make an excellent side dish as an accompaniment to roast fowls.

---

221. *Mutton, Beef, or Veal Sausages.*—Make a stuffing or force-meat of one tumbler of fine bread crumbs, one egg, pepper and salt to taste; onion or eschalot minced, one tablespoonful; a teaspoonful of parsley chopped very fine. Fry this stuffing, stirring constantly, five minutes. Cut large thin slices of cold fresh meat, a little underdone; lay a teaspoonful of the force-meat in the middle of each slice; roll it tightly and carefully, so

as to prevent the stuffing from oozing out at the ends. Wrap a narrow tape or good string around each piece, giving them a shape to resemble stuffed sausages; fry in hot lard, turning them; very little cooking will be required. Serve upon a hot flat dish. Garnish with lemon cut in slices and green sprigs of parsley. Serve with a piquant sauce.

---

222. *Soyer's Meat Fritter Receipt Modified.*—Put a pound of stale bread to soak in just enough sweet milk or water to moisten it; the same quantity of cold boiled or roasted meat; if baked or roasted meat is used, pare off any hard skin; use sufficient fat from the meat; chop in small dice rather fine; press the water out of the bread. Put in a clean frying-pan two ounces of butter or lard, two teaspoonfuls of chopped onion, and fry two minutes; add the bread, stir with a wooden spoon until the bread is somewhat dry, then add the meat. Season the mass with a teaspoonful of salt, half a teaspoonful of pepper, and half a grated nutmeg. Stir all together thoroughly, and break in two eggs beaten together a few minutes; mix this rapidly with the bread, and pour out into a dish immediately to cool. Roll it into egg-like shapes; dip in raw egg, flour them, and fry a light brown color. Serve upon a napkin. Send to table with it a tureen of tomato sauce. This makes a good stuffing before made into balls.

---

223. *To Prepare Chickens for Frying.*—After they are cleaned cut off the feet, then the limbs. Cut a slit at the bottom of the breast bone; take out the intestines, being careful not to break the gall-bag; divide the breast; cut the back in two pieces; separate the neck from the merry-thought. Take the giblets, viz., the heart, liver and gizzard; cut the gizzard open, empty it, and remove the sand; wash all well, and, strewing over a little salt, let it remain, if for breakfast, over night. Chickens are not good cooked immediately after being killed. When circumstances compel the cooking directly they are killed, either fry them be-

fore the animal heat has escaped, or as soon as killed throw them into a tub of cold water before picking them; keep them in this condition until needed, then pick and clean them.

---

224. *To Fry.*—Roll each piece in flour or corn meal; fry in plenty of boiling lard. Should the lard become hot enough to scorch the outside, lessen the fire; turn frequently; cover the pan with a tin plate; fry slowly. "To boil in lard" is the proper way to "fry" chicken. To make the gravy: Pour off the lard, strain it, and keep it for other purposes. Put a large tablespoonful heaped of butter into the pan; rub into it a dessert-spoonful of flour; set this upon the fire; stir it while melting, and until the butter has a rich golden color. Season with pepper and salt. Pour in half a tumbler of boiling water; as soon as it boils up once, pour it over the chicken. Send a dish of rice, hominy, or hominy cakes to table as an accompaniment

---

225. *To Fry Chicken in Batter.*—Half fry the chicken by the foregoing receipt; then dip it in a thin fritter batter and finish the frying. The gravy may be made as for the fried chicken, or in either case the lard used in frying will answer; add a little flour, stirring it in smoothly, and pour in half a tumbler of boiling water. Never pour gravy over meats fried in batter, but send it to the table in a sauce-boat.

---

226. *To Brown Fricassee Chicken.*—Cut up the fowl as for frying; roll the pieces in flour. Put a large tablespoonful of lard into a spider or shallow oven, and when boiling hot lay the chicken in; let it fry slowly until a good brown color upon both sides. If the taste of onion is liked, cut up one fine of the silver-skin variety. Draw the chicken one side and fry this a light brown, stirring it frequently. Stir it with the chicken; dredge in a dessert-spoonful of flour smoothly, and pour in a pint of boiling water; cover with the oven lid, and stew gently a quarter of an hour. The onions may be omitted if not agreeable, and a tea

spoonful of parsley used for seasoning and added with the boiling water. A tablespoonful of curry powder mixed with the flour used for thickening the gravy will convert this into a dish of curried fowl.

---

227. *To Fricassee Old Chickens.*—First stew them until tender. With a sharp knife remove the largest bones; flour the pieces and fry them a light brown color, and pour into the frying-pan a tumblerful of the broth they were stewed in. Dredge in an even tablespoonful of flour, cover the pan with a lid, and stew until the gravy is thick enough. Pour this over the fowl, and serve hot. Onion shred fine may be used if the flavor is relished, or parsley chopped fine.

---

228. *Turkey Cutlets.*—Kill a large gobbler; hang him up several days before using; then, with a sharp knife, take as many cutlets from the thighs and breast as may be needed, and fry or fricassee them. Continue to cut them until all that will answer the purpose is used, then put the carcass, dissected, into the soup-kettle, with a slice or two of ham or fresh meat; it will aid in making good soup. Serve without gravy, and pour over melted butter. Season upon the plate with French mustard or any kind of catsup preferred. Should the common gravy be preferred, make it as for brown fricassee.

---

229. *Croquets of Poultry.*—Take any kind of cold fowl; remove the skin and sinews; chop the meat very fine; pound it in a marble mortar, or grind it; soak an equal quantity of stale bread in just sweet milk enough to moisten it (this should be soaking while the meat is being prepared). Press the milk out of the bread, adding nearly an equal quantity of butter; work into the mixture the yolks of three eggs boiled hard and grated; season with nutmeg, salt and pepper. Beat the whites of two eggs to a froth; stir them into the mixture; mold in a wineglass, or make in cakes or balls and fry in hot lard. If the mixture is too stiff, moisten with a little cream. Take them up clear of

grease—a perforated skimmer will do this better than a spoon; lay a napkin upon a flat dish, and lay the croquets upon that. Garnish with lemon cut in rings, parsley or celery; serve pickle with it in a separate dish. A handsome way of serving croquets or meat salads, is to form upon a flat dish, the shape of the dish, a wall two inches high with rice boiled soft, or Irish potatoes boiled, mashed and rubbed through a colander; add a little milk to make them soft enough to be rubbed through. Boil three or four eggs hard; take the yolks out carefully and grate them fine; cut the whites in rings of uniform size; put the yolk evenly upon the outside of the wall. Put the dish a few minutes in the stove, merely to harden not brown the wall. Place the rings tastily around the wall upon the outside, sticking a row of cloves upon the edge to keep them in place. The space inside may be filled with croquets-salad, force-meat balls or small birds, making a beautiful supper dish.

231. *Rice Croquets.*—Wash and pick well a teacup of rice; boil it in three tumblerfuls of sweet milk; season with salt, pepper, and nutmeg if liked. Stir the rice frequently when it is nearly done, to prevent its scorching. When thick and dry, spread it upon a dish to cool. Chop fine, and pound in a marble mortar, oysters, and any kind of cold fowl, fresh meat, liver, kidney or fish, equal quantities; a teaspoonful of butter heaped. Make the rice into balls; hollow each one, and in the centre put a sufficient quantity of the meat mixture to nearly fill the opening; close the hole securely, roll the balls in the beaten yolk of egg, then in bread crumbs, and fry in boiling lard. These may be varied by seasoning the rice with lemon, vanilla, or with cheese, and stuffing the balls with any kind of jelly, jam, or dried fruit. These make a nice dessert, with arrowroot or cream sauce.

231. *Brain Croquets.*—Let the brains—calf or hog—soak an hour, to remove all coagulated blood; parboil them five or six minutes; take them up and season highly with pepper; salt to

taste; just sage enough to be recognized; a third as much bread or cracker crumbs as brains. Work all together with two table-spoonfuls of sweet, rich cream, and the white of an egg whipped to a strong froth. If too moist, add a little more bread crumbs; make into balls, roll them in raw yolk of an egg and bread crumbs, or sifted corn meal, and fry.

232. *Force-meat Balls.*—Take half a pound of veal or very tender beef, half a pound of bacon or nice kidney suet if preferred; beat them fine together in a marble mortar, or grind them in a sausage grinder; add a small teacup of bread crumbs moistened with cream. Season with half a nutmeg, half a teaspoonful of mace, an even tablespoonful of chopped parsley; pepper and salt to taste. Work all together with a well-beaten egg. If the paste is too stiff add another egg or only the yolk, or a little more cream. If not stiff enough they will fall to pieces. Fry in hot lard. They should be the size of a nutmeg, if for soup; larger, if to be served with roast.

233. *To Fry Ham.*—Cut the ham in thin slices; pare off the skin. If the ham is old or very salt, lay the meat in tepid water an hour before frying. Put in the spider or frying-pan, a teaspoonful of lard. When it is moderately hot put in the ham; turn frequently. Ham requires but little lard, but it is always best to have some. Always warm the pan before putting in the ham. To make the gravy: Dredge in flour enough to slightly thicken it—a teaspoonful of flour will be sufficient for half a dozen slices; pour in a wineglass of hot water, let it boil up, and then pour it over the ham, which has been taken out before making the gravy thick.

234. *Ham Fried in Batter.*—Take slices of boiled ham—they should not be cut large; season them with pepper; salt will probably not be needed. Make a thin fritter batter, dip the ham in and fry as directed in the receipt for frying ham. Take each

piece up separately with a perforated skimmer. Serve on a napkin laid in a shallow dish; or roll the ham first in egg, then in bread crumbs; press the crumbs on with the back of a spoon; if necessary, dip them twice. Only two or three minutes are required to cook them.

---

235. *Broiling.*—Broiling is an expeditious way of cooking meats, but is only suitable when the article cooked is to be eaten immediately. The apparatus necessary to conduct the process is extremely simple, being only a gridiron. The best kind have small concave bars, with a trough attached for catching the gravy, and should slant a little; that is, should be a little higher before. The legs should be of sufficient length to elevate the meat from six to eight inches above the fire. Always keep the gridiron bright and clean; the cook should never put it away after using it, without first thoroughly cleaning it. The fire must be well attended to; if the fire is poor and cannot be made better, abandon the idea of broiling upon a gridiron; the cooking can be more satisfactorily performed in an oven or frying-pan, by what M. Soyer calls "semi-frying or sauteeing." Good solid coals are absolutely necessary to success in broiling. Place the gridiron upon them after rubbing the bars with a little suet or lard, not enough to drip. The bars should be moderately hot before placing the meat upon them. If they are cold the meat will broil unequally, as the bars keep away as much heat as their breadth covers. Turn the article which is being cooked frequently. Some cooks say "they should not have a moment's rest." This is, I suppose, an exaggerated expression, simply meaning that rapid and frequent turning is best. The cook should so arrange her business as *not to leave* the gridiron a moment from the time the thing to be cooked is laid upon it until it is sent to the table upon a hot dish under a well-fitting cover; and it is due to the cook that the mistress of the house should not permit the dish to chill upon the table through the inattention or carelessness of servants or any useless ceremonies of the table. " Depend upon it there is a great deal of domes-

tic happiness in a well-dressed mutton chop, on a tidy breakfast table. Men grow sated of music, are often too wearied for conversation, however intellectual; but they can always appreciate a well-swept hearth and smiling comfort. A woman may love her husband, may sacrifice fortune, friends, family and country for him; she may have the genius of Sappho, the enchanting beauties of Armida; but a melancholy fate awaits her if she fail to make his home comfortable, and his heart will inevitably forsake her. Better submit to household duties, even should there be no predilection for them, than doom herself to a loveless home. Women of a higher order of mind will not run this risk; they know that their *feminine*, their *domestic duties*, are their *first duties*."

---

236. *To Broil Beef Steak—Mrs. H.'s Receipt.*—Cut the steak in slices about half an inch thick; place them upon the gridiron, and allow them to remain until thoroughly hot; then remove and place between two flat surfaces (the bottoms of earthen plates will answer); press firmly until you have extracted as much as possible of the juice of the meat; replace upon the gridiron, and broil until sufficiently cooked. In the meantime add to the juice of the meat a little butter and black pepper; heat and mix, and pour the gravy thus made upon the steak after you have placed it upon the dish in which it is to be sent to the table. The best steaks are cut from the ribs of the sirloin.

---

237. *To Broil Beef Steak, No. 2.*—The meat should be hung several days before using, if the weather is cool. Having hung long enough, cut the steaks half an inch thick, three inches wide, and five inches long. Thus divided, it is a good size for managing on the gridiron, and as much as a person would care to have on their plate at once. Should one part be thicker than the rest, roll it with a rolling-pin, or *very gently* beat it out to the same thickness. The practice of beating steak is very injudicious, "it breaks the cells which contain the juices;" this escaping, the meat becomes dry and tasteless; better always give the meat time to

become tender and ripe for the gridiron. Sweep the hearth clean; give the dust a few minutes to settle; prepare a bed of brisk solid coals; have the gridiron looking as bright as a mirror; rub the bars well with brown paper, or grease them slightly with suet or lard, not enough to drip, for this falling on the coals would produce smoke. Place the gridiron on the coals, and as soon as hot (not hot enough to scorch) lay on the steak, and turn frequently with meat-tongs or a knife. A fork, if inserted in the steak, will injure its condition by making "taps to let out the juice." I am conscious of repeating this caution often; I have done so because of the great carelessness of cooks in this matter. To have the most palpable duties performed satisfactorily requires "line upon line and precept upon precept." The dish upon which the steak is to be placed must be hot; put in the dish a large slice of good, sweet butter, and add two tablespoonfuls of tomato or mushroom catsup; stir these together as the butter warms; lay in the slices, and turn each slice over, so that all may be covered alike with the gravy. This should be done very hastily, and the steak sent immediately to the table; small space should be allowed between the broiling and the eating, to have it in perfection. With a well prepared sauce and proper accompaniments there is not a more elegant breakfast dish, and when the meat is juicy and tender, and the broiling performed with skill and dispatch, there is not a more delicate way of preparing this deservedly popular dish. The steak is *underdone* if, upon cutting, red gravy flows; a few more moments should be allowed for dressing, as the rare appearance of meat of any kind is disgusting to persons of good taste.

---

238. *To Broil Steak Another Way.*—This can be done very conveniently upon the stove by using the batter-cake griddle. Heat it *very hot;* while the griddle is being heated, place in an earthen dish a large tablespoonful of butter into which a dessertspoonful of flour has been stirred, a teaspoonful of salt, half a teaspoonful of pepper, two tablespoonfuls of mushroom, tomato

or walnut catsup; place this dish on the coolest part of the stove. The griddle being ready, lay on the steak, and turn the pieces constantly with tongs or a knife; when it feels firm when pressed it is done; then lay the pieces in the dish, putting some of the gravy on each steak; serve upon a hot dish. This is a simple but excellent way of cooking steak. For steak to be delightful and delicate, the meat should be juicy, kept until ripe; the griddle hot; the meat turned constantly; the seasoning of the right kind and quantity; the dish upon which it is to be served, hot; nursed with care from beginning to end; and lastly, eaten as soon as cooked. The advantage of placing the meat upon a very hot griddle, is, that the fibres on the surface contract, and this almost entirely prevents the natural juices from escaping, and in proportion to the loss of the juice the meat becomes dry and tasteless.

---

239. *Another Way.*—Cut the steaks an inch thick; make a few incisions in each piece of meat; this must be done after the meat has hung as long as is prudent. Prepare a marinade, by mixing in a deep dish two tablespoonfuls of salt, one of pepper, two of vinegar, four of mushroom catsup; turn the pieces in the mixture; let it lie all night; dust each piece lightly with flour, and broil over a quick fire; serve on a hot dish and butter well. This is a good breakfast dish, and is best cut from the ribs of the sirloin.

---

240. *To Broil Round Steak.*—Cut a pound and a half of steak from the round; saw neatly through the bone; let it be from three-quarters to an inch thick, cut of the same size. When the steak is large and thick, the process of broiling must be *slower* than for thinner pieces, and the turning less frequent. If there is a diversity of tastes in the family, one end, by placing it nearest the fire, can be cooked as much more than the other as is desired. The cook must acquaint herself with the tastes of those for whom she works, and spare no pains to please. Pepper the steak well when first put down; have the dish upon which it is to be served

warm, and when the steak is moved, should there be any gravy about it, hold the pieces between the steak tongs, over the warm dish, and let it drip. It requires practice and close attention to decide upon the exact moment when the steak is done, neither over or underdone. When it is just ready to be dished, season with salt, and lay bits of butter on the dish and over the steak. Onions, curry powder and mushrooms are used for seasoning; but as tastes differ as much as faces, it is a good arrangement to serve with sauces separately. Among the receipts for sauces will be found several good for steaks, chops, etc. The housewife should select different ones for different times, and thus give a pleasing variety to the same dish.

241. *Another Way of Cooking a Pound or More of Steak.*— After hanging until tender, season with onions, pepper, salt, etc.; lay it on a well-covered stew-pan; set it on the fire, *without water;* it must have a *strong heat, but not burn;* turn frequently until done, and serve with its own gravy.

242. *To Cure Beef for Broiling.*—After the steak has hung as long as it can, without spoiling, cut it in pound pieces, and to every piece rub on a teaspoonful of salt, one of black pepper, and as much saltpetre pulverized as can be held between the finger and thumb; rub this on well. Lay them upon a dish, and cover with a thin muslin cloth, that will protect it from the flies, without excluding the air. Set the dish in a cool place. Let it remain two days (unless it will taint, then less time), turning them over every day. The second night hang the pieces in a dark, cool place. Next morning broil as much as may be needed.

243. *Another Way.*—When kept until there is danger of tainting, bake half done and broil; pour over melted butter. Spiced underdone beef is excellent broiled and buttered, or broiled until brown upon both sides. Put in a stew-pan with a little water or cold gravy, butter and pepper, and stew ten minutes.

244. *To Broil Dried or Jerked Beef*.—Cut the slices thin; lay them an hour in tepid water; then broil them until thoroughly hot; turn the pieces once. Put them upon a hot dish; butter well, and serve.

---

245. *Veal Cutlets*.—Cut the steaks from the fillet (upper part of the leg); divide the meat into three parts. There is a natural indication of where the division should be. The flat square piece is best for cutlets. Cut them half an inch thick. Mix together in a deep earthen pan a teaspoonful of salt, half a teaspoonful of pepper, a tablespoonful of butter into which has been rubbed a dessert-spoonful of flour; catsup, if liked. Heat the gridiron warm; lay the cutlets upon the bars; turn once; then lay them in the gravy; put them again on the gridiron; turn once. Continue this until the cutlets are done. Lay them on a hot dish; pour the gravy over, and serve. This quantity of seasoning will answer for a pound of cutlets. Veal should be hung, and wiped dry every day it is kept. Never lay it upon wood; this keeps it moist.

---

246. *Broiling Cutlets*.—M. Soyer gives a very delicate way of broiling cutlets. Any kind of fresh meat will answer:—

When the meat has been kept long enough to be tender, cut and broil them *slightly*. Lay them in a seasoning of bread crumbs, an egg beaten, salt and pepper (a little nutmeg, if liked), a tablespoonful of butter, a few mushrooms chopped, or onions, if preferred. Let them stand until cold; place a small quantity of the seasoning, well mixed, upon each cutlet, and rolling them securely, wrap in well buttered foolscap paper, by laying the meat on one end of the paper, bringing the other end over, and folding the edges so that none of the gravy can escape. Place them upon a gridiron at least eight inches above the fire, and broil slowly half an hour. Be careful that the fire does not blaze. Remove the papers, and serve upon a hot dish. A thin slice of pork or bacon, wrapped with the cutlets, is an improvement

247. *Veal Steak* (*Excellent*).—Take a handful of any scraps or stringy parts of veal, two or three slices of pork, three table spoonfuls of chopped onions, salt and pepper; put them in a stew-pan with two tumblerfuls of hot water. Cover the stew-pan and let it simmer until the juice is all extracted from the meat. Strain the broth; wipe out the stew-pan; return the broth to it. Stir into the stew-pan a tablespoonful of butter, into which has been worked a teaspoonful of flour, two teaspoonfuls of French mustard. Let this simmer slowly.

Have the cutlets cut ready; heat the gridiron while the broth is simmering; broil them upon both sides a light brown color. Drop them into the gravy after it is strained, and stew ten minutes. Instead of broiling, the cutlets may be first fried.

---

248. *Steak "Devilled."*—Cut a round steak weighing a pound; saw through the bone. Broil slowly, basting frequently with a sauce made by mixing thoroughly a large tablespoonful of butter, a tablespoonful of good English mustard, a wineglass of good strong cider vinegar, half a teaspoonful of Cayenne pepper, the same of black, or, instead of the pepper, use an even tablespoonful of curry powder, and a slight flavoring of tomato catsup. This style of cooking steak is called "*devilling*." The seasoning should be highly pungent, so as to leave no doubt of its *paternity*. Underdone meat may be warmed with this style of seasoning, upon the table, in a chaffing-dish, *a-la-blase*. A very good proportion for a dish containing half a dozen slices, is one tablespoonful of butter, three of vinegar, one teaspoonful of loaf sugar powdered, and stirred into the vinegar, one tablespoonful of French mustard, or less of the English; season highly with black and Cayenne pepper. Put this mixture in the chaffing-dish. When it melts stir it well, and lay in thin slices of cold ham, veal, venison, etc.; cold turkey legs, liver, kidneys, are all good prepared with this seasoning. When kidneys are broiled, a very small wire should be run through them to prevent their curling.

---

249. *Mutton Chops*—Are cut from the best part of the neck, with a bone in each chop; beat the bone flat with a wooden mallet. Trim the sharp end of the bone round and scrape it. If there is too much fat, trim off some; broil plain, turning frequently. Have the gridiron prepared according to the directions given for broiling. If the meat has not been kept until tender, beat the meat slightly; but it is best to keep the meat hanging several days before it is used. In dishing, turn the sharp ends of the bone in; use a hot dish; pour over melted butter; season upon the plate with any kind of catsup, or made sauce preferred. They are excellent laid in melted butter, rolled in fine bread crumbs or corn meal; the first is best; turn frequently, and be sure the bread does not scorch. They may, if the trouble is not objected to, after being laid in butter, be seasoned with curry powder, or simply pepper and salt; lay in buttered paper; pin the paper securely; twist the ends; broil upon the gridiron carefully; turn frequently. The paper must not burn, it would injure the taste of the meat. Serve, when sufficiently done, without the paper, upon a hot dish. Make a broth by boiling in a stew-pan any scraps of the meat useless for any other purpose. Strain this when the juice of the meat is extracted. A pint of broth will be sufficient. Make it rich with butter. Season with wine or catsup. Send to the table in a sauce-boat. Rice or hominy, and hot Irish potatoes, should accompany them.

---

250. *Mutton Steaks.*—Cut them from the leg, half an inch thick; pepper well; broil quickly, turning frequently; baste well with butter. Should the fire blaze up, remove the gridiron until it is put out. Strew over the coals a little ashes. The taste of those for whom they are prepared should be consulted as to how much the steak should be cooked. When sufficiently done, place in a hot covered dish, and pour over caper sauce, or serve with mushroom sauce. Turtle and rabbit steaks are excellent prepared in this way.

---

251. *Mutton Cutlets.*—Cut them from the round or thick part of the leg; roll them slightly with the rolling-pin; pepper, and dust very lightly with flour. Lay them upon a dish until you can put in a stew-pan or gravy-kettle a tablespoonful of onion shred fine (if the flavor of onion is liked), three tablespoonfuls of vinegar, three of tomato catsup, pepper and salt to taste, one even tumbler of melted butter, six tablespoonfuls of warm water; stew together until the onion is tender, and the gravy thickens a little, stirring frequently. Broil the cutlets nicely. Take them up on a hot dish, and pour the gravy over them. Lamb and venison steak may be prepared in the same way. Send with them a dish of hot Irish potatoes.

---

252. *To Grill a Shoulder Blade of Lamb or Pork.*—Separate the blade bone from the ribs. Stew it half done with very little water; keep the stew-pan covered. When half done take it up; gash it over; broil slowly, basting frequently with a sauce made as for the "Devilled Steak." Pour over, after it is dished, any sauce that remains. Serve hot.

---

253. *Pork Steaks.*—The tenderloin is best for these. Cut them thin; pepper, and dust lightly with flour. They require longer broiling than any other fresh meat, and are not good unless well done. Sprinkle over a little salt just before they are done. Rub into a tablespoonful of butter a teaspoonful of powdered sage; place this upon a hot dish; lay the steak upon it; turn each piece once; cover the dish, and serve immediately. Fried apples or sweet potatoes are good eaten with pork steak. The sage may be omitted if not relished.

---

254. *Pork Sparerib*—is excellent broiled. Baste constantly with butter. Very few persons baste it sufficiently, hence it is not unfrequently brought to the table dry and tasteless. It requires neither gravy nor seasoning.

255. *To Broil Ham.*—Cut the slices thin and of a uniform size. Should one part be thicker than another, roll the thick part with the rolling-pin. If very salt, soak, an hour at least, in tepid water. Broil over a brisk fire, turning almost constantly; when done, butter and pepper well. An omelet, or eggs cooked in some way, should always accompany broiled ham, unless when it is served for supper. A nice breakfast dish.

---

256. *Broiled Sweetbreads.*—As soon as taken from the animal lay them in warm water; then wash them well; soak until the blood is removed; parboil them five or six minutes; take them up, and drop them in cold water; slice them; remove all strings and gristle. Broil over good solid coals; turn frequently. Have a few slices of fresh butter upon a warm dish; lay the sweetbreads upon it; turn once. Pepper them well, and serve immediately. Oyster sauce is an elegant accompaniment.

---

257. *To Broil Chickens.*—The fowl must be fat and young; no other kind is fit for the gridiron. After it is picked, open it by cutting down the back; remove the intestines; wash it well; keep it at least twelve hours, if the weather will admit. Warm and grease the gridiron; lay the fowl down with the inside next to the fire. Have a small oven lid, washed upon the inside perfectly clean, and wiped dry until it will not smut; put this upon the chicken; weight this down with a flat-iron. Broil slowly. When done—and it is seldom well done—pour over the fowl melted butter. Stew the giblets half done; then pepper them well, and finish upon the gridiron.

---

258. *To Smother Fowls.*—This is an excellent way to cook young ducks, turkeys, guinea fowls, etc. Clean the fowl as in the foregoing receipt. Dust it well with flour. Put it in a shallow oven or stove-pan; pour in a tumbler of warm water; cover with an oven lid, or a plate if cooked in the stove. As soon as the fowl is warm, begin to baste with fresh good butter; continue to baste frequently until it is nearly done. Remove the cover and brown the fowl. Dredge the fowl with flour, sprinkling very little into the gravy. Cook the giblets with the fowl; mince them; add to the gravy, and pour over the fowl. This mode of cooking is between baking and broiling, and is a more satisfactory process than plain broiling. Squirrels, and the hind legs and loins of rabbits, are good cooked in this way. Serve with the game a piquant sauce.

259. *To Broil Squabs, Birds, etc.*—Squabs, or young pigeons, are sometimes objected to as having a soft, immature taste. The reason of this objection is, they are cooked too young. Their finest growth is when they are *just full-feathered*. When they are in pin feathers, they are flabby; when they are full-grown, and have flown some time, they are tough. It is a good plan to mark them before they can fly, by cutting off a toe. In that way their age can be kept. Pick them; open them upon the back; clean and wash well. Broil upon a clear fire, turning frequently, and each time basting with butter. Lay toast upon the bottom of a hot covered dish (a chafing-dish is best); melt together a tablespoonful of butter, into which has been stirred half a teaspoonful of flour and a wineglass of sweet milk. When just ready to boil, place the squabs upon the toast, and pour over the sauce. Cover up the dish, and serve immediately. This receipt will answer for any kind of small, tender bird. Serve with tomato sauce or catsup.

260. *To Barbecue Any Kind of Fresh Meat.*—Gash the meat. Broil slowly over a solid fire. Baste constantly with a sauce composed of butter, mustard, red and black pepper, vinegar. Mix these in a pan, and set it where the sauce will keep warm, not hot. Have a swab made by tying a piece of clean, soft cloth upon a stick about a foot long; dip this in the sauce and baste with it. Where a large carcass is barbecued, it is usual to dig a pit in the ground outdoors, and lay narrow bars of wood across. Very early in the morning fill the pit with wood; set it burning,

and in this way heat it very hot. When the wood has burned to coals, lay the meat over. Should the fire need replenishing, keep a fire outside burning, from which draw coals, and scatter evenly in the pit under the meat. Should there be any sauce left, pour it over the meat. For barbecuing a joint, a large gridiron answers well; it needs constant attention; should be cooked slowly and steadily.

---

261. *Meat Pies.*—Considering the popularity of these dishes, few make their appearance upon the table unless *illy prepared*. In nine cases out of ten they are either tough and leathery, or so rich that it is beyond the capacity of a stomach of good powers to digest. The top crust (usually) is hastily baked, scorched and blistered; the bottom crust not baked *at all*, or *insufficiently*, and thoroughly saturated with rich gravy. These are the *extremes;* but how few avoid them! Where the meat is cooked in the pastry, I think they cannot, under any kind of management, be heathful, particularly for children and dyspeptics; but with care and judgment they may be made savoury and relishing.

A less objectionable way of preparing them is to bake them in a mould; stew the flesh or fowl, add the seasoning, and pour it into the pastry after it is done. For instance:—

---

262. *An Oyster Pie.*—Make a light puff paste dough; cover it, and set it in a cold place an hour; line a drum-shaped mould with the paste; brush the edge next to the bottom, on the inside, with the white of an egg; lay upon the bottom a piece of the dough rolled round to fit, and let it turn up half an inch upon the inside; press it against the sides upon which the white of the egg is, so as to cement them together. Lay across the top of the mould, crossed in different directions, large broom straws, washed clean. This will support the lid, and prevent its falling in. While the pastry is baking get the oysters ready; put enough to fill the mould in a stew-pan; they must be well covered with their own liquor. Grate in the yolks of two hard

boiled eggs; rub into a large tablespoonful of fresh butter a dessert-spoonful of flour; put this to the oysters. Stew five or six minutes, or until the oysters begin to shrink; add a wine-glass of rich, sweet cream. As soon as the mould is ready, take off the top crust; remove the pastry from the mould, and put it in a handsome circular, deep dish. Pour in the oysters; replace the top crust, and serve *hot*. If left standing too long, the bottom crust will imbibe so much of the gravy as to make it heavy and sodden. Some persons like this pie seasoned with mace—use it if relished. Instead of the straws to support the lid of the mould, slices of light bread are sometimes used to fill it. When the crust is done, remove the bread and pound it fine for soups, puddings, etc., etc. Send part of the gravy to table in a gravy-boat, using only enough in the pie to moisten the meat well.

---

263. *Veal and Oyster Pie.*—Cut thin slices of veal from the neck; stew them until tender; season highly with pepper; salt to taste. Put the oysters in a separate stew-pan; add a lump of butter rolled in flour. Bake the crust in a mould as for the oyster pie. After the crust is baked remove it from the mould; put it in a deep dish to suit the shape of the mould; put in a layer of veal and one of oysters, repeating until all are in; the oysters must be on top. Stir into the gravy (mix the two gravies) the beaten yolks of two eggs; let it stew just long enough to take off the raw taste of the egg; pour it into the pie; replace the lid, and serve *hot*. Chicken and oysters, and fish and oysters, are used together for pies, and are much relished; combine the ingredients and seasoning to suit the taste; wine and catsup may be used in the gravy if liked. The whole of the gravy should not be served in the pie; send part in a gravy-boat. Birds stewed and seasoned highly are good for these pies.

---

264. *Chicken Pie.*—Cut up the chicken as for frying. Stew it gently with a seasoning of pepper and salt until the fowl is nearly

done. Boil two large Irish potatoes until they can be mashed smooth (first remove the skin); work to the potato as much flour as will make a smooth dough; lay this aside for the dumplings. Make the crust with a quart of flour, a teaspoonful of soda, a small teacup of lard, a teaspoonful of salt, and buttermilk enough to make a smooth dough. Roll out the dough for the bottom and sides a quarter of an inch thick; line a deep earthen dish with it. Cut the pieces intended for the sides in long strips (it is best made without piecing); put them around carefully. Roll a circular piece; lay this on the bottom. Lay in the chicken carefully; sprinkle in a little flour. Cut the potato paste in strips three inches square; put in a layer of these. Hard-boiled eggs sliced, or cold Irish potatoes sliced, may be laid over the dumplings; then another layer of chicken, dumplings, &c. When the dish is full, take some of the broth that the chicken was stewed in and melt in it a large tablespoonful of butter; pour over the chicken, and sprinkle over a little flour. Roll out a piece of the dough (or if it is wanted *extra* nice, make the upper crust of puff paste) large enough to cover the top of the dish; cut it round, to fit; notch the edge in any tasteful way; cut a slit in the centre, and bake, without blistering, to a light brown color. Shallow pies are very good made in soup plates or tin pie plates; may be kept a day or two in cool weather, and warmed over.

---

265. *Veal or Mutton Steak Pie.*—Cut the steak in small pieces; beat it gently, and stew until tender, with a seasoning of salt, pepper, and (if spice is liked) half a grated nutmeg. Make the crust as for chicken pie. Line the earthen dish with it; lay in the steak; sprinkle over with flour, and lay over bits of butter. Cut in hard-boiled eggs and Irish potatoes. Pour the dish three parts full of the broth after all the meat is in; put on the upper crust; cut a slit in the centre that the steam may escape, and bake.

Venison pie made in the same way is very good. Pies may

also be made of pork, seasoned with onions; and of rabbits or squirrels. These should all be boiled until tender; put inside the crust and baked or stewed until the meat is ready to fall from the bone; seasoned highly with onions, Irish potatoes, parsley, marjoram, tomatoes with a little sugar stirred to them, a little mace or nutmeg, if liked, and catsup or wine. Serve in a "vol-au-vent," or large mould made of light puff paste, as for the oyster pie—the stew, just before serving, poured into it, using very little gravy in the pie, sending most of it in the gravy-boat.

---

266. *Rice Chicken Pie.*—Cut up the chicken as for frying. Stew it with the giblets (and a little cold ham cut up fine) until the meat will leave the bones easily. Pick off the meat in large strips, leaving only the meat on the small part of the pinions. Season the gravy with curry powder, or highly with pepper, a large tablespoonful of butter, an onion and a little parsley, if they are liked. Boil a pint of rice with a little salt; put a layer of this; then all of the chicken; pour in the gravy, and add a thick covering of the rice. (This may be too much rice, the quantity will depend upon the size of the fowl.) Bake half an hour, or less time, in a moderate oven, or in a stove not too hot. For baking this, use a deep earthen dish, and send to the table in it.

---

267. *Pot Pies* (*"so-called"*)—Are best made in a *deep oven*, large or small, to suit the quantity made. Line the sides with the dough; lay the meat or poultry (or they may be used together) on the bottom of the oven. Never put pastry at the bottom, and it is best to stew beforehand the meat or poultry to be used until half done, stewing the seasoning with them; add butter, slice in raw Irish potatoes, an onion, potato dumplings by the receipt given for dumplings to chicken pie. A few mushrooms may be added, or oysters. The seasoning should be varied. The mistress of the house need be at no loss to give variety to these family dishes. A raised crust made with butter milk and soda makes the most healthful pastry, and, when made

with very little handling, is very good. Potato paste is **also** very suitable. When the meat, gravy, and dumplings are all in (the oven should be three parts full of broth), sprinkle in flour, and lay over an upper crust which lacks an inch, all around, of fitting. When the pie is done, take off the top crust in a clean plate. In the dish in which the pie is to be served, lay the meat; put the side crusts around, and lay the lid or upper crust over the whole. Send the gravy to the table in a sauce-boat or small tureen. Fish pies are good made in this way. Only large fish are used.

---

268. *Calipash.*—The upper shell of the turtle is called the calipash—the under, the calipee. Scrape the meat from the calipash; immerse the latter in tepid water; rub and wash it until the shell is entirely clean; wipe it dry; cover the inside completely with a light puff paste. Take enough of the nicest part of the turtle (using the coarser pieces for soup) to fill the shape; put this meat in a stew-pan, with a seasoning of salt, pepper, mace, or any sweet herb used in cooking which may be preferred. For pound of meat take a quarter of a pound of good fresh butter; rub into it a dessert-spoonful of flour; drop this into the stew-pan; cover with cold water. Put on the lid of the stew-pan, set it on the stove or on a trivet before the fire; stew gently, skimming off all impurities until the meat is tender. Add a wineglass of mushroom catsup or any kind preferred, the same of Sherry wine. Stir all up and pour into the shell or calipash. Put on an upper crust, making it large enough to fit exactly; notch it around tastily; cut a slit in the centre. Should there not be gravy enough, pour in sufficient boiling water to answer. Bake a light brown. Send to the table on a square dish to fit, as nearly as can be, the shell. When well arranged, this is a beautiful as well as savory dish.

---

269. *Irish Potato Pie.*—Use any kind of cooked meat; if underdone, all the better. Cut in slices, thin and of a uniform size; butter each piece well; on one side pepper well. Have ready a

quart or more of Irish potatoes—the quantity must depend on the size of the dish in which it is to be served, and this should be an earthen one. Salt and strain the potatoes through a colander Put a layer an inch thick on the bottom of the dish; lay on this the slices of meat, then small bits of butter; pour in a tumblerful of broth, made of gravy saved with the fresh cooked meat of which the pie is made; or if no gravy has been saved, make of the trimmings of the meat as much as may be needed, and, if not rich enough, add a little butter; or half broth and the rest hot cream. Put on a top crust of the strained potatoes. Place the dish in the stove or oven a quarter of an hour. Serve hot.

---

270. *Salmagundi.*—Boil two calf's feet; take the feet out when done; reduce the broth to a quart. The feet may be fried and used, first removing the bone. Let the broth become cold in an earthen vessel; scrape off all the grease; wipe the top of the jelly with a coarse towel; put the cake of jelly into a kettle lined with tin or porcelain; season it with two lemons cut up (removing the seed), fine blades of mace, a stick of cinnamon, pepper (white pepper is best), and salt to taste. Beat to a froth the whites of six eggs; stir these to the jelly just as it melts; it must then be left to clarify and not stirred again. When it simmers long enough to look clear at the sides, strain it through a flannel bag before the fire; do not squeeze the bag. Suspend it by running a stick through a loop made by tying the bag; rest each end of the stick upon a chair, and throw a table-cloth over all to keep out the dust. If the jelly does not run through clear the first time, pour it through the jelly-bag again. Set this aside.

Prepare the meat and seasoning for the pie. Put into a stew-pan slices of pickled pork, using a piece of pork four inches square; if it is very salt, lay it an hour in tepid water. Cut up two young, tender chickens—a terrapin, if it is convenient—two or three young squirrels, half a dozen birds or squabs. Stew them gently, cutting up and adding a few sprigs of parsley. Roll into half a pound of butter two tablespoonfuls of flour; add this to the stew; let it stew until the meat is nearly done. Line a fire-proof dish, or two fire-proof dishes (this quantity of stew will fill two common-sized or quart dishes;) with good pastry; mix the different kinds of meats; put in Irish potato dumplings; season to taste; pour in the gravy and bake. When done, remove the upper crust when the pie is cold and pack in the jelly, heaping the jelly in the middle. Return the crust and serve cold or hot. The jelly will prevent them becoming too dry. They are good Christmas pies and will keep several days. Very little gravy should be used, and that rich. Should there be too much, leave the stew-pan open until reduced sufficiently. This kind of pie keeps well if made in deep plates, and by some is preferred to those baked in deep moulds.

---

271. *Meat Puffs.*—Roll out a sheet of good paste; cut it into circular pieces by pressing upon the dough with a saucer; pass a sharp knife round the saucer. Lay upon the half of each circular piece a spoonful of any kind of meat, poultry, fish, oysters, lobsters, clams, etc., minced fine, and seasoned to taste. Wet with wine or catsup; lay over the other half; crimp the edges, and bake or fry. Serve hot or cold.

---

272. *Meat Puddings.*—These may be made of any kind of scraps of fresh meat—skin or gristle will not answer. A pound of meat will make a good-sized pudding. Chop the meat in very small pieces; flour them well, and season with salt, pepper, a little parsley and eschalot minced fine; form it into a ball, using a little water to wet up the meat sufficiently to form the ball sprinkle a coat of flour over, and let it stand until the paste is made. Make this by Receipt No. 4 in the receipts for pastry. Roll out a circular piece of dough sufficiently large to inclose the ball; lay the meat in the centre of the dough, and carefully and securely close the edges, lapping them as little as possible. Flour a pudding-cloth well; inclose the lump of dough in it, allowing a little room to swell; tie it carefully; boil briskly in

plenty of hot water to cover it. An hour of steady boiling will suffice for a pudding containing a pound of meat and the seasoning. Keep the vessel covered. When done, take the bag out, dip it in cold water, and serve in a hot dish exactly suited to its size. I insist upon this, having seen the pudding brought to table in a dish so much too large as to make a very ridiculous figure. This receipt will answer for any kind of combinations of meat, head, tongue, oysters, poultry, liver, kidneys, ham, etc., and, instead of forming the meat into a ball, roll out the crust a quarter of an inch thick; spread the meat and seasoning over; roll the pudding; tie it in a cloth, closing the ends well, and boil. Much of the palatableness of this dish depends upon the sauce. Let it be rich, and well seasoned. Directions are given in the sauce receipts.

---

273. *Another Style of Pudding.*—Make it as a pie; tie a cloth over so as to prevent the water getting in, and boil; or boil it in a mould; line the sides and bottom of the mould; add the meat, seasoning to taste; cover tight with a well-fitting cover; boil and turn out. Serve with drawn butter.

---

274. *Virginia Chicken Pudding.*—Stew two young chickens cut up as for frying; season well with butter, pepper, salt, parsley, and onion shred fine. Make a batter of a quart of milk, six eggs beaten well; stir to the eggs smoothly nine tablespoonfuls of flour; thin with the milk. Take the chicken from the stew-pan when tender, leaving out the necks; place the pieces in an earthen dish; pour over the batter, and bake until the pudding is firm. It should not be suffered to stand long before being eaten, or it will be tough. A tureen of rich sauce should accompany it, using as much of the broth in which the chicken was stewed as is needed for the foundation of the gravy; add catsup of any kind. Instead of chicken, or combined with chicken, oysters, beef steak, veal, or any kind of game, may be used.

---

275. *Potato Pudding with Meat.*—Boil half a dozen large Irish potatoes; mash them through a colander; add two beaten eggs, butter, and milk to make a thick batter; season highly with pepper and salt. Lay slices of underdone meat upon the bottom of an earthen dish; pour over a layer of the batter, then meat, until the dish is full, having the batter upon the top; bake a light brown; very little cooking is necessary.

---

276. *Pease Pudding.*—Soak nice white peas (of the kind called Cornfield) several hours in plenty of water; tie them in a cloth, allowing room to swell; boil; when tender, turn them out; mash them; season with pepper and salt; tie in a scalded cloth; boil half an hour. From time immemorial this has been considered a proper accompaniment to boiled pork.

---

277. *Tomato Meat Pudding.*—Cover the bottom of a pudding-dish with bread crumbs; put on them a layer of underdone meat cut in thin slices, then a layer of tomatoes peeled and sliced; to a pint add an even tablespoonful of sugar; then a few bits of butter, pepper and salt, a little onion if agreeable; then bread crumbs, meat and tomatoes, repeating until the dish is full; put over a coat of bread crumbs; bake until a light brown. Serve hot.

1. Cheek; 2. Neck; 3. Shoulder, having Four Ribs; 4. Clod, or Front Shoulder, 5. Back Shoulder; 6. Fore Shin, or Leg; 7. Brisket; 8. Flank; 9. Standing Ribs; 10. Sirloin; 11. Sirloin Steak; 12. Rump; 13. Round; 14. Leg, or Hind Shank.

278. *Beef.*—The head is good stewed, boiled, baked, potted,

or for mince pies. To clean it, without removing the skin, put it in enough lukewarm water to entirely cover it; set the vessel where it will boil up once, just enough to scald the head. Take it up; scrape it well; when clean, wash and wipe dry; split the head and jowl apart; take out the brains; cleanse the inside from all coagulated blood; boil head and brains. Clean the feet in the same way.

Another way: Sprinkle powdered rosin over the whole head; scald in hot water; scrape clean; wash and soak well.

The neck is stewed or used for soups. The ribs may be boiled, or boned, stuffed and baked, or roasted. Shin for soup. (Take out the marrow before cooking, and stew, strain, and flavor it for hair grease.) Flank is good collared. The sirloin is to be baked or roasted. The best steaks, called "Porter-house" steaks, are cut from the sirloin, using the ribs for soup. The tenderloin makes excellent steak. Rump may be used for steak, or be roasted, baked, daubed, made a-la-mode, or corned. Round is used in the same way. The heart is good stuffed and baked, or roasted, and boiled makes excellent mince-meat. The liver and sweetbreads may be baked, fried, stewed, and, with the addition of a few oysters, make good pies and puddings. All bones, gristle, and scraps may be boiled, with a seasoning of herbs and spices, to a jelly; then cut into small pieces, dried, and used in making soup; when prepared in this way it is called "Portable Soup." In the hands of an economical, good manager, almost every part of the animal may be turned to good account.

As soon as the animal is cleaned and the intestines removed (all the fat upon them should be saved), let the tripe receive immediate attention, and the head and feet be cleaned. As soon as the animal is quartered, cut out the kidneys; hang the meat as long as it will keep without salting; wipe it dry. When cut up, put the steak in a bag; suspend it; salt the meat, and cover, to protect from flies; sprinkle over the top pieces black pepper beaten fine, and salt. Lay over branches of pine top; a part may be jerked, pickled or dried. The best beef has a bright red color; the fat white;

the grain coarse, and yielding readily to the pressure of the finger. Beef is in perfection when about four years old. The age of the animal may be ascertained by feeling the bone that runs through the ribs. If a four year old, the bone will be soft and tender; it grows harder with age. Stall-fed beef is much esteemed; allow the ox (generally an old one) to become poor, then fatten it well. Says M. Soyer: "The best plan to judge of the flavor is to look at the tongue; if it is plump, and has a clean, bright appearance, and the fat at the end is of a pinkish white, then the meat will turn out good; but if the tongue should look dark, and the fat dead white, then the meat will eat hard and flavorless. Cover the raw side of the hide with ashes, and send it to the tanner.

---

279. *To Corn Beef for Winter Use.*—Prepare the brine the first of November. Get a thirty gallon cask; let it be tight and clean; put into it fifteen quarts of salt, fifteen gallons of cold water, one pound of pulverized saltpetre, and to every gallon of water an ounce of carbonate of soda; stir well and frequently until the salt is dissolved; remove all scum. Keep the vessel well covered with a coarse cloth, and in a cool place. This may be made a week or two before it is needed. The animal being well fattened, kill it upon a cold day. Hang it two days without salt; on the third cut it up; salt it, fleshy side down, in a tub that will let out the bloody brine. Let it remain (well covered) ten days. Unpack it upon a cold day; wipe each piece, and add to the brine. Put a weight upon the meat to keep it under the brine. In a week it will be ready for use. Skim the brine occasionally. If it becomes at all sour, pour it off and boil, adding a little salt and soda, skimming well. Keep the cask in a cool, dry place, well covered. Tongues and mutton hams may be put in this brine.

---

280. *To Pickle a Hundred Pounds of Beef or Pork.*—Six gallons of water, nine pounds of salt, three pounds of brown sugar, one quart of molasses, three ounces of saltpetre, three ounces of

red pepper, one ounce of potash. Boil and skim well; let it get cold. Let the beef hang twenty-four hours after being killed; salt it two days; let the bloody brine run off; wipe each piece with a damp cloth; pack it in a cask; put weights upon it; pour over the brine. In five or six weeks re-boil; skim well, and when cold pour over the meat. It should be entirely covered with brine, and a cloth kept over it. If pork is intended for bacon, hang it to smoke for three or four weeks, the time depending upon the size.

281. *Spiced Beef.*—Make a brine with half a pound of salt, half an ounce of saltpetre, half a pound of sugar, a tablespoonful of cloves, the same of allspice and black pepper; crack the spice (do not beat it); boil five minutes in a pint of water; when cold, rub it upon ten pounds of beef. Turn it every day for two weeks. When ready for use, bake it in a deep dish; pour in the brine; to which add two tumblers of water; cover over the top with suet or slices of cold fat bacon. Let the meat become cold in the brine.

282. *To Dry Pickle Beef or Pork.*—Sixteen quarts of salt, three ounces of saltpetre, for every hundred pounds of meat. After the meat has hung and dripped until all the animal heat is gone, cut it into proper pieces; rub each piece well with salt; sprinkle salt on the bottom of a water-tight cask; pack in a layer of meat edgewise; take a maul and beat it down well; sprinkle over evenly a little saltpetre; fill all the interstices with salt; continue this until all the meat is packed in very solidly; cover two or three inches on the top with salt; put a weight on the top of the meat; throw a cloth over, or put on a good wooden top, and keep in a cool, dry place. Meat pickled in this way needs very little soaking before boiling, and, if the directions are followed, will be found to keep well.

283. *To Cure Beef Hams for Winter Use.*—After the beef has hung long enough for the meat to be tender, cut the hams from the hind quarter; with a sharp knife cut out the bone. Mix one quart of good salt, half a pound of brown sugar, one ounce of

saltpetre; lay this thickly over the inside of the hams. They should then be rolled by a strong hand, and firmly wrapped with a strong twine string, beginning at the hock; salt well upon the outside; put them upon a dish (they should not lie upon wood); cover with a thin cloth; turn every day for ten days; then suspend them in the smoke-house, and smoke slightly. For cooking, cut the slices thin, and broil. They will be found excellent. If the last of the meat becomes dry, use it for chipping.

---

284. *To Jerk Beef.*—Slice pieces from the round, or fleshy part, two inches thick. Make a scaffold in the open air, where the rays of the sun will fall directly upon the meat. The scaffold should not be covered with solid plank, but with narrow strips of wood. Dip the pieces of meat in salt and water; lay them upon the scaffold, and smoke. Be careful the fire does not blaze. The flies must be brushed away constantly. Turn it frequently; or it may be jerked without smoking, merely exposing the meat to the sun when the weather is warm and dry. When the outside of the meat hardens, string it, and hang in a cool, dry place. Always trim off the hard outside skin before cooking. Besides being broiled, it may be boiled or stewed. When hard, lay it in tepid water half an hour before broiling. It is not necessary to do this when cooked in either of the other ways.

---

285. *To Clarify Suet.*—Cut as much of the kidney suet as is wanted for culinary purposes; remove all the thin membrane that covers it; wash it; put it in a gravy-kettle or well tinned stew-pan; simmer slowly, stirring constantly to prevent its burning. When the suet is dissolved, and the cracklings float on the top, it is done; strain it into an earthen dish; when cool, pack away in jars; cover from the air; when used, shave very thin with a sharp knife. Suet may also be kept a few weeks by rolling it in flour, and protecting it from dust and air. The tallow is made by the first receipt, using all the grease from the intestines and every part of the animal.

286. *To Clarify and Harden Tallow.*—Melt ten pounds of tallow and two of beeswax together. Have ready two gallons of boiling water; as soon as the tallow melts pour over it the boiling water; let this boil two hours; remove the pot from the fire. In another pot put four pounds of alum; pour upon it three gallons of water. When the tallow becomes cold take it up; scrape off any sediment upon the bottom of the cake, and put it in the alum water. Boil eight hours steadily; skim off all impurities; replenish, if necessary, with hot water. Let the tallow cool, and if not satisfactorily white, add more alum to the water—about two pounds—and re-boil it. I have seen candles made in this way—the tallow re-boiled twice—equal to the adamantine. Make the wicks of soft twisted thread; they burn brighter if dipped in turpentine, and dried well.

---

287. *Confederate Candles.*—To two pounds of tallow add a teacup of strong lye (from hickory or ash ashes); simmer over a slow fire, when a greasy scum will float on top; skim this off as long as it rises; this grease will make soap. Mould your candles as usual.

---

288. *To Make a Cheap Sick Room Taper.*—Into a saucer half full of lard insert a piece of newspaper made of a sugar-loaf shape by cutting a small square and twisting it around the finger; put the broad end in the lard; let the taper end be an inch above the lard. Another way: Put a sycamore ball in a saucer of melted lard; when completely saturated, light it. Another: Tie a piece of soft cloth over a large button, leaving an inch or two of the cloth above the button for a wick; put it in a saucer; half fill with lard, and light it.

These little scraps of information, though very simple, are worth gathering up, as persons are sometimes unexpectedly placed in circumstances which render them valuable.

1. Loin, best end; 2. Loin, chump end; 3. Fillet; 4. Hind Knuckle; 5. Fore Knuckle; 6. Neck, best end; 7. Neck, scrag end; 8. Blade Bone; 9. Breast, best end; 10. Breast.

289. *Veal.*—The loin is the best piece for roasting; the fillet is stuffed and roasted; steaks, cutlets, collaps, etc., are taken from the fillet or thigh; chops from the neck, best end; the shanks for soup; the remaining pieces may be stewed or used for pies, ragouts and force-meat balls; the head is good stewed, potted, baked or boiled; stuff and bake the heart, or boil and use for mince pies. The liver and sweetbreads of the calf are much more delicate than when the animal is older. Boil the feet; make jelly of the liquor; fry, fricassee or stew the meat. Make tripe of the stomach; bake or stew the tongue. Veal of itself is an insipid meat, but, well seasoned, is not only very delicate and agreeable to the palate, but pleasant to the eye. The calf should be fattened upon the mother's milk, and killed when ten weeks or three months old, and when in perfect condition for the table, the grain will be close and firm, the flesh a delicate red, and the fat white; the kidneys should be covered with white, thick fat; the liver firm, and free from spots. Always hang the meat, and wipe it dry every day with a coarse cloth. It taints easily if permitted to rest upon wood and never turned or wiped.

---

290. *To Prepare Rennet.*—A rennet is the stomach of a calf, prepared in this way: Empty the stomach as soon as the animal is killed; wipe it dry upon the inside; sprinkle salt over it; let it lie five days; then shake off the salt; stretch it, and dry it. A piece three inches square will turn a quart of sweet milk.

Wash the rennet; soak in a teacup of tepid water an hour; pour the water to the milk; stir well; set in a warm place until the curds form. Make custards in this way: One quart of new milk, half a pint of cream; prepare the rennet as directed; add to the milk and cream mixed, stirring well; flavor with wine; sweeten to taste; grate in a nutmeg. Pour in custard-cups; set near the fire until the curd is firm; then set on ice or in a cool place. The rennet should be very slightly washed.

1. Leg; 2. Shoulder; 3. Loin, best end; 4. Chump end; 5. Neck, best end; 6. Breast; 7. Scrag end.

291. *Mutton.*—A saddle of mutton is two loins. The leg and loin are considered the best pieces. The leg may be boiled, baked or roasted; the loin is usually baked or roasted. The shoulder may be baked or roasted, or separate the blade-bone from the ribs and grill, or broil the blade-bone; broil, fry or stew the ribs. The neck affords several savory dishes; cut chops from the best end; spice and bake as mock venison; use for ragouts, stews, etc. Use the shanks and scrags for soup. Mutton hams are fine pickled a few days, then slightly smoked and used for broiling. Mutton is in the greatest perfection at four years old. The grain should be firm, but tender to the touch, of a dark, clear red, the fat firm and white. Mutton suet is useful for many purposes. Save all the surplus fat; stew it; strain from the cracklings; pour it into bowls to cool, and pack it away closely.

292. *Lamb.*—A lamb is usually divided into four quarters, which may be boiled, baked or roasted. The fore-quarter is

sometimes divided, using the ribs for chops, and grill the shoulder blade; the pluck consists of the heart, liver and lights; the fry is composed of the bowels, sweetbreads and kernels; the head is good stewed or boiled; the broth of it makes good soup. Some very thrifty, economical housewives use the feet of the sheep, called "*trotters*"—the liquor in which they are boiled makes a beautiful amber-colored jelly. Lambs should be killed when four or five months old, and weigh from twenty to thirty pounds. Save the suet.

---

293. *Venison.*—The shoulder should be roasted, or used for stews, puddings and pies; the neck for steak or stews; the haunch roasted or baked; the scrag and shins for soup. Buck venison is best. If young, the cleft in the hoof will be small and smooth; if old, large and rough. "The fat should be white, the lean very ruddy." The hams are good dried and chipped.

1. Ham; 2. Side or Middling; 3. Shoulder; 4. Chine or Backbone; 5. **Head and Jowl.**

294. *Pork.*—The hams and shoulders are salted and smoked; the sides pickled or smoked. The chine is the part of the backbone that lies next the head. It is usual to cut out the backbone whole, and then separate them before cooking. The chine is baked, boiled or stewed; the smaller bones stewed or boiled. It is best to take the ribs from the sides, and broil, bake, or roast them; the feet are good soused; the small intestines used for chitterlings; the liver fried or broiled; the harslet stewed; the head and ears made into cheese or scraffle; the jowl salted and smoked; the tongues salted and boiled, as beef tongues. Broil

or fry the kidneys, first passing a wire through to prevent their curling; the brains may be fried with eggs, or pickled to imitate oysters. The fat must be taken from the intestines, and that which is in a sound, healthy condition, must be put to soak to convert it into lard. The poorer parts use for soap, or stew and keep for greasing wagons and other plantation purposes.

295. *To Try the Fat.*—The lard for cooking is made from the leaf fat, the fat from the chine, head and trimmings of the joints, etc.. Wash it well, and soak twelve hours; if put to soak in the evening let it remain until next morning; wash it in tepid water, changing it twice; cut it in small pieces; pour a little water in the bottom of the kettle to prevent the fat from scorching (very little water is necessary); cut in small pieces; boil briskly until the oil from the meat is nearly extracted, and the process almost completed; then reduce the fire; stir frequently, turning the meat up from the bottom; when done, the cracklings will be a good brown, and float to the top and break crisp. Great care must be taken after the oil begins to look clear, to prevent its burning (the least taste of that kind will injure its quality); at the same time the cracklings must be thoroughly done, the water entirely evaporated, or the lard will turn sour. Strain first through a colander, pressing the oil out; then place a muslin or other thin cloth over the mouth of the jar, and strain again. To prevent the jars breaking in very cold weather from the freezing of the lard, put a stick as large as a man's wrist through the centre of the lard just as it begins to harden. When cold, withdraw the sticks; use seasoned wood—pine will not answer. Stoneware answers better on some accounts for keeping lard than tin. When jars are emptied, have them scalded and sunned immediately; repeat this just before using them again. A little lye will aid the cleansing. The lard from the intestines must be well soaked, washed and kept separate, and boiled by itself. By nice, careful management it may be made to answer for frying meats. Save the oil from the feet; clarify and bottle it. When jelly is to

be made of the liquor the feet were boiled in, there must not be any salt about them. The trimmings of the backbones, joints and tenderloins are used for sausages. There should be a pound of fat to two of lean. Never use leaf fat; in sausages it runs to gravy when cooked, leaving the meat dry and lean.

---

296. *To Cure Bacon.*—The first requisite in making good bacon is, that the hogs be in good condition; then, that they should be killed when the wind sets *decidedly* in the north; take advantage of the beginning of the cold weather; never kill upon the wane or decrease of the cold. After the animal is slaughtered, it should immediately be put in a vessel containing sufficient hot water to scald it well; turn once; scald the feet. It is possible to have the water too hot; extremes must be avoided. A scaffold, or platform made of plank, poles or rails, should be in readiness to receive the animal as soon as it is withdrawn from the water; then the scraping must be begun, taking care not to cut the skin; pour over, from time to time, hot water; a great deal of scraping and washing is necessary to clean the skin as it should be. Always scrape and clean the feet, head and ears, at the same time the hog is cleaned. When in proper condition, hang it; remove the intestines; wash every part well, using several waters; repeat this until the inside is entirely clean; wipe with coarse, clean cloths. Let the hogs hang in the open air until all are slaughtered and cleaned. The intestines should be received in tubs, put in charge of careful hands. The fat must be first saved, and put to soak; the intestines intended for sausage cases and chitterlings should be emptied and cleansed; the balance emptied, washed, and stewed for soap-grease; the maws are used for chitterlings; spread a little lime upon the inside of those intended for chitterlings; after lying a few hours, scrape and soak them. A little lime rubbed upon the inside of the articles used for chitterlings and tripe cleanses them much sooner, and gives a much better flavor than mere scraping and soaking.

---

297. *To Cut up the Hog.*—Remove the head; split the jowl and upper part asunder; take out the brains and tongue; cut out the backbone. Divide the remainder of the hog into six parts— the shoulders, middlings and hams. Round the hams; use the trimmings of the joints and the tenderloins for sausages. On the under side of the hams the bone *slightly projects;* saw this even with the meat; it is of no advantage to the ham, and a good hiding-place for skippers. Remove the spareribs from the middlings. Spread the meat until all animal heat is out, first sprinkling it over with salt.

---

298. *To Salt Pork.*—Have suitable tables or platforms ready; begin the salting by giving the shank end of each joint a smart rap upon the table, so as to loosen the joint; work the hock backwards and forwards to ascertain if this is done. The advantages of this is, the salt penetrates sooner. Rub the salt in well; pack in boxes or pits dug in the dirt floor of the smoke-house five or six feet deep; line the pits with plank; the plank should be at least a foot above the surface of the ground; cover the bottom with salt; pack the joints as soon as they are properly prepared, skin side down. When saltpetre is used, apply it by taking a pinch between the finger and thumb, and sprinkling evenly over the joints after they are salted, and before packing. Between each row of meat pack in salt, and when the last is in, cover well with salt, and then with fresh pine tops. If hogsheads are used for packing the meat, bury them in the ground to about a foot of the top. In four weeks the meat will be ready for hanging. It should be taken up on a cold, windy day. Shake off the salt; wash the hams as expeditiously as possible; hang the meat, hock down; smoke several hours each day until cured. The best plan for smoking is to have a furnace upon the outside, and attached to the smoke-house, a flue conducting the smoke inside. The smoking is an important matter; meat is often spoiled from being over-heated when the fire is made inside. When the fire is made inside, dig a pit two feet deep; make the fire in the bottom; clean it out each day. Joints should never be hung immediately over the pit, as the fire often blazes; and the smoke is warmer as it first rises from the pit. A little red pepper thrown upon the fire, or a few dry China berries, will drive off the flies. When sufficiently smoked, put the hams into bags made of thick Osnaburgs; tie them securely; whitewash the outside with a paste made of lime; hang immediately, hock side down. The remainder of the meat may be hung or packed away in ashes; if permitted to hang, there is some loss from dripping. If there is reason to fear the joints are tainted, run a sharp knife into the meat at the hock-bone; if an unpleasant odor is perceived, the meat is not doing well. A friend who is remarkably successful in curing bacon, tender, juicy, and of fine flavor, furnishes me the following receipt for curing hams: "Cut and round the hams smoothly; salt, and rub well; pack down; and the first favorable weather, after eight or ten days, take the joints up and *re-salt* them; in three or four weeks hang them and smoke gently. To protect them from insects, as soon as they are sufficiently smoked, put them into sacks, and lime the sacks." After the meat is taken up to smoke, it is a good plan to sprinkle the inside of each ham immediately after being washed with pulverized black pepper, to protect them from flies. The skipper-fly usually makes its appearance the last of February or early in March, according as the weather is more or less cold. It is very desirable to smoke and pack the meat away before that time. Sugar is sometimes used in curing meat—a pound to two pounds of salt, or a pint of syrup to two pounds of salt.

299. *To Cure Hams.*—Spread upon each ham the following mixture, and let them remain until the next day: One small spoonful saltpetre, one large spoonful of sugar, one large spoonful of molasses, a teaspoonful of red pepper, rubbed well together; then salt down and pack away as you do other meat. This is a good plan in localities where there is very little cold weather.

300. *To Preserve Hams by Packing in Ashes.*—Make a scaffold around the inside of the smoke-house; put as many tiers as may be needed, making them of very narrow strips of plank, so that when the hams are placed upon them, they will be supported only at the ends and in the middle, with space between each tier to allow a free circulation of air. Cover each ham well with dry leached ashes; place upon the thin strips of plank, skin-side down. When hogs are killed late in the season, before the meat is sufficiently smoked, and the skipper-fly begins to make its appearance, take the joints down; ash them well; hang again, and complete the smoking; then lay away, well ashed, upon the tiers. There is no better plan for those who like meat preserved in ashes.

---

301. *To Pot Meat.*—This is an economical way of using up scraps of cold meat, fowls, or fish. Cut up all the meat, separating it carefully from the bones; scrape off any gravy or hard skin that may remain after being cut or picked up. Gravy or stuffing would make the meat sour if kept over two or three days. Different meats may be potted together. First grind the meat by running it through a sausage mill. Pick out all the gristle; then pound it in a marble or wooden mortar, moistening it from time to time with clarified butter, adding any spice or herbs required for seasoning. It should be well beaten. Dr. Kitchiner, who recommends meats prepared in this way for invalids and persons of weak digestive powers, says: "There is no grease so good to use in the pounding as 'elbow grease.'" When reduced to a smooth paste, pack in small jars; cover an inch with clarified butter; tie a bladder or oilcloth over; keep in a dry, cool place.

---

302. *To Clarify Butter for Potting.*—Simmer the butter gently in an open vessel; when the water has evaporated (which may be known by the bubbling ceasing) take it off the fire, and let it remain undisturbed half an hour; the curd will settle at

the bottom. Bottle and cork tightly, and keep in a cool place. Butter prepared in this way will keep well, and is valuable for enriching stews, hashes, etc. Will make good cake and pastry. Potted meats should always be put cold in the jars, and packed firmly.

---

303. *To Pot Calf's Head.*—After the head is well cleaned, taking off the skin, nose, and ears; put it to boil with two of the feet, which have been well cleaned. Boil until tender; remove the pieces from the liquor; when cold, scrape off all grease that may adhere; take out all bones; put the meat back into the pot with the herbs intended for seasoning, and enough of the liquor to cover the meat, after skimming off the grease that floats on the top; boil half an hour. Take up the meat in a clean colander; let the liquor drain until the meat is dry and cold. Run through the sausage mill; then pound in a marble or wooden mortar, adding the spices and a little clarified butter from time to time. When a smooth paste is formed, pack in a mould; cover so as to exclude the air; mix the spices; half a teaspoonful of cloves, a whole teaspoonful of mace, cinnamon and allspice, one and a half of pepper to one pound of meat; salt to taste. Serve with pickle. If the meat does not turn out well, wrap a hot towel around the sides of the mould, or set a minute or two before the fire, turning it. Potted meats are excellent for sandwiches. Use the broth for soup.

---

304. *To Pot Ham and Tongue.*—Beat together well a pound each of cold lean ham and tongue; season with spices, if liked. When a smooth paste, pack in jars, by the foregoing receipts. Fowls, fish, with a little lean ham or tongue added, may all be potted. Suit the taste in making the combinations as well as in selecting the seasonings. Two ounces of clarified butter will be the proper quantity for one pound of meat, unless the meat is very rich; then less butter should be used. It is convenient to have these made dishes on hand, as, in case of having company

unexpectedly, additions may easily be made to lunch, dinner, or supper.

---

305. *To Pot Beef, Veal, Lamb.*—Cut the meat in slices; salt and pepper them. Put a layer of meat in the bottom of a double boiler or in an unglazed jar. If a jar is used, set it in a pot of boiling water; season between each layer of meat with spices; when closely packed, pour over a pint of good Madeira wine. Boil until the meat is tender, then pot as directed; or put the meat and seasoning in an earthen dish; put a thin crust of coarse flour and water over the top to bake. Take it from the gravy; when cold, pot it; use the gravy for soup.

---

306. *To Collar Meat.*—This is done by picking the meat into small strips; while hot, spread layers upon the bottom of a pan; sprinkle over mixed spices; fill the vessel with alternate layers of meat and spices; put on weights sufficient to press the meat into a solid cake. When cold, to be eaten with pickle, lemon-chow, etc.

---

307. *To Collar Flanks of Beef.*—Salt the two flanks; sprinkle over a little saltpetre; turn them every day for eight or ten days (if the weather is cold enough). At the end of this time wash the meat well; boil it until tender. Have ready half a teaspoonful of pounded and sifted cloves, the same of allspice, one teaspoonful each of cinnamon and mace. When the meat is tender, take it up and pick it to pieces as expeditiously as possible, removing the skin and gristle. Put a layer of the meat (mixing the fat and lean judiciously) on the bottom of a pan; sprinkle over pepper and the mixed spices evenly. When the meat and seasoning is all in, put a sheet of tin or a piece of board that will not give it a disagreeable taste. Place weights upon the board, and let it remain until the meat is perfectly cold. Serve with pickle. Another way is to boil the flanks; spread them out; trim off the fat when there is too much; remove all skin and gristle; spread

over the spices and pepper, and, beginning at one end, roll tightly; wrap with tape; put under weights; when cold trim the edges; garnish with sliced lemon.

---

308. *To Collar a Leg of Pork.*—Take out the bone; stuff with a mixture composed of two teaspoonfuls of powdered sage, one teaspoonful of pounded mace, one nutmeg grated fine, a dozen cloves, the same of allspice, a teaspoonful of cinnamon, salt to taste, a tablespoonful of pepper, half a pound of butter, one tumbler of fine bread crumbs; mix well; spread evenly on the inside of the pork. Wrap it to look as nearly as possible as it did before the bone was removed. Tie it tightly with tape; put it in a pan with a little water. Bake two hours. Press it by placing weights upon it. To be eaten cold.

SAUCES, STUFFINGS, AND GRAVIES.

"The most homely fare may be made relishing, and the most excellent and independent improved by a well-made sauce."

Upon many tables the only gravy which makes its appearance is the grease or drippings from the meat, thickened with a paste of water and flour, or the *pure unadulterated* grease minus the thickening. I earnestly advise all housewives to make themselves familiar with the art of preparing different kinds of sauces. I have seen the character of *poor* steak, joints, and puddings *in part* redeemed by a well selected, well prepared sauce.

---

309. *White Sauces for Boiled Meats or Poultry—Egg Sauce.*—Rub together smoothly a large tablespoonful heaped with good butter, two teaspoonfuls of flour. Pour into the stew-pan a tumbler of fresh sweet milk; set this upon the stove or upon a trivet, with a shovelful of fire under. Drop in the butter as soon as the milk boils up; shake the stew-pan. As soon as the butter melts, pour in a tumbler of sweet cream; only keep upon the fire long enough to scald the cream. Have ready the yolks of four or five hard-boiled eggs cut up; the whites of two; stir into the sauce just before pouring into the tureen; salt if needed. This preparation may be poured over boiled meats or poultry, sending a part of it to the table in a boat or tureen. Double the receipt if necessary.

---

310. *Celery Sauce.*—Boil the white parts of six stalks of celery (first cutting them in small pieces) in two tumblerfuls of the broth the meat was boiled in, or any pale broth (veal is best), or boiling water alone will answer. Add salt to taste; cover the stew-pan and let it simmer gently until tender. Rub a heaped teaspoonful of flour into a piece of butter the size of a hen's egg; strain the water from the celery upon this. Remove the celery

from the stew-pan, wipe it out, return the broth, add a tumbler of sweet cream or rich fresh milk; let this simmer gently five minutes, and serve. When fresh celery cannot be obtained, use the extract or the seeds bruised; tie them in a thin muslin cloth that they may be easily removed.

---

311. *Lemon Sauce.*—Make the sauce in the same way as the celery, boiling the peel of the lemon until sufficient flavor is imparted; add enough of the juice to make a pleasant acid, just before serving. Cauliflower may be used instead of the lemon, for variety.

---

312. *Oyster Sauce.*—A tumblerful of oysters; strain the liquor, pick out all the shells. Put the liquor in a stew-pan with one or two blades of mace; salt to taste. To a piece of butter as large as a hen's egg, rub a teaspoonful of flour; add this to the liquor with a tumblerful of sweet cream or milk. When this is just ready to boil, put in the oysters, first mincing them. Simmer gently until the oysters are well scalded, and pour into a gravy tureen. When made of canned oysters, stew entirely in milk or a pale broth.

---

313. *Caper Sauce.*—Melt a quarter of a pound of butter, into which two teaspoonfuls of flour has been rubbed; add two tumblers of sweet milk, or half water (all milk is best). Add six or eight tablespoonfuls of capers.

Mock caper sauce is made by adding pickles cut up; radish pods or nasturtions are good as substitutes for capers.

---

314. *Caper Sauce, No 2.*—Make two tumblerfuls of thin pap boil it until it looks transparent; add to this a tumblerful of butter, six tablespoonfuls of capers strained from their liquor. Pour part over the meat; serve the remainder in a sauce tureen.

Egg sauce is made in this way, adding them boiled hard and cut up fine.

SAUCES, STUFFINGS, AND GRAVIES.

315. *Onion Sauce.*—Slice two medium-sized white onions; lay them in water ten minutes. Boil them soft in clear water; pour off this water, and add as much sweet milk as is needed for the sauce. Rub to a tablespoonful of butter a teaspoonful of flour; add this to the onion and milk. Shake the stew-pan well while it is simmering, which should be from five to six minutes. Salt to taste. Strain and serve hot in a gravy-boat or tureen.

---

316. *Mushroom Sauce.*—Wash and pick a pint of mushrooms; rub them with salt, and immediately throw into cold water. When all are cleansed, put them to boil in a covered stew-pan, with sweet milk or pale broth; salt to taste. When the mushrooms are tender, strain the liquor from them; wipe out the stew-pan and pour back the liquor. Add butter, with a little flour rubbed into the butter. Stew until thick enough.

---

317. *Parsley Sauce.*—Boil three sprigs of parsley in a tumblerful of water ten minutes. Pick off the leaves, chop them fine, and salt to taste. Wipe out the stew-pan, return the water, and add to it an equal quantity of sweet milk. Make a paste of a teaspoonful of flour and a little cold sweet milk; when the milk boils, stir in the paste. Add a tumblerful of good fresh butter, then stir in gradually the minced parsley.

---

318. *To Make Parsley Crisp.*—Wash it clean; shake well in a dry towel until the water is absorbed. Lay a sheet of writing paper upon the bottom of a stove-pan; lay the parsley upon it; turn frequently until crisp. Garnish meats with it.

---

319 *Wine Sauce for Venison or Game.*—Put a tumbler of hot water or pale broth into a stew-pan; stir to it two tablespoonfuls of fine bread crumbs, one teacup of butter, the grated rind of a lemon, and a blade of mace; let these simmer five or six minutes. Stir into a teacup of Port wine a dessert-spoonful of loaf sugar; pour this into the stew-pan, shake it round, and as soon as the

wine is hot, pour it into a tureen. Serve hot. A little acid jelly put in the bottom of the tureen before pouring in the sauce, and then stirred into it well, is an improvement.

---

320. *A French Fish Sauce.*—Beat the yolks of two raw eggs; season them with salt, pepper, and two tablespoonfuls of vinegar. Scald it; stir well; add the grated peel of a lemon. Add slowly two tablespoonfuls of fresh olive oil, stirring constantly until well mixed. Add the juice of the lemon, or vinegar, to make a piquant sauce. Color green with spinach juice.

---

321. *Sauce for Boiled Fowls.*—Beat the yolk of an egg; add to it a tumbler of melted butter, one wineglass of sweet cream; stew five minutes. Season any way liked. This makes a nice sauce for pork chops, if seasoned with sage.

---

322. *Bread Sauce.*—A tumbler of bread crumbs; pour over them two tumblers of boiling milk or pale veal broth. Let this stand until the bread has absorbed the gravy; stew five minutes. Make it sufficiently rich with butter; season in any way liked; salt to taste.

---

323. *Dr. Kitchiner's Receipt for White Sauce.*—Cut in small pieces two pounds of lean veal and half a pound of ham. Melt two ounces of butter; let all simmer until the meat almost sticks. (Great attention must be paid to prevent its sticking; should it occur it will spoil the stock.) Make a paste, using three tablespoonfuls of flour and sufficient water; stir this into the stew-pan, and add three pints of hot water or hot broth. Stir all well together, and continue to stir frequently. Cover the stew-pan, and set it upon a corner of the stove where it will boil gently two hours. Season with an onion cut up fine, twelve grains of allspice, the same of cloves, two blades of mace, black pepper, a little red pepper, a few sprigs of parsley, and thyme. When the broth is reduced to a quart, skim off the fat; strain the broth,

and keep it in a cool place. When ready for use, add a pint of sweet cream, and simmer until thick enough. Pour part over the meat; send the remainder to table in a tureen.

---

324. *To Make Sauce to Pour over Boiled Fowls or Meat.*—One pint of fresh sweet milk; stir to it slowly a pint of boiling water; rub to two heaped teaspoonfuls of butter two even teaspoonfuls of flour; put this to the milk. Stew it until of the consistence of cream, shaking the stew-pan frequently. Season with salt and the juice of a lemon. If a whiter sauce is preferred, use more milk. If it is preferred to have it colored, beat up the yolks of two eggs; pour the sauce to them slowly, beating and stirring rapidly. Put the stew-pan on the stove long enough to take off the raw taste of the egg; one or two minutes will suffice. Pour a part of the sauce over the meat as a veil; season the rest in any way liked, and send in a tureen.

---

325. *Brown Sauces—Tomato Sauce.*—Skin a tumblerful of tomatoes; chop them fine; cut up a small silver-skinned onion; season with salt, pepper, and a dessert-spoonful of sugar. Put these into a stew-pan with a tablespoonful of butter; add two tablespoonfuls of grated bread crumbs, a wineglass of water; stew gently an hour, keeping the stew-pan covered; shake it frequently. Just before serving, stir in two eggs beaten several minutes.

---

326. *Lobster Sauce.*—Boil the lobster very well done; mince the meat; take out the coral and eggs, and pound them in a mortar (the coral gives a fine red color to the sauce). Rub to the coral a piece of butter the size of an egg. Put a pint of the broth in which the lobster was boiled in a stew-pan; thicken it with a paste made of water and a teaspoonful of flour. Let this simmer two or three minutes; add as much meat of the lobster minced as is required; let all heat well, and add the butter just before serving. The fine red color of the coral will be lost if it boils. Use hen lobsters for sauce.

327. Sauce for Lobster.—Mash fine the yolks of two hard-boiled eggs, a tablespoonful of water and the coral of the lobster, a teaspoonful of made mustard, two tablespoonfuls of salad oil, and five of vinegar. Pepper and salt to taste.

---

328. Sauce of Anchovies, Shrimps, or Clams.—Rub into a tumbler of butter a teaspoonful of flour; pepper and salt to taste. Put a tumbler of water in the stew-pan; add the butter and seasoning; simmer five minutes. Add the meat of anchovies, shrimps, or clams.

---

329. Mint Sauce.—Three tablespoonfuls of fresh mint chopped fine, five tablespoonfuls of vinegar, two teaspoonfuls of sugar dissolved in the vinegar. Serve with roast lamb or chops.

---

330. Apple Sauce.—Stew or bake acid apples; when done, mash and strain them. To a pint add a small piece of butter; sweeten to taste; grate over it a little nutmeg; serve with pig, goose, or ducks. Dried apples and peaches stewed, and sweetened and seasoned with lemon or orange peel, or nutmeg, makes a good accompaniment to fresh meats. Stewed cranberries make a superior sauce for meats or poultry.

---

331. Horseradish Sauce.—One teacup of grated horseradish, one wineglass of good cider vinegar, into which has been dissolved a dessert-spoonful of loaf sugar, the same of mustard, a teaspoonful of salt; stir this to the horseradish. Serve with hot or cold meats.

---

332. Mustard Sauce.—Stir to a teacup of vinegar a teaspoonful of mustard, one of salt, two of loaf sugar pulverized, one tablespoonful of butter; put all into a stew-pan, and let it simmer until boiling hot. Beat in a bowl the yolks of two eggs; stir the vinegar to them, stirring slowly and constantly. Return the mixture to the fire, and when boiling hot, pour into a tureen and serve. This is a good sauce for broiled meats, hashes, ragouts, or game. If fresh olive oil is used instead of butter, this makes an excellent sauce for salad, or cold slaw.

---

333. *Pickle Sauce.*—Into a tumblerful of melted butter stir a large tablespoonful of chopped mustard pickle, with a tablespoonful of the vinegar; stir three minutes, or until thoroughly hot.

---

334. *Curry Sauce.*—Add to a pint of broth or melted butter an even tablespoonful of curry powder; wet into a paste with cold water; or boil in the broth an apple or an onion cut up; when soft enough to mash fine, strain; wipe out the stew-pan; return to the stew-pan, and add the curry powder; simmer two minutes. Parboil the onion before adding it to the broth; this is more delicate than to add it raw.

---

335. *Sauce for Barbecues.*—Melt half a pound of butter; stir into it a large tablespoonful of mustard, half a teaspoonful of red pepper, one of black, salt to taste; add vinegar until the sauce has a strong acid taste. The quantity of vinegar will depend upon the strength of it. As soon as the meat becomes hot, begin to baste, and continue basting frequently until it is done; pour over the meat any sauce that remains.

---

336. *Sauce for Steaks, Chops, and Fried Chicken.*—After the steak is sufficiently fried, take it up on a hot dish; set it covered where it will keep warm; strain the grease in which it was fried; return only a tablespoonful to the pan; if liked, a little onion may be cut up, and added; fry a golden color, stirring frequently. For a pound of meat, use a large tablespoonful of butter; put this into the frying-pan; sprinkle in a heaped teaspoonful of flour, stirring it to a smooth paste; pour in a tumblerful of hot water; stir it well; shake the pan and let it simmer until of the consistence of cream.

---

337. *Brown Sauce.*—Cut up a tumblerful of red onions; fry it in a large tablespoonful of butter; sprinkle to the butter an even tablespoonful of flour (browned), making a smooth paste. Be careful the butter does not burn; that would ruin the flavor of the sauce; pour in a pint of boiling water or broth. Let this simmer until it thickens slightly. When water is used, more butter is required than for broth; season with salt and pepper. Put in the tureen a large tablespoonful of French mustard; no other mustard will answer the purpose so well; pour upon this the sauce, mixing well. Onions, when used in sauces or gravies, are more delicate to be parboiled one or two minutes; this is necessary when using the red onion. The white has a more delicate flavor.

---

338. *Brown Onion Sauce.*—Fry the onion. Into another frying-pan put a few slices of ham or any kind of meat, adding to it a teaspoonful of lard. Let it fry until brown, turning frequently to prevent its scorching; when a dark color, pour over the meat a tumbler of hot water; stir it until it is well mixed with the meat; add this to the onion; stew two or three minutes; strain, and mix with it an even tablespoonful of French mustard, or a wineglass of catsup or Port wine.

The trimmings of any kind of fresh meat, or any good bones cracked, may be boiled, and the broth used for gravy, sauces, or soup; also essence of ham, the top of the pot skimmed and strained, and remains of gravy should be carefully saved in covered earthen vessels, kept in a cool place, and used to aid gravies, or for the soup-kettle. "Wilful waste makes woeful want."

---

339. *Browning for Sauces.*—The flour used for thickening should be spread upon the bottom of a tin pan, placed upon the stove; *stir constantly* until of a good brown color. Keep it in a tin dredging-box ready for use. Sugar may also be used. Dr. Kitchiner's receipt for preparing this is: "Take half a pound of pulverized loaf sugar; add to it a wineglass of cold water; put this into a stew-pan; simmer slowly, stirring constantly with a wooden or silver spoon until of a light brown color, and it begins to smoke; add to it an ounce of salt, and dilute it with water until it is of the consistence of cream. Let it boil; take off the scum, and bottle it. To make a small quantity for immediate use, put a teaspoonful of pulverized loaf sugar in a large iron spoon, with as much water as will dissolve it; hold it over a hot fire until it is a dark brown color. Use for browning soups and sauces. Mix it well with a tumblerful of broth before adding to the soups or sauces.

---

340. *Plain Gravy for Roast Meat.*—Take up a tumblerful of the gravy; set it aside; when cool, remove the cake of grease. Put the gravy in a stew-pan; set it on the fire; dissolve half a tablespoonful of browned sugar in half a tumbler of the gravy. It should be hot; if there is not sufficient extra gravy for this, use hot water; pour this to the gravy in the stew-pan; let it simmer five minutes. If a richer gravy is preferred, add as much as is liked of the solid grease which was removed; unless the plates are hot this will congeal, and look like tallow. The unseasoned taste of roast or baked meat gravies are generally preferred. Catsups or mustards may be added upon the plate.

---

341. *Gravy, No. 2.*—Put into a stew-pan an even tablespoonful of hard butter; when it melts, stir to it slowly two teaspoonfuls of flour; when well mixed, add a little of the gravy slowly, stirring well; then more gravy, until a tumblerful is stirred in; simmer five minutes; skim off the fat as it rises. It will probably be too rich.

---

342. *To Make Gravy for Ham.*—When the ham is sufficiently cooked, remove it immediately from the frying-pan. To a tumbler of gravy sprinkle in slowly, mixing smoothly with the gravy, a teaspoonful of flour; pour in half a tumbler of boiling water; shake the pan well; let it simmer a minute; pour in a gravy boat.

343. *Beef Steak Gravy*—Is made in the same way when the steak is well rolled in flour; less flour is required in making the gravy. When onions are used, first slice, and pour boiling water over them; let them stand five minutes; drain the water from them; fry a light brown color in the gravy, before adding the thickening; withdraw them before dredging in the flour.

---

344. *Gravy that will Keep Several Days.*—Lay in a stew-pan or suitable vessel half a pound of lean, juicy, fresh meat of the poorest pieces or trimmings; over this put half a pound of pickled pork, or a little less bacon of the side meat. Cut up two medium-size onions and a few sprigs of parsley. Pour into the vessel a tumblerful of boiling water (not more than this); cover the vessel, and let the meat stew, turning it once, until it is a rich brown color; then pour in boiling water enough to just cover it; let it simmer an hour; remove the meat; thicken the gravy slightly with a paste made of brown flour and water; let this simmer half an hour; add any essence of ham or good gravy that may be saved for such purposes. Put in an earthen vessel well covered, and exclude from the air. Warm it before serving; season with any catsup liked. For making all brown gravies, fry the meat first, and pour over hot broth, gravy or water; use the browned sugar or flour for coloring and thickening. Kidneys, livers, necks of poultry, the scraggy parts of the necks of animals, may be used for making the stock for gravy.

---

345. *Gravy for Baked Fowls.*—Put the neck and giblets to stew; add salt to taste. In half an hour take out the neck and giblets; thicken with a paste made of flour and water while the broth is boiling; add a tumbler of the gravy to the same quantity of the broth; let it simmer until thick as rich cream; cut up the giblets; add to the gravy. Should there be too much grease, skim it off. Gravies are often served with an amount of grease floating upon the top that renders them repulsive rather than in viting. Seasoning of any kind of vegetable or catsup may be used—not, however, in sufficient quantities to overpower the natural flavor of the gravy.

---

346. *Gravy for Baked Pig.*—Boil the harslet until tender mince the liver and heart very fine. Put a tumblerful of the broth they were boiled in into a stew-pan; thicken it with two teaspoonfuls of flour; wet into a paste with a little of the broth; stir to this an equal quantity of the pig gravy; season with sage; simmer two or three minutes; salt and pepper to taste; add the minced liver; serve in a tureen. The remainder of the harslet may be hashed; add to it any gravy not required for the pig, should any remain. Make the brains into a pancake; fry, and garnish the dish with it, cutting it into small shapes; use alternately sprigs of parsley; or, if the brains are not used in this way, stew them until done; mash them, and add to the gravy.

---

347. *Gravy for Tripe, Cow Heel, or Calf's Head.*—Boil and thicken two tumblers of beef or veal gravy; add the grated rind of a lemon, a teaspoonful of curry powder; or season highly with red and black pepper if the curry is not liked; simmer ten minutes; add catsup to taste, and the juice of a lemon. If wine is preferred, add a wineglass of Madeira instead of the catsup.

---

348. *Stuffings—For a Boiled Fowl.*—Moisten a pint of bread crumbs with hot milk; melt in the milk a tablespoonful of butter; salt and pepper to taste; mince fine as many oysters as bread crumbs (or Irish potatoes boiled and mashed fine, as bread crumbs, if it is not convenient to use oysters); mix well, and stuff, allowing a little room for the stuffing to swell; close the aperture well so as to allow as little water as possible to get into the fowl.

---

349. *For Baked or Roast Fowls.*—Moisten bread crumbs, hard biscuit or crackers, with boiling water; let it stand until the bread can be mashed to a paste; add a spoonful of butter before the boiling water is poured on; season with salt and pepper, and minced eschalot, onion, or parsley cut up fine. After mashing the bread, mix with it one or two eggs; put a teaspoonful of lard into the frying-pan; when hot, pour in the batter, and fry until dry, stirring constantly; use while hot. A richer stuffing is made by using the yolks only of four or five eggs; milk and flour for a batter, the consistence of fritter batter; salt and pepper to taste; onion if liked. Pour into a greased pan; when brown on one side, turn it; take it up when a good brown color; mash it up while hot with a tablespoonful of butter. The fowl should never be crammed tight with stuffing; room should be left for it to swell. Put the stuffing in before putting the fowl to roast or bake; it will be better if the fowl is stuffed an hour or more before it is cooked. I have known many cooks to half cook the fowl and then stuff. The longer the stuffing remains in the fowl, so that it is not kept long enough to sour, the more completely the flavor of the seasoning is imparted to the meat. When the fowl is ready for the table, if the stuffing is performed skilfully, there will not be the least appearance of it visible upon the outside. This stuffing, or any other, may be seasoned with mace, or nutmeg if liked, or with cauliflower chopped, mushrooms, almonds, potatoes, as persons may fancy.

---

350. *Stuffing for Pig.*—Use equal quantities of cold hominy (or rice) and flour; mince a few eschalots or an onion, a few sprigs of parsley, a little sage, salt and pepper; make this into a dough; bake it a light brown; while hot, mash it with sufficient butter to make it rich enough; stuff while hot; or use for the dough half flour and half corn meal.

---

351. *Potato Stuffing.*—Bake or boil dry Irish potatoes; mash and strain them through a colander; mix with them an equal quantity of bread crumbs; grate, and add three hard-boiled eggs; mix with a large tablespoonful of butter. If not sufficiently moist add a little cream; season to taste—a delicate and delicious

stuffing. When batter-bread muffins, etc., are used, save some for stuffing; corn meal batter-bread makes a fine pig stuffing. Meats are sometimes added to stuffing. Sausage-meat is considered good to add to stuffing for baked turkey, also grated ham, or tongue. All stuffings made of cold breads, and moistened with milk or water, are richer for being fried a few minutes after they are mixed and seasoned, stirring constantly. Stuffing should not, as a general thing, be bound together with raw egg; it is lighter without.

352. *Stuffing for Fish.*—Butter slices of stale bread upon both sides; saturate them with wine, catsup, or cream, as preferred. Cut again in smaller slices, and lay inside the fish; this also makes a good stuffing for game.

353. *M. Soyer's Receipt for Stuffing for Goose.*—For a middling-sized fowl cut up a pound of onions; a teaspoonful of pulverized sage if dry, two if green, and minced fine; one teaspoonful of salt, one of brown sugar, one of pepper. Set this over a slow fire; let it stew fifteen minutes; then, with a spoon, stuff the bird while the onion is hot.

VEGETABLES.

"Man has been called in relation to his diet Omniverous, from his being adapted to live on every kind of food; whereas most other animals are confined to one. In man it is evident from his anatomical structure that he was intended to feed promiscuously on animal or vegetable food, as choice impelled.

"No animal can live happily except in conformity to the laws of his constitution; it follows, therefore, that man requires mixed food. A proper balance between the two kinds of food should be observed if we desire to live a natural and consequently healthy life.

"A well arranged dietetic scheme ought to consist of such a combination of the albuminous, oleaginous and farinaceous constituents as is most appropriate to the requirements of the system, and it is not only necessary for the healthy support of the body that the food ingested should contain an adequate proportion of alimentary constituents, but that those should be in a wholesome or undecomposing state.

"It cannot be questioned that articles originally good and wholesome may derive a poisonous character from changes taking place in their own composition—a peculiar ferment is sometimes generated which the stomach is not able to bear."

---

354. *Vegetables.*—Vegetables intended for dinner should be gathered early in the morning. A few only can be kept twelve hours without detriment. "When fresh-gathered they are plump and firm, and have a fragrant freshness no art can give them again when they have lost it by long keeping, though it will refresh them a little to put them into cold water before cooking." A little soda in the water they are cooked in will help to preserve the color of those that are green. They lose their good appear-

ance and flavor if cooked too long, and are indigestible if not cooked enough; close attention and good judgment are necessary to know the proper time to take them up. Always drain the water from them well before sending to table; have the dishes hot upon which they are placed, and never send them to table until the meats are served; when sent in too soon, and often uncovered, they become chilled and unfit for use. Always put vegetables to boil in hot water.

355. *Asparagus.*—When cut below the ground, skin the white part, or it will be tough; cut as nearly as possible the same length; turn the points together, and tie in bunches. Have a stew-pan of boiling water salted; lay the asparagus in; boil briskly half an hour; toast slices of light bread; pour over a little of the asparagus water; butter it well; put the asparagus on the toast; serve hot. The toast may be omitted if not liked. Or, cut the stalks above the ground—this is more tender, but not so pretty; cook in the same way; and it is good cut in small pieces, stewed with pepper, salt, butter, and just water enough to cover them. Make a paste of a little of the water and a teaspoonful of flour; stir to the stew; let it simmer five minutes. Take them up as soon as done; too much cooking injures the color and flavor. Asparagus is good boiled tender, cut up and dressed as a salad, with hot vinegar, egg, butter, pepper and mustard. To be eaten hot.

356. *Burr Artichokes.*—The burr or globe artichoke should be well washed; put to boil in plenty of hot water, slightly salted; boil until tender, which may be ascertained by drawing a leaf; trim the points; serve with melted butter, in a tureen. A separate plate should be provided to serve them upon.

357. *Jerusalem Artichokes.*—These may be sliced, and boiled like turnips, or cooked in any way Irish potatoes are. They require longer boiling. They are considered particularly good boiled and dressed as a salad.

358. *Beets.*—Dig them carefully, so that the fibres are as little broken as possible; if careless about this, red beets, when cooked, lose their fine color. Wash them well, and put them to boil in hot water from one to two hours, according to size. Press them without piercing or breaking the skin, to ascertain if they are done; when they yield readily to the pressure, take them up in a pan of cold water; rub off the skin, slice them, and dress with butter, pepper, and salt when young and tender, or with salt, pepper, and vinegar if preferred. Old beets lose their sweetness, and are best dressed with hot spiced vinegar, into which has been stirred a little sugar. They may be eaten cold when dressed with vinegar; they may be boiled, or baked and grated, and dressed as a salad. Beets have a finer flavor baked than boiled; it requires longer time to cook them in this way. Be equally as careful not to break the skin or fibres. Beets may be preserved through the winter by hilling, as sweet potatoes are for winter.

---

359. *Beans.*—String them carefully; wash well, and boil them briskly in an open vessel half an hour, or until tender; some varieties requires longer boiling than others. The water in which they are put to cook should be boiling and salted; when tender, take them up in a colander; drain the water carefully from them, and transfer them to a hot covered dish; pour over melted butter. Some persons prefer their being boiled with a piece of bacon, the side meat is preferred; either way is good. The meat should boil half an hour before the beans are put in. Beans may be saved for winter by packing them in salt, a layer of each; the beans should not be strung. Gather them at the age for boiling. When used, soak them until fresh enough.

---

360. *Lima, or Butter Beans.*—When fully formed, and before the hull turns yellow, shell them; wash well, and put them to boil in hot water, sufficiently salted to season them. When tender, pour off nearly all the water; make the remainder of the

broth rich with butter, and serve upon a hot dish. Never pepper them unless with white pepper; the small black particles of the common pepper upon so white a vegetable gives them an untidy look.

361. *Succotash.*—Boil butter-beans shelled (dried or green) half an hour; salt the water; then add half as much green corn cut from the cobs. Boil the cobs a few minutes when the beans are first put to boil. Take out the cobs; add the corn; to half a gallon of the succotash add a paste made of two tablespoonfuls of flour, and water sufficient to form the paste; season with salt and butter enough to make it as rich as may be liked. This is also very good boiled in the broth in which poultry has been boiled, or cooked with a small piece of pork. Succotash may be made of dried beans, and corn dried for winter use; soak them an hour before using. Dried beans are excellent baked with pickled pork.

362. *Brocoli.*—Gather hard heads; peel the stalks; boil in salted water briskly, leaving the vessel open twenty minutes, or until tender; take them up and pour over melted butter. Serve hot.

363. *Cabbage.*—Take off the green leaves; quarter the heads; wash them well, examining between the leaves for insects; let them lie in cold water until it is time to put them to boil; cut off part of the thick stalk, or the leaves will be overdone before the stalk is tender. Put in boiling water, sufficiently salted; it should be well covered with water; if too little is used, the cabbage will be strong. Some kinds of cabbages require to be first parboiled, then put in another water; always using boiling water. When tender, take them up in a colander; drain off all the water; put them upon a hot dish, and cover with slices of butter, putting some between the leaves. It is also liked boiled in the liquor in which bacon has been boiled; when cooked in this way, take up the meat, the flavor of the cabbage would injure the meat; skim off all impurities on the liquor, and put the cabbage in; boil

briskly; and when done, they will sink to the bottom; take them up immediately into a colander, and drain well. Serve in a hot dish, and never in the same dish with the meat.

The remains of cabbage used at dinner is sometimes chopped fine, and fried with a little butter or lard, and served as a breakfast dish.

---

364. *To Stuff Cabbage.*—Strip off the green leaves; examine and wash well; lay in cold water until ready for use. Cut out the heart, or centre, leaving two or three rows of leaves. Scald the cabbage well; when the leaves wilt from the scalding, there will be less danger of their breaking. Chop the leaves fine; add to them any scraps of cold meat or poultry; season high with pepper and salt; and if the flavor is liked, an onion, shred fine; bind the whole together with a raw egg, worked in; a few bread crumbs may be added. Make this into several balls, or one large ball, and put in the centre of the cabbage; fold the leaves over carefully; wrap well with thread; over this put a thin netting or muslin; tie it securely, and boil until the cabbage is tender. Drain it from the water; serve upon a hot dish, with melted butter poured over. Remove the cloth and strings before pouring over the butter.

---

365. *Hot Slaw.*—Cut the cabbage in four quarters; after washing it carefully, parboil ten minutes. Take it out of the water; cut in thin slices; put it in a stew-pan; season with salt; add a wineglass of hot water, an even tablespoonful of butter; cover the stew-pan, and let the cabbage stew until tender; stir it frequently from the bottom. When tender, which will probably require an hour's steady stewing, add as much vinegar as will give the mass a pleasant acid taste.

---

366. *Cold Slaw.*—Cut a head of hard white cabbage into very fine shavings. It is seldom shaved fine enough. For a quart of the cabbage take the yolks of three eggs, beat them well; stir into

a tumbler and a half of vinegar two teaspoonfuls of loaf sugar, a tablespoonful of olive oil, one of thick, sweet cream, or a piece of butter as large as a walnut, a heaped teaspoonful of mustard, salt and pepper to taste; mix with the egg, and put this sauce into a stew-pan; when hot add the cabbage; stew until thoroughly hot, which will only require four or five minutes. Toss it up from the bottom with a silver or wooden fork. Take it up and set where it will become perfectly cold, on ice is best. The quantity of vinegar will depend upon its strength.

367. *Sauer Kraut.*—Quarter a dozen hard heads of cabbage; cut off the stalks closely; sprinkle salt in the bottom of a cask; pack the cabbage down firmly; put over another layer of salt; when all are in, cover with a heavy weight. Keep the cask in a cool place. In four or five weeks the pieces will be ready for use.

To cook sauer kraut: Soak in plenty of water until fresh enough. Boil until tender, with bacon, pickled pork, or in water salted; and, when tender, add butter when boiled in water. After being boiled, it may be fried with a small piece of butter or lard.

368.—*Cauliflower.*—Remove all green leaves. To look well this vegetable should be very white. Boil it in water salted, or half sweet milk; when tender, put over it, while hot, slices of butter, putting some on the inside. This vegetable is fine in soups, to season meat sauces, for salads and pickle.

369. *Carrots.*—Carrots require longer cooking than any other vegetable. When young, they only require to be washed before being cooked. Old carrots should be cut into slices, and stewed until tender; season with salt and butter. Carrots are good in soup, and are better grated; they give a rich color to soups.

370. *Celery.*—This is usually served without being cooked, but may be stewed. Cut the root in small pieces; add water to

cover it; season with salt; simmer until nearly done; add butter, into which has been rubbed a little flour. When sufficiently cooked, just before taking it up, add a wineglass of sweet cream.

---

371. *Cucumbers.*—Gather them early in the morning; put them in water. An hour before they are to be served, peel and cut them in thin, round slices; cover with cold water until a few minutes before sending to the table. Pour off this water; add a third as much white onion, cut in thin slices, as cucumber. The onion should be skinned and kept in cold water until used; season with salt, pepper and vinegar. Cucumbers may also be stewed as squashes, and seasoned with butter, or sliced lengthwise, rolled in corn meal, salted and fried.

---

372. *Corn.*—Gather the ears when the grains are full of milk, but before they are hard; remove the shuck and silk; put the corn in boiling water, with a little salt in it; boil half an hour if the corn is young. Serve the ears hot as they are boiled, or cut them from the cobs with a sharp knife; put in a deep covered dish; season with salt, pepper, and butter. Sugar corn is best for the table.

---

373. *Samp.*—Take the corn when the grains are full, but milky; with a sharp knife shave off the corn to the cob; be careful not to cut the cob (that would injure the taste of the corn); scrape out the milk. Put it all in a stew-pan; pour over four times its bulk of boiling water; add salt to taste. Let the mass boil four hours, covered; boil slowly. Eat with butter; or pour into pans; cut in slices, when cold, and fry. Stir frequently when the corn is nearly done.

---

374. *To Stew Corn.*—Cut it from the cobs with a sharp knife; put it in a stew-pan with the milk which came from the corn, and to each quart of corn, half a tumbler of water; stew until done, which will require from a half to three quarters of an hour;

depending upon the age of the corn. When done, season with pepper, salt, and butter. Or, put the corn, after it is cut from the cobs, into a frying-pan; add a tumbler of water to a quart; stew half an hour, stirring frequently; season with pepper and salt; add a piece of lard or butter as large as a walnut, and fry until a light brown color, or less if preferred. Corn may be roasted by laying it on the gridiron, after removing the shuck; turn it often until the grains are all a light brown color; eat with salt.

375. *Green Corn Fritters.*—Six ears of boiled corn grated, three eggs; beat the yolks; mix with the corn; season with pepper and salt; add two even tablespoonfuls of sifted flour; beat the whites to a stiff froth, and add last. Fry as fritters, in hot lard. Serve upon a napkin laid upon a flat dish. Another way: Grate four ears of corn; beat five eggs separately; stir the yolks with the corn; two teacups of flour, sour milk sufficient to make a batter thick as rice batter cakes, half a teaspoonful of soda; add the whites last, beaten to a stiff froth. Fry as fritters, or bake as griddle cakes.

376. *Green Corn Pudding.*—Two well beaten eggs, two tumblers of grated corn, half a tumbler of milk, tablespoon a little heaped of butter, pepper and salt to taste. Bake.

377. *Green Corn Pudding, No. 2—Mrs. C.'s Receipt.*—One pint of green corn grated, one large teacup of cream, one heaped tablespoonful of flour, one tablespoonful of good butter, four well beaten eggs, salt to taste; bake half an hour without scorching. This may be used as a dessert, with a good sauce.

378. *Green Corn.*—Green corn may be kept for winter use by parboiling it. Cut it from the cobs, and dry in the sun; keep in paper bags, in a dry place. Soak it and use with dry beans to make succotash. Another way: Remove all the green shuck but the

layer next the cob; tie the open end securely, wrapping the string around the whole ear; pack in salt. Sweet corn is best for preserving in this way.

---

379. *Eschalot.*—A species of onion. They are good in the spring. Strip off the outside skin; cut off all the green part; boil in salted water; serve with melted butter; or cut them fine, using a little of the green top joining the root; put them on the fire in cold water in a frying-pan; when the water is nearly ready to boil, pour it off; add a few slices of pork or bacon, and fry, turning them frequently. Some persons eat them raw, served with lettuce, radishes, and water-cresses. They may be used for seasoning in the place of onions.

---

380. *Endive.*—This is only used for salad. In the fall and spring (have two plantings) tie up the heads, and bleach them · they become beautifully white and crisp. Serve it as a salad with the same sauce used with lettuce salad.

---

381. *Egg-Plant.*—The purple is best. Peel and parboil them; mash fine; season with salt, pepper, and a little onion, if the flavor is not disliked; add butter to make it moderately rich. Put this mixture in a deep earthen dish; grate over it bread crumbs, and bake a light brown color.

---

382. *Egg-Plant, No. 2.*—Peel the egg-plant; parboil it five or six minutes; cut the slices crosswise; season with pepper and salt. Beat up an egg or two, as may be required; roll the slices in the egg and then in fine bread crumbs. Fry a light brown in hot lard. Serve on a flat dish, upon the bottom of which is a folded napkin. They should not be piled. Send to the table as fast as cooked. They must be thoroughly done.

---

383. *Egg-Plant, No. 3.*—Cut a round piece from one end of the plant; with the handle of a spoon scoop out the inside. Par

boil the shell in water, a little salted, five minutes; take it out, plunge it in cold water. Stew the inside with a little onion, pepper and salt, until done. Beat one or two eggs; add to the stew with butter to season it properly—for the inside of one egg-plant a heaped teaspoonful of butter will be sufficient, and one egg; mix well, and stew until dry, adding half as much bread crumbs as egg-plant; stuff the shell with this; a little minced veal, ham, tongue, or poultry may be added to the stuffing, and is an improvement. Tie on the piece cut off. Put the egg-plants to bake in a dish, the bottom of which is covered with slices of bacon; bake an hour; serve on a flat dish whole; remove the string and top piece. The egg-plant is sometimes cut in half, lengthwise, the contents removed, and stewed as above; the half pieces parboiled until tender in water salted; then stuffed with a rich force-meat; a coating of egg spread over the open side, bread crumbs sprinkled over; put in a dish with slices of cold ham, and baked until tender; either way is good.

384. *To Fry Plain.*—Peel the egg-plant; cut it in thin slices; strew salt between the slices; let them remain an hour; parboil them five minutes; roll each slice in flour or corn meal; fry a golden color in boiling lard; turn the pieces once; serve upon a napkin.

385. *Greens.*—Kale, or cole, mustard, cabbage sprouts, turnip tops, to any of which may be added a few beet tops, the young shoots of the poke plant, all make good spring greens. Pick and wash them; let them lie in cold water at least an hour before they are used. Put them on in plenty of boiling water, salted; boil briskly twenty minutes; they will sink to the bottom when done. Take them up in a colander; press the water from them; put upon a hot dish; cut across the leaves in several places with a sharp knife; pour over melted butter; dress with poached eggs, either placed upon the dish of greens or served in a separate dish. They are not good unless served hot. Some

persons prefer greens boiled with a piece of bacon or hock bone of ham. No matter in what way they are cooked, poached eggs should accompany them.

---

386. *Leeks.*—These are a species of onion, and more delicate than any of the tribe. They are ready for use early in the spring. Skin them; lay in cold water an hour; boil in salted water until they yield readily to pressure. Put them upon a hot covered dish; pour over melted butter.

---

387. *Lettuce.*—This vegetable is usually served in a raw state, as a salad; but is sometimes cooked, cut up, seasoned with salt and pepper, fried with pork until wilted, or stewed with asparagus, green peas, and slices of lamb or mutton. For salad: Make a sauce; put it upon the bottom of the salad bowl. Gather the lettuce early in the morning. Wash them well, but very delicately, as they are easily bruised. Lay the heads in ice-cold water; keep in a cold place, or they will not be crisp. If the heads are large, divide them, but use the knife carefully; much pressure will destroy the crispness of the vegetable, without which a salad is valueless. Ten minutes before dinner is served, clip the lettuce with a sharp pair of scissors kept for this purpose; they are best long and slender. The clipping should be done by "fairy" fingers. Put the lettuce (while clipping it) upon a clean towel; then strew it lightly over the sauce, which has already been placed upon the bottom of the sauce-bowl. If convenient, now set the bowl upon ice until needed. In serving, toss the lettuce with the sauce lightly, stirring from the bottom, using a wooden fork and spoon. Separate plates should be used for serving the salad.

---

388. *To Make the Sauce.*—One teaspoonful of mustard, one of salt, two of loaf sugar pulverized, a tablespoonful of olive oil, a teacup of vinegar; mix these together; put in a stew-pan until scalding hot. Beat two eggs well; pour to them the hot vinegar,

stirring constantly until the danger of the eggs curdling is over. It must be entirely cold before being applied to the lettuce.

Another Sauce: For a quart of lettuce boil three eggs until the yolks are hard; separate them from the whites; mash them smoothly with the back of a wooden spoon; mash a small Irish potato with a large tablespoonful of thick sweet cream; strain the potato through a sieve; mix with the egg; add a teaspoonful of mustard, one of loaf sugar heaped, a teaspoonful of salt, a wineglass of good apple vinegar. Put this sauce on the bottom of the salad bowl. There is a prejudice with many against the use of olive oil; this is needless if the oil is fresh; no taste of it is discernible. The clarified essence of ham may be used in its place. Butter does not answer well. When cold, the particles harden, and separate from the vinegar. The sauce, by some, is preferred without oil or butter, using only salt, pepper, vinegar, and sugar. It is well to dress one salad bowl with the lettuce whole, mixing in radishes, celery, cresses, and young eschalots, leaving a few inches of the green tops; season extempore upon the plate to taste, sugar, mustard, etc., being at hand.

---

389. *Winter Salads*—May be made of beet roots boiled and grated, artichokes in the same way, endive cut up (after being bleached) as lettuce; with these mix the sauce thoroughly with the vegetables. Irish potatoes boiled and mashed, seasoned with salad sauce (butter may be used with them) is very good cold, but much better hot. After seasoning, return to the stew-pan until hot. Reserve in every case the whites for ornamenting. Cut them in rings; lay over the salad with sprigs of parsley.

---

390. *Mushrooms.*—Great care should be used in gathering them. There is a poisonous kind nearly resembling the edible kind, and fatal mistakes have occurred. The good are first very small, of a round form, with small stalk; the upper part and stalk are white; the under, a salmon color, and, as they increase in size, become brown. They grow rapidly, and are found in open

fields or pastures; reject those found in shady places. The smell of the genuine mushroom is pleasant. They are indigestible. They may be cooked in a variety of ways. To broil: Select large ones; lay the flaps on the gridiron; broil until thoroughly hot. Serve with butter, pepper, and salt.

---

391. *To Stew.*—Take the large buttons; peel them; cut off the stalks; put them in a stew-pan with a tablespoonful of vinegar, butter, salt, and pepper, according to the quantity cooked. Cover the stew-pan, and let them cook until tender; add another piece of butter, into which has been stirred a little flour; let this become hot. Lay a few slices of toast (which should be prepared while the mushrooms are being cooked) in the bottom of a hot, deep covered dish. Pour over the contents of the stew-pan, and serve immediately.

---

392. *To Bake Mushrooms.*—Rub off the skins of the large flaps with salt and a piece of coarse clean cloth; trim the fringe from the small ones; cut off the stalks; lay them upon their back in an earthen dish. For a pint, use a large tablespoonful of fresh butter, with an even tablespoonful of brown flour stirred to it; put some of this upon each mushroom; bake until tender, which will require from twenty to thirty minutes. Serve upon toast; first dip the toast in boiling water.

---

393. *Nasturtion.*—The blooms are gay, and make a fine relish eaten with cold, light bread, buttered. They make a beautiful breakfast dish. This vegetable is seldom used, however, but for pickling; for this, gather the pods when fully grown. They serve as a good substitute for capers in making sauce.

---

394. *Ochra.*—Gather only the young pods. They should be very little washed, and not suffered to remain a minute in water, and never trim them until after they are washed, as they lose much of the fine mucilage that makes the vegetable so valuable.

It may be used in soup, or to make gumbo (which is a thick soup), and stewed, fried, etc., and may be dried and preserved as a winter vegetable. Receipts for soup and gumbo have already been given.

395. *To Stew Ochra.*—Cut it in round slices; put it in a stew-pan; for a quart, add a wineglass of hot water, a tablespoonful of butter, into which has been rubbed an even teaspoonful of flour; salt and pepper to taste. Cover the stew-pan, shake it occasionally, and stew until tender; serve in a hot covered dish. A few tomatoes and a little onion stewed with the ochra is an improvement. This is excellent used as a sauce for plain boiled rice.

396. *To Fry Ochra.*—Boil a quart; strain it well from the water; mash it smooth; season with salt and pepper. Beat in one or two eggs, and add flour (about half a tumbler of sifted flour) to make the batter stiff enough to fry as fritters. Serve on a flat dish upon a napkin. They should not be piled; send in as fast as fried.

397. *To Dry for Winter Use.*—Quarter them; use only those that are tender; string them; hang them in an airy room until dry. To cook them, soak twelve hours.

398. *Onions.*—For seasoning, the red onion will answer; but only use the white silver-skinned for boiling, stewing, etc. Take off the outer skins until the white solid part is reached; cut off a slice, top and bottom. Put them to boil in a covered vessel; pour over hot water to cover them; add a little salt to the water. When done, take them up with a perforated skimmer entirely clear of water; dress with melted butter.

399. *Onion Custard.*—Skin and slice ten medium-sized white, silver onions; fry them in fresh butter; as soon as of a golden

co'or, drain them from the butter; mince them very fine. Beat four eggs; stir to them slowly, stirring constantly, two tumblers of sweet milk; stir all to the onions; season with salt, pepper, and nutmeg. Pour in an earthen dish that will just hold it, and bake fifteen minutes. Fried onions are relished by some persons.

---

400. *Onion Stew.*—Cut up six white onions, medium-size; slice as much Irish potatoes after peeling. Put all in a stew-pan; pour over a pint of hot water; season with salt and pepper; cover close; simmer gently; when nearly done, add a tablespoonful of butter, with a heaped teaspoonful of flour rubbed into it, and half a tumbler of sweet cream. Stir from the bottom to prevent its scorching, and when just ready to boil, pour into a hot covered dish; serve immediately. This is a fine accompaniment to boiled poultry or mutton.

---

401. *Irish Potatoes.*—" Next to bread, there is no vegetable article, the preparation of which, as food, deserves to be more attended to, than the potato." The Mercer is the best variety used at the South. The large yellow is a good potato, and is earlier than the Mercer. The peach-blow is also a good variety. To cook them when very young, wash them; scrape off the skin; put them in a stew-pan; cover with hot water; boil gently until tender; pour off the water; add to a quart of potatoes a heaped tablespoonful of butter, with a teaspoonful of flour rubbed into it; pour in a tumblerful of sweet cream or milk; stew, uncovered, five minutes; serve in a hot dish.

---

402. *To Boil Potatoes Fully Grown.*—First assort them, and boil together those of the same size. Common sense teaches that this ought to be done, since when large and small go to the kettle together the small ones are spoiled before the larger ones are sufficiently cooked. Wash them well in several waters. Put them to boil in hot water to cover them, slightly salted. Use an iron vessel. Keep the boiler covered a quarter of an

nour, then leave it open until the potatoes are done to the centre; try one with a fork. Pour off every drop of the water that can be; set the vessel on the coolest part of the stove; leave it open ten minutes. Pour them into a colander; skin rapidly, putting them into a hot dish. Some cooks pour them from the boiling water into cold water; this is done to make the skinning easier. After this, the next step should be to throw them to the pigs, as they absorb the water, and are rendered hard and sodden, and unfit for the table. Serve with melted butter. Potatoes should never be sent to the table until the plates are served with the first course of meat, then they should make their appearance smoking hot. The practice in very many families is to put all the vegetables upon the table at once. This is wrong. Send them as they are needed, particularly in cold weather. When the ham is served, send the cabbage and beans; serve those vegetables generally relished with that particular kind of meat. With boiled pork, beef, mutton, etc., send turnips, potatoes, etc., and so with the variety of meats.

403. *To Steam Potatoes.*—Put them in a steamer, and set it over a boiler; when done, leave the steamer uncovered. The boiler should be partly filled with water, and kept boiling steadily until the potatoes are cooked.

404. *To Boil Old Potatoes.*—Boil them by the foregoing receipt. Have a coarse clean towel in the hand, and as each potato is removed, wring it in a corner of the towel; slip the skin off and they are delightfully mealy. Serve with melted butter, on a hot dish. When potatoes are old they are good baked and served in their jackets. Eat with cold butter.

405. *To Stew Potatoes.*—Peel and slice them thin, put them in a stew-pan, cover with sweet milk, or half milk and water. Butter to season them, with a little flour rubbed to the butter; add this to the potatoes; salt and pepper to taste; stew until the pota-

toes are soft. They may be sliced and stewed in very little water, then dressed with butter and cream.

---

406. *To Scollop Potatoes.*—Boil, and mash them with the end of a rolling-pin until perfectly smooth; season highly with salt, pepper, butter, and two or three hard-boiled eggs chopped fine (three eggs for a quart of mashed potatoes); fill an earthen dish with it. Bake long enough to form a slight crust, and just before being sent to the table.

---

407. *Potato Salad.*—Mash and strain the potatoes through a colander; make them rich with butter; season with a sauce made by mashing the yolks of three hard-boiled eggs for a quart; a teaspoonful of unmade English mustard, pepper and salt; a teacup of good apple vinegar; a teaspoonful of loaf sugar may be added to the vinegar; mix this thoroughly with the potato. Put it in a stew-pan and when hot serve; ornament the top with rings cut out of the white of the egg and sprigs of parsley. Some persons prefer this cold; it is good either way.

---

408. *To Fry Potatoes.*—Boil and mash them; season with salt and pepper; make into cakes as large as the top of a tumbler; roll in flour and fry a light brown color. Very little frying is necessary. Serve upon a napkin placed upon the bottom of a flat dish. They should not be piled; serve as fast as fried. Cold potatoes may be sliced and fried.

---

409. *To Bake Sweet Potatoes.*—Take them of the same size; wash them well; cut off the ends; put them in an oven or stove-pan. For a peck of potatoes, pour in the oven a tumbler of hot water; turn them once when half done; bake slowly. If an oven is used, put fire on the lid. When done they may be served in their jackets, or peeled, and sliced; put a layer on the bottom of a shallow earthen dish, then a few bits of butter, a little sugar, a slight seasoning of cinnamon or nutmeg; another layer of potato

VEGETABLES.

and seasoning until the dish is filled. Set it in the oven until hot and serve.

---

401. *To Roast Sweet Potatoes.*—Sweep a hot hearth well; lay on the potatoes; cover with hot ashes; let them remain until tender. Irish potatoes may be cooked in the same way.

---

411. *To Fry Sweet Potatoes.*—Take large potatoes, peel and slice them; fry them in hot lard, turn often, salt each piece slightly; serve on a napkin. A good breakfast dish.

---

412. *To Stew Sweet Potatoes.*—Slice them half an inch thick; stew with pork chops, or pieces of the tenderloin. Take all up together when done. Season the gravy with cream, a little parsley minced fine, salt and pepper.

Potatoes are liked peeled and roasted under meat. The large-sized ones should not be used for this style of cooking; the medium size is best.

---

413. *Green Peas.*—Shell them; wash them well; put them in a stew-pan; cover with boiling water and stew covered until tender; add salt to the water. They should be boiled fast to retain their color; half an hour will generally be sufficient time, but try one or two. Drain off the water; pour them into a hot covered dish and dress with fresh butter. When a little old, boil them with a very small piece of super-carb. soda; a little sugar when they begin to lose their sweetness. A double kettle, putting the peas inside without water, boils them well. Since the season for green peas I have met with the following receipt; it may or may not be good. Try it.

Cover the bottom of the stew-pan with lettuce leaves; pour in the peas; add for each quart of peas a tablespoonful of butter; salt to taste; the butter being salted, very little will be required. Cover the stew-pan; set it over a moderate fire; shake it frequently, and once or twice stir from the bottom. Should there be too little moisture after cooking a while, add more butter. Serve when tender; use a little sugar if liked.

---

414. *Hopping John.*—Pick out all defective ones from a quart of dried peas; soak them several hours in tepid water; boil them with a chicken or piece of pickled pork until the peas are thoroughly done. In a separate stew-pan boil half as much rice dry; take the peas from the meat, mix them with the rice, fry a few minutes until dry. Season with pepper and salt. This may be made of green English peas.

---

415. *Dried Peas.*—Soak several hours in water; pick out all defective ones; put them in hot water; boil until tender. Dress with butter, or boil with a piece of pickled pork; drain from the water through a colander before adding the butter. Salt to taste.

---

416. *Pumpkin.*—Cut the pumpkin open; take out the seed, but do not scrape the inside; peel the rind off; cut in small pieces. Put them to stew in a covered vessel, with very little water; stir often from the bottom, to prevent its scorching. When done it may be kept several days in a cool place; use an earthen vessel. Dress with butter and a little sugar and ginger, as a stew, or fry with a little sweet lard, or use for making puddings and custards.

---

417. *Winter Squash and Cashaw*—May be used in the same way. The cashaw is also good cut in half, the seed removed, baked with the rind on; when done, scrape out the inside, and season to taste with butter, pepper, and a little sugar.

---

418. *Parsnips.*—Scrape them, and split them a few inches only when young; when old, slice them. Stew them, covered with water, until tender—half an hour will be sufficient time for young roots; much longer for older ones. Dress with butter, salt, and pepper.

419. *To Fry Them.*—Boil whole ones until tender. When cold, slice a quarter of an inch thick; season with salt and pepper, and fry in boiling lard. Take the pieces up with a perforated skimmer. Serve hot.

---

420. *Parsnip Fritters.*—Boil enough parsnips to make two tumblerfuls, when mashed and rubbed through the colander; season with salt and pepper; add one well-beaten egg, and flour enough to hold it together (half a teacup full will be sufficient); fry in thick cakes. Serve as fast as they are fried. The sugar parsnip is best.

---

421. *To Fry Them in Batter.*—Make a thin batter. Boil the parsnips in salted water; slice them; dip the pieces in batter; take up some of the batter with each slice. Fry in boiling lard, a light brown color.

---

422. *Radishes*—Are served in a raw state. Gather them early in the morning; break off part of the long tap-root, and cut off all the top except an inch or two; wash them well, and keep in ice-cold water until it is time to serve them. Put them upon a salad bowl, with lettuce, cresses, etc., or in glass stands. The crimson ones are highly ornamental. Radishes are more digestible if grated and seasoned with salt and pepper; used as a salad.

---

423. *Spinach.*—Wash the leaves in several waters; keep it in cold water until it is time to put it to boil. Put it in hot water, slightly salted; have just water enough to cover it. Cover the stew-pan, and boil briskly until the leaves are tender; they will sink when done. Pour into a colander, and press the water out. wipe out the stew-pan; cut up the spinach fine; put it in the stew-pan; season with pepper and butter enough to make it rich. When thoroughly hot, stir the butter in well, and serve hot. Have ready as many poached eggs as may be needed, and lay over the top of the spinach. Serve upon a separate plate, helping each plate to an egg, which should be cut up and well mixed with the spinach. Spinach may be boiled with bacon, but is no' so delicate. The dish may be garnished with hard-boiled eggs sliced, instead of the poached, if preferred. When well boiled and served, this is the most delicious of the spring greens.

424.—*Salsify.*—Scrape the roots well; cut off the tops close to the root; slice them long, or circular. Stew until tender; salt the water; drain them from the water. Wipe out the stew-pan; return the salsify to it, and add sweet milk enough to cover it. To three tumblerfuls of the salsify add a piece of butter as large as a large hen's egg; rub into it a teaspoonful of flour; season with salt and pepper; let this stew five minutes, covered; shake the pan well twice; remove it from the fire, and add vinegar, to give a pleasant acid taste. Serve hot, in a covered dish. This is called "mock oyster."

---

425. *Salsify Fritters.*—Scrape the roots; stew them until they can be mashed well; rub them through a sieve; season with salt and pepper. To three tumblerfuls add a well-beaten egg, a teaspoonful of butter, half a tumbler of flour; mix well, and fry in thick cakes, in boiling lard. The salsify may be grated without being cooked. Make a batter with one or two eggs, *sour* milk, a little soda, and to a tablespoonful of the batter add a teaspoonful of the grated salsify; fry in hot lard. Serve upon a napkin placed in the bottom of the dish. The grated root has more of the taste of the vegetable than that which has been cooked.

---

426. *Squash.*—Gather them as long as the outside skin can be easily punctured; after that they are too old. Peel and slice them; keep them in water until time to cook them—from half an hour to three quarters is sufficient, depending upon the age and size. Salt the water they are boiled in. Put them to cook in hot water; keep the vessel covered. When tender, empty them into a colander, and press the water out; mash them; wipe out

the stew-pan; return the squash, and season with cream, butter salt, and pepper. Squashes are also very nice sliced, parboiled until tender, pressed between two plates until dry, dipped in thin batter, and fried. Serve them as fast as fried; they should not be piled. They may also be mashed, and made into fritters, in the same way that the salsify fritters are. Winter squashes require more cooking, and should have the seed removed.

---

427. *Tomatoes.*—Gather them ripe; scald them until the skin can be removed. They may then be prepared in a great variety of ways.

---

428. *To Stew.*—To a dozen large tomatoes mince a good-sized onion (or less if preferred), and if the flavor of onion is not liked, omit it altogether; a tablespoonful of good brown sugar, a teaspoonful of pepper, salt to taste, a teacup of bread crumbs, a large heaped tablespoonful of good butter. Put in a covered stew-pan, and cook an hour; shake the pan well and frequently. Beat up the yolks of two or three eggs, and, just before serving, stir them rapidly to the tomatoes; let them remain a minute, and serve in a small tureen, or covered dish. This is a fine accompaniment to all kinds of baked or roast meat. Tomatoes are best cooked a long while.

---

429. *To Bake Tomatoes.*—Peel and mince enough to fill a quart dish; season them with sugar, mace, pepper, salt, and a little minced onion. Put a layer of bread crumbs upon the bottom of the dish; then a layer of tomatoes, a little butter, another of bread crumbs, until the dish is full; bread crumbs must be strewn thickly over the top; lay over bits of butter. Bake in a moderate oven, two hours.

---

230. *To Stuff.*—Take very large ones; half them; take out the seed; mince a little fowl, grated ham or tongue; season

highly with Cayenne pepper, salt to taste, onion and parsley minced; stuff with this. Spread over the force-meat raw egg and sift over bread crumbs. Put them in a stew-pan, with slices of fresh meat at the bottom, or cold ham. Pour over hot water to cover the meat before putting in the tomatoes; set the skin side down. Stew half an hour; add a little butter. Serve with or without the meat, in a hot, covered dish.

---

431. *Ochra and Tomatoes.*—Use half of each; season with salt and pepper; skin the tomatoes; slice the ochra; add a little onion; add a little sugar to the tomatoes. Stew without water, three quarters of an hour; add a piece of butter the size of a walnut to each quart of the mixture, when first put in the stew-pan.

---

432. *Tomato Salad.*—Scald and peel them; slice them thin; season with salt, pepper, sugar, and a little onion; add very little vinegar.

Tomatoes are excellent seasoned and boiled in a double kettle a long time—for a quart, two hours. Their own juice will be sufficient fluid.

---

433. *Tomato Fritters.*—Take equal quantities of tomatoes (skin and mince fine, and strain them from their liquor) and green corn very tender; scrape it from the cob with a sharp knife; use the milk of this. Season with sugar, salt, and pepper. Add for a quart of the mixture two well-beaten eggs, one tumbler of sweet milk, and flour enough to hold the mass together. Fry in thick cakes in boiling lard.

---

434. *Tomato Leather.*—Mash fine; strain through a sieve; add a little sugar; grease panes of glass; spread over the mixture, and dry. This can be used in soup or stews.

---

435. *Tomatoes.*—Tomatoes may be kept in different ways for winter use. Gather them just ripe, with the stems; put them in

a glass jar and cover with weak vinegar; soak before using. Tomatoes may be easily kept in self-sealing cans, and will well repay the trouble and expense. A good receipt for canning fruits and vegetables, and also for bottling them, may be found in this book. Tomatoes may be kept in salt. Gather them just before they are fully ripe; keep on the stems; put a layer of salt, then one of tomatoes. Keep well covered in a cool place. Soak before using.

---

436. *Tomato Paste.*—Skin and cut up ripe tomatoes; salt them to taste. Let them stand twelve hours; strain them from their liquor; use this for catsup. Put the pulp in a double kettle or unglazed jar; season with sugar, pepper, mace, or nutmeg; to a quart of tomatoes add a tumbler of good apple vinegar. Stew, stirring frequently, until this thickens to a paste; it will require two or more hours, depending on the quantity made. Dry it upon dishes, then pack in wide-mouthed glass bottles; cork well and keep in a dry place. A piece four inches square will season a gallon of soup. It will be found to be very useful for winter soups and sauces.

---

437. *Turnips.*—Peal and slice a quarter of an inch thick; keep them in cold water until the hour for cooking. Put them in hot water to cover them, slightly salted; stew until tender. If young it will require from twenty to thirty minutes; longer time for older ones. When tender, lay the slices in a hot, deep dish; pour over butter to make them rich; serve hot.

Another way: Slice them and boil with pork; mash them, and rub through a colander. Put them in a stew-pan with a little of the skimmings of the pot; salt and pepper. When thoroughly hot, serve. Always serve on a separate dish; never under meat.

---

438. *Water Cresses.*—Serve raw, with lettuce, parsley, and radishes

STORE SAUCES.

439. *Tomato Catsup.*—To every gallon of tomatoes sliced, add five tablespoonfuls of salt, two of Cayenne pepper, two of black pepper ground, one teaspoonful of mace, one of allspice, one of cinnamon, half a one of cloves, two large onions sliced, one tumbler of good brown sugar, one quart of good apple vinegar, one large tablespoonful of ground mustard (a little garlic is sometimes used). Put all these well mixed in a stew-pan; simmer gently four hours. Stir frequently, to prevent its scorching. Strain; when cold, bottle; use new corks. It is poor economy to use old corks.

Another way: A gallon of tomatoes, a quart of apple vinegar, three tablespoonfuls of ground black pepper, three of salt, three of English mustard, two of mixed spices, a teacup of onion, a teaspoonful of Cayenne; boil slowly half the day; stir often; strain and bottle. Boil in a covered stew-pan. Never use a copper or brass vessel; iron lined with porcelain is best.

---

440. *Mrs. A.'s Receipt for Green Tomato Sauce.*—Slice thin a peck of green tomatoes. Make the winter's supply just before the frost falls upon them. Put the tomatoes in layers, with salt, twenty-four hours; drain through a sieve. Boil in a gallon of good apple vinegar an ounce each of mace, allspice, black pepper, half an ounce of cloves, a tablespoonful of celery seed, two of mustard seed, half a dozen pods of green pepper, and a pound of brown sugar. After the spices are well scalded in vinegar, strain it on the tomatoes; return all to the stew-pan; scald them well, but no more. When cold, mix in a small box or mustard bottle, and cork well.

---

441. *Chetney Sauce* (*Imitation*).—Eight ounces of tart apples, the same of salt; a quarter of a pound each of tomatoes, raisins, and brown sugar; a tablespoonful of Cayenne pepper; garlic and onion, tablespoonful each. Bruise these, and cover with three quarts of good apple vinegar. Grate the rind of four lemons; add the juice, removing the seed. Put in a jug, set near the stove, and shake well twice a day for a month. Strain the juice through a flannel bag without squeezing. This makes an excellent fish sauce, using a teaspoonful to a tumbler of broth or melted butter. Bottle and cork well. What remains in the bag answers well for "devils," grills, barbecues, etc.

---

442. *Pepper Catsup.*—Take any quantity of red or green pepper pods; slit the pods; boil in sufficient water to cover them. Stir and mash them while boiling; strain through a colander, then through a sieve. To two quarts of this pulp, add one quart of vinegar, two or three garlic buttons minced fine, a small onion cut up, one tablespoonful of salt, one of cloves, the same of allspice. Boil one hour; if too thick, add more vinegar. The red pods make a beautiful red catsup.

---

443. *Imitation Worcester Sauce.*—One gallon of ripe tomatoes washed and cut up. Pour over three quarts of water; let it boil down half. Stir occasionally to prevent the tomatoes from sticking. (A double vessel is valuable in preparing these sauces.) Strain through a sieve; add two tablespoonfuls of ginger, two of black pepper, two of salt, one of cloves, one of red pepper. Boil down to a quart; add a tumbler of vinegar. Strain, bottle, and cork tight.

---

444. *Cucumber Catsup.*—Grate two dozen grown cucumbers and six silver-skinned onions; sprinkle half a tumbler of salt upon them. Prepare them in the evening, and early in the morning lay them on a sieve and let them drain. Soak a teacup of white mustard seed; drain them from the water, and add to the cucum bers a wineglass of whole pepper-corns. Put them in a jar; cover with vinegar. Keep in a wide-mouthed jar in a cool, dry place; cork well.

---

445. *Dr. Kitchiner's Receipt for Mushroom Catsup.*—Gather the right kind in September; full-grown flaps are best. Put a layer of these on the bottom of an earthen dish; sprinkle them well with salt; put alternate layers of mushroom and salt. Let them lie three hours. Pound them in a mortar; repeat this for two days, stirring them well. Pour them into an unglazed jar; to each quart add an ounce and a half of black pepper, and an ounce of red pepper. Cover the jar close; set it in an oven in water; make the water boil two hours steadily. Strain through a sieve, without squeezing. Put it in a stew-pan; boil gently half an hour; strain again. Put it in a jar to settle, adding a tablespoonful of brandy to each pint of catsup. Rinse half pint bottles with brandy before bottling. It is best to keep it in small quantities. It must be well cooked and sealed, and kept in a cool, dry place. Examine it from time to time, by placing a strong light behind the neck of the bottle. Should any dross appear, boil again. A tablespoonful of this will impregnate a tumblerful of sauce. After the juice is strained, dry the mushrooms, and make powder. Just before the boiling is finished, great care is necessary to prevent the catsup from burning. A double kettle is a very suitable vessel in which to boil these catsups.

---

446. *Walnut Catsup.*—Take the walnuts when a pin will pass through them; pound them slightly. Put in an unglazed jar a layer of walnuts, and a slight sprinkling of salt; repeat until the walnuts are disposed of. Let it stand a week; strain off the juice. To every gallon add a pint of eschalot or onion cut fine, one ounce of cloves, the same of mace, allspice, ginger, and black pepper, and one clove of garlic cut up. Boil until reduced one third. When cool, bottle; cork well, and seal. Keep in a cool, dry place Age improves this.

447. *Lemon Catsup.*—Roll well half a dozen lemons to increase their juice; grate off the peel; squeeze out the juice; remove the seed; add a tablespoonful of grated horseradish, the same of ground ginger, half as much mace and cinnamon, one grated nutmeg. Pour over a pint of vinegar; scald five minutes. When cold, strain and bottle. Use to flavor piquant sauces.

448. *Pudding Catsup.*—Mix together half a pint of noyau, a pint of Sherry or other white wine, the yellow peel of four lemons pared thin, and half an ounce of mace. Put the whole in a large bottle, and let it stand for two or three weeks; then strain it, and add half a pint of capillaire, or strong sugar syrup of curacoa. Bottle it, and it will keep three or four years. It may be used for several dishes, but chiefly for pudding sauce, mixed with melted butter.

449. *Noyau.*—Blanch and beat a pound of bitter almonds or peach kernels; mix with the grated rinds of three lemons three pounds of loaf sugar, one tumblerful of honey, one gallon of brandy, one quart of rose-water; put in a jug, and cork tight. Shake it well every day for a month. Then strain it; add another quart of rose-water; mix well; bottle and cork, and cement the stopper. Keep in a dry, cool place.

450. *Capillaire.*—Eight pounds of loaf sugar pulverized; wet with three pints of water, and three eggs well beaten. Let it boil up twice; skim and strain it; flavor with two wineglasses of orange-flower water. Bottle, and use it as a summer drink with a little lemon juice and ice water. Sweeten pudding catsup with it.

451. *Ratafia.*—Beat fine a pound of bitter almonds, one ounce of nutmeg, one pound of loaf sugar, one grain (apothecary) of ambergris. Infuse three weeks in brandy. Strain and bottle.

452. *Orgeat*—A pleasant drink for summer. Take half a pound of sweet almonds blanched, half a dozen bitter almonds or peach kernels. Beat them with orange-flower water to prevent their oiling; add one tumbler of water, half a tumbler of orange-flower water. Strain it; add a pound of loaf sugar. Boil ten minutes, and skim. When cool, bottle it. Use one tablespoonful to a glass of ice water, or freeze it.

---

453. *To Make Curry Powder.*—Three ounces of coriander seed, the same of turmeric, one ounce each of ginger, black pepper, mustard, allspice, and of cumin and cardamom seed half an ounce. Beat; sift well; bottle, and cork tight. A teaspoonful will season a pound of meat. It is usual to add a little acid with curries, apple, or lemon minced. Rice should always accompany curried meats.

---

454. *Soy.*—One pound of salt, two pounds of sugar; fry this a quarter of an hour over a slow fire, stirring constantly; one tumbler of essence of anchovies, a dozen cloves, one tablespoonful each of thyme, sweet basil, and marjoram. Pour over all three pints of boiling water. Boil until the salt is dissolved. When cold, strain and bottle; cork tight. Use to flavor gravies and sauces.

To Flavor Vinegars for Salads and Sauces.—These are very convenient articles for flavoring salads, etc.; one or two receipts will answer for any kind of vegetable or sweet herb liked.

---

455. *Sweet Basil Vinegar.*—Fill a wide-mouthed jar with the green leaves; let it steep ten days; strain it on to fresh leaves; steep a week; strain and bottle. A tablespoonful will flavor half a gallon of soup. Horseradish, cucumber, eschalot, mint, garlic (celery seed will answer in place of the green celery), are all prepared in the same way. When making chow, use the trimmings and peel of the horseradish to flavor vinegar.

---

456. *Pepper Vinegar.*—Put into a quart bottle thirty small

pods of green or red pepper (make of both kinds separately). Set the bottles in an oven in water; make the water boil. When the peppers are thoroughly hot, pour in good vinegar to fill the bottle; cork tight. In the centre of the cork insert a goose quill or reed three inches long, open at both ends; through this the vinegar may be poured when using it. Stop with a good cork when not in use.

---

457. *To Prepare Mustard for the Casters.*—Make a smooth paste of one heaped tablespoonful of mustard flour, half a teaspoonful of fine salt, the same of loaf sugar, three tablespoonfuls of water or sweet cream. Only make sufficient to last two days. Another way is: Use vinegar in place of the cream. Celery or horseradish vinegar answers the purpose well. If the vinegar is too strong, dilute it.

---

458. *Mustard that will Keep Good a Month.*—Dissolve three ounces of salt in a quart of hot vinegar; pour the vinegar hot upon a teacup of horseradish. Cover it closely; let it stand a day and night. Make a smooth paste of this vinegar, and good flour of mustard, beating it well; put it in a wide-mouthed glass bottle; cork tight. In addition to these catsups, sauces, and vinegars, the store-room should be supplied with caviare for fish, which is made of the roe of sturgeon, Worcester sauce, Tarragon vinegar, French mustard, etc., etc. Having a good variety of these, it will always be easy to give a different flavoring to soups and sauces.

---

459 *Brandy (Good French) aad Wine*—Should be kept for cakes, etc. Steep spices in it ten days; strain and bottle; use three ounces of any kind of spice to a quart of wine or brandy; slightly bruise the spice. Steep the different kinds of spices separately. At the end of ten days, strain and bottle; cork tight; label each bottle. This is a neat and convenient way of using spices for seasoning. The tincture of lemon is made by

putting the yellow part of the lemon peel into brandy or wine until it is strongly impregnated with the lemon flavor. Grate off the outside of the lemon upon lumps of loaf sugar; pack in a glass jar, and use in cakes and desserts.

460. *To Keep Lemon Juice.*—To every pint of juice (sever lemons will generally make a pint—roll well before squeezing) put a pound of double-refined sugar; stir until dissolved; bottle it in small bottles; pour over the top of the juice, after it is bottled, a teaspoonful of olive oil. When wanted for use, apply a piece of cotton until it absorbs the oil.

461. *Chicken Salad.*—For a pound of chicken, after it is minced, use six eggs; boil them hard; separate the yolks and whites; mash the yolks to a smooth paste with the back of a wooden spoon; add half a tumbler of good sweet olive oil (or rather more melted butter), half a tumbler of vinegar (celery vinegar is best), two even tablespoonfuls of dry mustard flour, a tablespoonful of loaf sugar (dissolved in the vinegar), a teaspoonful each of pepper and salt; wet the mustard to a paste; stir all these together. Mince a third as much white lettuce, cabbage, or celery as meat; mix well with the meat, tossing them together with a wooden or silver fork; add the sauce just before serving. Garnish with sprigs of green parsley and the whites of the eggs cut into rings. Salad is very pretty served within potato or rice walls ornamented tastily.

462. *Lobster Salad.*—Boil a hen lobster. When done, remove the meat from the shell; mince it; rub the coral to a smooth paste with a tablespoonful of olive oil or melted butter; add the grated yolks of three hard-boiled eggs, one teaspoonful of mustard, salt and pepper to taste, and a wineglass of good cider vinegar. Mix the sauce well with the meat; add a third as much white lettuce or celery, cut up fine just before serving. Salmon salad may be made in the same way. Garnish with lemon sliced and

green parsley or celery. Make salmon salad with the same seasoning.

---

463. *Meat Jelly.*—To make a quart of this jelly: Melt it, and season with two lemons cut in slices, remove the seed; a teaspoonful of black pepper, bruised slightly; a blade of mace, stick of cinnamon, one onion, a sprig of parsley, thyme, sweet basil, salt to taste, two tablespoonfuls of celery vinegar, the whites of five eggs beaten to a froth. Let it stew gently, *without stirring,* until the jelly looks clear; strain once or twice through a jelly-bag. Set a turkey, birds, fish, etc., intended for a party-supper, under this while being dripped. Let the jelly be thick enough upon the article to form a thin veil; color with cochineal a flesh or pinkish color; sea green, for fish, may be colored with spinach juice, or juice from beet tops. This jelly is also excellent in Christmas meat pies, salmagundi, etc., intended to be kept several days; it not only seasons them finely, but keeps the meat moist. It is highly ornamental as a garnish for cold meats.

---

464. *To Bone a Turkey.*—Clean the turkey; remove the intestines; cut off the first joints of the legs; cut down the backbone; very carefully raise the meat from the backbone on each side; unjoint the wings, leaving the small part of the wing bone; raise the meat carefully from the breast, using a sharp knife with a narrow blade. The meat being now detached from the bones, and those unjointed, draw out the frame; only the merrythought will remain, which can be easily cut out. Break up the bones; put them in a stew-pan; cover them with cold water, and stew while the turkey is being stuffed with a rich force-meat. First sew up the slit and any holes that may have been accidentally made, making the stitches on the inner side. The force-meat may be of well-seasoned sausage meat, or veal minced fine, and seasoned with spices to taste, or with mace only, or use sweet herbs. After it is stuffed, so as to look as before the bones were removed, put it in a large stew-pan, that will just hold it without

cramping; strain over the gravy from the bones. If this does not cover the fowl, add warm water; add any vegetable or sweet herbs liked, several slices of cold boiled bacon, and a few slices of veal. It will require from an hour and a half to two hours gentle stewing. Let it cool in the liquor; take up the fowl; scrape off the gravy; melt and strain the gravy. Season it to taste, if not already sufficiently seasoned; boil it down to a jelly. Strain over the fowl, or serve around it, upon the dish.

---

465. *To Make Tough Meat Tender.*—If an old fowl, as soon as it is killed immerse it with the feathers on in a jar of weak ley; let it remain twelve hours. For steak and younger poultry, rub over the steak and the inside of the fowl, saleratus or soda. To stew immediately after killing, cook before the animal heat is extinct.

---

466. *To Keep Eggs during the Winter.*—Brush them over with oil; pack them in boxes of dry charcoal; turn the small end down.

Another way: Oil them; pack in boxes, and turn each egg twice a week. If the eggs are kept in one position, the yolk will in a short time settle upon the shell, and spoil. Hens understand this, and turn over the eggs upon which they set daily.

Another way: Bore auger holes large enough to hold the eggs in poplar plank (pine will not answer, it gives a bad taste to the eggs), or any kind of seasoned plank that will not impart the peculiar taste of the plank; make shelves of this plank in a dry place; brush the eggs over with oil; set them with the small end down in these auger holes. In very cold weather, cover them with a double blanket. They may for some purposes be scalded in boiling water, and packed in salt, charcoal, or bran, and turned frequently—or keep them in strong brine.

---

467. *Rice Flour Cement.*—Mix the flour (as much as is needed) with cold water; pour into boiling water; let it simmer until a transparent paste is formed. When cold use it.

468. *Waterproof Cement.*—To a tumbler of sweet milk, put as much good vinegar; scald it until it curdles; strain the whey from the curds, and mix the whey with the whites of five eggs; beat them well together; add quicklime, sifted through a sieve, until the mixture is of the consistence of thick paste. With this broken cracks in vessels of all kinds can be mended. It resists the action of fire and water.

---

469. *To Render Water Soft for Washing.*—Where there is lime in the water, this method of preparing water for washing will be found useful: Stir a pint of fresh slacked lime to a gallon of water; let it settle; pour it off from the sediment carefully, and immediately bottle, and cork it tight. Add a tumblerful of this lime water to the hard water; stir it well together; let the sediments settle; then pour off the water through a Canton flannel cloth.

YEAST AND BREAD.

"Bread should have the first place on our table, and in all discussions of dietetics and cookery. ''It is the staff of life,' the main reliance of the muscle and bone. 'That person who habitually eats good bread,' says a distinguished physician, 'ought never to complain much of indigestion, for poor bread is one of the principal causes of dyspepsia.' If it be true, and I presume no reflecting mind doubts it, that 'the highest success in life finds its only sure basis in physical vigor, and that this physical vigor depends mainly upon the quality of food thrown daily into that great human laboratory, the stomach—is it not a matter of paramount importance that every article of food, especially bread, be so prepared as that it may fulfil completely its functions in the system?" The author of Hints upon Cookery says truly "a culinary reform is demanded," and very gracefully concludes by invoking the aid of each mistress of a family to closely superintend, and, to some extent, even assist in the preparation of meals, at least until our cooks shall have become better instructed and more skilful than at present. What he says of his fair readers, may, I hope, with with equal propriety be said of mine, that "they are not among those who are ashamed to know how to make a loaf of bread or to stir a batch of biscuit with their own hands. Even the kitchen is a place of dignity and honor in their presence when love sanctifies the baking and boiling." Four things are requisite to have good bread, viz.: good flour, good yeast, good baking, and that the dough should be WELL KNEADED.

---

470. *To Make Hop Yeast.*—Put a handful of hops into a stewpan; peel and slice two large Irish potatoes; add them to the hops; pour over them two quarts of water, and boil until the potatoes are soft. Make in an earthen bowl a smooth paste of

a pint of flour and cold water. Strain the hop-tea upon the paste. Stir it well; wash the stew-pan, and pour the batter into it. Simmer ten minutes, and pour back into the bowl, and when lukewarm, add a teacup of brown sugar or half as much syrup, a tumblerful of good yeast, and set it to rise where it will be warm, and kept of a uniform temperature. When well risen, make up part of it into leaven. This is done by sifting corn meal, and pouring in liquid yeast to make a rather stiff dough. Work it well; roll into a long piece as thick as a man's wrist, and cut with a knife into thin cakes. Sprinkle a large dish thickly with flour; lay the cakes on, meeting but not touching; set them in a dry, warm place, where the wind will blow freely upon them. In winter they may be dried in the sun. Turn them several times each day, and when nearly dry, roll them to a powder with the rolling-pin. Expose them to the air till quite dry, and pack in a jar with a tightly-fitting cover. Two tablespoonfuls will be sufficient for a quart of flour. Dissolve the leaven in a tumblerful of tepid water or milk (water is best in summer, milk in winter). Keep the leaven in a dry place, well protected from the air. It is well to have a good supply of this always on hand. For immediate use, put part of the yeast into a wide-mouthed glass bottle; stop loosely until fermentation ceases, then stop well, and in winter keep in a warm place. It is a common error with cooks to *overheat* bread and yeast. A uniform blood heat is necessary to success in bread-making. Change the vessel in which the yeast is kept; wash it with hot water in which a teaspoonful of soda to a quart has been dissolved. Sun it half an hour. In this way the vessel may be kept sweet and clean. Peach leaves will answer for this yeast as well as hops; a handful of leaves to a quart of water.

471. *Irish Potato Yeast.*—At twelve o'clock in the day, mash very smooth a boiled Irish potato; mix with it a tablespoonful of liquid yeast or a teaspoonful of the powdered leaven; if necessary, use a little water. Mix this well with the potato in a soup-

plate; turn a plate over it; set in a warm place if the weather is cold. At night make up the breakfast bread with this preparation, leaving a tablespoonful to start the yeast again. If for tea, make the yeast after breakfast. When the yeast is good it will increase somewhat in bulk and crack open over the top. This is a *simple* and *excellent receipt.*

---

472. *To Make Bread with Irish Potato Yeast.*—Sift one quart of flour; rub into the flour a piece of lard as large as a hen's egg; add a teaspoonful of salt. Beat one egg in a bowl with two level tablespoonfuls of sugar; then add two heaped tablespoonfuls of potato yeast. Beat a little, and pour the mixture into the flour; add a tumbler of tepid water; knead the *dough well.* Grease a tin bucket; put in the dough, greasing it slightly on the top. Cover, and set it to rise. When risen, make into rolls, placing them so as to touch in the pan they are to be baked in. Cover, and when risen near the top of the pan, *bake quickly.* If the weather is very warm, make up the bread between eleven and twelve o'clock. It will be ready to make into rolls between three and four o'clock. This makes DELICIOUS BREAD.

---

473. *Sweet Potato Yeast.*—Bake or roast sweet potatoes (white Bermudas are best) enough to make a pint of potatoes after being rubbed through the colander. Pour over this a pint of boiling water, a pint of cold water, a teacup of good hop yeast, or half a cup of leaven; mix well together. Pour it in a wide-mouthed jar; stop lightly till it rises. Keep in a moderately warm place in winter, and a cool place in summer. The bread may be made up entirely with this yeast, always reserving a cupful to start the yeast. Make it fresh every two or three days. Irish potato yeast may be made in the same way.

---

474. *Milk Yeast.*—Early in the morning put into a stew-cup, lined with porcelain or tin, two teacups of fresh milk; let it boil up once, and then pour in a teacup of cold water; stir in the milk

one teacup of corn meal, and flour enough to make a smooth batter, about the consistence of fritter batter; add a teaspoonful of salt. Set the mixture in the sun, if a bright summer day, or where it will keep of a regular tepid heat till risen. As soon as the yeast rises, make up the dough with it entirely. Put the bread in the oven or pan in which it is to be baked; keep it moderately warm; bake as soon as it rises sufficiently. Bread made of this yeast is very good, but does not *keep well*. A pint of yeast will wet two quarts of flour. A little warm water poured in to rinse the vessel in which the yeast was, may be used if necessary in wetting up the bread. Use a piece of lard the size of a hen's egg to each quart of flour. When the bread is done, take it out of the pan and set it upon one end. After remaining in this position a quarter of an hour, turn it, and never let it set flat on anything, until cold, as the under part will absorb the dampness or sweat. If there should be a hard crust in consequence of baking too fast on the top, upon removing the bread from the oven wrap it in a damp cloth, and set it up.

---

475. *Corn Meal Yeast.*—Half a pint of corn meal made into a batter, with equal parts of sweet milk and warm water, a large tablespoonful of good brown sugar, and a teacup of good yeast. When well risen, add corn meal sufficient to make it almost dry; then spread it upon dishes to dry, in the *air* (not the sun); keep in a dry place, well covered. A handful will make up three pints of flour.

---

476. *Magic, or Cold Yeast.*—This yeast is superior to any I have ever used, in warm or even moderately warm weather. It is more reliable, and less troublesome. I confidently recommend it after long experience in its use. Take one cup of fresh sweet milk, one of cold water, two tablespoonfuls of nice sugar, and flour enough to make a moderately thin batter; make it in a covered jar or mug, and set in the safe, or some cool place, if the weather is warm, where it must remain undisturbed for two days.

On the morning of the third, add two more tablespoonfuls (even full) of sugar and two teaspoonfuls of salt; set it away as at first until 11 o'clock. Make up rolls, or any kind of bread liked; bake when light; unless tea is very early, the bread may be made still later, and first put down in a lump, and when this rises, mould it, and bake at the second rising. To continue the yeast from day to day, when the batch of dough is made at eleven, stir the yeast well before pouring it into the flour; reserve a teacup until next morning; then add to it a teacup of water, a tablespoonful of sugar, and flour enough for a batter of the consistence of that first made. It will be ready at the time it is needed. If more is required, use more water—the milk is only used in starting the yeast. Change the vessel every two days. If the yeast becomes a little sour, stir in half a teaspoonful of soda; should it look brisk and lively after the soda is stirred in, the yeast is good; if not, discard it, and make fresh yeast. In *very cold weather* the yeast and dough must be put on the hearth, though not very near the fire. This yeast requires so little time to raise bread, that for breakfast I set a sponge at nine o'clock at night, and make the bread early in the morning. A sponge is set in this way: Take a tumblerful of sweet milk or cold water, one of the magic yeast, pour them (well stirred) into a small jar; beat in flour enough to make a smooth batter, not very thick; remove the spoon, sprinkle flour over the top of the batter; cover it well, and if the weather is warm, put it in a cool place. Early in the morning, taste the batter; if at all acid, stir in a little soda; make into dough, either for Sally Lunn, French rolls, or in any way preferred, adding a small piece of lard, or butter, and an egg if liked; mould the dough; let it set until it rises; bake in a rather quick oven. The dough must be *well worked* at first until it blisters, pulling it to pieces, and working in the flour slowly, and until the dough is a little stiff. I never add a particle of flour when working bread the second time (deeming it unwise to throw in fresh material after fermentation has commenced), and only handle it enough to mould.

477. To Set a Sponge for Light Rolls with Yeast that Requires to be Kept Warm.—Into a pint of tepid water, or fresh sweet milk, beat as much sifted flour as will make a stiff batter; add a tumblerful of lively, brisk yeast; stir all well; sprinkle flour on the surface of the batter; cover well, and set it to rise. When the sponge rises so as to make cracks through the flour, sprinkle over it a teaspoonful of salt; beat into the sponge a tumbler of tepid water; in another vessel beat up two eggs well; pour part of the sponge to the eggs until a smooth batter is formed (a tablespoonful of sugar may be used if liked); then stir the egg into the remainder of the sponge; beat all well together. Sift two quarts of flour; rub in well one tablespoonful of lard, the same of butter; make a hole in the middle of the flour; pour in the yeast; work the flour in gradually; knead the dough well. Few persons are aware how much the grain of the bread is improved by being well worked. Never wet up all the flour at once; reserve a third to work in; sprinkle the flour on the board; work it in the dough well. Pull the dough to pieces; turn it inside out; work again; each time sprinkling the flour upon the board until it is all worked in, and the dough looks light and spongy. Grease a pan; mould the dough either in long, round, or twisted rolls; lay them in the pan, so that they will touch; let them rise. If the sponge is good it will not require over half an hour to raise the dough after it is moulded. Bake in rather a quick oven. Should the oven or stove be too hot, lay over the bread a sheet of paper; should a hard crust form, the bread will not be light. When a sponge is set, the dough should only rise once; when made without a sponge, it must rise first undivided, then moulded, and set to rise the second time. Every kitchen should be supplied with a smooth poplar or marble board, upon which the bread should be worked, first mixing in a tray until the dough is cleared from the hands; then flour the board well, and work as directed. It requires some experience to know when to work the dough the second time, for if allowed to rise too long it will lose its sweetness, without always becoming sour. When, unfortunately, the dough is permitted to remain until sour, pull it open, dissolve half a teaspoonful of soda for a quart of flour, in a wineglass not quite full of warm water; pour over, and work in well.

---

478. *To Know when the Oven or Stove is Hot Enough for Baking.*—Sprinkle in a little flour; if it turns slowly a good brown color, the oven is right; if it burns immediately, it is too hot. Leave the door of the stove open a few minutes to allow it to cool. It will be right when you can hold your hand in to count twenty. But this is not a reliable rule, since some persons endure heat better than others. Baking may be done in the stove, in a brick or iron oven; if a brick oven is used, kindle the fire when the dough is put to rise; by the time the bread has risen, the oven will be ready; when the oven is hot enough, clean it out, and give the dust a few moments to settle before putting the bread in. When an iron oven is used, set the bottom side up before the fire until well warmed; in putting coals under, mash the larger ones with the back of the shovel, that all may be of the same size; where one or two larger coals than the rest are left under the oven, cake or bread is very apt to bake with large holes, or as cooks express it, "blow up" in holes. At first the heat should be strongest at the bottom of the oven; put the oven lid on cold, or slightly warm; cover it with hot embers; heat gradually. Baking can only be learned by experience. It is a good plan to heat the flour very hot before making it up. After sifting, I always place the flour well spread in the sun, or before the fire, taking care it does not scorch.

---

479. *French Rolls.*—One quart of flour, one or two eggs beaten with an even tablespoonful of sugar; dissolve a yeast cake, or, if the leaven is pulverized, two tablespoonfuls in a tumbler of tepid water; stir this well, and pour it to the eggs. Sift the flour into the tray; reserve a third of it to work into the dough after the flour is wet up. Into the remainder of the flour sprinkle a tea-

spoonful of salt, and rub in well a heaping tablespoonful of butter or lard; pour the yeast in, and stir the flour in gradually. When the dough can be rubbed from the hands, flour the board or bottom of the tray, and begin to work the dough upon it; sprinkle down more flour; pull the dough to pieces; repeat this until all the reserved flour is in; continue to work the dough until it feels light and spongy to the touch. The dough for light rolls should be softer than for loaf bread. Grease the pan in which the bread will be put to rise; lay the dough in; press it down with the hand until it covers the bottom; lightly touch it over with lard, to prevent a crust from forming. Throw a clean towel over. Set it to rise where it will be kept moderately warm. When it has risen, immediately take it from the pan, and roll it in a round strip; pull it into pieces of uniform size (and never very large); mould them into long or round shapes; grease the pan slightly in which they are to be baked; lay the rolls in, touching. Let them rise again, which should be in half an hour; bake in a quick oven, not hot enough, however, to blister or burn.

480. *Secession Biscuit.*—These are made precisely the same as light rolls, only moulded differently. After the second rising, grease the bottom of the oven or pan in which they are to be baked; work each piece of dough separately, and make them as common soda biscuit are shaped; lay them in the oven or pan; they should not touch. Let them rise fifteen or twenty minutes; bake in a quick oven. They are not so good when permitted to stand any length of time.

481. *Potato Bread.*—Rub half a dozen Irish potatoes, peeled, through a coarse sieve; mix them thoroughly with twice the quantity of flour; add one egg, a tablespoonful of butter, a teaspoonful of salt, a tumbler of tepid water or fresh sweet milk, in which has been dissolved a tablespoonful of leaven; make a smooth dough; after being well risen, mould into loaves or long rolls; let them rise again; bake in a rather quick oven. This bread keeps well.

482. *Sally Lunn, No. 1.*—Into one quart of sifted flour rub a large heaped tablespoonful of butter, or half butter and lard, a teaspoonful of salt. Into a pint bowl break two eggs; beat them several minutes; pour to them a teacup of good yeast. Make a hole in the middle of the flour (reserve a tumbler of the flour before rubbing in the shortening); pour in the yeast and egg. After stirring them together well, work the flour in until a soft dough is formed; sprinkle the board; work the dough well until the reserved flour is all in, pulling the dough to pieces. When more wetting is needed in first making the dough, use tepid sweet milk in winter, water in summer. When the working is finished, the dough should be rather soft. Let this rise in a lump. Divide the dough in four equal pieces; roll the same size. Grease two shallow pans; on the bottom of each lay a piece of the dough; spread over the surface a thin coat of lard. Lay over the remaining pieces of exactly the same size and thickness. Care should be taken to make them fit well. Fold the dough as it is lifted from the board; lay half on first, then the other half; throw over a clean towel; set the pans where the dough will keep at an even temperate warmth. When risen, bake in a quick oven. Take them from the pans; shake gently the pieces apart; butter the bottom piece well by laying over slices of fresh butter; replace the top pieces; cut in slices; serve warm. The slices should not be removed when put upon the table, but cut for convenience of serving.

---

483. *Sally Lunn, No. 2.*—Take a small tumbler of new milk and boil it. When cool, add to it two eggs well beaten, a cake of leaven (dissolve this in the milk), and flour enough to make a stiff batter. Make it up at nine o'clock at night; next morning stir in a tablespoonful of melted butter; grease a mould; pour in the batter, and set in a warm place to rise; when well risen, put it to bake. You can add sugar and spice, and make this a sweet cake if you like. If at all sour, stir in a little soda, dissolved in a tablespoonful of warm water.

484. *Sally Lunn No. 3.*—One quart of flour, three eggs, one tablespoonful of butter; add half a cup of good yeast. Mix at ten o'clock A. M., for tea, as soft as you can with the hands.

---

485. *Receipt for Split Rolls.*—One egg, one tablespoonful of sugar well beaten together, and one yeast cake dissolved in a cup of warm milk; add flour to make a stiff batter. Set to rise at ten o'clock in winter and twelve in summer; then work a heaping tablespoonful of butter in flour enough to make up the yeast; roll out the dough an inch thick, and spread butter on it; fold it in half, and cut any shape you fancy. Let them rise in the pan in which they are to be baked. Bake quick.

---

486. *Rockbridge Alum Sally Lunn.*—One tumbler of yeast, one of sweet milk, five eggs beaten well, ten ounces of butter, two of sugar; mix into a stiff batter and let it stand in a warm place until it rises. Beat it down. Put in the pan it is to be baked in; let it rise again, and bake in a quick oven.

---

487. *Bread without Yeast.*—Take so much milk or warm water as will wet up the flour you wish to use. Salt rather more than is used for common bread. Stir in flour to make a paste about as thick as griddle-cake dough. Put this paste in a tin bucket, and set in a pot of warm water near the hearth or stove where the water will keep about milk warm. This will give the paste an even temperature. In four or five hours this well rise, and foam like yeast. Pour it into your tray, and work in flour enough to make bread. Put in the pans they are to be baked in, and set them in a warm place. Cover with paper or cloth, and let them rise; when risen, bake in a quick oven. A piece of lard or butter the size of a large walnut for each quart of flour, may be used, if preferred. Try it both ways.

---

488. *Sponge Biscuit.*—Put a pint of fresh sweet milk to warm in a stew-pan; drop in two heaping teaspoonfuls of lard. When the lard has melted, sift a quart of flour into a pan; a teaspoonful of salt, a teacup of brisk, lively yeast; pour on the milk; make a stiff batter. When risen, grease the stove-pan, warm it slightly, and drop the batter on in large spoonfuls. Let them set a few minutes where they will be merely warm, no more; then bake in a quick oven. Send immediately to table, as they are not good if kept until a hard crust forms. These may be baked in cups.

---

489. *Light Bread.*—To three pints of sifted flour, pour one pint of tepid milk or water and a tumbler of good yeast. Beat well and set it to rise in a moderately warm place; make this at night. In the morning, stir to the sponge a pint of warm water and two teaspoonfuls of salt; work in as much flour as will make a rather stiff dough. Work it well; mould it into loaves; let it rise; bake in a moderately quick oven. Use, when cold, for dinner-bread. It makes good toast when stale.

---

490. *Crumpets.*—One quart of sifted flour, one large tumbler of sweet milk (warm the milk); beat in a bowl two eggs; stir to them one small-sized teacup of good yeast. Make a stiff batter of the flour, eggs, and milk, beating all well together. Sprinkle over the top a slight coat of flour; leave the vessel (covered) where the batter will rise. Grease and heat the batter-cake griddle; pour on a large tablespoonful; bake rather slowly; when done on one side, turn. Butter and send to the table hot. Very few cooks manage the buttering well. They either put on enough to render the cakes disgustingly rich, or butter unequally, or put the butter in a tin vessel, place it on the stove or fire until it turns to oil, and then pour it profusely over the cakes. In buttering, as the cakes are removed one by one, lay over each very thin slices of cold butter. It should be done on the gridiron, piling them as they are buttered; immediately transfer them to a hot plate, and serve. The taste of oiled butter is very disagreeable, and should never be used for cakes or waffles. If it is preferred to have the

butter warm, put it in a small well-tinned sauce-pan, and place this in a "bain marie" or hot water bath, or put the butter in a deep plate and set it over a vessel of hot water.

---

491. *Flannel Cakes.*—Put a quart of sweet milk in a stew-pan; set on the stove to warm; drop into it a large tablespoonful of butter, or a little less lard. Beat up four eggs well; pour to them a tumbler or half a pint of good brisk yeast; then the milk, and flour enough to make a stiff batter; let it rise. Just as you are ready to fry them on the griddle, if at all sour, strew over the surface a teaspoonful of soda finely pulverized; beat it in, and fry immediately. In all the receipts given for crumpets, flannel cakes, etc., the cold yeast may be used unless the the weather is very cold. Very excellent cakes may be made by taking a teacup of dough from the breakfast-bread. Rub the dough to a batter with milk; beat up an egg; melt and stir to the egg a teaspoonful of hard butter; add flour to make a batter as stiff as for flannel cakes; fry in the same way, or make it a little stiffer; let it rise, and bake in a shallow pan in a quick oven. If at all sour, stir in half a teaspoonful of soda just as it is put to bake. This batter may be baked in muffin-rings.

---

492. *Raised Waffles, No.* 1.—Make a batter rather stiff, with three tumblers of sweet milk, two well-beaten eggs, a teaspoonful of salt, as much melted lard as can be dipped up in a tablespoon, and a tumbler of good yeast. Beat the flour in gradually until a stiffish smooth batter is formed. Set it to rise; when well risen, heat the irons; grease them slighly; pour in batter enough to fill them, but not to overflow; put them on a bed of coals; turn in two or three minutes. Bake on the reverse side in the same way. Slip the waffle from the irons on to a warm plate and butter it. Have a stew-pan of hot water on the stove; set the plate over the mouth of it until two or three are baked, which should be done as expeditiously as possible. Send to the table, and continue to send this number until all the batter is used. This is a much better plan than to

bake and send all at once. Though a delightful cake when well made and eaten fresh, it will soon spoil by standing.

---

493. *Rice Waffles, No. 2.*—Beat together two eggs; a teaspoonful of salt. Into another pan mash smoothly a teacup of warm, well-boiled rice. Stir to this until melted, a teaspoonful of lard; add alternately a tumbler of sweet milk and flour, to make a batter rather stiff; mix all together well. It requires an equal quantity of flour with the rice, or perhaps a little more flour. When the flour is very dry and light, it requires, if measured, more than it does of flour that is heavier.

---

494. *Rice Waffles, No. 3.*—Put a pint of sweet milk in the stewpan; a teacup of boiled rice; add to it a tablespoonful of butter; as soon as the butter melts, take the pan from the fire; beat four eggs well, and stir to them alternately—making a smooth batter—the milk and one quart of sifted flour; salt to taste. Bake and serve hot.

---

495. *Rice Flour Waffles, No. 4.*—Make half a tumbler of nice corn meal mush. While it is warm, stir to it a dessert-spoonful of butter. Make a smooth batter by beating in well two eggs, one pint of rice flour, one even teaspoonful of soda sifted in with the flour, and sweet milk to make a thin batter; salt to taste. Just before baking, stir in two teaspoonfuls of cream of tartar, previously dissolved in warm water. This is an excellent receipt for a batter-bread. Bake in a quick oven in a pan two or three inches deep. Eat hot.

---

496. *Quick Waffles, No. 5.*—One pint of buttermilk, one pint of sifted flour, one egg, one tablespoonful of melted lard, a large teaspoonful of soda. Send them to the table as fast as baked. They are very light and good while fresh, but spoil very soon if permitted to stand.

---

497. *Sweet Potato Waffles, No. 6.*—Two tablespoonfuls of

mashed, baked sweet potato, one of butter, stirred to the potato while hot, one of sugar, one egg, one pint of sweet milk, six table spoonfuls of sifted flour; mix well, and bake. These may be made without the egg, using four tablespoonfuls of flour.

---

498. *Mush or Hominy Waffles, No.* 7.—One pint of hominy or a teacup of mush, half a pint of flour, two eggs beaten separately, an even tablespoonful of lard stirred to the hominy; add sweet milk to make a thin batter; salt to taste.

---

499. *Mrs. R's Waffle Receipt, No.* 8.—One pint of flour, a handful of corn meal; sift them together. Beat the yolks of two eggs; make a batter of one pint of sour milk, teaspoonful of soda, and the mixed flour and meal; add one tablespoonful of lard after it is melted, then pour all to the beaten eggs; stir well together; salt to taste. Bake quick; serve hot.

---

500. *Muffins, No.* 1.—One pint and a half of sweet milk warmed, a piece of lard or butter the size of a large hen's egg melted in the milk, one large teaspoonful of salt, a small teaspoonful of soda (even full and well pulverized). Beat up with three eggs a tablespoonful of sugar; make to the eggs a batter with the milk and flour alternately, to form a stiff batter—so stiff as to be just able to beat it; stir in a tumblerful of good yeast; set the batter in a warm place to rise. When well risen, beat it down; let it rise again; be careful not to disturb it after the second rising more than is necessary to pour it into the muffin-rings. The rings should be prepared by greasing, and laying them upon the bottom of a stove-pan which has been greased, or an iron oven. In either case, the oven or pan should be well warmed at the bottom before the batter is poured in.

---

501. *Muffins, No.* 2.—A pint and a half of flour, one pint of sweet milk, three eggs, one yeast cake (three inches square) dissolved in the milk; let it rise. Just before baking, beat in a

teaspoonful of sugar and half a teaspoonful of soda; bake in a quick oven.

---

502. *Muffins, No. 3.*—Three tumblers of sifted flour, three eggs beaten well together, a tumbler half full of melted lard or butter, salt to taste, one tumbler of sweet milk, a yeast cake as large as the top of a tumbler. Set the batter to rise. When risen, pour in muffin-rings; bake in a quick oven.

---

503. *Muffins, No. 4.*—One pint of milk, one tablespoonful of hard butter; soften it, by placing the vessel containing it on the stove; two eggs well beaten, two wineglassfuls of good brisk yeast; flour to make a thick batter. When it rises, pour into the muffin-rings.

---

504. *Muffins, No. 5.*—At nine o'clock at night make a batter, by mixing two well-beaten eggs, a pint of sweet milk, a dessert-spoonful of butter or lard, a heaping pint of flour, half a tumbler of good yeast, salt to taste, half a teaspoonful of soda, or a teaspoonful of lime water. In the morning pour into the muffin rings (prepared as directed in the preceding receipt) without stirring. Bake in a quick oven.

---

506. *Muffins without Yeast, No.* 6.—Beat separately three eggs, make a smooth batter, by mixing a pint of flour with the eggs, and adding half a pint of sweet milk, or enough to make a thin batter; butter the size of a hen's egg; salt to taste. Heat the oven or pan in which the muffins are to be baked; grease the rings; place them upon the pan. Dissolve in half a wineglass of warm water two teaspoonfuls of cream of tartar; stir this to the batter, and, just before pouring the batter into the rings, stir in a teaspoonful of soda. Bake quick, without blistering. When eaten, they should be torn open. To cut them open with a knife, is an offence so grave that the cook will find it difficult to forgive. The batter for raised or yeast muffins should be thick; it becomes

thinner by fermentation. When made of soda, let the batter be thinner, and always beat the eggs separately, which is not necessary when yeast is used. Very good muffins may be made by using fewer eggs. To one quart of flour, measured after sifting, mix a teaspoonful of salt, a pint of sweet milk, or a little more if necessary; two eggs beaten separately, the whites added last; half a teacup of melted butter, or a little less lard. Dissolve two teaspoonfuls of cream of tartar in warm water; stir it in, and then add a teaspoonful of soda; thin batter; bake quick.

506. *Corn Meal Muffins, No. 7.*—One pint of sifted corn meal, a teaspoonful of soda, two tablespoonfuls of lard after being melted, two eggs well beaten, as much sour milk as will make a batter the consistency of pound-cake batter. Bake with a moderately hot oven in muffin-rings.

507. *Mixed Muffins, No. 8.*—Two eggs beaten separately, one pint of sweet milk, half a pint of flour, the same of corn meal, sifted together, two tablespoonfuls of melted lard; salt to taste.

508. *Hominy Muffins, No. 9—Mrs. W.'s Receipt.*—Two eggs, two tablespoonfuls of hot hominy, with a level tablespoonful of melted lard stirred in, two tablespoonfuls of sifted corn meal, two of flour, salt to taste, sweet milk to make a thin batter. Bake in small pattie-pans in a quick oven.

509. *Muffins, No. 10—Mrs. H.'s Receipt.*—Two eggs beaten separately, two teaspoonfuls of yeast powder, two tablespoonfuls of melted lard, one teaspoonful of salt, sweet milk and flour to make a moderately stiff batter. If the milk is a little acid, stir a little soda to it. When it is not convenient to use yeast powder, use as a substitute one teaspoonful of soda to two of cream of tartar.

510. *Batter-Bread without Eggs.*—Two tumblerfuls of sifted corn meal (even full), two of buttermilk, one teaspoonful of salt,

a piece of lard the size of a walnut melted and stirred in; grease a stove-pan (it must be shallow), and just before pouring in the batter, stir in half a tumbler of tepid water, a teaspoonful of soda dissolved in it. Bake in a hot oven.

---

511. *Breakfast Cakes.*—Dissolve a yeast cake two inches square, or a heaping tablespoonful if powdered, and the leaven is very good (use a little more if the yeast has been made some time), in half a teacup of warm water. Take a pint of fresh milk, and with flour make a soft dough; set it to rise. When well risen, work to the dough one egg well beaten, two large tablespoonfuls of melted butter. After mixing (no more flour should be added), put the batter or soft dough into cups; let them set to rise ten minutes. Bake in a quick oven; serve hot. Turn them out of the cups, handling them very delicately.

---

512. *Snow Flakes—Mrs. R.'s Receipt.*—One quart of sifted flour, one quart of sweet milk, salt to taste, six eggs beaten separately, one tablespoonful of melted lard. Just before baking, stir in one heaping dessert-spoonful of yeast powder. Bake in small patty-pans in a quick oven; grease the pans slightly. This is a delicate, and, when well made and baked, a beautiful dish.

---

513. *Soda Biscuit.*—Put in the sifter one quart of flour and one even teaspoonful of super-carb. soda; sift these together; rub into the flour thoroughly a piece of butter the size of a hen's egg; salt to taste; wet the flour with sour milk until a soft dough is formed; make it into thin biscuit, and bake in a quick oven. Work it very little. Always reserve a little flour before putting in the soda to work into the dough, and flour the board.

---

514. *Yeast Powder Biscuit.*—A quart of flour, a piece of lard rubbed into it as large as a hen's egg, a teaspoonful of salt (a neat way of adding the salt is first to dissolve it in a little water), a heaped-up teaspoonful of yeast powders. Wet up the flour with

sweet milk, and work just enough to mix; roll thin; prick with a fork, and bake in a quick oven. If it is not convenient to use the yeast powders, take two teaspoonfuls of cream of tartar, mix well with a teaspoonful of soda; add to the flour.

---

515. *Hard Biscuit.*—Measure a quart of flour, and one tumblerful over; reserve this. In the quart of flour rub a large tablespoonful of butter (or rather less of lard), and a teaspoonful of salt; wet to a soft dough with warm sweet milk; knead it well, working in slowly the reserved flour; sprinkle the biscuit-board with flour; beat the dough, turning it, pulling it to pieces (sprinkling on flour as may be needed), until the dough is well blistered. Roll it out; cut with a knife or biscuit-cutter, and bake in a moderately warm oven.

---

516. *Crackers, No. 1.*—Rub six ounces of butter into two pounds of sifted flour; dissolve a teaspoonful (level full) of soda in a wineglass of buttermilk; strain this through a fine sieve to the flour; add a teaspoonful of salt; beat well; roll thin; bake. If not crisp when first baked, put them again into a slack oven, and merely heat over.

---

517. *Crackers, No. 2.*—One pint of flour, the yolk of one egg; beat to this a dessert-spoon even full of fine sugar, one teaspoonful of butter, salt to taste; the same of lard, mixed together; wet with sweet milk to a stiff dough; beat well; cut with a wineglass; bake in a moderately hot oven. These are excellent if well made.

---

518. *Crackers, No. 3.*—One quart of flour, two ounces of butter, half a teaspoonful of salt, a level teaspoonful of soda dissolved in warm water, sweet milk enough to make a stiff dough; beat well with a pestle. Cut with a wineglass after rolling the dough thin.

---

519. *Crackers, No. 4.*—One teacup of sweet milk, half a tea-

spoonful of soda, one of cream of tartar, one tablespoonful of the white of an egg, first measuring and then beating it; a tablespoonful of butter, a little heaped teaspoonful of salt; mix very stiff; beat well; roll thin, and bake. Make these with arrow root flour, instead of flour.

---

520. *Tea Bread.*—Three tumblers of sifted flour, a teaspoonful and a half of cream of tartar, half a teaspoonful of soda, tablespoonful of butter rubbed to the flour, and a teaspoonful of salt. Rub the cream of tartar into the butter; dissolve the soda in a half tumbler of sweet milk; add this and a full tumbler of milk to the flour. Make a soft dough; roll an inch thick; press a saucer upon it, passing a knife around the saucer each time it is pressed, to cut the cakes the shape of the saucer; prick them, and bake in a hot oven.

---

521. *Mrs. W.'s Thomas-Bread Receipt.*—A tumbler of sweet milk, two eggs well beaten, salt to taste, two tablespoonfuls of melted butter or lard, two even tablespoonfuls of dry sugar, a dessert-spoon even full of yeast powder, flour to make a stiff batter; bake as soon as the powder is in.

---

522. *Clabber Bread* (*excellent*).—Beat four eggs separately, two teacups of clabber, one tablespoonful of butter (very slightly heaped, and placed in a pan upon the stove long enough to soften), a teaspoonful of soda, the same of salt; mix with flour to a stiff batter; grease the pan in which the bread is to be baked; pour in the batter; let it stand an hour, and bake.

---

523. *Rice Flour Loaf Bread.*—To one quart of rice flour, add an even teaspoon and a half of dry soda if the teaspoon is small; two eggs well beaten, separately; two tumblers of sweet milk, a teaspoonful of butter; put upon the fire in the pan in which the bread is to be baked, long enough to soften the butter. Have the pan made warm, and set in the oven or stove, where it is to

be baked. When the batter is ready, stir in half a teaspoonful of tartaric acid; pour into the warm pan, and bake immediately.

Another way: To half a tumbler of nice corn-meal mush, add a dessert-spoon even full of butter, two eggs beaten separately, one pint of rice flour, teaspoon of soda sifted in with the flour, salt to taste, sweet milk to make a thin batter; just before baking, stir in two teaspoonfuls of cream of tartar dissolved in warm water.

---

524. *Corn Meal Batter Bread.*—One pint of clabber or buttermilk, the same quantity of sifted corn meal, teaspoonful of soda, salt to taste, four eggs, well beaten, added last. To beat separately is best.

---

525. *Rice Bread.*—Three teacups of rice flour, one of wheat flour, one heaping teaspoonful of cream of tartar rubbed into the flour, two well-beaten eggs, a tablespoonful of butter, one half teaspoonful of soda, and sweet milk enough to make the batter the consistency of pound-cake.

---

526. *Rice Pan Bread.*—Two tablespoonfuls of hot hominy, one of butter; when cold, add one pint of rice flour, and make a batter with sweet milk.

---

527. *Hominy Bread.*—Two eggs beaten light, two cups of cold boiled hominy, one of corn meal, a tablespoonful of melted lard, and sweet milk for a thin batter.

---

528. *Egg Bread.*—One pint of sifted meal, nearly a pint of buttermilk, one egg, a lump of lard the size of a small walnut, and a teaspoonful of salt. Just before baking, add a teaspoonful of soda dissolved in two tablespoonfuls of warm water. If the milk is sweet, add two teaspoonfuls of cream of tartar.

529. *Batter Bread.*—One quart of corn meal, pour on it a pint of boiling sweet milk; stir in a teaspoonful of salt, one even tumblerful of hard butter; stir this into the hot mush; beat five eggs well, and stir into the batter. Bake in shallow pans, not over two inches deep, and fill them even full. Grease the pans before pouring in the batter.

---

530. *Rice Corn Bread.*—One pint of boiled rice, one pint of corn meal, a dessert-spoonful of lard, one pint of buttermilk (or sour milk), two eggs, beaten well; mash the rice smooth; add the lard to it; stir in the last a teaspoonful of soda; bake *in shallow pans*. This may be made with sweet milk, leaving out the soda, substituting yeast powders, or double the eggs, and add a little more rice and meal.

---

531. *Risen Corn Bread*—May be made with yeast and a little shortening. By some esteemed very good bread.

---

532. *Cheese Biscuit.*—One pound of flour, half a pound of butter, half a pound of grated cheese; make up quick, and with very little handling, as puff paste. Roll thin; cut and bake in a quick oven. Salt to taste.

---

533. *Buckwheat Cakes.*—Sift together one quart of buckwheat flour and a teacup of corn meal. In cool weather make up a moderately thin batter with lukewarm sweet milk; salt to taste. In warm weather it is best to use water, the milk would sour; add half a tumbler of good lively hop yeast (hop yeast is best for buckwheat); make it up in a jar (covering closely) at 9 o'clock at night. The next morning beat in three eggs; let it set fifteen or twenty minutes; just before frying, stir in a teaspoonful of soda, first sprinkling it over the batter. Dip out with a ladle, putting the same quantity in each cake, and not enough to make them very large; when very large, they become cold before they can be eaten; nothing is poorer than cold buckwheat cakes. Hot separate plates should be placed for serving them in, and nice syrup and drawn butter put upon the table, to be eaten with them (if liked); only one or two for each person should be sent in at once. And in taking them from the griddle always put them upon a hot plate.

---

534. *Buckwheat Cakes Without Yeast.*—Make the batter, as in the above receipt, with sweet milk; dissolve in the milk two heaped teaspoonfuls of cream of tartar; teaspoonful of soda; it should be thinner than when made with yeast. Mix the batter just before using it; fry immediately after adding the soda, and if a large quantity is made, divide the batter and soda; put half of the soda in one vessel; use this, and add the second portion to the remainder of the batter; or use sour milk and soda.

---

535. *Superior Wheat Flour Batter Cakes.*—One quart measure of flour, three parts full; three tablespoonfuls of sifted corn meal, two or three eggs, beaten separately; make a moderately stiff batter with sweet milk, two teaspoonfuls of soda sifted with the flour and meal, one teaspoonful of tartaric acid dissolved in water, or a heaped dessert-spoon of yeast powder; stir the soda in just before frying; never stir after it effervesces. Good cakes may be made by this receipt, substituting sour milk for the acid, and less soda.

---

536. *Rice Griddle Cakes.*—One pint and a half of cold boiled rice; put to soak an hour in warm water enough to cover it. Mash the rice well, and make a batter, just before using, with one quart of sour milk, one light quart of flour, salt to taste, and two eggs well beaten. The batter should be moderately thick. Stir in a teaspoonful of soda just before frying. Fine batter cakes may be made of stale, light bread; trim off the crust; soak the bread, and make it by the above receipt. Sour bread may be used to advantage in this way

---

537. *Another Way to Make Griddle Cakes.*—Dissolve a tea

spoonful of soda in a teacup of buttermilk. Beat well four eggs; stir to them the teacup of soda and buttermilk, and one table spoonful of butter; soften it by setting it on the stove; stir in a quart of flour alternately with two more cups of buttermilk. Bake, turning once; pile them on the griddle, putting a thin slice of butter between each cake.

---

538. *Batter Cake.*—One egg, one dessert-spoonful of butter, one pint of flour, three quarters of a pint of sour milk, a teaspoonful of soda, dissolved in a little warm water; add just before serving; salt to taste.

---

539. *Clabber Cakes.*—One large teacup of clabber, nine tablespoonfuls of sifted flour, salt to taste; let this set an hour before using. Dissolve a teaspoonful of soda in a wineglass of sweet milk; add this last, and fry as batter cakes immediately.

---

540. *Soda Batter Cakes.*—Two eggs well beaten, one tumblerful of sour milk, flour to make a stiff batter, a teaspoonful of soda; or make them of sweet milk and yeast powders, or one teaspoonful of soda, and two of cream of tartar.

---

541. *Hominy Cakes.*—One pint of cold hominy, half a pint of flour, one egg, one tablespoonful of melted lard or butter, sweet milk to make a batter rather thin, a teaspoonful of yeast powder.

---

542. *Batter Cakes Without Eggs.*—To one pint of sifted flour add as much buttermilk as will make a rather stiff batter; salt to taste. Divide the batter in two separate pans; measure a teaspoonful of soda; divide this, putting into one pan half the soda; use this; add the soda to the other pan, and fry from that until the batter is used. Send to the table hot; they are not good if left to stand.

---

543. *Risen Batter Cakes.*—Four eggs well beaten, one pint of

sweet milk, a pint and a half of flour, a teaspoonful of salt, a wineglass of good yeast; make the batter at 9 o'clock at night. In the morning, stir in a small teaspoonful of soda, just before frying.

544. *Rye Batter Cakes.*—Warm two tumblers of sweet milk, with a teaspoonful of salt; beat two eggs well; make a thin batter with rye flour, the eggs and milk well stirred together; add a teaspoonful of soda. Fry in rather small cakes. Rye and corn meal batter cakes should be made thin; flour cakes moderately stiff.

545. *Corn Meal Batter Cakes.*—One egg, one teaspoonful of lard stirred into a tablespoonful of hot mush, salt to taste, one pint of sweet milk, corn meal to make a thin batter, an even teaspoonful of yeast powder (or the yeast powder may be omitted, using another egg); beat them well. These batter cakes may be made of sour milk and soda, but are not generally considered so good. Rice or hominy may be used instead of mush.

546. *Rice Flour Batter Cakes.*—Beat three eggs separately; make a batter rather stiff, by stirring to the yolks of the eggs alternately a large teacup of rice flour and milk. To a tumbler of hot rice, or small hominy well boiled, add a heaped dessert-spoonful of butter or lard; stir in the whites of the eggs beaten to a stiff froth; mix well with the yolks. Fry on the griddle.

547. *Rye Bread.*—One pint of rye flour, one of good corn meal, salt to taste, a piece of lard or butter as large as a walnut, a teacup of good yeast, milk or water to make a stiff dough; work it well; set it to rise; when well risen, form into loaves; let it rise again. Bake in a moderately quick oven.

548. *Rye Drop Cakes.*—Two eggs well beaten, a pint of rye flour, salt to taste, a teaspoonful of sugar, sweet milk to make a rather

thin batter, a teaspoonful of yeast powder stirred in last. Bake in small shallow tin pans in a quick oven. Or mix one pint of rye flour, one of corn meal, one tablespoonful of syrup; mix with milk a teaspoonful of yeast powder; let it remain an hour before baking.

---

549. *Buttermilk Cakes.*—One quart of flour and an even teaspoonful of soda sifted together, a heaped teaspoonful of salt; rub into the flour well a piece of lard or butter the size of a large hen's egg; wet to a rather soft dough with buttermilk; work until the dough is smooth; roll out an inch thick; cut, by pressing a saucer on the dough; cut around with a sharp knife. When all are cut, prick them with a fork, and bake in a quick oven.

---

550. *Short Hoe Cakes.*—One quart of flour and one teaspoonful of salt dissolved in a wineglass of water; rub in the flour till thoroughly mixed; a large tablespoonful of butter or lard; pour in the salt; wet up with cold water; only work the dough enough to be smooth; roll an inch thick or less, and bake.

Another way: To one pound of flour rub in well three-quarters of a pound of butter and one teaspoonful of salt. Beat the yolks of two eggs well; pour to the eggs half a tumbler of sweet milk; stir them well together; wet up the flour with it to a rather soft dough; use more milk, if necessary. Handle the dough lightly, and very little. Roll into round cakes; prick them with a fork; bake in a moderately hot oven.

---

551. *Johnny Cake.*—One pint of boiled rice or hominy, one egg, one tablespoonful of butter, salt to taste, flour enough to make a soft dough; roll half an inch thick; bake quick, without blistering; serve hot. Tear the cakes open, and butter. Cut the cakes four inches long and three wide.

---

552. *Corn Meal Johnny Cakes.*—Make three tumblers of sifted corn meal into a soft dough with one egg well beaten, and mixed

with a pint of sweet milk; salt to taste. Spread the dough over a hot griddle. When one side is a light brown, turn it; serve hot, sending to the table only one at a time; let others succeed rapidly until all are served.

553. *Plain Corn Bread.*—Plain corn bread should be made with cold water; the dough stiff, and well worked with the hand; made into pones; baked in a hot oven, and not allowed to remain in the oven until the crust becomes too hard to be eaten.

554. *Victoria Wafers.*—One pint of sweet milk, one teaspoonful of salt, one teaspoonful of butter, flour enough to make a very thin batter. The wafer-irons should be very shallow.

555. *Corn Meal Wafers.*—Three tablespoonfuls of sifted corn meal, one tablespoonful of flour, one of melted lard, salt to taste; sweet milk to make a thin batter. Fry a light brown color in shallow irons. These must be eaten as soon as fried; they become tough very soon. The irons should always be hot and well greased before the batter is put in.

556. *Wafers.*—To a quart of sifted flour, rub in three-quarters of a pound of fresh butter. Dissolve a large teaspoonful of salt in a tumbler of cold water; wet the dough with this. Use more water if necessary to make a moderately stiff dough; work it very little; divide into pieces, which, when rolled very thin, will just cover the inside of the wafer-irons. Heat the irons and grease them; lay in the dough; close the irons tightly. Should the dough be too large for the irons, trim it off after they are closed. Lay on hot embers; turn in two or three minutes. They should be of a light brown. If properly made and cooked are very crisp and nice. The dough may also be rolled the size of a saucer, and baked in an oven or stove; or cut in diamond-shapes and fried in boiling lard; taken up with a perforated skimmer and served on a napkin.

557. *Milk Toast*.—Cut four slices from a stale loaf; place them in a toaster, or prop them before the fire, turning each piece until a light brown color. Have a pan ready with a tumblerful of hot sweet milk. Dip each slice in quickly; lay one upon the bottom of a hot dish; lay over thin slices of fresh butter, then another piece of toast, until all are arranged in this way. Send, under a cover, to table. Toast should be eaten when fresh made.

Another way: Toast the slices; dip them in hot water or milk, and pour over a small teacup of melted butter, for three long slices. The butter should only be set in boiling water, and remain until melted. It should never be set immediately upon the fire.

Another way: Cut from a round or square loaf of stale bread, four slices a quarter of an inch thick. Toast them (using toasting-forks) a yellowish brown color; put them in a hot dish that will hold them without dividing. Put in a stew-pan a pint of rich, sweet milk, and a quarter of a pound of butter, a teaspoonful of salt, a tablespoonful of flour made into a paste, with a little cold milk added as the milk in the stew-pan boils up; simmer two or three minutes; pour over the toast, and serve immediately.

---

558. *Queen's Toast*.—Toast the bread by the foregoing receipts. Beat together two eggs; pour to them gradually, and mixing well, a pint of milk. Have ready half a pound of sweet lard or butter, boiling; soak the bread until it looks entirely moistened with the milk and egg, but not until it is so saturated as to fall to pieces. Drop the toast into the boiling lard; turn the pieces; very little frying is necessary; serve upon a soft napkin, with cream sauce or good syrup. This may be made of very stale bread without toasting, merely frying it.

---

559. *Toast and Cheese*.—Butter the bread; grate cheese, and spread thickly upon it; toast before the fire; serve hot.

Another way: Put two ounces of cheese (sliced thin, if soft;

grated, it hard), a piece of butter the size of a hen's egg, into a stew-pan or chafing-dish; whip together an egg and a wineglass of Madeira. When the cheese and butter melt, stir in the egg and wine gradually, mixing it well. Season with pepper and nutmeg, if liked. Spread immediately upon hot toast, and serve.

Another way: Toast the bread on both sides, and butter it; toast a slice of cheese on one side; lay that next the bread; toast the other side with a salamander or hot oven-lid; spread over French mustard; serve hot. These preparations must be eaten as soon as ready; if kept, the toast becomes hard; this may be remedied by pouring over a little hot cream and butter sauce. Dry toast should not be prepared until the moment it is wanted.

---

560. *To make Stale Bread Taste as if Fresh.*—Steam the bread, not permitting the water to reach it. When thoroughly hot, wrap it in a thin cloth, and stand it on the end. A stale loaf tied in a cloth and boiled an hour, makes a nice pudding. Use a rich butter sauce.

---

561. *To Boil Grits.*—Wash them in several waters, rubbing between the hands well until all the bran is separated from the white of the grain. When perfectly white and clean, pour over boiling water; let it set a few moments. Put the grits to boil in a well-covered stew-pan (lined with tin or porcelain is best); cover with plenty of water. Salt the water to taste; boil until the grain is soft, keeping the cover on. Should there be too much water when the grits are nearly done, take off the cover until the water is sufficiently reduced; if there is a deficiency, supply it by adding hot water. Grits should be boiled slowly, to give them time to swell, and plenty of water used. The hominy when done should be moist, neither very dry nor wet.

---

562. *Hominy Cakes.*—Mash a tumbler of cold hominy with a teaspoonful of butter; work into it the yolk of one egg; form the

cakes by packing in a wineglass; roll them in flour; fry in plenty of hot lard. Salt to taste.

---

563. *Ley Hominy.*—To a gallon of shelled corn, add a quart of strong ley. Boil together until the husks begin to come off the corn; rub the grains of corn between the hands, to entirely remove the husk; wash it well, and boil in plenty of water until the grains are soft. It requires long boiling. As water may be needed, replenish with *hot* water. Boil in it sufficient salt to season. When nearly done, stir it from the bottom to prevent its burning. Before using it, mash it slightly with a wooden mallet, and fry in a small quantity of lard or butter. It will keep several days in cold weather. Put it in a covered earthen bowl or jar. Very fine hominy is made by pounding the grains of corn in a large wooden mortar. It is moistened with a little warm water to facilitate the removal of the husk, and fanned several times during the process. When the grains are sufficiently cracked and free of husk, wash it well and boil until soft. Boil salt in the hominy. Keep it in an earthen dish, covered. When wanted for the table, mash the grains and fry in lard or butter until the side next the pan has formed a good crust; lay a plate upon it and invert the frying-pan, or it may be seasoned with butter and only kept on the fire until hot. These are nutritious dishes for breakfast. The large hominies are used principally in cold weather, grits or small hominy all the year round, being fresh-boiled every day.

---

564. *Macaroni.*—Wash half a pound of macaroni; boil it in plenty of water until tender; lay in a shallow earthen dish a layer of the macaroni (the pieces should be broken the same size), one of grated cheese, and salt to taste. Lay over slices of butter; cover with sweet milk or cream. Bake in a moderate oven, ten or fifteen minutes. Serve hot. Another way is, to arrange alternate layers of boiled macaroni and grated cheese. Pour over a custard made of three well-beaten eggs, two table

spoonfuls of stale grated bread, one tablespoonful of butter, and half a teacup of cream or sweet milk. Bake half an hour, or until the custard is set. If boiled too long, it will lose its shape; if baked too much, it will be dry and tough. It may be boiled tender, put in a shallow dish with alternate layers of cheese, covered with milk, bread crumbs over this, and over these thin slices of butter. Bake until the butter melts and the bread crumbs are slightly brown.

---

565. *Dr. Kitchiner's Macaroni Pudding.*—Simmer half a pound of macaroni in plenty of water (salted to taste) until tender, but not enough to lose its form or make it too soft; strain the water from it; beat up the yolks of five eggs, the whites of two. Take a half pint of good rich cream, a breast of cold fowl, three slices of cold ham; mince the meat fine; grate three tablespoonfuls of Parmesan or Cheshire cheese; season with pepper and salt. Mix these with the macaroni. Put all into a buttered pudding-mould; set this in a pan of boiling water, and let it steam an hour. A double kettle may be used. Serve hot with rich gravy. To make the gravy: Two yolks of eggs; half teaspoonful of salt; one lemon cut up, seeds removed; tablespoonful of butter. Season with white pepper. Put it on the fire until the butter melts, stirring constantly, or the egg will curdle; stir to this a tumbler of sweet cream, boiling hot. Serve immediately. If sweet milk is used instead of cream, melt a teaspoonful of butter in it. This makes a nice fish sauce when well seasoned.

---

566. *To Make Vermicelli.*—Thicken three or four eggs with flour to a stiff dough; roll it in thin sheets; the thinner the better. Spread them to dry, turning them. When dry, which may be done before the fire or in the sun (it will require at least an hour—it is important they should be very dry), roll each piece like a scroll, and shave it in thin slices; shake these apart. When the soup is nearly done, boil them in it a quarter of an hour. What

remains, if all is not needed, may be kept two or three days in a dry place.

---

567. *Cheese Stewed.*—If the cheese is hard, grate it; if soft, cut it in thin slices. To a quarter of a pound, add a tumbler of sweet milk, half a teaspoonful of salt, and half a tumbler of fine bread crumbs. Rub a teaspoonful of mustard flour or French mustard into the butter, half a teaspoonful of pepper (white pepper is best); put these ingredients into a stew-pan lined with porcelain or tin; stew until the cheese melts. Beat an egg well, stirring it rapidly and thoroughly into the cheese. Let it remain on the fire one minute; pour into a deep dish and serve immediately. Dry grated cheese is a pretty supper dish; shape it in wineglasses; turn upon a flat dish.

---

568. *Welsh Rarebit (called Rabbit) to be Prepared on the Table.*—Cut or grate a tumblerful of good cheese. Put it in a chafing-dish; add a piece of butter the size of a large hen's egg; light the lamp to the chafing-dish; put it in the proper place. Stir the cheese and butter together until they have melted; season with salt and pepper. Now stir to the cheese a wineglass of good Madeira wine, and one well beaten egg; mix these to a smooth paste. Remove the lamp, and serve. Thin dry toast should be served with the cheese.

---

569. *Eggs.*—To boil, should be fresh. If put in tepid water, four minutes will set the whites, five minutes will set the yolk, ten minutes will boil them hard. When put in boiling water, the white hardens too fast for the yolk; tepid or warm water is best. I have sometimes boiled them in this way: Place the eggs in cold water; when the water first begins to bubble, the whites will be well set. Fresh-laid eggs require longer boiling than those a little old. Large eggs require more time than those of less size,

570. *To Scramble Eggs.*—Put a teacup of sweet milk into a stew-pan; rub a teaspoonful of flour into a piece of butter the size of an egg; add this to the milk; salt to taste. Beat half a dozen eggs light; stir to the milk. As soon as the whites are well set, pour over buttered toast. Serve hot. The toast may be omitted. This is a much more delicate way of cooking than to scramble them in lard or butter without the milk.

---

571. *To Poach Eggs.*—Have a pan or skillet half full of boiling water; break as many fresh eggs into it as will lie side by side, they should not touch; let them remain undisturbed until the whites are set well. Take them up when done; trim the ragged parts, so as to make the eggs round. Pour over each egg a teaspoonful of melted butter. In taking them up, use a perforated skimmer.

---

572. *To Fry Eggs.*—Put a piece of lard or butter the size of a large walnut in a frying-pan; put this on the fire. When the lard is hot, break the eggs one by one carefully into the lard; sprinkle over salt and pepper. When the eggs are done, take them up immediately; serve with fried ham. When the eggs are not perfectly fresh, break each one into a saucer before cooking; one bad egg will spoil all the rest. Do not turn them.

---

573. *To Fricassee Eggs.*—Boil them ten minutes, or entirely hard. Take them up, and drop them into cold water until they are cool enough to remove the shell. Beat up one raw egg; roll the hard-boiled first in the raw egg, then in bread crumbs; let them dry, turning them. Fry in hot lard. Serve as an accompaniment to roast or baked meat, with rich gravy. They may be cut in half; remove the yolk, and fill each end with a rich force-meat; join them or not, as preferred; roll in raw beaten eggs; then in bread crumbs, and fry.

---

574. *Another Way.*—Boil them hard; cut a slice off the large end, so that the egg will set firmly, first removing the shell; arrange them tastefully upon a small circular dish; garnish with sprigs of parsley. Serve with rich gravy. Eggs are good boiled hard, and cut in slices, with a sauce made of one white onion, sliced thin, and fried slightly in a dessert-spoonful of butter, into which has been stirred a teaspoonful of flour, half a teaspoonful of salt, the same of pepper. When the onion has stewed two or three minutes, pour in, slowly (stirring), a tumbler of sweet milk. Chop very fine two sprigs of parsley; add it to the sauce. Let all stew five minutes; put the eggs in a deep dish; pour over the sauce. A very good accompaniment to boiled meats. It is very fine, eaten with cauliflower or white cabbage.

575. *Pickled Eggs.*—Have ready a quart of good apple vinegar, by scalding in it one dozen cloves, half a nutmeg, a dozen grains of allspice, half a teaspoonful of pepper, two teaspoonfuls of flour of mustard. Boil a dozen eggs hard; shell them, and lay in a glass jar; pour over the hot vinegar; turn them occasionally; keep the jar well covered. Serve with pressed or collared meat, head-cheese, Hunter's beef, etc.

567. *Omelette.*—Break six eggs separately; beat the whites to a stiff froth; stir the yolks well; season with one teaspoonful of salt, half a teaspoonful of pepper, a tablespoonful of parsley minced fine. Put into a stew-pan one tumbler of sweet milk, reserving a wineglassful of the cold milk to wet into a paste a tablespoonful of flour. When the milk is boiling hot, stir in the paste; let it simmer two minutes; take it from the fire; add to it a tablespoonful of butter. When the butter dissolves, and the milk is blood warm, stir it to the yolks; half a tumbler of grated ham, cold beef tongue, dried grated beef, or venison, or cheese may be added if liked; very little minced onion may be used, if the flavor is agreeable. The parsley, onion, grated ham, etc., may all be omitted if not liked. Add the well-beaten whites last. Have a small frying-pan ready. It

should be well washed, and rubbed very dry; put in the pan a teaspoonful of fresh butter; set it on a moderate fire; while the butter is heating, beat to the eggs half a teaspoonful of yeast powders. Fry on one side; hold over the upper side a hot oven-lid or a salamander; roll the omelette. *Serve upon a hot dish.* They should not be piled. Send two or three to the table at each time of sending. An omelette should be half an inch or more thick; should not be greasy, burnt, or kept upon the fire until too hard; a light brown is the proper color. When it is not convenient to use yeast powders, substitute soda and cream of tartar—an even teaspoonful of cream of tartar, and a quarter of a teaspoonful of soda. It requires two persons to fry the omelettes and manage the salamander; it should be done very expeditiously, as well as carefully. It is not necessary to roll them; some persons prefer it should not be done.

577. *Rice Omelette—Mrs. B.'s Receipt.*—One teacup of boiled rice, one teacup of sweet milk, three eggs well beaten, a level tablespoonful of butter; season with grated ham, a little minced onion, pepper, and salt to taste. Bake a light brown; much cooking will spoil it.

578. *To Boil Rice.*—Pick out all discolored grains; wash it well in two waters; soak an hour before boiling. Twenty minutes before serving, stir it slowly into boiling water, previously salted. One pint of rice will require four tumblers of water. When done, pour immediately into a clean colander, and set it upon the coolest part of the stove. Toss it up lightly with a silver or wooden fork. Every grain should stand distinct. Boil it in an open stew-pan, lined with tin or porcelain. This is the way it should be cooked when eaten with meats.

A healthful and favorite dish for children, is to boil it in water until half done, using less water than in the first receipt; then add sweet milk, a spoonful of butter, and two or three eggs; sweeten, and spice to taste. Cold rice may be used in a variety of ways: Sliced and fried, seasoned as croquets, moulded in a wineglass, or in any way liked; rolled in flour, and fried; made into custards, batter bread and batter cakes, waffles, stuffing, etc.

---

579. *Sandwich.*—Slice loaf bread or cold biscuit; butter one side very thin; lay upon this thin slices of lean ham, or any kind of fresh meat or poultry; roll the bread. Serve for tea or lunch.

Another way: Slice the bread very thin; grate a quarter of a pound of dry cold ham; mix with a tablespoonful of pickle minced very fine, a teaspoonful of mustard, half a teaspoonful of pepper, cream, a tablespoonful of butter slightly heaped; add to it the ham and seasoning; mix well, and put a layer between the slices of bread. Anchovies and sardines picked from the bones, prepared in the same way, are good; also spiced oysters, shrimps, etc.; they should be minced fine. Grated beef tongue makes excellent sandwich. Never use gristle or tough pieces of meat. The yolks of hard-boiled eggs (one to each tablespoonful of butter) grated and creamed with the butter, is an improvement.

PASTRY.

"Whether rich or poor, young or old, married or single, a woman is always liable to be called to the performance of every kind of domestic duty, as well as to be placed at the head of a family; and nothing short of a *practical* knowledge of the details of housekeeping can ever make those duties easy, or render her competent to direct others in the performance of them.

"How indispensable a part of female education is Domestic Economy! How absolutely such knowledge is needed in this land of *freedom* and *independence*, where riches cannot exempt the mistress of a family from the difficulty of procuring efficient aid, and where perpetual change of domestics renders perpetual instruction and superintendence necessary."

---

580. *Puff Paste, No. 1.* — Never attempt this in warm weather unless you are supplied with ice; then keep the butter in ice-water until hard and firm. Mix it in a cool place, as far as possible from the fire, and use ice-water to wet the flour. Handle as little as possible, and, after the dough is formed, put it in a pan; cover it with a towel, and set the pan upon ice. In winter it is less difficult to make. Sift one pound and a quarter of flour; reserve the quarter of a pound. Work all the buttermilk out of a pound of butter, which divide into four equal parts. Rub one-fourth of it into the pound of flour until it has a granulated look. Wet this into a smooth dough a little stiffish, with a tumblerful of cold water in which has been dissolved a teaspoonful of salt. Subdivide the remaining three-fourths of the butter so as to form six parts. Roll out the dough half an inch thick; upon which place one of the sheets of butter, rolled to just the size of the dough; sprinkle this with part of the reserved flour;

fold twice, and turn so that the points will be to and from you. Flour the rolling-pin, and, pressing evenly upon it, roll *from* you until half an inch thick. Great care is necessary to prevent the butter from bursting through. Repeat this process as many times as there are divisions of butter; and as the necessary handling will impart a little warmth to the dough, and as it is important that it should be *kept* as cool as possible, after each rolling place it upon a dish or pan, and set it upon ice or in a cool place for a quarter of an hour at least; a longer time if the delay will not be inconvenient. In two hours use it, cutting off just enough for each pie. A plainer crust is better for an under crust, using the puff paste only for covering, or to make open tartlets or puffs. *Handle as little as possible;* use, in rolling, *only* flour enough to prevent surfaces of the dough from adhering to the pastry-board or rolling-pin. For a pastry-board, marble is *decidedly* best; but well-seasoned poplar will answer. Judgment must be used in wetting up the dough, as some flour requires more water, some less.

---

581. *A very Light, Crisp Paste, No. 2.*—To a pound of sifted flour allow three-quarters of a pound of butter; reserve a tumblerful of flour to use in rolling. In wetting it up, use the white of one egg beaten to a stiff froth, and enough water to make it into a stiffish dough. Then manage in all respects as directed in the foregoing receipt. Pastry should be made soon in the morning. Have everything in readiness before beginning, as the work cannot be done too expeditiously.

---

582. *A Good, Plain Crust, No. 3.*—A quart of sifted flour, a quarter of a pound of lard, the same of butter, a teaspoonful of salt; reserve a little of the flour to use in rolling; work the butter into the remainder. Dissolve a piece of sal-volatile the size of a large nutmeg in half a tumbler of water; add this to the flour, using as much more cold water as is necessary to wet the dough to a proper consistence; roll the dough; spread half the lard upon it, to within half an inch of the edge, turning up the edge to pre

vent the lard from oozing out. Sprinkle with flour; fold twice, and roll. Repeat this process with the remaining lard, and set in a cool place for half an hour or more before using. This answers well for an under crust where the real puff paste is used for the upper.

---

583. *A Good Crust for Meat Pies, No. 4.*—Half a pound of lard rubbed into a quart of flour; dissolve a teaspoonful of soda in a wineglassful of water; add this to the flour, and wet up with sour milk to a smooth dough.

---

584. *An Easy Way of Making Crust for Plain Family Pies, No. 5.*—Use the weight of nine eggs in flour, and of four eggs in lard or butter. If butter is used, the weight of eight eggs in flour will be enough.

---

585. *Potato Paste for Dumplings, No. 6.*—One pint of Irish potatoes mashed and strained; double the quantity of sifted flour; an even tumblerful of good, firm butter; wet up with sour milk, into which has been stirred enough soda to sweeten it.

---

586. *A Plainer Potato Paste, No. 7.*—Equal quantities of mashed Irish potatoes and sifted flour; wet up with sour cream, into which has been stirred sufficient soda to sweeten it. Always use salt in making dough—a teaspoonful to a quart of flour.

---

587. *A Suet Paste for Boiled Dumplings, No. 8.*—Pick and chop fine half a pound of beef suet; add to it a pound and a quarter of sifted flour and a teaspoonful of salt. Mix up with a tumblerful of sweet milk or water. Beat it well to incorporate the suet and flour.

---

588. *A Potato Paste for Meat Stews, No. 9.*—A common-sized tumblerful of mashed potatoes rubbed through a colander; add sufficient flour to enable you to roll well; salt as you judge suffi-

cient—about a teaspoonful. Flour your board and pin well before rolling.

---

589. *Risen Paste, No.* 10.—Dough, made as for light rolls, *after it has risen well*, makes a good crust for meat pies, and for common fruit pies and dumplings.

Pastry should be baked in a quick oven; not, however, hot enough to blister or scorch. Should there be any appearance of that, protect it with a sheet of letter paper.

Never use rancid butter or lard!

In *summer* it is extremely difficult to make good puff paste. Fruits, custards, and puddings, are much more easily prepared, and make more elegant desserts.

In baking fruit pies be very careful not to let the juice spill in the oven. The burnt syrup imparts a disagreeable taste. It is well to elevate the plates a little above the bottom of the stove or oven, to prevent burning the under crust.

PIES.

590. *Cranberry Pie.*—Pick the unsound fruit out carefully; wash and stew until soft; sweeten to taste. Line pie-plates with a good puff paste; fill three-fourths full with the fruit, always heaping it a little in the middle. Put in not quite a tumblerful of the juice; put over an upper crust, pinching the edges well together, and cutting a slit in the middle to allow the steam to escape. When done, sprinkle thickly with pulverized loaf sugar, and serve with cream sauce, flavored with nutmeg.

---

591. *Blackberry Pie.*—Gather the berries carefully, without bruising, as they are better without being washed. Line a pie-plate with good crust. Put in a layer of the berries, then one of sugar, and dust over with a little flour. (Five tablespoonfuls of good brown sugar and an even tablespoonful of flour will be sufficient for a large pie.) In this way fill the plate nearly full, heaping the fruit a little in the middle; add half a tumbler of water, and put on the upper crust, pinching the edges together, and cutting a slit in the centre; serve with cream sauce. This sauce is a good accompaniment to all fruit pies.

Any kind of fruit pies, such as cherries, raspberries, plums, etc., are made by the foregoing. A coat of grated or pulverized sugar gives a nice finish to the pie.

---

592. *Apple Pie, No.* 1.—Line a deep plate with good crust, first greasing the plate slightly. Cut in thin slices ripe, juicy apples; fill the plate, putting in alternately apples, sugar, and spice (a tumbler of brown sugar will season a quart of apples of pleasant taste); grate over half a nutmeg, the same of cinnamon, the same of coriander seed (if they are liked), half a tumbler of water; put over the upper crust. Bake three-quarters of an hour.

593. *Apple Pie, No. 2.*—Fill a soup-plate with tart apples sliced thin; pile the apples up in the middle; put over them a crust of good pastry, greasing the edge of the plate slightly to prevent the crust sticking; trim the dough off evenly, allowing size sufficient to cover the apples well. Let it bake until the crust is a light brown color and the fruit tender. Remove the crust carefully, first passing a knife between the plate and crust. Invert the crust; season the fruit to taste, and spread it upon the crust; grate nutmeg over. Eat with rich cream or mock-cream sauce.

---

594. *Mock-Apple Pie.*—One large grated lemon, three large soda crackers, two even tablespoonfuls of butter, two teacups of sugar, one egg, a wineglass of water poured over the crackers. These will make two pies, baked with two crusts.

---

595. *Peach Pie.*—These may be made like apple pie. There is a very popular pie for common, every-day use, called "Cut and Come Again." To make it: Line the inside of an oven with risen dough or paste made by Receipt No. 4. Fill the oven with good, ripe, juicy peaches, sliced thin; put in a little water; cover with a crust, and bake in a moderate oven until the crust is done; remove the upper crust; sweeten and spice the fruit; spread it upon the upper crust, and lay the side crust around. This is best cold, and may be kept in a cool place for several days. Eat with cream sauce.

---

596. *Rhubarb Pie.*—Take the tender stalks of the rhubarb; remove the skin; cut the pieces an inch long. Line the pie-plate with paste; put a layer of rhubarb and a layer of sugar, sprinkled over thick; continue this until the paste is nearly filled. Sprinkle grated lemon peel and pulverized coriander seed between each layer for flavoring; a heaped teaspoonful of flour to each pie sprinkled between the layers; add half a teacup of water; put on an upper crust, pinch the edges down carefully, and

cut a slit in the centre. Bake *slowly* an hour. In all pies where there is not sufficient fruit to prevent the crust from falling in, before placing on the upper crust, cross three stout straws on the top of the pie-plate to support the crust. When the pie is done, the crust may be loosened with a pen-knife or other small instrument sufficiently to enable you to remove the straws. Tin plates are better than earthen for baking pies.

---

597. *Sliced Potato Pie.*—For baking this, a plate deeper than the common pie-plate is necessary. Bake medium-sized sweet potatoes not quite done; yams are best. Line the plate with good paste; slice the potatoes; place a layer upon the bottom of the plate; over this sprinkle thickly a layer of good brown sugar; over this place thin slices of butter, and sprinkle with flour, seasoning with spices to the taste. A heaped tablespoonful of butter and a heaped teaspoonful of flour will be sufficient for one pie. Put on another of potatoes, piled a little in the middle. Mix together equal quantities of wine and water, lemon juice and water, or vinegar and water, and pour in enough to half fill the pie; sprinkle over the potato a little flour, and place on the upper crust, pinching the edges carefully together. Cut a slit in the centre, and bake slowly for one hour.

---

598. *Imitation of Mince Pie.*—An excellent imitation of mince pie may be made by placing between the layers of potatoes a layer of raisins, currants, and chopped apples, seasoning precisely as for a mince pie.

---

599. *Pie-Melon Pie.*—Peel the fruit and cut out all the seed part; cut in slices about a quarter of an inch thick; scald them. Put them in a stew-pan, and cover with cold water, in which has been dissolved enough of tartaric acid to make it pleasantly acid. When the fruit is tender, sweeten it to taste, and bake between two crusts. A little grated lemon peel may be added, if liked.

600. *Mince-Meat Pies.*—To prepare the meat: Chop fine two pounds of lean, tender beef, cold, boiled, or baked; remove all skin and gristle. (The tongue and heart of a very young beef, boiled tender, makes the *best* mince-meat.) Mince fine half a pound of suet, one pound of raisins, seeded; one pound of dried currants, washed and picked; half a pound of citron, sliced thin, the same of candied orange or lemon peel; one pound of clean, moist brown sugar; the juice of six lemons, the rinds grated (throw away the pulp); two nutmegs beaten; one ounce of salt, one of ground ginger, the same of coriander seed, pounded and sifted; half an ounce of allspice and cloves each. Mix the meat, fruits, and spices well. Pour upon the sugar a pint of wine and half a pint of brandy; add the fruits to the meat; pour over the wine and brandy. When it is well mixed, pack it in small jars, and pour over the top of the meat the best syrup an inch thick; cover closely, and keep the jars in a cool place. When ready to make the pies, line pie-plates with a good crust; add to a pint of the mixture a pint of tart apples chopped, a wine-glass of rose-water. Fill the crust half full; lay over bits of butter; put in more meat to nearly fill the plate; cover with puff paste; cut a slit in the middle, and bake. They keep well. Warm them before using. I have eaten very good mince pies made of the flesh of rabbits. Cold fowls are sometimes used to make pies for immediate use. An excellent way to keep the meat a few weeks is to spice the meat, pack it away, covering closely with syrup, and add the fruits, wine, and brandy when the pies are made.

Mince pies without meat may be made of apples, using the mince-meat seasoning. Sweet potatoes, sliced or grated (half done), are good used in the same way.

Never attempt to keep the meat more than a month or six weeks in this climate.

---

601 *Remarks upon Pies and Tarts.*—Pies are sometimes brought to the table looking very awkwardly, caused by the

upper crust being cut too small. To prevent this, roll out the paste for the covering; fold it as you remove it from the board; lay on the pie one half; then turn the other half over; press around the edge of the plate; do not pull the dough; if too large, trim it by slanting the knife towards you; notch the edge of the pie with the back of the knife-blade, or pinch the upper and lower crust together.

Tarts differ from pies in this respect: they are baked without an upper crust. Sometimes the fruit is baked with the crust, or the crust may be first baked, and then filled with any kind of stewed or preserved fruit. *Tartlets* are baked in small patty pans, and filled with any kind of preserved fruits or jellies. They should be made of the best puff paste.

---

602. *Icing or Meringue for Tarts.*—A meringue spread upon the top of these open pies gives them a very elegant finish. Make the meringue in this way: Whip the whites of eggs to a stiff froth. To this add, for each egg, a tablespoonful of pulverized loaf sugar. Whip this in, and flavor with lemon, vanilla, or rose-water, or any flavoring preferred. Spread this, with a knife, carefully upon the fruit; return the tart to the oven, and let it remain until the meringue becomes of a very pale brown color. The effect is very fine when the meringue and the crust are of the same shade. (Should the cook, however, inadvertently allow the crust to burn, she need not consider herself obligated to blacken the meringue.) The whites of two large eggs made into a meringue will cover two large tarts.

To ice tarts: Whip the whites of two eggs to a solid froth; spread this over the fruit; sift over it powdered sugar, very thick. Press it down; sprinkle a little water over the sugar, to slightly moisten it. Put the tart in the oven for ten minutes. This is Dr. Kitchiner's receipt, which I have used many years.

Tarts and tartlets are best eaten cold.

PUDDINGS.

"Method is essential to the dispatch of all business; for what is well arranged proceeds with ease and regularity."

I have often been asked, "What is the difference between puddings and custards, as, in the receipts usually given in Cookery Books, there seems but little distinction made?"

My classification is simply this: Puddings are baked without crusts and usually in deeper vessels; are generally served hot and eaten with sauces. Custards, on the contrary, are, as a general thing, baked in rich paste, and usually served cold.

Boiled puddings and custards require no classification.

All puddings made with soda and sour milk should be baked in a quick oven. The eggs should be beaten separately; the flour and whites added alternately, putting in at least a third of the flour last, or the whites will float upon the top, and as soon as the pudding is exposed to the air, will fall. Beat the yolks well; add a little flour and a little salt; then pour in a small quantity of milk, if it is used; pour very little milk at once or the batter will be lumpy. When half of the flour is used with the milk, stir in the whites, beaten to a stiff froth; then the remainder of the flour, and, should any milk remain, stir it in last. Just before baking, if soda is used, sprinkle it over the top and beat it in quickly, or dissolve it in the last milk added. Batter for puddings should always be strained through a hair sieve. No matter how carefully it is prepared, there will be lumps which can be removed only by straining, and which, if allowed to remain, would render the pudding more or less heavy. When fruit is used, it should be prepared the day before it is wanted. Seed the raisins; wash and pick the currants and dry them, so that there will be no hindrance when the hour for making the pudding arrives. Fruit should be floured, or it will sink to the bottom. The oven must not be quite so hot for a fruit pudding as for one without. Should the pudding brown too fast after it has risen and a crust begin to form, lay over it a sheet of letter paper. If the paper is put on too soon, the batter will adhere to it, and, in raising the paper, the crust will be broken.

For boiled puddings, follow the directions for mixing baked puddings. For a bag, use a square of coarse, thick linen. It should be boiled, rinsed well, dried, ironed and put away carefully as soon as used. Strong tape should be kept for tying. Before pouring the batter in, scald the cloth, lay it in a bowl, flour it well and evenly; pour the batter in, gather up the ends carefully, allowing room for it to swell (some kinds of batter require more room than others, corn meal more than wheat flour). Tie securely. Put a small piece of dough (made by stirring a little flour and water together) directly over the place where the cloth is tied, and tie above the dough with a piece of broad tape, so as to make a long loop. Run a flat stick through this loop, strong enough to support the weight of the pudding, and long enough to reach across the top of the vessel in which it is boiled. Suspend the bag in a pot of boiling water so that it will not touch the bottom. It must be completely immersed in water and kept so during the process. Should the water become too much reduced, replenish with boiling water, a kettle of which should be kept for this purpose. When the pudding is taken out of the pot, lay it for a few minutes in cold water, to disengage it from the cloth. All the pans, rolling-pin, board, and strainer, in short, everything to be used must be perfectly clean and ready for use, so that no time is lost in "running round" looking up things. All materials should be fresh and good. In summer lay the eggs in cold water. Always sift and sun the flour, or heat it before the fire.

---

603. *Plain Baked Pudding.*—One pint of sifted flour, a quart of sour milk, and seven eggs. Beat the eggs separately, then stir them together; add the flour, and a little salt (a quarter of a tea-

spoonful), the milk last. Grease the mould in which it is to be baked. Have the oven or stove ready for baking. Stir in a teaspoonful of soda, which has been dissolved in a tablespoonful of warm water; pour the batter into the mould, and bake quick. Eat with liquid sauce.

---

604. *Mrs. W.'s Baked Pudding.*—Eight eggs, beaten separately; eight tablespoonfuls of sifted flour, as full as can be dipped up; three tumblers of sweet milk, a dessert-spoonful of butter; beat well, and bake in a quick oven. Eat with wine sauce.

---

605. *Baked Pudding (excellent).*—Two tumblerfuls of sifted flour, the same of sweet milk, five eggs, beaten separately. Mix the eggs; add the flour; then the milk; strain it. Butter a deep earthen dish; stir rapidly into the batter a teaspoonful of yeast powder, and pour into the dish. Bake in a quick oven. Eat with a liquid sauce. These puddings should be put to bake when the rest of the dinner is ready to be taken up. If long exposed to the air, they fall.

---

606. *Bread Pudding.*—Pour over twelve tablespoonfuls of fine light bread or cracker crumbs, three tumblerfuls of boiling sweet milk. Let it stand covered until half an hour before dinner. Then mix with six eggs well beaten, nine tablespoonfuls of sugar, a small grated lemon, three tablespoonfuls of butter, *not* heaped. Bake in a moderate oven. To ascertain whether a pudding is done, pierce it near the centre with a large straw or knife-blade; if no batter adheres to it, the pudding is done.

---

607. *The Queen of Puddings—Mrs. C.'s Receipt.*—One pint of bread crumbs; pour over them a quart of hot sweet milk; beat a tumbler of sugar to the yolks of four eggs; add to the milk, while warm, a piece of butter the size of a large hen's egg, and the grated rind of a lemon. Mash the bread smoothly. When saturated with the milk, pour it on the eggs, stirring well.

Butter a deep earthen dish; pour this mixture in, and bake until the custard is firm (if baked too long, or if the oven is too hot, it will be watery). Take it out of the oven, and spread over the top a layer of jelly, marmalade, or sweetmeats of any kind. Beat to a stiff froth the whites of four eggs; add to them the lemon juice, and for each egg a tablespoonful of powdered loaf sugar. Pile this over the pudding, and return to the oven long enough to color it a delicate brown. Serve cold with arrow-root or cream sauce.

608. *Cake Pudding.*—Put a layer of stale sponge cake, a layer of raisins, currants and citron mixed, or any kind of fruit liked (apples sliced thin or stewed are very good); another layer of cake. Pour over this a rich custard made of a quart of milk and the yolks of six eggs; sweeten, not so much as for boiled custard. Flavor to taste, and bake. Serve with wine sauce. (Stale rusks may be used for this pudding.)

609. *Bread and Butter Pudding.*—Butter a deep pudding-dish; line the bottom with thin slices of light bread, well buttered; upon this, a thick layer of currants, raisins, and citron; another layer of buttered bread. Make a custard by beating six or eight eggs, with a quarter of a pound of nice sugar and a quart of milk. Pour half this custard on the bread in the pudding-dish, and let it stand half an hour. Pour over the remainder of the custard, and bake in a moderate oven. Large crackers may be split and buttered, and used in the same way. Serve with mock cream or arrowroot sauce.

610. *Poor Man's Pudding.*—Pour one quart of hot sweet milk over a pint of stale bread or biscuit crumbs; let them soak an hour; sweeten to taste. Beat two eggs well; mix with the bread; stir all well. Season with orange peel, dried, beaten fine and sifted. Bake half an hour, just as dinner is ready. It should be eaten as soon as done, with solid butter sauce.

611. Chambliss Pudding.—Three eggs, a small teacup of butter, a teacup of crushed sugar, two teacups of sifted flour. Beat the yolks of the eggs with the sugar; cream the butter and flour together, adding the flour as in making a cake; add the whites last. A dessert-spoonful of yeast powder. Pour in a buttered pan, and bake in a quick oven. Eat with transparent sauce.

612. Buttermilk Pudding.—Six eggs, beaten separately; four teacups (common-sized) of sugar, beaten with the yolks of the eggs; cream one and a half teacups of butter; add, alternately, the eggs and six teacups of sifted flour; thin with a teacup and a half of sour buttermilk. Flavor with lemon. Stir in last a teaspoonful of soda. Eat with sauce.

613. Molasses Pudding.—One pint of good syrup, a common-sized teacup not quite full of melted butter, two well-beaten eggs, a tablespoonful of ginger, one tumblerful of sour milk, and a teaspoonful of soda; mix all together, with flour enough to make a batter the consistence of pound-cake batter. Bake for an hour, in a deep, buttered pan. Turn it out; grate sugar over it, and eat with a rich sauce.

614. French Black Pudding.—Beat the yolks of four eggs, with a teacup of good brown sugar; add alternately enough flour to make a batter the consistence of pound-cake, one tumblerful of good syrup, and half a tumbler of sour milk. Pour into the batter, when well mixed, a gill of brandy. Stir in a teaspoonful of soda, then the whites of the eggs, beaten to a froth. Grease a pan; pour in the batter; bake quick. Turn it out; grate loaf sugar over it, and serve with wine sauce.

615. Taylor Pudding.—One cup of butter, creamed; two cups of sugar, beaten with the yolks of four eggs. Add this to the butter; stir all well together; add alternately the whites, beaten to a stiff froth, and six even teacupfuls of sifted flour; thin with two cups of buttermilk. Dissolve a large teaspoonful (not heaped) of soda in a wineglass of warm water, and add last. Bake in a quick oven, not hot enough to scorch. Eat with liquid sauce.

---

616. *Charleston Pudding.*—Beat six eggs separately, adding three teacups of crushed sugar to the yolks. Cream together four teacups of flour, one of butter, and one of sweet milk. Sift a teaspoonful of soda with the flour. Dissolve two teaspoonfuls of cream of tartar in a small wineglass of cold water. Add, lastly, the whites beaten to a stiff froth; stir them in lightly. All the beating to the pudding must be done before the whites are added. Bake, and turn out. Sift over it fine loaf sugar. Eat with sauce.

---

617. *Corn Meal Pudding, No.* 1.—One pint of sifted meal, one tumbler of good molasses, one pint of sweet milk, a quarter of a pound of butter, grated lemon peel or powdered mace to flavor it. Boil the milk; while hot, pour it upon the meal, and mix well. Warm the butter. Stir to the molasses half a teaspoonful of soda. Beat the eggs separately; add the eggs when the mush is cold. Mix all well. Bake in a buttered dish. Eat with a rich liquid sauce.

---

618. *Corn Meal Pudding without Eggs.*—Seven heaped tablespoonfuls of sifted corn meal, two dessert-spoonfuls of lard or butter, heaped; a tumblerful of molasses, two teaspoonfuls of powdered ginger, a quart of hot sweet milk. Mix well, and pour into a buttered dish, and just as it is put into the oven, stir in not quite a tumblerful of cold water. Bake half an hour. Serve with a rich sauce.

---

619. *Apple Pudding* (*excellent*).—Peel and core eight or nine pleasantly acid apples, of rather small or medium size. Put them into a stew-pan with half a tumbler of water, a wineglass

of wine, a heaped tablespoonful of crushed sugar, a small stick of cinnamon, a blade of mace, a little lemon peel. Put the cover on the stew-pan, and stew slowly, until the apples are tender. Take them up, and let them get cold. Fill the bottom of an earthen dish with the apples, and pour over them a rich custard made by beating together the yolks of eight eggs, and the whites of four. Scald a quart of milk; sweeten to taste, and stir to the eggs slowly, stirring constantly. Bake in a moderate oven. An oven too hot will make the custard watery. Serve with solid sauce, if the pudding is eaten hot; liquid sauce, if cold.

A similar pudding may be made by pouring over the apples a thin batter, instead of a custard. The proportions for this are one tumblerful of sifted flour, three tumblerfuls of milk, four eggs, beaten together. Make a smooth batter, and pour over the apples when they are cold.

---

620. *Apple Pudding*, No. 2.—Butter thickly the inside of a small earthen baking-dish; cover the bottom and sides thickly with grated bread crumbs; press them on. Nearly fill the dish with acid apples stewed, spiced, and sweetened. Cover half an inch thick with bread crumbs; lay over bits of butter. Bake slowly half an hour. Turn out, and eat with sauce.

---

621. *Tapioca Pudding*, No. 1.—Pour a quart of milk over a tumbler of tapioca. The milk should be boiling hot, and sweetened to the taste. Beat six eggs well, and when the milk is nearly cold, pour it slowly upon the eggs, stirring rapidly; season with nutmeg and cinnamon. Bake a quarter of an hour, and serve with rich sauce.

---

622. *Tapioca Pudding*, No. 2.—Soak a tumblerful of tapioca for one hour in two tumblerfuls of milk. Put in a stew-pan half a dozen medium-sized tart apples, peeled and cored; the cavities filled with sugar and a little powdered cinnamon. Pour to them a tumblerful of water; cover the stew-pan, and stew until the

apples are tender. Take them up; put them in a fire-proof dish; pour over them any syrup that may remain in the stew-pan; add to the tapioca another tumblerful of rich, sweet milk; pour over the apples, and bake. Eat with rich, solid, butter sauce.

---

623. *Rice Flour Pudding.*—Into a pint of boiling milk stir a paste made of five tablespoonfuls of rice flour; wet up with cold milk; add to the milk, while warm, a heaped tablespoonful of butter; add a pint of cold milk. Beat six eggs with four heaped tablespoonfuls of crushed sugar, add them to the batter; mix well; season with nutmeg. Butter a deep earthen dish; pour the batter in, and bake until the pudding is firm, which will probably take half an hour. Eat with rich cream or mock-cream sauce.

---

624. *Grated Potato Pudding.*—One pint of sugar, half a pint of molasses, one large spoonful of butter, and a pint of sweet potatoes, grated. Mix well, and add sweet milk enough to make quite thin; season with orange peel, beaten fine, and ginger. After it is mixed, add to it three well-beaten eggs. Bake in a very slow oven to allow it to candy over the top.

---

625. *Sweet Potato Pudding.*—Take half a pound of sweet potatoes; wash them, and put them into a pot with a very little water—barely enough to prevent their burning. Let them simmer slowly for about half an hour; they must be only parboiled, otherwise they will be soft, and make the pudding heavy. When they are half done, take them out; peel them, and, when cold, grate them. Stir together to a cream half a pound of butter and six ounces of powdered sugar; add a grated nutmeg, a large teaspoonful of beaten mace, the juice and grated peel of one lemon, a wineglass of rose-water, a glass of wine, and a glass of brandy. Stir these ingredients together. Beat eight eggs very light, and stir them into the mixture alternately with the potato, a little of each at a time. Having stirred the whole very hard at the last, pour into a buttered dish, and bake three-quarters of an hour. To be eaten cold.

626. *Secession Pudding (excellent).*—Four teacups of sifted flour, three of dry crushed sugar, one of sweet milk, one teaspoonful of soda, two of cream of tartar. Stir the soda in the flour; dissolve the cream of tartar in a little cold water; six eggs beaten separately. When the buttermilk or clabber is used, omit sweet milk and cream of tartar. Buttermilk may be used instead of cream of tartar. Eat with a rich sauce.

---

527. *Sunderland Pudding.*—Six eggs, three tablespoonfuls of sifted flour, one pint of milk, a pinch of salt. Beat the yolks well; mix them smoothly with the flour, then add the milk. Lastly, whip the whites to a stiff froth; beat them in, and bake immediately. Eat with liquid sauce, flavored with vanilla.

---

628. *A Superior Bread Pudding.*—Three pints of milk scalded, a teaspoonful of salt, elven ounces of grated bread. Pour the hot milk over the bread at least an hour before the pudding is made. A good plan is to put the bread to soak before you rise from the breakfast-table. To make the pudding, add half a pound of sugar, a quarter of a pound of butter, five eggs, well beaten. Flavor with mace, and bake three-quarters of an hour. Eat with rich sauce.

---

629. *Rice Pudding.*—A quarter of a pound of rice, boiled until soft. While boiling, stir frequently, to prevent scorching. While warm, add to it a quarter of a pound of butter. To six eggs, beaten separately, and afterwards mixed, add a quarter of a pound of sugar, a wineglass of rose-water, or any flavoring preferred. Eat with transparent sauce.

---

630. *Vermicelli Pudding.*—Mix with three eggs enough flour to make a stiff dough; roll it out into two very thin sheets; cut into narrow strips, and dry them in a stove or oven. After they are dried, drop them into hot water, and boil three minutes. Drain the hot water from them, and pour them into a pan of cold water. Beat six eggs with six even tablespoonfuls of good sugar.

Take a heaped tablespoonful of butter; divide it into small bits or slices; place upon the bottom of an earthen baking-dish a layer of the strips of dough; upon this bits of butter; then a layer of raisins; then another layer of the strips, and so on until the dish is half filled. Over this pour the custard. A very few minutes will be sufficient to bake it. To be eaten as soon as baked, with a rich cream or arrowroot sauce.

631. *A Custard Pudding.*—One quart of milk, eight eggs, eight tablespoonfuls of flour; wet up the flour with sufficient milk to make it into a paste; put the remainder of the milk on to boil. As it boils, stir in the paste; let it boil five minutes; then pour it off. When cool, add the eggs, previously well beaten; flavor to taste. Butter earthen cups; pour the custard into the cups, and grate a little nutmeg over it. Fill a stove baking-pan to the depth of an inch with boiling water; set the cups in it, and bake until the custard is firm enough to turn out. Serve with transparent sauce.

632. *A Quick Pudding.*—Mix three tablespoonfuls of flour with three of sweet milk. Put a quart of milk to boil, and, as it boils, stir in the paste. Beat three eggs well, and add the milk to them when tepid. Bake in a buttered earthen dish, and as soon as baked, eat with a rich butter sauce.

633. *California Pudding.*—One egg, one cup of sugar, half a cup of butter, all creamed together. One cup of sweet milk, four cups of flour, one teaspoonful of soda, and two of cream of tartar, or a dessert-spoonful of yeast powder. Bake in a quick oven, and eat with transparent sauce.

634. *A Good Cheap Pudding.*—Two tumblers of sifted flour, one of crushed sugar, one egg, a light tablespoonful of butter, a teacup not quite full of sour milk, a small teaspoonful of soda, a teaspoonful of essence of lemon; cream the butter, sugar, and

egg together well; stir the soda to the flour, and add alternately the flour and the milk until all are mixed. Have ready a buttered dish, and bake immediately in a quick oven. Eat with a sauce.

---

635. *Boiled Puddings.*—I omitted to mention in the proper place that a mould is sometimes used for boiling puddings. I greatly prefer a bag. When the mould is used it should have a well-fitting cover, or be carefully tied over with a strong linen cloth, as the smallest quantity of water getting in would spoil the pudding.

---

636. *Currant Pudding.*—One pint of bread crumbs, six eggs, two tablespoonfuls of flour, one of sugar, a dessert-spoonful of butter, half a pound of currants. Cover the bread crumbs with a quart of boiling milk; add the butter; beat the eggs and sugar together; add the flour. When the milk is nearly cold, pour it slowly to the eggs, stirring constantly, to make a smooth batter; strain through thin muslin. Flour the currants well; add lastly. Scald the bag; flour it well on the inside; pour in the batter, and boil two hours. Serve with a rich sauce.

---

637. *Quaking Pudding.*—One quart of milk, nine eggs beaten separately, nine tablespoonfuls of flour, half a teaspoonful of salt. Boil two hours. Eat with a rich sauce.

---

638. *Cracker Pudding.*—Pour over four soda crackers a pint of boiling milk. When cool, mash well. Beat four eggs well; stir to them a tablespoonful of flour. Mix all well, and boil an hour. Eat with rich sauce.

---

639. *Boiled Plum Pudding.*—Two tumblers of fine bread crumbs, one tumbler of sifted flour, half a pound of raisins, seeded and cut in half; the same of currants, picked and dried; a large piece of citron, cut into strips. Chop half a pound of dried beef suet; soak several hours in a tumbler of brandy or wine, a table-

spoonful of mace and cinnamon mixed. Add to the batter one beaten nutmeg; two grated lemons, removing the seed; ten eggs beaten well with a tumbler of sugar. Pour upon the bread two tumblers of rich milk, very hot; mash it, and mix the ingredients, first flouring the fruit well, or it will fall to the bottom. Stir the pudding well; scald your pudding-bag; lay it in a bowl; flour it thickly; pour in the batter; tie well, and follow the directions for boiling. Serve with a rich sauce, for which a variety of excellent receipts are given in this book.

This pudding will require six hours constant boiling. Lay it in a pot of boiling water, and turn several times before suspending it. Some persons boil without suspending, turning the pudding frequently, and putting a plate at the bottom of the pot to prevent the bag from scorching. Always lay the pudding in a pan of cold water a few minutes before turning it out of the bag. Butter is sometimes used instead of suet, using rather less butter. If any of the pudding is left, tie in a cloth and re-boil an hour.

---

640. *Dr. Kitchiner's Plum Pudding.*—Suet chopped fine, six ounces; raisins, seeded and cut, six ounces; the same of currants, washed and dried; bread crumbs, three ounces; the same of flour, three eggs, half a nutmeg, a teaspoonful of mace and cinnamon mixed, half a teaspoonful of salt, a tumbler of milk, four ounces of sugar, a little citron and orange peel. Beat the eggs well; add the spice; mix the milk in by degrees; then the rest of the ingredients. Boil in a cloth, as already directed, in plenty of water. It must boil steadily, or the pudding will be heavy. Boil six hours. Prepare everything the day before it is wanted.

---

641. *A Simple Fruit Pudding.*—One pint of sour milk; half a pound of flour, half a pound of light bread crumbs, a pound of raisins (seeded and cut), or a pound of dried peaches, or peach chips cut very fine; six ounces of crushed sugar, six ounces of suet, or butter, a teaspoonful of soda. Mix very thoroughly, and boil briskly three hours. Eat with wine sauce.

642. *Mrs. P.'s Plum Pudding.*—Roll a pint of crackers; pour on them a quart of milk, in which has been melted half a cup of butter. Add four tablespoonfuls of crushed sugar to five eggs, and beat well. Mash the crackers well in the milk, and pour to the eggs. Pour a part of the milk from the crackers on half a tumblerful of flour, so as to form a paste, and add to the other ingredients. Add a wineglass of wine, half a grated nutmeg, a quarter of a pound of raisins, a quarter of a pound of currants, and two ounces of citron. Flour the fruit well before adding. Boil two hours, and serve with a rich sauce. This pudding is also good baked.

---

643. *A Cheap Currant Pudding.*—Three eggs beaten separately, three tablespoonfuls of sugar beaten with the yolks, a small tablespoonful of butter, a saucer of currants, a tumbler of bread crumbs, a heaped tablespoonful of sifted flour, three tumblerfuls of sweet milk, a wine glass of wine. Boil one hour and a half. Eat with sauce.

---

644. *Almond Pudding.*—Blanch a pound of almonds; beat them to a paste, pouring in, gradually, two tablespoonfuls of rose or orange water, to prevent their oiling. Stir to them two tumblerfuls of rich cream, two wineglasses of milk, two of wine, ten eggs well beaten, one tablespoonful of arrowroot flour, one of bread crumbs. Boil half an hour. Eat with arrowroot sauce.

---

645. *A Charlotte.*—Make a paste by receipt No. 6 or 8. Roll out a quarter of an inch thick, and spread to within an inch of each edge with stewed cranberries, blackberry or raspberry jam, or any kind of stewed or preserved fruit, jelly, or marmalade. Roll carefully; fold around it a strong cloth or napkin, and tie securely at each end. If it is a large Charlotte, boil two hours. Eat with solid butter sauce.

DUMPLINGS, ETC.

646. *Boiled Apple Dumplings.*—After making the paste, divide into as many pieces as there are apples. Pare and core medium-sized apples that are easy to cook; sweetenings will not answer. Fill the cavities with marmalade or jelly. Roll the pieces of paste to about the size of a small saucer; put the fruit in the middle; draw the paste around, enclosing the fruit well. The edges of the dough should nearly meet, not lap. Tie in thin muslin, separately; drop into a pot of boiling water. Three quarters of an hour will be required to boil them. They are pretty boiled in coarse knit or crocheted cloths. Serve with hard butter sauce.

647. *Apple Dumplings (Stewed).*—Pare and core the apples; put them in a stew-pan, and parboil them a little. Fill the cavities with any kind of sweetmeats. Roll out pieces of potato paste to the size of a common saucer; place an apple upon each piece (some persons stew the fruit first, and place about a heaping tablespoonful upon each piece of paste); close the edges of the paste around the fruit. Put the dumplings in a large fire-proof dish without piling. Make a sauce of enough water to cover the dumplings; sweeten to taste; add for a dozen dumplings half a pound of butter; flavor with a tablespoonful of powdered cinnamon. Pour this over the dumplings. Set the pan or dish in the stove or oven; stew three quarters of an hour Turn them once, when half done. Serve the liquor in the dish for sauce. Should the water become too much reduced, add a little water, just enough to make the sauce.

648. *Apple Dumplings (Baked).*—Make a paste by receipt No. 2. Pare and core the apples, filling the cavities with sugar, and flavored with essence of lemon. Enclose the apples sepa rately in the paste; put them in a tin pan, and bake them. Serve hot, with rich, solid butter sauce.

---

649. *Snow Balls.*—Wash and pick half a pound of rice; boil it, covered with water, ten minutes; drain through a sieve, and spread on a dish to dry. Peel and core six apples, medium-sized. Divide the rice into six parts; envelop each apple in a portion of the rice (the cavities in the apples first filled with powdered sugar and cinnamon). Tie separately in cloths, loosely. Boil one hour. Eat with a rich sauce.

---

650. *Fritters.*—Three eggs, three tumblerfuls of sifted flour, two tumblerfuls of milk (sour milk or buttermilk); beat the eggs separately, adding to the yolks, alternately, the flour and milk. Stir in an even teaspoonful of soda. Whisk the whites to a stiff froth, and stir lightly into the batter last. Have ready a pan of boiling lard, and drop the batter in by spoonfuls; color a light brown on both sides. Cover the bottom of a dish with a napkin, and place the fritters upon it, and send to the table hot. These are nice eaten with molasses sauce, or with sugar, acidulated with lemon juice; vinegar or wine may be substituted for the lemon juice. These fritters may be varied by adding to the batter any kind of fruit sliced very thin or grated, or any kind of sweetmeats, taking care to dip up some of the fruit in each spoonful of the batter.

---

651. *Bell Fritters.*—Put into a stew-pan a piece of butter the size of a large hen's egg; pour over it a pint of boiling water, and set it upon the stove until it is ready to boil. Stir in a pint of flour, making a smooth paste. Let this remain on the fire a few minutes, stirring all the time to prevent its sticking to the vessel; when thick as mush, remove it from the fire. When milk-warm, beat in one egg at a time until five are added; put in a teaspoonful of salt. Put a pint of lard in a small, deep vessel. Make the fritters in small balls, about the size of a

small hen's egg, and drop into the boiling lard. Fry a delicate brown, and serve upon a dish the bottom of which has been covered with a napkin. Eat with cream and sugar sauce.

---

652. *Bread Fritters.*—Cut stale light rolls or rusks into slices half an inch thick. Beat two eggs, and add to them a tumblerful of rich milk, sweetened to taste and flavored with cinnamon or mace. Pour this mixture over the bread; turn the slices once, and when saturated (but not soft enough to break) drop into boiling lard. Fry to a delicate brown on both sides, and eat with wine sauce, or molasses sauce.

---

553. *Pancakes.*—This is a good proportion for pancakes: A quart of sifted flour; enough milk to make the batter the consistence of thick cream (pancake batter should always be thinner than that for fritters); salt to taste; three eggs beaten separately. Put a piece of lard the size of a nutmeg into a frying-pan, and, when hot, pour in about two tablespoonfuls of the batter—the batter spread over the bottom of the frying-pan; the quantity will depend upon the size of the pan. When brown on one side, turn it; and when both sides are a delicate brown, fold twice and place in a covered dish. Send them to the table as soon as three or four are prepared; follow these with others as expeditiously as possible. Do not commence baking until the last meat course is nearly through, as they are not good unless eaten hot. Use the same sauce as for fritters.

Pancakes are sometimes served without being folded, and a little powdered sugar flavored with cinnamon or nutmeg sifted over each pancake. They are then called a "quire of paper pancakes."

---

654. *Puffs, No.* 1.—These are made of pastry rolled to the size of a saucer. Spread, to within a quarter of an inch of the edge, on one-half the paste, any kind of stewed or preserved fruit; turn over the fruit the other half of the paste. Either bake or fry. These are good cold, either with or without cream sauce.

655. *Puffs, No. 2.*—One quart of milk, one pint of sifted flour, four eggs beaten separately, and then stirred together; stir alternately to these the flour and the milk. When the batter is well mixed, strain it. Butter cups and pour into them the batter two-thirds full, and bake in a quick oven. These should not be made until dinner has been sent to the table. To be eaten hot, with wine sauce.

CUSTARDS.

ALL custards made of milk and eggs should be baked in a moderate oven. If baked too rapidly they are almost sure to be tough and watery. Custards are best baked without a bottom crust, lining only the sides and edges of the plate with the puff paste. Several layers of the paste (rolled very thin) placed around the edge and extending far enough to allow the custard to conceal where they terminate, give an elegant finish. Some persons are in the habit of notching and otherwise ornamenting the edges of the paste. This is highly improper; the puff paste should be handled as little as possible, so as to preserve the flaky texture of the crust. Custards are best eaten cold, but should not be kept too long. If served warm they will require an under crust.

---

656. *Lemon Custard, No. 1.*—Three lemons, six eggs, two cups of nice sugar, and two cups of cold water. Roll the lemons well; cut them in very thin slices, and press out the juice. Beat the eggs separately; stir the water and lemon juice together. Beat the sugar and the yolks of the eggs together; add, lastly, the whites well beaten. Bake in a rich paste.

---

657. *Lemon Custard, No. 2.*—The yolks of eight eggs, half a pound of butter, three-quarters of a pound of sugar, and two good lemons. Grate all the yellow in, and then add the juice. Bake in a rich paste.

---

658. *Orange Custard, No. 1.*—The yolks of eight eggs; before breaking them, balance their weight with sugar; balance the weight of three with butter. Cream the butter, sugar, and yolks together. Grate the outside peel of two oranges; add this with

their juice. Line the plate with puff paste as in the preceding directions; pour in the custard, and bake.

---

659. *Orange Custard, No. 2.*—Cream half a pound of sugar with half a pound of butter; add the grated rind and juice of two oranges, and one wineglass of mixed wine and brandy. Beat six eggs light, and pour on gradually. Bake as directed in the preceding.

---

660. *Cocoanut Custard, No. 1.*—The whites of eight eggs beaten to a froth, eight tablespoonfuls of powdered loaf sugar, four tablespoonfuls of melted butter, the white part of a large cocoanut grated, a wineglass of wine. Bake in puff paste.

---

661. *Cocoanut Custard, No. 2.*—A heaped tablespoonful of butter, creamed; one pound of crushed sugar; nine eggs, beaten separately; the grated meat of a large cocoanut. Cream the butter and sugar together. Mix the cocoanut and eggs, and stir to the butter with a wineglass of rose or orange water. Lastly, stir in lightly a tumblerful of rich cream. Bake half an hour in puff paste.

---

662. *Almond Custard.*—Blanch a quarter of a pound of sweet almonds; the same of bitter almonds or peach kernels; a quarter of a pound of powdered white sugar, and two ounces of butter. Beat the almonds to a paste, adding rose or orange water to prevent their oiling. Cream the butter and sugar together; stir in the almond paste by degrees until worked in smoothly; add the whites of six eggs, beaten to a froth; beat in very lightly four even tablespoonfuls of sifted flour, dipped up lightly. Bake half an hour in puff paste. Sift loaf sugar over when cold.

---

663. *Citron Custard.*—The yolks of twelve eggs, three-quarters of a pound of sugar, half a pound of butter. Beat the yolks and sugar very light; cream the butter; stir all together. Place

strips of citron on the bottom of pie-plates, lined with puff paste; pour over the custard. In pouring the custard be very careful not to drop any upon the outside pastry, as it gives it a very untidy appearance.

---

664. *Transparent Custard.*—Beat well with half a pound of crushed sugar the yolks of eight eggs; set upon the fire the pan containing them, and add, in small pieces, half a pound of butter; stir constantly until the butter melts; remove it from the fire, and stir in a wineglass of thick cream. Flavor to taste, and bake in puff paste. Citron or other sweetmeats placed at the bottom, may be used with this batter.

---

665. *Mock-Lemon Custard.*—To six tablespoonfuls of grated apple (horse-apple or any ripe, pleasant apple will answer—sweetenings should never be used for cooking or drying); one grated lemon peel and pulp; not quite half a common-sized teacup of butter; two eggs, well-beaten; sugar to taste; a wineglass of thick cream, stirred in last. Bake in puff paste.

---

666. *A Delicious Apple Custard.*—Six acid apples of medium size; a tumblerful of crushed sugar; three tablespoonfuls of butter, very little heaped, or two tumblerfuls of very rich, thick cream; six eggs; one lemon peel grated; half the juice. Peel the apples and grate them. Cream the butter and sugar together. Beat the eggs separately, and mix as for cake. Bake in puff paste. This quantity will make two custards.

---

667. *Apple Custard.*—Take half a dozen tart apples; peel and core them; cook them in a little water until soft. Mash them very smoothly; sweeten and spice to taste; beat in five or six eggs. Bake in puff paste. One gill of cream improves this. In using cream for custards or puddings, add it last, as much stirring converts it into butter.

---

668. *Mush Custard* (*excellent*).—One pound of smooth mush (sift the finer part of the corn meal); stir to it a quarter of a pound of butter. Beat separately six eggs; with the yolks a pound of crushed sugar. Mix all as for a cake. Grate the rind of one lemon; add this, and the juice to the mush. Bake in a rich paste.

669. *Dried Apple Custard.*—One pint of dried apples, mashed and strained; two eggs beaten with the apples; sweeten and spice to taste. Add half a tumblerful of cream or rich milk. Bake in a paste, and when done, cover with a meringue, according to directions given under the head of Tarts.

670. *Breckenridge Custard.*—The yolks of six eggs; three quarters of a pound of sweet potatoes (yams are best) boiled and strained through a colander; three-quarters of a pound of butter, creamed soft with a pound of powdered sugar. Mix all together, as for cake; spice with nutmeg; flavor with lemon or vanilla. Bake in a rich crust.

671. *Potato Custard.*—One teacup of boiled or baked sweet potatoes, mashed and strained; one teacup of butter; the same of sugar; three eggs well beaten. Cream the potato and butter together; beat the eggs and sugar together; mix them; flavor as may suit the taste. Bake in a rich crust.

672. *Irish Potato Custard.*—Mash very smoothly a pound of Irish potatoes; cream with it half a pound of butter. Beat three eggs with half a pound of sugar. Mix all well; flavor with wine and nutmeg. Bake in puff paste. Sprinkle loaf sugar over when done. Excellent, either hot or cold.

673. *Pumpkin Custard.*—Pass a pint of boiled pumpkin through a colander, and add to it a pint of cream. Beat eight eggs, and add them gradually to the other ingredients, stirring

constantly. Then stir in a wineglass of rose-water, a teaspoonful of powdered cinnamon, and a grated nutmeg. Lay a paste in a buttered dish, and bake three-quarters of an hour.

---

674. *Rice Custard.*—Pick and wash well one tumblerful of rice; boil it dry in a pint of milk or water. Take it up; mash well and strain through a colander; add a pint of sweet milk and half a tumblerful of melted butter. Beat three eggs well; add to the rice when it is cool; sweeten and flavor to taste. Bake in puff paste.

This may be baked without a paste, and raisins or currants added, if liked. If used, stir them in when the custard is at least half done; if added earlier, they will settle at the bottom. Should be eaten with cream sauce.

---

675. *Vanilla Custard.*—Make a quart of milk into a thick mush with flour. While hot stir into the mush a tablespoonful of butter. Set it off until cold; add to it six well-beaten eggs; sugar to taste; flavor highly with vanilla; bake in rich pastry.

---

676. *Bartow Custard.*—One quart of sweet milk, three tablespoonfuls of rice flour, half a pound of sugar, quarter of a pound of butter, six eggs, a teaspoonful of salt, two tablespoonfuls of orange-water, half a grated nutmeg. Mix the flour with a little of the milk to the consistence of cream; set the remainder of the milk in a tin pan upon the stove; as it boils, stir in the paste. Let it simmer two or three minutes, stirring constantly; remove it from the fire, and add the butter and salt. Beat the eggs and sugar well together until they are perfectly light, as for cake. When the milk is cool, pour it slowly to the eggs, stirring constantly until it is all well mixed; add the flavoring. Line the plates with puff paste, and bake in rather a quick oven.

---

677. *Egg Custard.*—One quart of milk, one tablespoonful of flour, one ounce of butter, six ounces of sugar, six eggs. Put the

milk over the fire until it boils. Mix the flour with a little cold milk, and stir the paste to the boiling milk. Let it remain on the flour two or three minutes; then remove it, and stir in the butter. Beat the eggs separately, the sugar with the yolks; then stir the yolks and whites together, and pour the milk to them when it is nearly cold. Strain the mixture; use any flavoring liked. Line pie-plates with puff paste; pour in the custard, and grate nutmeg over the top, and bake until the custard is set.

It is not absolutely necessary that the eggs should be beaten separately; but it *is* necessary that they should be *thoroughly* beaten.

This custard is delicious poured in a buttered dish and baked without a crust. In this case, use four ounces of sugar, and serve hot with a rich, solid butter sauce.

---

678. *A Simple Egg Custard.*—Four eggs, four tablespoonfuls of crushed sugar, an even tablespoonful of butter, one of flour, mixed to a paste with a little cold milk. Put a pint of milk in a stew-pan, and set on the fire. As it boils, stir in the paste, and simmer for two or three minutes; remove it, and add the butter. Beat the eggs and sugar together, and pour the milk to them when it is cool. Bake in a paste.

---

679. *Jelly Custard.*—One cup of fruit jelly; one cup nearly full of crushed sugar; one tablespoonful of butter; three eggs, beaten separately. Flavor with lemon, and bake in puff paste.

---

680. *Cracker Custard.*—Make a rich lemonade with two lemons and one pint of water; sugar to taste. Add four grated Boston crackers, one tablespoonful of butter, and a little mace. Bake in paste.

---

681. *Molasses Custard.*—One cup of syrup, one of sugar, three eggs, half a cup of milk, a tablespoonful of butter. Flavor with ginger, orange, or lemon, and bake in a paste.

SAUCES.

"A great deal of the elegance of cookery depends upon the accompaniments to each dish being appropriate and well adapted to it."

ALL butter sauces should be made of good, fresh butter. Nothing good can be made of rancid butter; the taste cannot be disguised. To melt or draw it well, constant attention during the process is necessary. Should it oil, add to it immediately a tablesponful of cold water, and pour it into an earthen bowl, stirring well. For the taste of burnt butter there is no remedy; it is unfit for use; therefore be particular in placing it upon the fire never to set it upon a blaze or very hot coals. It is a good and safe plan to put the vessel in which the butter is to be melted into another containing boiling water. A double kettle or a hot water bath answers this purpose well. A stew-pan lined with porcelain is also a suitable utensil for the boiling of sauces, and one should be kept for this purpose alone. In many kitchens there is not a single vessel suitable for preparing these delicate, and, as they should be considered, indispensable accompaniments to meats, puddings, etc.

To melt butter properly: Put into a stew-pan two ounces of butter, a large tablespoonful of flour or corn starch, arrowroot, or potato starch, two tablespoonfuls of milk. When the butter begins to melt, stir all well together; add six tablespoonfuls of hot water; cover the stew-pan, and stir all well together; let it boil up. When of the consistence of cream, pour it out, and flavor or season in any way desired. Butter mixes better with milk than with water; but in transparent sauces water alone must be used, as milk will render it cloudy.

---

682. *Transparent Sauce.*—A piece of butter the size of a large

egg, a common-sized saucer of sugar, a tumbler nearly full of water. Put them all in a stew-pan together, and stir well. Simmer gently five or six minutes. Beat the yolk of an egg in a bowl; pour the sauce very slowly upon it, stirring hard. When all is in, return the mixture to the stew-pan; stir constantly until it is thoroughly hot; pour it into the tureen. Flavor with lemon, orange, or vanilla, and grate nutmeg over.

---

683. *Sponge Cake Pudding Sauce.*—Two cups of butter creamed with a cup of sugar; beat together, in a deep bowl or dish, the yolks of two eggs. Put the butter in a well-lined stew-pan; set this in boiling water. Stir the butter constantly until it has melted; pour it slowly to the eggs, stirring hard. Return it to the stew-pan; pour in a teacup of boiling water. Let it simmer three or four minutes, shaking the pan or stirring it frequently. Flavor with any of the extracts, and grate over nutmeg.

---

684. *Mrs. B.'s Sponge Cake Sauce Receipt.*—Two tablespoonfuls of powdered loaf sugar, six of cold water. Boil a few minutes; stir in two heaped teaspoonfuls of butter. As soon as the butter melts, stir well, and season with wine and nutmeg.

---

685. *Sauce for Boiled Pudding.*—Cream together a tumbler of good fresh butter, the same of powdered sugar; stir to them half a tumblerful of hot water; mix well. Place the stew-pan containing this mixture upon the stove just long enough to heat thoroughly, adding the grated rind of a lemon or orange, or flavor with extract of lemon. Put upon the bottom of the sauce tureen a tablespoonful of currant or apple jelly; pour the sauce over it, stirring and mixing well—or the jelly may be omitted and wine used instead.

---

686. *Arrowroot Sauce.*—Wet up half a teacup of arrowroot

with a teacup of cream, milk, or water, as preferred; two large tablespoonfuls of sugar, and nutmeg to taste. Boil four or five minutes; serve hot. Should it become too thick, thin with cream. Flavor with rose or orange water, or wine, if preferred, using pale Sherry; more sugar if liked.

---

687. *Wine Sauce for Puddings.*—Stir together one teacup of butter, two of good sugar (loaf is best), and an even tablespoonful of flour. Put these into a stew-pan, and stir to it half a tumbler of boiling water. Let it simmer a minute or two; pour in half a tumbler of wine. Serve in a sauce tureen; grate nutmeg over. If preferred, use less water and more wine.

---

688. *A Good Sauce.*—One tumbler of wine and one of sugar; stir together, and heat to the boiling point; stir slowly to the well-beaten yolks of four eggs. Put on the fire long enough to take off the raw taste of the egg. Grate in lemon; add a tablespoonful of the juice, or orange peel or nutmeg. Serve hot, in a covered tureen.

---

689. *Cream Sauce.*—Stir together a tumblerful of rich, thick cream and a tumbler lightly full of fine white sugar; grate over it nutmeg. Serve cold, with fruit tarts.

---

690. *Mock Cream Sauce.*—To two tumblers of sweet milk, stir in loaf sugar enough to sweeten it well; put it on the fire. Beat together the whites of two eggs, and the yolk of one. When the milk becomes hot, pour it slowly to the eggs, stirring constantly. Return it to the stew-pan; scald it, shaking the stew-pan frequently. Serve in a sauce-boat. Flavor in any way liked.

One egg will be sufficient if you use a large tablespoonful of potato or corn starch, arrowroot, or flour. Wet this up with a little of the milk, cold, and pour into the sauce when it boils up, stirring well.

691. *Syllabub Sauce.*—Cream seasoned as for syllabub makes fine sauce for delicate custards, fritters, and pancakes.

---

692. *Sauce of any kind of Jam.*—Put into a small stew-pan half a tumbler of Sherry wine, in which has been dissolved an even teaspoonful of powdered sugar. Mix in well two tablespoonfuls of jam. Warm gently; use with delicate custards or puddings.

---

693. *Butter Sauce.*—Half a tumbler of butter, a tumbler of sugar; mix well, and stir to the yolks of two eggs; pour over a tumbler of boiling wine; boil one minute, stirring well. Serve with plain boiled pudding.

---

694. *Hard Sauce.*—Cream, until white and spongy, one teacup of butter, two of loaf sugar, pulverized. This sauce requires *to be creamed well.* Stir in as much wine as it will take, or season with any of the extracts. Place it, lightly heaped, on a glass or silver plate. It makes an elegant sauce for bread puddings, or for any kind of boiled pudding. This sauce may be varied by stirring to it a large tablespoonful of very stiff apple or quince jelly, or the grated rind and juice of an orange or lemon.

---

695. *Egg Drawn Butter.*—Beat one egg light; add to it a tumbler of cold water. Set it on the stove in a stew-pan; boil slowly until it thickens; stir in a dessert-spoonful of butter. To this may be added wine and sugar. Serve with puddings.

---

696. *Sauce for Tarts.*—Make a thick boiled custard; for a pint, use the yolks of four eggs, a tablespoonful of corn starch; wet with cold milk, and add to the boiling pint of milk. Pour into an open stand when cool. Sweeten and flavor to taste. Make an icing of two of the whites beaten stiff; spread over the custard, and scorch with a hot salamander or shovel.

CAKES.

THE process of the compounding and baking of cakes being a delicate operation, it should not be left to careless hands, but should be carried on under the close supervision of the housewife. Says Mrs. Hannah More: "Those women who are so puffed up with conceit of talents or position as to neglect the plain duties of life, will not often be found women of the best abilities. It is best to begin cake-making as early after breakfast as is convenient. Have everything in readiness. When there is fruit to be used, prepare it the previous day. By all means be supplied with well-balanced scales, as in cake-making nothing should be done by guess-work, and measuring is much less exact than weighing. Be sure that all your materials are good. *Never* use rancid butter. Sift and sun the flour well. In summer, place the eggs in cold water a little while before using—the whites froth better. When soda and cream of tartar are used in batters, the soda should be carefully sifted with the flour, as the smallest lump will make a yellow place in the cake. Dissolve the cream of tartar in a little water. Sal volatile is often used in the place of soda. A bit the size of a nutmeg will be sufficient for a pound of cake. Yeast powders are also very good. For beating the whites of the eggs an egg-beater of wire is best. When one cannot be procured, a large silver fork is very good. A good substitute for an egg-beater is a bunch of white oak splits tied near one end. The whites should be whipped to a very solid froth. When they will adhere to the dish or a knife-blade, inverted, they are well beaten. Never commence beating them until the yolks and sugar are finished beating, as, if beaten too soon, they will fall. Always use a wooden paddle for beating cake; the warmth of the hand renders the batter oily. Wash the butter in cold water; cream it, pouring off every particle of water. In cold weather, wash in tepid water, or place near the fire, where it will soften enough to cream. For mixing the batter, an earthen bowl is best.

To mix cake: After creaming the butter, add the flour by degrees, creaming together until half the flour is used. Beat the yolks and sugar, adding the sugar gradually until the mixture is white and spongy. The principal *beating* of the cake should be put upon the yolks and sugar. After they are beaten sufficiently, add them to the butter alternately with the remainder of the flour. In all cakes where butter is used, the whites must be added last; as soon as they are well incorporated with the batter, put the cake to bake. In sponge cake, at least a third of the flour must be added after the whites, or the cake will fall. Fruit should be well floured before adding to the batter. Butter the pans after covering the bottom with foolscap paper, rubbing the butter on with a cloth, that there may be no lumps. The excellence of cake depends quite as much upon the baking as upon the proper mixing of the ingredients. Good judgment and close attention are absolutely essential, but experience alone can render one an expert cake baker. If an oven is used, let the bottom be warm before placing the cake in it. Put the lid on cold, and cover evenly with hot embers. Keep the oven at a moderate heat until the cake is well risen; then increase the heat, and bake as quickly as possible without burning. If baked too slowly, the butter becomes oily, and settles in streaks through the cake. Never attempt baking cake in a stove while the cooking of a meal is in progress, as, under those circumstances, it is impossible to regulate the heat properly. To prevent burning, it is well to elevate the cake a little from the bottom of a stove or brick oven by placing the pan upon muffin-rings, or a trivet; or, in an iron oven, throw a little ashes or sawdust into the bottom before putting in the pan.

To ascertain the degree of heat of a stove or brick oven, put in a small bit of dough; if it gradually assumes a light brown color it indicates a condition proper for the reception of the cake. Never suffer the heat to diminish while the cake is baking, as it will cause it to fall. It is, of course, sometimes necessary to raise the oven-lid or open the stove to look at the cake; but never suffer it to remain open longer than is absolutely necessary, as contact with the air will cause it to fall. When the cake is done, it will shrink from the sides of the pan. To ascertain the fact more satisfactorily, pierce with a straw near the centre; if no batter adheres to the straw, the cake is done. Always turn cakes upon a soft tablecloth to cool, turning them twice or three times, or oftener, that they may not become heavy from the absorption of the steam which they emit. Fruit cake must remain in the pan to cool, as in removing it, it would be almost certain to break from its own weight.

To prepare cake for icing: Trim off carefully all the burnt or uneven places; brush off the crumbs, and dust evenly with flour.

Sponge cake requires a quicker oven than any other. Tea cakes require quick baking. Pound cake, a more moderate heat. Fruit cake, more moderate still. Molasses cake is more easily scorched than any other. In baking large cakes, a pan with straight sides is best—a tube in the centre.

697. *Fruit Cake, No. 1.*—Sugar, one and a half pounds; butter, the same; flour, the same; eighteen eggs; of raisins and currants mixed, three pounds; citron, half a pound; one tumbler of brandy, two tablespoonfuls of cinnamon, the same of mace, the same of cloves, and a   teaspoonful of soda. For any fruit cake an almond icing is best, as the ordinary icing becomes discolored.

698. *Fruit Cake, No. 2.*—Twelve eggs, fourteen cups of flour, seven cups of sugar, three cups of buttermilk, three cups of butter, three light teaspoonfuls of soda, one tablespoonful each of cloves, mace, and cinnamon; one pound each of currants and raisins, half a pound of citron, and half a tumblerful of brandy.

699. *Black Cake.*—One pound of plain pound-cake batter, two

pounds of raisins, stoned; two pounds of currants, picked, washed and dried before using; half a pound of citron, cut in small pieces; season highly with nutmeg, cinnamon, and a little cloves, and allspice. After the batter is made, and the spices added, and before putting in the fruit, stir a teaspoonful of soda into a saucer of molasses; stir this into the cake. Stir in the fruit (previously well floured) *quickly*, and set to baking as soon as possible; bake slowly. If the fruit is burned at the bottom, it imparts a bad taste to the cake.

---

700. *Confederate Fruit Cake.*—The weight of twelve eggs in butter, flour, and sugar; one tablespoonful of spice, half a tablespoonful of cinnamon, the same of mace, the same of cloves, one nutmeg, a wineglass of brandy, and two pounds of currants, or of dry peach chips cut very fine.

---

701. *A Cheap Fruit Cake.*—One pound of sugar, one pound of flour, one pound of raisins, three quarters of a pound of butter, four eggs, a teacup of buttermilk, a teaspoonful of soda, wine and spices to taste.

---

702. *Currant Cake.*—One pound each of butter, flour, and sugar; six eggs, one tablespoonful of powdered cinnamon, one nutmeg, a piece of sal volatile the size of a nutmeg, dissolved in warm water; one pint of sweet milk, two pounds of dried currants. Bake in a moderate oven.

---

703. *Pound Cake, No. 1.*—One pound of butter, one of sugar, one of flour, twelve eggs, one teaspoonful of soda, two of cream of tartar. The soda and cream of tartar must be dissolved separately; the latter in about half a teacup of water, the former in a little less. Beat the yolks and sugar together; the flour and butter together; the whites beat separately to a stiff froth. When all are well beaten, mix the eggs into the butter and flour thoroughly; add the seasoning to your taste; and, lastly, mix in soda and cream of tartar. Bake rather quickly.

704. *Pound Cake, No. 2.*—One pound of flour, one pound of sugar, three-quarters of a pound of butter, the whites of sixteen eggs, the yolks of four. Beat sugar, yolks, and butter together until all are nicely creamed; then mix the well-beaten whites alternately with the flour; add the juice of one lemon and one teacup of sweet milk.

---

705. *Plain Pound Cake.*—Three-quarters of a pound of butter; one pound of sifted flour; one pound of sugar (pulverized, loaf, or crushed); ten eggs. Beat the sugar with the yolks until very white; cream the butter; add to it the flour alternately with the egg and sugar. Add the whites lastly, and do not beat the batter after they are mixed with it; squeeze in the juice of one lemon and a wineglass of good brandy.

---

706. *General Gordon Cake.*—Three-quarters of a pound of butter, one pound of sugar; cream them well together; break in one egg at a time until you have used ten; beat well, and add a paper of corn starch; add a teaspoonful of yeast powder. Flavor with vanilla. Bake quickly.

---

707. *Corn Starch Cake.*—One pound of sugar, half a pound of butter; six eggs, beaten separately; three-quarters of a pound of corn starch; three tablespoonfuls of flour. Flavor to taste. Bake in small shapes or cups.

---

708. *Cocoanut Cake.*—½ pound of butter, one pound of flour, one pound of sugar, one pound of cocoanut, one wineglassful of rose-water, ten eggs. Peel the brown skin off the cocoanut and grate it; spread it on a dish to dry. Beat the butter and sugar to a cream; whisk the eggs, and add to it, and stir in the flour; add gradually the grated cocoanut and rose-water; beat the mixture well for ten or fifteen minutes; butter a pan; line the sides with thick paper well-buttered; pour in the mixture, and bake in a moderate oven nearly three hours.

709. Almond Cake.—One pound of sugar, three-quarters of a pound of butter, three-quarters of a pound of flour, ten eggs. Mix as pound cake; then add half a pound of almonds, beaten fine (blanched), one tablespoonful of rose-water.

---

710. Almond Sponge Cake.—Beat fine, with a wineglass of rose-water, two ounces of almonds, half sweet and half bitter; one pound of sugar, ten eggs, beaten separately; add, lastly, half a pound of flour.

---

711. Sponge Cake, No. 1.—One pound of sugar, seven eggs, half a pound of flour. Pour upon the sugar half a tumblerful of water; put in a sauce-pan, and set on the stove until the sugar is well dissolved and the syrup begins to bubble on the top; then set aside. While it is cooling, beat the yolks well, and when the syrup is tepid add them to it, beating very thoroughly. Then add the whites whipped to a stiff froth; add the flour last, stirring it in very lightly. Flavor with anything you like. Bake in a quick oven.

---

712. Sponge Cake, No. 2.—Twelve eggs, the weight of these in pulverized loaf sugar, the weight of eight in sifted flour, the juice of a lemon. Beat the yolks well; add to these the sugar, and beat well. Whip the whites to a froth, and add first flour, then whites, adding flour last. Bake in a quick oven.

---

713. Georgia Sponge Cake.—Twelve eggs, the weight of these in sugar, the weight of six in flour. Separate the eggs, leaving out the yolks of two. Beat the yolks well; then add the sugar by degrees. Beat very thoroughly; then add the whites, beaten to a stiff froth, and, lastly, the flour, stirring it in as lightly and quickly as possible. Flavor with a tablespoonful of brandy and any extract preferred. Bake in a quick oven.

---

714. Croton Sponge Cake.—Six eggs, half a pound of butter one pound of sugar, one pound of flour, a teaspoonful of soda, two of cream of tartar, one cup of sweet milk. Rub the butter and sugar to a cream; beat the eggs separately; mix the cream of tartar with the flour; dissolve the soda with the milk, which must be added last. Almonds blanched and beaten may be added to this.

---

715. *Indian Pound Cake.*—One pint of sifted meal, half a pint of flour, nutmeg, and cinnamon. Beat eight eggs, half a pound of sugar, half a pound of butter, and stir in gradually the meal and flour. Beat all together well, and bake an hour and a half. Must be eaten soon after it is baked to be nice.

---

716. *Jelly Cake, No. 1.*—Beat three eggs thoroughly; add one cup of sugar and one of flour. Stir these well together, and add one teaspoonful of cream of tartar and half a teaspoonful of soda, the latter to be dissolved in a very little water. Bake in two pie-tins, as evenly and quickly as possible, taking much care that it does not bake too hard around the edges. A sheet of writing paper laid over the top will prevent it from burning or scorching too much. Have ready a clean towel or cloth, and when the cake is done slip it out, bottom side upon the cloth; then spread the uppermost side quickly with currant or other tart jelly, and, commencing at the end, roll it up so as to form a long, compact roll. To use, slices are cut from the end of the roll.

---

717. *Jelly Cake, No. 2.*—Half a pound of white sugar, one-fourth of a pound of butter, eight eggs beaten separately; one pound of flour, juice and grated rind of one lemon, half a teaspoonful of yeast powder. Beat and mix well as for pound cake, and bake very thin on tins. While hot, spread each layer with tart jelly or marmalade, placing one layer upon another until there are half a dozen thicknesses. Ice the top, or sift loaf sugar very thickly upon it.

718. *Silver or Bride's Cake.*—The whites of sixteen eggs beaten to a froth; stir to them one pound of pulverized loaf sugar Cream together three-quarters of a pound of butter and one light pound of sifted flour; add all together. *Use no spices.* Flavor with lemon, vanilla, or rose. Almonds blanched and pounded are an improvement. Use rose-water with the almonds to prevent them from oiling.

---

719. *Golden Cake.*—Made by the same receipt, using the yolks instead of the whites; add a grated lemon.

A very beautiful jelly cake can be made by reserving a little of the batter from each of the foregoing, and baking thin, as in directions for jelly cake, placing the silver and golden cakes, alternately, with jelly between.

---

720. *Citron Cake.*—One-third of a pound of butter, one-third of a pound of sugar, half a pound of flour, four eggs, half a wine-glass of brandy, half a pound of citron.

---

721. *Spice Cake.*—Three cups of butter, six cups of sugar three cups sour milk, twelve (light) of flour, twelve eggs, three small teaspoonfuls of soda, sifted in the flour; one small teaspoonful of cloves, three of cinnamon, five of ground orange peel, three of nutmeg, one of allspice.

---

722. *White Cup Cake.*—Four teacups of sifted flour, two of loaf sugar, one of butter, one of sour cream or rich milk, a small teaspoonful of soda, the whites of six eggs, well beaten. Flavor with lemon.

---

723. *Cup Cake.*—One cup of butter, two of sugar, three of flour, four eggs, one teaspoonful of soda, one cup of sour milk. Flavor as you please. This cake makes an excellent pudding eaten with wine sauce.

---

724. *Cocoanut Tea Cake.*—Beat together one pound of sugar half a pound of butter, six eggs, tablespoonful of yeast powder, and flour to make a soft dough. Grate two cocoanuts; stir them to the batter; mix thoroughly; roll out, and cut into cakes, and bake in a moderate oven.

725. *Superior Tea Cake.*—Two pounds of flour, one of dry sugar, half a pound of butter, five eggs, beaten separately; a dessert-spoonful of hartshorn or sal-volatile, rolled fine, dissolved in a little warm water. Flavor with mace or cinnamon. Roll very thin, and bake quick.

726. *Plain Tea Cake.*—Three teacups of dry sugar, one of butter, one of sour milk, three pints of flour, three eggs, well beaten; half a teaspoonful of soda. Flavor to taste; roll thin, and bake in a quick oven.

727. *Ristori Cake.*—One teacup of butter, three of sugar, six eggs, four teacups of flour, one cup of sweet milk, one teaspoonful of cream of tartar, half a teaspoonful of soda, half a nutmeg, a wineglass of rose-water. Bake in a moderate oven.

728. *Loaf Cake.*—Two pounds of flour, one of butter, one of sugar, one of raisins, one tumbler of yeast, two tumblers of sweet milk, three eggs. Beat the eggs and sugar together. Mix all the ingredients well together, and set it to rise. After it has risen, work in the raisins (previously seeded and cut.) When it has risen the second time, set it to baking, as you would light bread. A wineglass of brandy improves it. The raisins may be omitted, or any other fruit substituted.

729. *Forrest Cake.*—After the dough for light bread or rolls has risen the first time, take from it about three teacupfuls. Beat three eggs thoroughly and add to them three cups of sugar, beating well. Cream one cup of butter and add to them the sugar and eggs, creaming all well together. Add the dough, and work well until you have made a smooth batter. Season with one nutmeg, a teaspoonful of coriander seed, powdered and sifted; the

same of cinnamon, the same of allspice. Add last a *small* teaspoonful of soda dissolved in a tablespoonful of warm water. It is better to stand and rise about fifteen minutes before baking; but if fruit is added, it should be baked as soon as the fruit is worked in or it will sink to the bottom.

---

730. *Doughnuts.*—Half a pound of butter, three-quarters of a pound of sugar, three tumblerfuls of sweet milk, two eggs beaten with the sugar; a tumblerful of yeast, flour enough to make a dough as soft as for soda biscuit; flavor with mace, cinnamon, or any spices. Set it to rise, and when it has risen well, roll out and cut in diamonds or small squares, and fry in boiling lard, turning frequently. When a light brown, take them out and lay on a soft cloth to absorb the grease. When cold, heap in a dish, sprinkling powdered loaf sugar thickly between.

---

731. *Doughnuts without Yeast.*—One teacup of sour milk, two of sugar, one of butter, four eggs, well beaten; one nutmeg or mace, two small teaspoonfuls of soda, flour enough to roll. Cut the same size, any shape you like. Fry in plenty of hot lard, turning constantly, and manage as above.

---

732. *Jumbles, No. 1.*—Three eggs, half a pound of sifted flour, half a pound of butter, half a pound of loaf sugar, one tablespoonful of rose-water, one nutmeg. Stir the sugar and butter to a cream. Beat the eggs light; add all to the flour, and stir hard with a knife. Sprinkle flour upon your board; flour your hands well; take up with the knife a portion of the dough, and lay it on the board; roll lightly with the hands into long, thin rolls. Cut into equal lengths; curl into rings; lay gently into an iron or tin pan, buttered (not too close, as they spread). Bake in a quick oven five minutes. Grate sugar over the top. The top of the oven should be nearly *red hot.*

---

733. *Jumbles, No. 2—Mr. S.'s Receipt.*—One pound of sugar,

one pound of butter. Cream these together until light; add eight eggs, well beaten; half a teaspoonful of soda, two pounds of flour. Make a funnel-shaped bag of thick cotton or linen jean, open at both ends; in the small end insert a tin tube; tie it in securely so that the batter will not escape; pour the batter in the bag, and press upon greased pans. Bake in a hot oven.

---

734. *Rusks.*—One and a half tumblers of flour, the same of sugar, two even tablespoonfuls of butter, yolks of three and whites of four eggs, two tablespoonfuls of wine, one teaspoonful of yeast powder. Cream butter and flour together; beat the eggs with sugar; beat the batter well. Bake quickly.

---

735. *Drop Cake.*—Weight of six eggs in sugar, the same of flour, the same of butter. Lay aside three of the eggs, and use three, well beaten separately. Make as pound cake; flavor with nutmeg. Drop a small spoonful on flour; roll with the hand into a twist; join the ends; sprinkle loaf sugar over and bake. Currants will improve them.

---

736. *Sugar Biscuit.*—Half a pound of flour, one-quarter of a pound of butter, one-quarter of a pound of powdered loaf sugar. Cream the butter; add the egg and sugar; then the flour and a tablespoonful of cream. Roll out the dough thin; cut with a wineglass.

---

737. *Sweet Wafers.*—Two ounces of butter, half a pound of sugar, half a pound of flour, five eggs, beaten separately. Bake in wafer-irons well greased, and roll over a knife.

---

738. *Marmalade Tea Cakes.*—One pound of butter, one pound of sugar, one pound and a half of flour, a wineglass of wine, cold water enough to make a stiffish dough. Roll into a paste about a quarter of an inch thick, and cut out with a tumbler. Prick them, and bake to a light brown in a quick oven. Spread over

the top a coat of marmalade, and on this a meringue, made of powdered loaf sugar and the whites of eggs, and flavored with lemon or vanilla. Return to the oven until this is a light brown color.

---

739. *Crullers.*—Six eggs, one cup of butter, one cup and a half of sugar. Beat eggs and sugar well. Stir the butter into flour enough to make a smooth dough. Roll, and cut into any shape, and fry in hot lard.

---

740. *Bunns or Rusk.*—Four eggs, three-quarters of a pound of flour, half a pound of sugar, two and a half wineglassfuls of rich milk, six ounces of butter, a wineglass and a half of yeast, if strong; more, if not very brisk; two tablespoonfuls of rose-water, one nutmeg, one large teaspoonful of mixed mace and cinnamon. Sift half a pound of the flour into a pan; the other half into a plate. Put the milk in a soup-plate; cut up the butter in it, and set on the stove until warm. Stir the butter into the milk, and set aside to cool. Beat the eggs; stir them into the milk, and put all into the flour. Put in the spice and rose-water; add the yeast. Stir all hard with a knife; add the sugar very gradually; if put in all at once, the bunns will be heavy. Then, by degrees, sprinkle in the other flour; stir all well together. Butter a pan; put in the mixtures; cover with a cloth, and set near the fire to rise. This will take about five hours. When risen, divide into pieces the size of a hen's egg; make into rolls, and put in the pan. Bake in a moderate oven.

---

741. *Bunns.*—One-quarter of a pound of sugar, the same of butter, one pound of flour, one egg, three wineglassfuls of milk, two of yeast, one teaspoonful of cinnamon; knead the dough well; let it rise; then divide in small pieces; knead each piece into a little round cake; lay in a buttered pan, and set in a warm place to rise; prick the tops with a fork. When risen, bake in a moderate oven.

Bunns may be glazed on the top with the white of an egg.

742. *Plain Bunns.*—One tumbler of sweet milk, three eggs, tablespoonful of butter or lard, six tablespoonfuls of sugar, beaten with the eggs until they are light; half a tumbler of good yeast, flour to make into rather a soft dough. Set in a warm place to rise. When risen, mould into rolls, as in the foregoing When risen the second time, bake as quickly as possible.

743. *Tip Top Cake.*—One egg, one tablespoonful of butter, slightly heaped; one cup of sugar. Cream all together until light and spongy; add, alternately, two cups of flour and a small teacup of sweet milk, a dessert-spoonful of yeast powder or half a teaspoonful of soda and one teaspoonful of cream of tartar; rub the cream of tartar dry in the flour; dissolve the soda in the milk. Beat all together, and flavor with rose-water or with any spice or extract liked.

744. *Southern Rights Cake.*—Four tea cups of sifted flour, five eggs, two teacupfuls of sugar, two teacupfuls of butter, one tablespoonful of sifted ginger, one teaspoonful of allspice, and one of cinnamon, a wineglassful of brandy, one teaspoonful of soda, one teacup, not quite full, of molasses (syrup will not answer); cream the flour and butter; beat the sugar to the yolks of the eggs; dissolve the soda in the molasses; whip the whites to a froth, and add last. Best baked in small pans.

745. *Railroad Cake.*—One large teacupful of sugar, a tablespoonful of butter somewhat heaped, two eggs, one pint of sifted flour, one teacup of sweet milk, one teaspoonful of soda, and two of cream of tartar, or a dessert-spoonful of yeast powders. Dissolve the soda in the milk, and rub the cream of tartar in the flour. Flavor according to taste.

746. *Nondescripts.*—Yolks of four eggs beaten light, one teaspoonful of salt, flour enough to form a stiff dough; beat the dough well, and roll as thin as tissue paper; cut out by a saucer, and fold twice. Cut with a knife into narrow strips, leaving them united at the extreme point. Fry in plenty of boiling lard. When taken up, sprinkle loaf sugar thickly over them. Instead of shaping as above, the dough may be cut in strips about an inch wide and four inches long, and fried as directed. The former, however, is prettier.

---

747. *Shrewsbury Cake.*—One pound of sugar, one pound of butter, one and a half pounds of flour, one egg, half a tumblerful of milk. Form into a soft dough; roll thin; cut into small cakes, and bake.

---

748. *Marvels.*—Three eggs, three tablespoonfuls of sugar, one tablespoonful of melted lard, flour enough to make it of the consistence of biscuit dough. Roll and cut in diamond shapes, or in strips about four inches long and three wide, subdivided into narrow strips connected at either end. Fry in boiling lard, and sift loaf sugar over them. These are pretty cut with a jagging-iron.

---

749. *Lady's Fingers.*—Make these of sponge-cake batter; form them an oval shape upon sheets of white paper slightly damp. Make them three inches long, of the same size and shape. When done, remove them carefully from the paper; cover the under side of one with jelly; lay on this another cake, putting the under side upon the jelly; fit them neatly. Sponge-cake is excellent made of half corn starch, the rest wheat flour, or arrow-root and flour. These may be cemented with icing, or the white of an egg, instead of jelly.

---

750. *Soft Ginger Cake.*—Four eggs beaten separately, three tumblerfuls of flour, one of butter, one of sugar, one of molasses, a teaspoonful of soda stirred well into the molasses, or two teaspoonfuls of yeast powders sprinkled into the batter; ginger, to your taste.

---

751. *Soft Ginger Bread.*—Two and a half cups of molasses,

one tablespoonful of butter, five eggs, one tablespoonful of ginger, one teaspoonful of soda, enough flour to thicken to the consistency of pound-cake batter.

---

752. *"Colquitt" Ginger Bread.*—Half a pound of butter, one quarter of a pound of brown sugar, one tablespoonful of ginger, one teaspoonful of cinnamon, six eggs, three gills of molasses, half a gill of milk, the grating of one orange, half a pound of flour, half a pound of corn starch, and a teaspoonful of soda. Beat the butter, sugar, and spice well together; mix the flour and starch. Beat the eggs, and add to them the starch and flour, half at a time. Stir the milk and molasses in; then the remainder of the flour and starch. After beating, add the soda. Line with paper, and grease the pan. Bake in a moderate oven.

---

753. *Mrs. H.'s Soft Ginger Cake.*—One cup of sugar, three of molasses, one of butter, one of sweet milk, three eggs, seven cups of flour, one teaspoonful of soda beaten well into the molasses; ginger and spice to taste.

---

754. *Fruit Ginger Cake.*—One pound of flour, one cup of sugar, two of molasses, half a pound of butter, six eggs, one pound of currants, the same of raisins, half a pound of citron, one tablespoonful of ginger, one teaspoonful of cinnamon and allspice, one teaspoonful of soda, and two of cream of tartar, or three teaspoonfuls of yeast powders.

---

755. *Superior Ginger Cakes.*—Four eggs, one cup of sour milk, one quart of molasses, one cup of sugar, one cup of butter, one cup of lard, one tablespoonful of ginger, an even tablespoonful of soda beaten into the molasses. The eggs and sugar should be beaten together as for cake; the butter worked into the flour. After mixing the ingredients thoroughly, handle as little as possible. Flour your board and rolling-pin *well*, as the dough should be as soft as can be handled. Roll a quarter of an inch thick; cut with any shaped tin, and bake in a quick oven.

756. *Ginger Crisps.*—One cup of sugar, two of molasses, one of butter, a teaspoonful of soda in a small quantity of water, ginger to your taste, flour to make a stiff dough. Roll very thin; cut with a wineglass, and bake in a quick oven.

---

757. *Ginger Crisps, No. 2.*—Two cups of molasses, one of lard, one tablespoonful of ginger, one dessert-spoonful of soda dissolved in a very little hot water, and enough flour to make a smooth dough. Roll thin.

---

758. *Ginger Nuts.*—Three and a half pounds of flour, one pound of butter, half a pound of sugar, one quart of molasses, five even tablespoonfuls of ginger, three teaspoonfuls of allspice, one of cloves, and two teaspoonfuls of cinnamon. Make a smooth dough; roll out, and cut about the size of a cent piece; wash over with molasses and water, and bake in a moderate oven.

---

759. *Miss Matilda's Ginger Cakes.*—Three quarts of flour, one teacup of lard, one quart of molasses, one tablespoonful of soda beat into the molasses, half a teacup of sour milk, and three tablespoonfuls of ginger. Roll half an inch thick; cut in any shape, and brush over with the white of an egg.

---

760. *Ginger Cake—Mrs. S.'s Receipt.*—Half a teacup of lard, a teacup nearly full of good brown sugar, half a teacup of sweet milk, a tablespoonful of molasses, an even tablespoonful of ginger, and half a teaspoonful of soda. Bake in a pan.

---

761. *Spice Ginger Cake.*—Five eggs, two teacups of butter, four of flour, two of sugar, one teacup not quite full of molasses, with a teaspoonful of soda stirred into it until it foams from the bottom; a wineglass of brandy, a tablespoonful of ginger, one of cinnamon, and one of allspice and cloves mixed. Add the whites frothed last; next to the last, the molasses. Fruit may be added.

ICING.

A STEW-PAN lined with porcelain or tin is the best vessel to use in boiling icing.

---

762. *Nonpareil Icing.*—One pound of the best loaf sugar; pour over it half a tumblerful of water; let it boil until it will fall in short drops from the spoon; pour it immediately into an earthen bowl, and when it is milk-warm, break into it the whites of three large, fresh hen's eggs; beat until stiff and white, adding half the juice of a lemon, or half a teaspoonful of cream of tartar. Flavor with extract of lemon, vanilla, or any flavoring preferred. It can be colored a delicate pink, if liked, with cochineal, strawberry juice or extract, or with the juice of a beet.

---

763. *Beautiful Icing.*—The whites of four eggs well beaten with one pound of loaf sugar pulverized and sifted, a teaspoonful of arrowroot, and one of pulverized and sifted white gum Arabic, and the juice of one lemon. Flavor with rose-water, or anything liked.

---

764. *Almond Icing.*—This can be made by either of the above receipts, by using to a pound of sugar, half a pound of almonds, sweet and bitter mixed, blanched and beaten to a paste, with a little rose-water. It is by far the best for icing fruit cakes, as it does not become discolored so easily as the plain.

In using icing, after the cake is floured, pour (if for a large cake) two or three tablespoonfuls on the top, and spread over evenly with a large-bladed knife, keeping a glass of water convenient, into which dip the knife for smoothing over any little inequalities that may appear. It is best dried in the sun if the weather will permit. If dried by the fire, care must be taken to prevent scorching. Should any of the icing remain, make of it macaroons, kisses, and meringues. In using almonds, always mix a few bitter ones, or peach kernels, with the sweet.

---

765. *Almond Macaroons.*—One pound of blanched almonds; beat to a paste, with rose-water, one pound and a half of loaf sugar pulverized, and the whites of seven eggs; mix well. Roll in flour a teaspoonful to each ball, and bake upon paper buttered. Bake in a quick oven. Cocoanut grated, and parched ground peas, are all good.

FANCY DISHES.

766. *Meringue—Mr. S.'s Receipt.* — Whites of eight eggs beaten stiff (they should be beaten entirely from one direction); one pound of pulverized white sugar; flavor to taste. Make a bag, funnel-shape, open at both ends; tie a tin tube in the small end; cover seasoned plank that will not impart a wood taste, with white paper; wet the paper with water, pour the meringue in the bag, lay the tube on the paper, and press out in any shape liked. Bake in a moderate oven. Make the bag of thick cotton or linen jean.

---

767. *Prune Meringues.* — Stew prunes enough to half fill a dish of suitable size; sweeten to taste; put them in the dish, and cover with a handsome meringue. This makes a very nice dessert.

Preserved cherries may be used in the same way.

---

768. *Lemon Soufflé.* — The yolks of three eggs, three ounces of sugar, and the grated rind of half a lemon. Beat these together well; add to them the whites of the eggs, beaten to a solid froth, and the juice of half a lemon. Put all immediately into a deep pudding-dish, and bake for ten or fifteen minutes. Serve with a sauce made of two well-beaten eggs, the juice and grated peel of half a lemon. Stir it over the fire till it begins to rise. Care must be taken not to let the soufflé get too brown. The safest way to cook soufflés is to set the dish over boiling water, and hold over a red hot salamander or large shovel until the egg is of a golden color.

---

769. *Trifle.* — Beat the whites of four eggs to a stiff froth; whip a pint of rich cream on a flat dish with a silver fork or egg-beater until very solid; then mix the two in a bowl, adding alternately cream and egg, a spoonful at a time; flavor to taste.

Serve in a glass stand, putting in a layer of cream, then one of almond macaroons or meringues. Prepare this just before serving.

---

770. *Syllabub, No. 1.*—One pint of thick cream (if it should be a little acid, stir in enough soda to sweeten it). Mix with the cream one quarter of a pound of white sifted sugar; let it stand half an hour; then add three wineglasses of Sherry or Madeira wine. Whip to a stiff froth, and fill the glasses. Either churn the cream, using a small tin syllabub churn (which can be procured at any tin-shop), or pour the cream upon a flat dish and whip with a silver fork or egg-beater. The latter is more tedious, but the syllabub is more solid.

---

771. *Syllabub, No. 2.*—Beat to a solid froth the whites of four eggs; mix with a pint of rich cream; sweeten with four tablespoonfuls of pulverized loaf sugar; add wine to taste, and whip to a stiff froth and fill the glasses. It should be whipped until very solid.

---

772. *Boiled Custard.*—Twelve common-sized teacups of sweet milk, twelve eggs, all broken together and well beaten; thirteen tablespoonfuls of sifted loaf sugar, beaten into the eggs. Put the milk on to simmer with a few sticks of cinnamon. After the eggs are well beaten, pour them into the milk, stirring the milk constantly until it begins to thicken. Pour it off, and set where it will become perfectly cold. Take of whipped syllabub enough to cover the tops of the glasses which you fill with the custards; place it on the bottom of a clean sifter inverted over a plate, and let it remain long enough to drip out any cream that the froth may contain. When well dripped, heap roughly upon the top of the custard in the glasses. The custard may be served in a large glass bowl.

---

773. *Plain Boiled Custard.*—Put to boil a quart of fresh milk.

Take two tablespoonfuls of corn or potato starch, farina, or arrowroot, or of wheat flour, and mix to a smooth paste with a little cold milk. When the quart of milk boils up, pour the paste to it, and let it boil five minutes. In a large bowl stir to the yolks of eight eggs eight heaped tablespoonfuls of pulverized sugar until they are mixed. (The yolks of the eggs should be beaten as little as will answer, as custards are much richer to retain as much as possible of the natural color of the egg.) When the milk is tepid, pour it to the eggs, and return to the kettle; throw in a stick or two of cinnamon, and boil according to the directions following this receipt. When the custard is done, pour it into an earthen bowl; stir steadily for a few minutes; then set it where it will become icy cold. Flavor with any extract liked.

The whites should not be beaten until just before the custard is to be served; then whip them to a solid froth, and flavor with the same flavoring used for the custard. They may be delicately colored with a teaspoonful of molasses, or with any of the coloring extracts, or with cochineal. Lay this upon the custard. Serve the custard in a large glass bowl or in custard cups. This custard is excellent poured into cups, the cups set in an oven or pan half filled with boiling water, and baked.

Directions for boiling custards: For this a double kettle is best; where this cannot be procured, boil in a tin bucket; set in an oven of water kept constantly boiling. Stir the custard well from the bottom, and when it begins to form like beads on the bottom of the spoon, lose no time in pouring it out. An earthen vessel is best for pouring it into, as it does not retain heat so long as tin. After pouring it out, stir steadily for five or six minutes, as it sometimes curdles after it is taken up. For making custards, perfectly fresh milk should be used. Should it be necessary to use that which has been standing, first add to it a little soda to prevent its turning.

774. *White Custard.*—The whites of eight eggs, one-quarter of a pound of sugar; whip as you would for icing. Boil a quart of

milk; add to it a tablespoonful of arrowroot; wet up with cold milk, and boil for five minutes. Pour off the milk, and when tepid, add it to the eggs, stirring well. Return it to the kettle, and boil ten minutes, stirring constantly. Pour it out, and when cool, flavor with vanilla or any thing preferred.

It is well to make this to serve with those baked custards in which only the yolk of the egg is used.

---

775. *Tapioca Boiled Custard.*—Put to soak in one pint of milk a tumblerful of tapioca. Let it soak at least an hour; then pour to it a quart of milk mixed with the yolks of six eggs. Put on to boil with a stick of cinnamon or a few fresh peach leaves, to flavor it. When the tapioca is soft, and the custard begins to thicken, take it up. Serve in custard-cups, grating a little nutmeg over.

---

776. *Floating Island.*—Place slices of sponge or Naples biscuit at the bottom of a large glass stand. Pour the dish half full of good boiled custard. Beat to the whites of the eggs six table spoonfuls of hog's foot or calf's foot jelly to a stiff froth. Place this irregularly on the top of the custard.

If it is not convenient to use either of the jellies mentioned, any kind of fruit jelly will answer, using four tablespoonfuls.

---

777. *Gipsy Squire.*—Saturate with Sherry wine a thin sponge-cake. Ornament the top with blanched almonds, sticking them in with the points upwards, and tastily arranged. Half fill a large glass bowl with good boiled custard, and carefully place the cake on the top of the custard, taking care that the bowl used is of a circumference somewhat larger than that of the cake.

---

778. *Muffled Cake.*—Place a thin sponge-cake in the bottom of a glass bowl. Nearly fill the bowl with rich boiled custard. Heap thick and high over this, syllabub from which the cream has been dripped through a sieve. Ornament this with small, thin bits of solid fruit jelly.

779. *Velvet Cream.*—Three-quarters of a pound of isinglass dissolved in a teacup of white wine, warm; strain it; mix with one pint of cream and the juice of one lemon. Sweeten to your taste, and when all is mixed together, pour into moulds.

---

780. *Swiss Cream.*—One pint of sweet cream, half a pound of loaf sugar, the yolks of eight eggs. Beat together, and simmer for a few minutes. Put one ounce of gelatine in a quart of water, and boil down to a pint. Pour the two mixtures together. Let it come to a boil; set it aside. When cool, flavor with lemon or vanilla. Put upon it syllabub from which the cream has been dripped through a sieve.

---

781. *Isabella Cream.*—One ounce of isinglass dissolved in half a pint of boiling water. After straining it, add one quart of cream, and stir till it boils. One teacup of crushed sugar is now put in, and the mixture a little cooled; then the beaten yolks of six eggs are gradually added, together with one glass of wine. The whole should be strained and stirred until almost cool, when it may be turned into a mould. This is a handsome dish, as the yolks of the eggs give it a fine, rich color.

---

782. *Bohemian Cream.*—Take four ounces of any kind of fruit which has been stewed soft with sugar; pass this through a sieve; add to half a pint of the fruit an ounce and a half of melted isinglass; mix it well; whip up a pint of cream, and add to it gradually the fruit and isinglass. Put it into a mould; set on ice or in any cool place, and when ready, dip the mould into warm water and turn out.

Grated pineapple will make the above cream most elegant. It is very nice made with apples or any good fruit, and almond cream, very nice, may be made by substituting for the fruit almonds blanched and pounded with rose-water.

---

783. *Apple Soufflé.*—Boil and sweeten the fruit; strain through a sieve. Put this into a deep dish. When cold, pour over a rich custard about two inches deep. Whip the whites of the eggs to a stiff froth, and lay, in rough pieces, on the custard. Sift fine sugar over it thick, and put into a slack oven for a few minutes.

---

784. *Egg Soufflé.*—Six eggs, beaten separately; with the yolks beat a tablespoonful of sugar to each egg, very thoroughly; mix very lightly with the whites; flavor with any kind of extract; put into a fire-proof dish, filling the dish, and heaping slightly. Put into a stove or oven of a very moderate heat, and let it remain until heated through, and a very light crust is formed over it. To be eaten immediately.

This is a very nice little dessert; serves well as an accompaniment to cake. Should not be made until after dinner has been sent in, as very few minutes are required for making it, and should be very closely watched while baking, as too great heat will quickly spoil it.

---

785. *Apple Float.*—One pint of dried apples, stewed, mashed, and strained; sweeten and flavor with nutmeg to taste. Beat to a stiff froth the whites of six eggs; add lightly to the fruit. Eat in saucers or strawberry plates, with rich cream sauce

---

786. *Apple Snow*—Is made by the same receipt, using green apples instead of dried.

---

787. *Float.*—Beat to a stiff froth the whites of four eggs flavored with a few drops of extract of lemon; sweeten a pint of rich cream; pour it over the eggs; add six teaspoonfuls of currant or some dark, acid jelly. Beat for an hour, until perfectly light. The cream will answer if a little acid.

---

788. *Charlotte Russe.*—Dissolve in a pint of water one and a half ounces of isinglass; let it boil until reduced one half. Boil, and flavor with vanilla, one pint of milk. Beat well the yolks

of six eggs, and stir into them half a pound of loaf sugar. Strain the milk into the eggs; let them simmer on the fire a few moments, but not boil. Strain the isinglass into the custard. Whip to a strong froth two pints of cream; lay this on the bottom of a sifter, inverted, to drip; then stir it into the custard, and set it away to congeal. (Flavor the cream with wine.) Put it into a mould to give it a pretty shape before it cools; or, if you prefer, make a mould of sponge-cake, by cutting out the centre, leaving the walls an inch or two thick. Or, make a mould of lady's fingers, by placing them upright inside, of any kind of a shape, cementing the edges with the white of an egg. After they are placed, set the mould on ice, and pour in the Charlotte russe just as it begins to congeal. Keep it on ice until just before serving. This may be iced.

---

789. *Another Charlotte Russe.*—Break up one ounce of Cooper's American isinglass (or use Cox's gelatine) in a tumbler of water; let it stand all night; then pour into it four tumblers of new milk; put it on to boil. When dissolved, pour it on the yolks of six eggs well beaten, with three quarters of a pound of loaf sugar. Pour it again into the kettle to boil. When it begins to thicken, and is nearly done, add the whites of six eggs well beaten. Stir it all the time, or it will be lumpy. When cold, add a pint of whipped cream, and drip it upon a sieve. Flavor with lemon or vanilla, and pour into moulds to congeal.

---

790. *Curds and Cream.*—Drip the whey from clabber through a perforated tin shape—a large heart shape is very pretty. Serve (when dry enough to turn out) with rich cream sauce, flavored with nutmeg. Sweet milk may be turned with rennet, using a piece two inches square to a quart of milk.

---

791. *Buttermilk Curds.*—Three pints of buttermilk, three tumblers of new milk. Boil the sweet milk with a stick of cinnamon; pour to the buttermilk hot; let it stand until the whey

is cleared from the curds; drip it. Eat with cream and loaf sugar. Flavor with nutmeg.

---

792. *Directions for Freezing Ice-Creams and Custards.*—Ice-creams, custards and water are so delightful and refreshing for summer desserts and tea, it is to me a matter of astonishment that every family is not supplied with a patent ice-cream freezer, of which there are many in the market. By the use of one of these, the process of freezing is rendered so much more expeditious and satisfactory as to more than compensate for the trifling expense involved in its purchase. If not provided with this convenience, a small quantity of ice-cream can be frozen in a tin bucket, taking care that there are no holes in it to let in the water, and spoil the cream. Set this bucket in a wooden tub or bucket several inches larger. On the bottom of this place a layer of pounded ice and salt; set in the bucket containing the cream, or custard, and pack closely around its sides a mixture of pounded ice and salt (mixed in the proportion of six pounds of ice to one of salt), extending to within two inches of the top of the freezer. Cover the freezer, and keep it in constant motion, removing the cover frequently to scrape the congealed cream from the sides with a silver spoon or wooden paddle, taking care to keep the sides clear, and stirring it well to the bottom. Keep the tub well filled with salt and ice outside the freezer, and take great care that none of the salt water gets in to spoil the cream. The outside tub or bucket should have a hole in or near the bottom, from which the bung can be removed to allow the water to pass out as the ice melts. After the cream is well frozen, it may be packed in moulds, and set in salt and pounded ice. When you wish to serve it, wrap the mould with a hot cloth, turn out the cream and serve immediately.

For making ice-cream, genuine *cream* is, of course, preferable. But in the absence of this, equal parts of milk and cream may be used; or, the milk may be heated, and, while hot, perfectly fresh sweet butter added to it in sufficient quantity to give it the richness of cream. Boiled milk or custards must be allowed to become perfectly cold before putting them in the freezer. Sour cream or buttermilk may be used by stirring into them enough soda to correct their acid before sweetening and flavoring. Custards and creams for freezing should be sweetened and flavored more highly than when not frozen. A half pound of powdered loaf sugar and four eggs will be sufficient for a quart of custard; stir the eggs and sugar together. Scald fresh sweet milk; pour boiling hot upon the eggs, stirring constantly. Flavor to taste, and when cold, pour into the freezer. Finish by the directions already given.

When flavored with fruit (if raspberries or strawberries), stem the fruit; mash it; add to each pint four tablespoonfuls of powdered loaf sugar; stir this into the fruit. Add a grated lemon to each quart. This is not absolutely necessary, but is an improvement; the custard is rather insipid without it. Let this set at least two hours before using. Strain the fruit, pressing it through a sieve. Use a pint of juice to a pint of custard. The color may be heightened by adding to the juice a little prepared cochineal; add more sugar if not sufficiently sweet. For pineapple custard, grate the fruit after peeling; it is better if one grated lemon is used to each pineapple. Soft peaches may be used, mashing and rubbing them through a sieve; mix with the cream or custard, and freeze. Apricots, apples, etc., or any fruit liked, may be grated or cooked, and then mashed, sweetened, and stirred to the cream or custard; let it remain until the flavor is sufficiently imparted, then strain, and put to freeze. The extracts and syrups of these fruits afford a good substitute when the fresh fruit cannot be procured. If a richer custard is preferred, use either of the three given in the receipts for boiled custards. The white custard is particularly fine when frozen. Flavor to taste, the flavoring giving the name to the custard.

---

793. *Milk Sherbet.*—Sweeten, and flavor the milk to taste; put it in the freezer just as it begins to freeze; add the juice of

three lemons (first roll the lemons before squeezing) to each gallon of milk; add a little of the extract of lemon. Stir all together well; flavor the milk by boiling the peel in it; then when cold, freeze.

---

794. *Lemon-Water Ice.*—Rub lumps of sugar upon the rinds of four lemons until a pound of loaf sugar is used; pour over it a quart of water; squeeze in the juice. Freeze, or make a lemonade, sweeter than when not intended to freeze, and more highly flavored. Freeze, and serve in glasses.

---

795. *Orange-Water Ice*—Is made in the same way as the lemon-water ice, using less sugar, and if the oranges are very sweet, use one lemon to four large oranges. After these preparations are nearly frozen stiff, stir into a quart the whites of two eggs beaten to a stiff froth. Mix thoroughly. Serve in glasses. Any kind of fruit ices may be prepared by adding to the water any syrup or jam of the fruit desired. Grate apples, sweeten, and freeze them; mash soft peaches, freeze them, and any kind of fruit liked.

---

796. *Sherbet.*—To six lemons and eight sweet oranges, sliced, and the seed removed, put one gallon of water, and sweeten to taste. Freeze, or use ice.

---

797. *Wine Ices*—Are made by taking as much lemonade as is required for freezing, making it not quite so highly flavored as for lemon ice—omitting one lemon, and adding claret or Sherry to taste. Add Jamaica rum to the lemonade, and you have Roman punch. Freeze, or use ice.

FRUITS, ETC.

"Nothing can be more delicious than fruit. It is a cheap mode of furnishing a dessert, or for the tea-table—wholesome, nutritious, and pleasant.

"Every species has a flavor peculiar to itself, and this variety renders them more pleasing. Thus God resembles a tender father, who provides not only for the support, but also for the pleasures of his children.

---

798. *To Prepare the Pineapple for the Table.*—An old writer (Sturm) says of this fruit: "That pride of vegetable life, and compendium of all the blandishments of taste—the pineapple." Peel them; slice thin; pile in layers, sprinkling between each layer powdered loaf sugar. A pound of sugar to a pound of fruit. Let this stand an hour or two before using. Some persons add wine. I protest against the adding of a single thing. "Loveliness needs not the foreign aid of ornament." Pineapples are best sliced lengthwise, so as to avoid the centre, which is hard and tasteless.

---

799. *Ambrosia*—Is made by placing upon a glass stand, or other deep vessel, alternate layers of grated cocoanut, oranges peeled and sliced round, and a pineapple sliced thin. Begin with the oranges, and use cocoanut last, spreading between each layer sifted loaf sugar. Sweeten the cocoanut milk, and pour over.

---

800. *Snow.*—Cocoanut grated; ornament with box-vine.

---

801. *Oranges.*—A pretty style of preparing oranges for the table is to cut the rind through with a sharp penknife into quarters, leaving the pulp whole. Peel off the rind, leaving it attached

to the orange at the stem end, and turn in the separated points, so as to form a cup-like receptacle for the fruits. Heap this in stands, and ornament with orange leaves, or some other bright, glossy leaves.

---

802. *Bananas.*—Bananas should be perfectly yellow. Strip them; serve upon a flat dish.

---

803. *Peaches and Cream.*—Peel soft juicy peaches, quarter them, put a layer of peaches, one of sugar, sprinkling it on very thick until the desired quantity is prepared. Spread thickly over the last layer of peaches powdered loaf sugar. Set the dish upon ice or in a very cool place an hour before using; do not bruise them. Some persons like them best mashed fine, sweetened, and a little grated nutmeg added; in either way serve in small deep plates; eat with rich cream.

---

804. *Raspberries and Strawberries*—Are also delicious. Cap them, wash very little; they must not be allowed to remain in the water a moment longer than necessary. Put layers of the fruit and powdered loaf sugar in glass stands. The fruit will wilt after the sugar is put upon them; this is particularly the case with strawberries. If they are to be kept several hours, it is best not to cap them (always wash them before capping) until an hour before they are to be served.

---

805. *A Pretty Dish.*—Pare and core, without splitting, some small-sized tart apples; boil them gently with one lemon for every six apples until a straw will pass through them. Make a syrup of half a pound of loaf sugar for each pound of apples; put the apples in unbroken, and the lemons sliced, and boil gently until the apples look clear. Take them up carefully, so as not to break them; add an ounce or more of clarified isinglass to the syrup, and let it boil up. Put the apples in a glass stand with a slice of lemon over each, and when the syrup is nearly cold, strain it over them. Eat with thick cream.

FRUITS, ETC.

806. *Watermelons*—Make a delicious dessert. A bright red watermelon makes a very showy appearance if cut through the middle, crosswise, in points. Cut a piece off each end so as to give both halves a level base to stand upon.

---

807. *Breakfast Fruits.*—Grapes, figs, and cantelopes are nice breakfast fruits, and may be served in this way: Remove the first course, and the white cloth; if the table is not a handsome one, it should be covered with a wine cloth, under the white tablecloth; always send colored doylies with fruit. Grapes may be tastily arranged with their leaves. Finger-bowls should be placed before each person, to be used after the fruit course is finished.

---

808. *Calf or Hog's Foot Jelly.*—To make clear jelly, great care is necessary in preparing the stock. Have no salt about the feet until after they are taken out of the liquor in which they were boiled. After taking them out, strain the liquor, and when it is cold, skim off carefully every particle of the grease. (This oil should be clarified and bottled, and answers many valuable purposes in a family.) After skimming, scrape over the top of the jelly, and then wipe it carefully with a coarse towel. It is sometimes necessary to melt it a second time, in order to clear it entirely of the grease. To two gallons of the jelly, six tumblerfuls of powdered loaf sugar, six tumblerfuls of wine (pale Sherry), six sticks of cinnamon, six lemons cut up, removing the seed (when lemons are scarce, good cider may be used, flavoring with extract of lemon). Wash and wipe carefully six eggs; beat the whites to a froth; crush the shells and put into the preserving kettle. As the jelly melts, mix all the ingredients well, and stir no more, as it would interfere with the clarifying process. When the jelly boils clear, remove the egg carefully; have ready a Canton flannel bag, made with a loop on each side, through which to run a stick for suspending it. Strain the jelly through this bag, and if it does not run clear the first time, strain it again; never squeeze the bag, but let it remain suspended from the stick (the ends of which are supported by chairs) until all the jelly has dripped out. In very cold weather it is necessary to suspend the bag before a fire, to prevent the jelly from congealing in the bag. While it is dripping, protect from dust, by covering the whole with a tablecloth.

---

809. *Gelatine Jelly—Mrs. W.'s Receipt.*—One box of Cox's gelatine, two quarts of water, one pint of wine, two lemons, one quart of sugar, one and a half sticks of cinnamon, one and a half dozen cloves, two blades of mace, the beaten whites and shells of six eggs; stir till it boils. Let it boil thirty minutes, and strain through a Canton flannel bag.

Cox's sparkling gelatine is a superior article, and the directions, which are very good, always accompany the packages.

---

810. *Lemon Jelly.*—One ounce of the best isinglass, one and a half pounds of loaf sugar, three lemons (pulp, skin, and juice), removing the seed. Pour on the isinglass a quart of boiling water; stir into this the lemon; add a glass of the best Sherry or Madeira wine. Strain into moulds. If the lemons are not fresh, add a little tartaric acid. If this does not congeal, dissolve, and add more isinglass.

Orange jelly is made in the same way, using oranges instead of lemons.

---

811. *Wine Jelly.*—One ounce of Cox's Sparkling gelatine, one pound of loaf sugar. Dissolve the gelatine in a pint of boiling water; add the sugar and a quart of white wine. Stir the mixture very hard, and pour it into a mould. When it has congealed, wrap the mould in a cloth dipped in warm water; turn out the jelly, and eat with cream.

---

812. *Blanc-Mange.*—Take a pint of calf's foot jelly after it is prepared; melt it, and mix with the yolks of six eggs well beaten, with two tablespoonfuls of sifted loaf sugar; put it into the kettle

again, and let it *just come to a boil.* Pour it into a mould, and set in a cool place, and stir for some time to prevent its curdling Eat with cream or custard, flavored with lemons. This may be made of Cox's gelatine. First make a pint of jelly, then add the eggs.

813. *Blanc-Mange, No. 2.*—One measure of calf's or hog's foot jelly after it is prepared, and one of cream. After they are melted together, flavor with sugar and wine to taste. Let it boil up once, and pour into moulds. Wet the moulds with cold water before using.

814. *Carrageen or Irish Moss Blanc-Mange.*—Pick and wash thoroughly one cup of Irish moss; pour to it one quart of milk. Sweeten to taste. Let it boil until it thickens; strain through a thin cloth, and pour into a mould. Very little boiling is necessary. Eat with sweetened cream or with custard.

815. *Corn Starch Blanc-Mange.*—Four or five tablespoonfuls of starch to one quart of milk; beat the starch thoroughly with two eggs, and add it to the milk, when near boiling, with a little salt; boil a few minutes, stirring it briskly. Flavor with rose, lemon, or vanilla, and cool in small cups or wineglasses. When cold and stiff, turn into a glass stand. Sweeten it while cooking, or use a sauce of sugar and cream.

Farina blanc-mange is made in the same way. Set on ice if convenient.

816. *Arrowroot Blanc-Mange.*—A teacupful of arrowroot wet up to a paste with a little cold water. Boil a quart of milk and pour to the arrowroot, stirring it well. Boil again until it thickens, and pour into cups or moulds. Flavor and sweeten to taste before boiling the second time. By the addition of a few eggs, and a little butter, this makes a very nice custard, baked in a rich paste.

Potato starch may be used in the same way.

817. *Isinglass Blanc-Mange*.—An ounce of isinglass (in warm weather an ounce and a quarter); dissolve in a pint of boiling water. Let it stand until cold; add a quart of milk and a stick of cinnamon. Boil until the isinglass is dissolved; sweeten and flavor to taste, and turn into moulds. Wet the moulds with cold water before pouring in the blanc-mange; it will turn out better.

---

818. *Ice Pudding* (*A Delicious Dessert*).—Make a rich boiled custard of a pint of milk, pint of cream, yolks of eight eggs; sweeten to taste. Beat smooth, adding rose-water, a quarter of a pound of sweet and bitter almonds; mix a quarter of a pound of raisins seeded, the same of currants, half as much citron and preserved orange peel; flour these well. Pour the custard hot over the fruit; mix well. When cool, add a pint of whipped and drained syllabub. Put it into any kind of mould of pretty shape, and freeze it. Serve with custard or syllabub sauce; flavor and sweeten to taste.

---

819. *Fruit Jellies*—Should be made with the best loaf sugar. The pulverized sugar is more or less adulterated. The fruit should be of good quality, and free from defects. Jellies should be made in a brass kettle, or in iron lined with porcelain. When brass is used, great pains should be taken to keep the kettle perfectly bright and clean. Jellies are best kept in tumblers, cups, or small moulds. The vessels should not be quite filled. Letter paper or tissue paper, cut to fit the top, should be wet in a little brandy, and laid on the jelly in the mould. Thicker paper should be cut of a little larger size, and pasted with the white of an egg over the tops of the moulds. Put up in this way, the jelly will keep for years. It should be set in a dry, cool place.

To know when jelly is done, drop a teaspoonful in cold water. If it drops clear from the spoon, and becomes of a proper consistency, take it off immediately. Should it unfortunately become ropy from boiling too long, it can be used to a very good purpose for preparing summer drinks, nectars, water ices, etc.

820. *Apple Jelly.*—Use apples of a pleasant acid. Peel and core them, and, as you cut them, throw the pieces immediately into cold water, to prevent their being discolored by the action of the air. When you have prepared as many as you wish to use, put them into the preserving-kettle, and pour over them just enough water to cover them. Cover closely with a plate, and let them boil without interruption until the apples are soft; then strain through a thin linen bag into some vessel that can be kept covered. The proportion for making the jelly: To two tumblers of the juice use one tumbler and a half of loaf sugar, pulverized. Measure the juice and the sugar in this proportion, and put into the kettle. Let this syrup boil for a few minutes; then strain through a jelly-bag. Return to the kettle two tumblerfuls of the syrup; this, boiled to the proper consistency, will form one tumblerful of jelly. After preparing the juice, and measuring the proportions, it is safe to make the jelly thus in small quantities.

Quince jelly is made in the same way. Never use the cores and seeds, as the effect of these is to cause the jelly to rope.

Strawberries, blackberries, raspberries, and grapes, all make very pleasant jellies. After washing the fruit, put it on to boil without any water, and when the juice is all extracted, strain and proceed as in apple jelly.

---

821. *Crab Apple Jelly.*—Wash the fruit and remove the stems and all defective parts. Cover them with boiling water, and let them stand until the water is cold. Put them in the kettle; cover with water, and turn a plate closely over them; proceeding in all respects as in the apple jelly, excepting that, being a very acid fruit, they require equal proportions of the juice and sugar. This jelly is nice to serve with baked or roast meats, as also is a jelly made from the wild plum. In straining the juice, never squeeze the bag; only take that which runs clear for the first quality of jelly.

---

822. *Orange Jelly.*—Use large oranges. From the stem end cut a piece of rind about as large as a ten-cent piece; insert the handle of a spoon, and with this remove all the pulp. Throw the rinds into salt water—they make an elegant preserve. From the pulp remove carefully all the seed, and then strain out the juice. To every quart of juice add an ounce of Cox's sparkling gelatine dissolved in a little boiling water. For the sweet oranges, use sugar in the same proportion as in making apple jelly; for sour oranges, use a pound of sugar to a pint of the juice.

PRESERVES, ETC.

For making preserves, a good quality of fruit should always be used, and good sugar. If loaf sugar is used, it will not require clarifying. For many of the small, dark-colored fruits, good brown sugar answers very well, and may be clarified for use in this way: To two pounds of sugar add a pint of water and the white of one egg. Stir all well together when first put into the kettle; after that it must not be stirred. Let it boil until the syrup looks clear, carefully skimming off the dross. Strain through a thin muslin cloth. In preparing the fruit, it should be thrown into water as fast as peeled, to prevent its being discolored by contact with the air. The usual proportion in making preserves, is a pound of sugar to a pound of fruit. There are a few fruits which require more sugar. In making the syrup, use a tumblerful of water to a pound of fruit. The syrup should always be boiled and strained before putting the fruit in it.

---

823. *Oranges Preserved Whole.*—After removing the pulp and juice, as in the directions for making orange jelly, throw the rinds in weak salt and water for twelve hours. Then take them out and boil them in clear water until tender, taking great care not to break them. (The more fully to prevent this, but few should be boiled at a time during the whole process.) For making your syrup, use the best loaf sugar, in the proportion of a pound and a half to a pound of the fruit. Put the sugar in the kettle, and cover with cold water. When it has boiled sufficiently to form a thin syrup, pour it, boiling hot, over the fruit, and set it away to stand twelve hours. Boil again, this time boiling the fruit for about half an hour. Pour the syrup over again, and let it remain twelve hours. Then return all to the kettle until the fruit is fully penetrated with the syrup and looks clear. Put up

in glass jars, and should the syrup appear thin after standing several weeks, boil again.

Lemons can be preserved in the same way.

---

824. *Citron Preserves.*—Take the citron melon; if not very large, cut through the melon crosswise in slices about a quarter of an inch thick; remove the outer rind and the seed, and notch the edge tastily. If the melon is too large for this, cut the slices of a convenient size. After preparing the slices, soak them for twelve hours in lime water (made by dissolving two handfuls of lime in three gallons of water), changing the pieces twice from top to bottom. Then soak in clear water, changing the water twice; then scald in alum water. Now place in the bottom of the preserving-kettle a layer of grape leaves, upon this a layer of citron, then a layer of the leaves, and so on until you have put in all your citron, with a layer of leaves on top. Pour in enough water to cover them, and boil for half an hour; then take out the citron, and plunge into cold water. Boil again with the layers of grape leaves, and plunge again into the cold water. Repeat this several times; then boil, for half an hour, in a moderately strong ginger tea.

To make the syrup: Use a pound and a half of loaf sugar to a pound of citron. After boiling, strain it boiling hot upon the fruit, and let it stand. The next morning boil until the citron is clear and tender. Citron should never be eaten until it is at least a month old. Watermelon rind, peeled and cut into fanciful shapes, may be preserved in the same way. Muskmelons, fully ripe, are sometimes used. They should be cooked without soaking, removing the inside soft part and the outside rind.

---

825. *Glass Melon.*—Gather the melons when fully grown, but before they turn yellow; scrape off the green part of the rind, and cut a small piece from the stem end of the melon. With the handle of a small teaspoon remove the contents; scald them in alum water; plunge them in cold water; let them remain until

cold. Scald them again in fresh water, boiling a few minutes; plunge again in cold water; repeat this four times. Make a thin syrup, allowing one pound and a half of loaf sugar to a pound of the melon. Scald the fruit in this; pour all into a tureen or deep covered dish; let it remain one night; next morning return to the kettle. Slice one lemon to two pounds of citron; remove the seed, and boil with the melons until they are tender.

826. *Pineapple Preserves.*—Wash the fruit and boil, without paring, until they are tender. Take them out, pare them, and slice lengthwise, so as to remove the hard centre. Make a syrup, using a pound of sugar to a pound of fruit; pour it, when boiling hot, over the fruit, and let it stand until the next morning. Then pour off the syrup from the fruit, and boil it until nearly thick enough, when the fruit must be put in and boiled in the syrup for fifteen or twenty minutes.

827. *To Preserve Strawberries.*—Take the weight of the strawberries in double-refined sugar. To each pound add a quarter of a pint of water; boil to a thick syrup. When it cools, pour it over the berries, and let them stand all night. Next morning boil the syrup and fruit ten minutes. Repeat this process for three days in succession. As the syrup becomes thinned by the acid juice which exudes from the strawberries, there would be danger of fermentation unless re-boiled as directed.

As this fruit is difficult to preserve from fermentation, it should be put up in air-tight cans or in small jars, and very carefully tied or sealed up. Keep them in a cool place.

828. *To Preserve Raspberries and Blackberries.*—For these fruits use an equal proportion of sugar. To each pound of the sugar add about a wineglass of water, and boil to a thick syrup. Put the fruit in, and let it boil for fifteen minutes; take it out with a perforated skimmer; spread on dishes, and let them stand in the sun. When the syrup has boiled to a proper consistency,

put the fruit in small jars, and pour the syrup over. Seal tightly. Small delicate fruits such as raspberries, blackberries, etc., require very little cooking. Long boiling impairs their flavor, and renders them hard.

---

829. *To Preserve Cherries*.—With a goose-quill, sharpened to a point as for a pen, remove the stones from a part of the fruit that you wish to use. Prepare a syrup in the same proportions as directed in the foregoing receipts, and when nearly thick enough, add the fruit, and allow it to boil briskly for thirty minutes; then remove with a perforated skimmer, and let the syrup continue to boil until of a proper consistency. Then pour over the fruit, and put up as directed in preceding receipts.

The reason for stoning part of the cherries, is that the seed contain so much Prussic acid that to allow them all to remain would impart too strong a flavor to the preserves.

---

830. *To Preserve Grapes*.—Grapes are preserved in the same way, without seeding them. Select, for preserving, fruit that is not entirely ripe, carefully removing all that are defective. The Scuppernongs are very nice.

---

831. *To Preserve Plums*.—For large, fine plums, that you wish to make particularly nice, remove the skins by scalding them. Make a syrup in the proportion of a pound of sugar to one of fruit, and when thick, pour it boiling hot over the fruit, and let it stand until the succeeding day. Repeat this for three successive days. On the third day put in the fruit and boil until they are done. This mode of preserving is preferred on account of the fruit breaking to pieces if preserved immediately. The boiling syrup poured upon them hardens the fruit.

Plums and damsons may be preserved in the same way with the skins on, and are very suitable for tarts and tartlets.

---

832. *To Preserve Muscadines*.—Wash the fruit carefully, and pulp them. They are prettier with the seeds removed, but the process is a tedious one. Collect the juice carefully with the pulps, and reserve the hulls for making vinegar, or for preserving with brown sugar for winter pies.

Make a syrup in the usual proportion—pound for pound. Put in the fruit, and boil until it looks clear.

---

833. *Crab Apple Preserve.*—Boil for a short time in clear water. Be careful not to boil too long, as the fruit mashes very easily. Just as soon as they are soft enough to admit of removing the cores with a goose-quill, push them out. Soak, for one night, in weak alum water; from this, soak in clear water for two hours. Make a syrup in the proportion of one and a half pound of sugar to one of fruit; put the fruit in, and let it boil until it looks clear. Take them out, and if the syrup is not thick enough, continue boiling until it is of proper consistency.

---

834. *To Preserve Figs.*—Take the fruit when not quite ripe. Soak for ten or fifteen minutes in weak, warm soda water to remove the skin; or peel thinly with a sharp penknife. To one pound of figs use three-quarters of a pound of sugar. When the syrup is made, put in the fruit, and let it boil until half done; take them up, and spread on a dish, and put in the sun. Let the syrup simmer slowly, always carefully removing any impurities that may rise to the surface. When clear, put in the figs; let them cook until transparent, taking them out separately when done. Set in the sun again; if the syrup is not clear, skim again; do not let it boil away too much. Put the figs in jars, and when the syrup is cold, pour it over them.

The small kind, called the Celestial fig, is better unskinned.

---

835 *Preserved Peaches.*—In selecting this fruit for preserving, the best are the yellow, freestone peach, before it is quite ripe, taking care they are yellow throughout, as those that are red next to the seed make a dark preserve. Peel them, and cut in

halves, throwing immediately into cold water to prevent their turning dark. Weigh the sugar in the proportion of pound for pound, and put down in alternate layers to remain all night. (It is best to prepare them late in the evening, and preserve early next morning.) In the morning, pour off the syrup, and clarify by using the white of an egg to a quart of juice. Skim while boiling, and strain through a thin cloth. Put in the fruit. Have ready a few peach kernels blanched, and put in with the fruit. Cover lightly with an earthen plate, and let them simmer gently until the peaches are clear, removing the plate occasionally to turn the fruit from the bottom. When done, take the peaches up, and spread on dishes, and set in the sun half an hour, letting the syrup continue to boil until thick enough. The peach mentioned in the beginning of this receipt is the variety that I prefer for preserving. The white English and the yellow clingstone are also very fine for this purpose. In cutting the fruit, take care to have the slices of a uniform thickness, or the thinner slices will boil to pieces before the thicker ones are done.

---

836. *To Preserve Quinces.*—Wash the fruit; peel it, and as you peel, throw in cold water. Cut in slices of uniform thickness; put them in a kettle, and cover with water; turn a plate over them, and let them stew until tender. Take them out, and into the water (allowing a tumbler of the water to a pound of sugar) in which they were stewed put the sugar in the proportion of pound for pound. Unless loaf sugar is used the syrup will need clarifying. Skim off the impurities, and when the syrup is clear put in the fruit; cover again with the plate and simmer gently until done. Take up with a perforated skimmer and spread on dishes to cool. Quinces will be very hard unless stewed before the sugar is added.

---

837. *Pear Preserves.*—Throw the pears into water as you peel them. Remove the cores or not as may be preferred. Preserve exactly as you would quinces.

MARMALADES, JAMS, ETC.

If put up in small quantities, and for immediate use, three-quarters of a pound of sugar to a pound of fruit is sufficient; but if it is desirable to keep them longer, a pound of sugar is a better proportion. As in preserves, the best sugar should be used.

---

838. *Orange Marmalade.*—For this, use the pulp that has been removed previous to preserving the rinds; carefully pick out all the seeds. If the oranges are sweet, three quarters of a pound of sugar is sufficient to a pound of fruit—for the sour orange, equal proportions will be required. Mix the fruit and sugar well; add half a tumblerful of water to a pound of sugar, and boil for half an hour, stirring a great deal to prevent their burning. A little of the peel, boiled in clear water, and shredded very fine before adding to the mass, gives an improved flavor to this marmalade.

---

839. *Apple Marmalade.*—Peel and slice the apples; weigh and put them into a kettle, and stew until tender. Mash them fine; add the sugar in the proportion of pound to pound. Let them cook slowly, stirring very frequently. By no means allow it to scorch, and when the mass has a jellied appearance, it is done. About half an hour will generally be found sufficient for making the marmalade, after adding the sugar.

---

840. *Quince and Peach Marmalade*—Are made in the same way. They should be put up in tumblers, or very small jars. They are very good for tarts and tartlets.

---

841. *Strawberries, Raspberries, Blackberries and Grapes*—All make nice marmalade or jam.

842. *Compote of Apples.*—To one pound of fruit, peeled and sliced, add one pound of sugar. Boil until the apples can be pierced with a straw. Take the fruit out, and place in a glass or other deep dish. Add to the syrup half an ounce of gelatine to a pound of the fruit, and boil for ten or fifteen minutes. Pour over the fruit when cool enough. The gelatine is not absolutely necessary, but it is a great improvement. Oranges may be done in the same way. Compotes may be made of small fruits, such as plums, apricots, damsons, etc., without peeling. They are delicious, and may be used as desserts, served with cream or mock-cream sauce.

---

843. *Frosted Fruit.*—Select perfect fruit of any small variety, such as cherries, plums, grapes, or small pears, leaving the stems on. Dip them, one by one, in the beaten white of an egg, or in a solution of gum Arabic, and from that into a cup of very finely pulverized sugar. Cover the bottom of a pan with a sheet of fine white paper; place the fruit in it, and set in a stove or oven that is cooling. When the frosting on the fruit becomes firm, heap them on a dish, and set in a cool place.

---

844. *Apple or Gooseberry Fool.*—Put the fruit in a stone jar, with a good quality of brown sugar in the proportion of half a pound to a pound of the fruit. Set the pan on the stove, or in an oven of hot water. Put a large spoonful of water in the bottom of the jar to prevent burning. When they are soft, pass them through a sieve. Have ready one teacup of new milk, the same of cream, boiled together, and left to cool. Sweeten the custard, and by degrees add the fruit. Nice dish for tea.

---

845. *To Bake Apples or Quinces.*—Core them, and fill the cavities with nice sugar. Sprinkle the outsides with sugar, and to a large dish containing a dozen, add a tumblerful of water. Set them to bake slowly. They may be served with meats, or as a dessert, with cream sauce. Use them cold.

Pears are very nice baked in the same way; but, being a rather insipid fruit, it is best to squeeze over them the juice of a lemon, throwing the peel into the water that is added to them.

---

846. *Stewed Peaches.*—Peaches also make a nice dessert, but are better stewed, peeling them, and removing the stones or not, as is preferred. These methods of preparing fruit are also nice for tea. Serve with them cream or mock-cream sauce.

---

847. *Candied Orange and Lemon Peel.*—Remove the pulp and inside skin; cut the peel in strips lengthwise; boil in clear water until tender. Make a syrup in the proportion of half a pound of sugar to a pound of the peel, adding to the sugar as much water as will melt it. Put in the peel, and boil over a slow fire until the syrup candies; then take them out; strew powdered sugar over them, and set in the sun to dry; or, if the weather will not admit of this, dry them in a warm oven or stove. These will be found very useful in making fruit cakes and puddings.

---

848. *Peach Chips.*—Peel good peaches, not too ripe, as in that case the chips will be very dark when dried. Slice the peaches *very thin;* have ready prepared a syrup made in the proportion of half a pound of sugar to a pound of fruit, and water enough to melt the sugar; the syrup must be very thick. Put in the chips, and scald them well. Remove them with a perforated skimmer, and dry in the sun. After they are dry, pack closely in jars, sprinkling finely powdered sugar between the layers. This preparation well supplies the place of raisins in making fruit puddings, and plain family fruit cakes.

---

849. *Peach Leather.*—Peel very ripe, soft peaches; mash them fine, and strain through a colander. If the peaches are not very sweet, add a little sugar. Butter well panes of glass, and spread the paste smoothly upon them. Put in the sun to dry; when dry on one side, turn it, and when perfectly dry, roll and keep in

boxes. When not convenient to use the glass, butter strips of cloth, and spread upon well-seasoned boards.

---

850. *To Dry Figs.*—Take ripe figs; dip them in moderately strong soda-water, and wipe them. Have ready a syrup made of half a pound of sugar to a pound of the fruit. When it is thick, drop the figs in, and let them scald well. Take them up, and place them in a dish with the stems up. With the bottom of another dish or plate press them gradually to a flat shape; sprinkle them with fine sugar, and set in the hot sun. Turn them with a knife, and sprinkle again with sugar. When dry, pack in boxes or jars, with sugar between the layers of figs. If the weather is damp, dry in a warm oven or stove.

---

851. *Tomato Figs.*—Use thoroughly ripe tomatoes; pour boiling water over them to remove the skin; weigh them; place them in a stone jar, with an equal quantity of good sugar. Let them stand two days; then pour off the syrup; boil and skim it until no scum rises. Pour it over the tomatoes; let it stand two days; boil, and skim again. After repeating this process for the third time, they are fit to dry, if the weather suits; if not, keep them in the syrup. They will dry in a week. Pack in boxes lined with white paper, putting powdered sugar between the layers of fruit. Should any syrup remain, it may be used for making common marmalade, or for sweetening pies.

---

852. *To Dry Citron or Watermelon Rind.*—After preserving place in the sun, and dry. They answer well in puddings and cakes as a substitute for the imported citron.

---

853. *To Dry Cherries.*—Stone the fruit, and scald in a thick syrup. Dry, and pack them away. Grapes may be done in the same way, without seeding. These are very nice to store away for winter use, and the housekeeper who is well supplied with such articles need never be at a loss for a dessert.

MARMALADES, JAMS, ETC.

854. *To Stew Dried Peaches and Apples.*—Examine the fruit well; wash well, rubbing it through the hands. Pour boiling water over it, and let it stand until the water cools. Put to stew with a little water in a preserving kettle, or a stew-pan lined with tin or porcelain; the latter is best. Put on the cover, or turn a plate lightly over it, and let it stew until soft. Then mash through a colander; sweeten to taste, and spice with anything preferred. Be certain never to stew fruit in an iron vessel, nor set it to cool in tin.

---

855. *To Save Fruit without Sugar.*—Put in wide-mouthed bottles; fill up with cold spring water. Put them in a vessel of water up to the neck; boil half an hour; tie bladders or oil-skin over tight, or cork and seal while hot. Let them set until cold. Keep in a cool place. Use as soon as opened. Pack hay around while boiling, to steady them.

FOR MAKING CANDIES.

856. *Sugar Candy.*—To three tumblers of good brown sugar, add one tumbler and a half of cold water, one tablespoonful of good vinegar, and a small teaspoonful of butter. Boil without stirring until it begins to rope. To pull it, begin as soon as it can be handled, and take hold of the mass only with the tips of the fingers; pull rapidly. Use no grease about the hands, or very little.

---

857. *To Make Ground Pea Candy.*—Parch, shell, and beat the peas. Take up the candy before it has boiled as much as in the first receipt, and use more butter; stir while boiling. When poured out, mix in the peas. Almonds and grated cocoanut may be used.

---

858. *Cocoanut Candy.*—Use equal quantities of loaf sugar and grated cocoanut; add enough milk of the cocoanut to moisten the sugar. Put it to boil, and stir almost constantly. When the candy begins to turn to sugar, stir in the cocoanut as quickly as possible. Pour it into buttered dishes. Cut while warm with a buttered knife. Parched ground peas (beat) may also be used.

---

859. *Molasses Candy.*—Half a gallon of West India molasses, one pound of sugar, a teaspoonful of essence of lemon, the juice of two large lemons (but this must not be added before the candy is nearly done); add the rind of one when the molasses is first put to boil; stir occasionally. Boil steadily three hours, or until upon cooling some on a plate it will be found stiff enough. Pour it off; pull as the sugar candy. Flavor with ginger, if it is preferred to lemon.

860. *Toffie.*—One pound of loaf sugar, three ounces of butter, and the grated rind of one lemon. Boil a quarter of an hour; pour into dishes slightly buttered. Cut in strips with a buttered knife, but do not attempt to raise them until cold.

A pound of thin shelled almonds will yield half a pound when shelled; if very thick shelled, it will require more.

---

861. *To Make Almond Macaroons.*—Half a pound of shelled almonds, a quarter of a pound of butter, the whites of three eggs, twenty-four large teaspoonfuls of powdered loaf sugar, a wine-glass of rose-water, a large teaspoonful of mixed mace and cinnamon. Blanch and beat the almonds the day before they are needed. Beat and sift the spice. Beat the eggs stiff; add to them gradually a teaspoonful at a time until all is in; beat hard; add the spice, dissolved in the rose-water; then the almonds. It should now look like a soft dough; if *too* soft, add a few more almonds. When mixed, take a little flour in the palm of the hand; take up a small lump with a knife; roll it on the flour in your hand into a ball; flatten it slightly. Have ready a long shallow tin pan buttered; lay the macaroons on it as they are formed; place them about two inches apart. Bake in a moderate oven eight or ten minutes, or until a pale brown color. The top of the oven should be hotter than the bottom. If baked too much they become very hard, and lose their flavor; if too little, they will be heavy. They should rise, and crack open somewhat. Grated cocoanut may be substituted for almonds.

TO CAN FRUIT AND VEGETABLES.

"The chief agent in the work of preservation is heat. If after the application of heat for a certain time (by which process the air is expelled) the article be sealed up hermetically, it will remain unchanged for an indefinite period."

"The fruit and vegetables should be canned as early as possible after being gathered.

"How to know that the can is hermetically sealed and that the contents will keep: The contents, as soon as they cool, will slightly shrink, leaving a vacuum, and the top and bottom of the can will become concave from the pressure of the external air. This shows that the sealing is complete. Set the can in a warm place, and if, after four or five days, the concave condition of the top and bottom remain, all is right."

Peaches should be peeled; if they are clear-stone, halve them; if cling-stone, cut in slices of uniform size. As you cut them throw them into water; first, however, weighing them. With sugar in the proportion of half a pound to a pound of the fruit, put them in a vessel, the fruit and sugar in alternate layers (some persons prefer less sugar; enough, however, must be used to make them palatable). Let them stand until all the sugar is dissolved. Then put all into a preserving-kettle, and let them remain until the fruit is thoroughly penetrated with heat; say, for half an hour. While the fruit is boiling hot, fill the cans, and seal immediately.

To can quinces it is necessary that the fruit, after being pared and cut into pieces of uuiform size, should be boiled in clear water until slightly tender. In the water in which they were boiled (allowing half a tumbler to a pound of sugar) dissolve sugar in the proportion of half a pound to a pound of the fruit. As soon as the sugar is dissolved, and the syrup begins to boil, return the quinces to the kettle, and boil for fifteen minutes. Can them while boiling hot, sealing immediately. Pears may be done in the same way.

Smaller fruits—raspberries, strawberries, blackberries, currants, etc., are done as follows: Pick and wash the fruit carefully, and weigh, allowing to a pound of fruit half a pound of sugar or less. Put the fruit and sugar in alternate layers in a vessel, and allow them to stand for one hour. Then put them in the preserving-kettle, and boil for ten minutes. While boiling hot, can and seal immediately. Use no water; they yield sufficient juice.

Corn, peas, and ochra should be boiled for half an hour in just sufficient water to cover them. Can and seal while boiling hot.

Of course the corn is cut off the cob before boiling. Asparagus will require boiling but fifteen minutes. Tomatoes should be scalded just enough to allow of removing the skins; then boiled for half an hour in their own juice, and canned boiling hot. In no case should salt be added.

---

862. *To Brandy Peaches.*—Use ripe fruit—not sufficiently so, however, to be soft. White English or yellow peaches are the best varieties for this purpose. Make a strong soda water, using two large tablespoonfuls of soda to a gallon of water. Put this into the preserving-kettle, and let it boil. While it is boiling, put in the peaches (previously weighing them), only three or four at a time, turning them. Let them remain long enough for the skin to be easily wiped off with a coarse towel. Rub off the skin, and throw them into cold water. If the soda water becomes too weak, add a little more soda. Make a syrup, using a pound of sugar to a pound of fruit; put the peaches in, and let them scald well; remove them, and continue to boil the syrup until it is quite thick. When the peaches are cold, put them in jars, and cover with peach brandy, and let them remain until the next day. Pour off the syrup when it becomes sufficiently thick. After the peaches have stood for one night, pour off the brandy; add the

syrup to it; stir well together, and return it to the peaches. The juice from the peaches will weaken the brandy, and it may be necessary to add more in the course of about two weeks.

No spices should be used in putting up the fruit; but after the peaches are eaten, the liquor may be spiced, and will make excellent cordial.

Cherries, plums, damsons, grapes, and pears, are all good put up in the same way. The pears must first be peeled.

WINES, CORDIALS, ETC.

863. *Grape Wine.*—The grapes should be gathered on a dry, clear day, after the morning dew has disappeared. Pick them carefully from the stems, selecting only ripe and perfect fruit. Mash them thoroughly, taking care not to bruise the seeds, as that would impart a bitter taste. After bruising, let the mass remain twenty-four hours. Strain through a colander or sieve, taking care that there is no grease about it. Sweeten the juice (for this the crushed sugar is best) until it will float an egg so as to show about the size of a twenty-cent piece. Put into jugs, filling them, and leaving the mouths unstopped, reserving a bottle of the juice to replace that which escapes from the jugs by fermentation. When fermentation ceases, pour the wine off into a large bowl, and clarify in the following manner: Wash sand (half a pint will be sufficient for five gallons of wine) until the water will run clear from it. Beat to this the whites of four eggs, and stir into the wine. When it has settled, and the wine looks perfectly clear, pour off carefully into clean jugs, putting a piece of muslin inside of the funnel. Cork the jugs tightly, and set in a cool place where they will not be disturbed until the last of October or first of November.

A few days before bottling, have the bottles that you wish to use well-washed, dried, and sunned. Provide *new* corks. Have everything in readiness before the bottling begins, including cement for sealing. Strain the wine again into large pitchers, taking particular care not to turn the jug back after beginning to pour from it, as it stirs up the sediment which is at the bottom of the jug. Cover inside of the funnel with a piece of muslin before placing it in the mouth of the bottle; fill the bottle, and cork immediately, driving the cork in with a wooden mallet or light hammer. (*Never use old corks.*) Cover the neck of the bottle with cement. Keep in a cool, dry place.

864. *Muscadine Wine.*—Gather the fruit ripe; bruise them without breaking the seed. (The Scuppernong grape makes wine of a beautiful Champagne color, as will also the pulp and juice of the muscadines if the hulls be rejected.) Put the mass in an open vessel, and cover with a cloth. Stir three times during the first twenty-four hours. Let it stand two or three days. Draw off the liquor clear; if in a wooden vessel, bore a hole near the bottom, and draw off carefully, passing it through a flannel cloth or bag. Add sugar until it will float an egg to the surface. Pour into a vessel prepared thus: Melt brimstone in an iron ladle, and saturate a cotton cloth with it. Set one end of the cloth on fire, and put it into the cask; put in the bung lightly until the rag is nearly consumed; then drive it in tightly. After the cask has remained thus for two or three hours, pour in the juice; leave out the bung, covering the hole to keep out dust and insects. The cask should be entirely filled with the juice, and added to, a little every day, from a bottleful kept for the purpose. Do this until it ceases to ferment. Then drive in the bung; have a gimlet-hole near the bung, and stop lightly with a peg to allow the gas to escape. In three weeks drive in the peg. Examine in December; pour into another cask similarly prepared. Repeat this some cold, clear day in March. Bottle when clear. When a small quantity is to be made, use jugs as in the receipt for grape wine.

865. *Blackberry Wine.*—Use ripe berries. To every gallon of the fruit pour half a gallon of boiling water. Let them stand twenty-four hours. After that time, pour off the juice (pressing the berries) through a colander into another open vessel. Strain again through a flannel or Canton flannel bag, and to every gallon of juice add two and a half pounds of good, clean sugar. Stir it

up well, and put into jugs, filling them entirely. Add a little more juice every day, from a bottleful reserved for the purpose, until fermentation ceases; then proceed precisely according to directions for making grape wine.

---

866. *Cider Wine.*—Fifteen gallons of cider, fresh from the press; to each gallon, add two pounds of good brown sugar. When the sugar has dissolved, strain the mixture into a clean cask. Let the cask want two gallons of being full; leave out the bung for forty-eight hours. Put in the bung, leaving a little vent until fermentation ceases; then bung up tightly. In a year it is fit for use. It needs no straining; the longer it stands upon the lees, the better.

---

867. *Tomato Wine.*—Let the tomatoes be fully ripe. After mashing well, let them stand twenty-four hours. Then strain, and to every quart of the juice add one pound of good sugar. Let it ferment again, skimming frequently; when clear, bottle. To use this, sweeten a glass of water to the taste, and add the tomato wine until sufficiently acid.

---

868. *Strawberry Cordial.*—To each quart of the juice allow a pint of white brandy, and half a pound of loaf sugar. Let it stand two weeks. Pin a piece of muslin in the bottom of a sieve; strain, and bottle.

---

869. *Blackberry Cordial.*—Put very ripe berries in a jar; cover them with good peach brandy. Cover well with oil-cloth; let it stand a week. Strain the brandy from the fruit. Put in a kettle a pound of crushed sugar for every quart. Add spices—one teaspoon of allspice, one of cinnamon, and the same of cloves; do not beat the spices. Pour on the sugar as much of the liquor as will dissolve it; as soon as it boils up, pour to the rest of the liquor; mix well, and bottle.

Peach cordial is good made in the same way, only cut up the

peaches and scald them when the sugar and spices are scalded. Any cordial may be made in this way.

870. *Blackberry Cordial, No. 2.*—Mash thoroughly with the hand, without bruising the seed, very ripe fruit. Put it in a kettle, and let it stew three hours, keeping the cover on the vessel; stir frequently. Add a tablespoonful of cinnamon and allspice, less cloves. Strain after it has boiled, and when cold, add to three quarts of juice one quart of good French brandy. Sweeten to taste with loaf sugar.

871. *Muscadine Cordial.*—Pulp the muscadines. A few of the hulls left will give the liquor a beautiful color. Let it stand twenty-four hours. Strain it, and to every three quarts add a quart of good brandy. Sweeten to taste with loaf sugar. Bottle, cork well, and keep in a cool place.

872. *Cherry Bounce.*—Stone half the cherries; fill the vessel half full of the fruit, putting down a layer of fruit and a layer of good brown sugar in the proportion of a quarter of a pound of sugar to a quart of fruit. Fill the vessel with good *apple* or French brandy; tie it up securely. Let it remain until the cherries look a pale red; then strain, and bottle. Use it by adding water to taste, and more sugar if liked. This may be made in a jug; should be covered or stopped well, or the brandy will lose its strength.

873. *Crab Apple Beer.*—Boil the fruit until the water is a pleasant acid; strain it. To a gallon, put a piece of yeast cake an inch square. Sweeten to taste. Use the second day.

874. *To Keep Cider.*—In the manufacture of pure cider, cleanliness is *absolutely necessary* in every step of the process. Let the fruit be washed clean; pick out all unsound ones. Let the press and casks be clean. Make that which is to be kept in cool

weather. Place he casks in a cool apartment. While the fermentation progresses, the casks should be full, that all impurities coming to the top may flow over through the bung-hole. After active fermentation has ceased, the cider should be drawn off from the settlings into other clean casks, when fermentation will again be active for a few days. When fermentation begins to cease, clarify. Stir to each barrel two ounces of isinglass, or the whites of four eggs. After the clearing process, which will be effected in a few days, take of the sulphite (not sulphate) of lime a quarter of an ounce to the gallon, which dissolve in a little of the cider, and thoroughly mix with the contents of the cask. When filled, so as to exclude all air, drive in the bung.

---

875. *Cherry Nectar.*—To four pounds of the fruit washed and picked (stone half the fruit) put three tumberfuls of white wine or good apple vinegar. Let it stand four days. Strain through a cloth, and to a pint of juice add a pound of loaf sugar. Boil in a porcelain kettle a quarter of an hour. When cold, bottle and cork it; keep in a dry, cool place. To use, pour a tumbler half full of the nectar; add a few pieces of ice; fill with very cold water. A refreshing summer drink.

---

876. *Raspberry Nectar.*—Pour over two quarts of ripe rasp berries a quart of good apple vinegar. Let it stand until the fruit ferments; then strain, and to every pint of juice add three quarters o a pound of loaf sugar. Simmer twenty minutes.

Strawberry, blackberry, etc., may be made in the same way. Use by half filling a tumbler, and adding ice-water.

These nectars may be made effervescing drinks by adding to the water sufficient soda. Put the vinegar in the tumbler; pour in the soda-water. When the taste of the fruit is not distinct, pour off the vinegar, and pour it over fresh fruit. Let it set a day, and strain.

---

877. *Lemonade.*—Roll half a dozen large lemons well; cut

them in thin slices (when the lemons are small, use eight); put a layer of sugar (use two tumblers of crushed sugar) and a layer of the sliced lemons; press the mass slightly; let them remain a quarter of an hour. Pour upon the lemons a gallon of cold water. Stir them from the bottom; add more sugar if not sweet enough. Put in the glasses (if convenient) small bits of ice, and pour in the lemonade, putting a slice of the lemon in each glass. Orangeade may be made in the same way of sour oranges, or if sweet, add two lemons to six oranges. Pomegranates also make a pleasant acid drink, prepared from the seed, sweetening to taste.

878. *Sherry Cobbler.*—Dash lemonade with Sherry wine; add ice.

879. *Lemonade au Lait.*—One tumbler of lemon juice, the same of Sherry wine, three quarters of a pound of loaf sugar, a quart of boiling water; mix, and when cold, add two tumblers of boiling sweet milk. Strain after it has stood twelve hours. Seven lemons will make a tumbler of juice. Preserve the peel, and dry, or infuse them in strong fourth-proof brandy, and keep it for flavoring cakes, puddings, and sauces.

880. *Cream Beer.*—Take six pounds of double-refined sugar, four ounces of tartaric acid, and two quarts of water; put this on the fire, and when just warm, add the whites of two eggs beaten to a froth. It must not come to a boil. Pour it off through a thin cloth, without squeezing. Flavor with lemon. Bottle, and keep in a cool place.

To use this: Pour into a tumbler two tablespoonfuls of this syrup; fill two-thirds full with water. Just as it is drunk, stir in half a teaspoonful of soda.

881. *Ginger Beer* (*superior*).—To six quarts of water add one ounce of cream of tartar, and two ounces of white Jamaica ginger; boil it ten minutes. Strain it; add to the liquor a pound of loaf

sugar. Put it on the fire; let it simmer until the sugar is dissolved. Pour into an earthen vessel, into which has been put two ounces of tartaric acid and the rind of one lemon. When lukewarm, add half a tumbler of strong hop yeast. Stir all well together, and bottle; tie down the corks tightly. Use in a few days.

882. *Ginger Beer, No. 2.*—One ounce of ginger bruised and boiled in a gallon of water, with the peel of two lemons; boil quarter of an hour. Pour out in an earthen vessel; when cool, add the juice, with an ounce of cream of tartar, and one pound and a half of good sugar. Add another gallon of cold water, the whites of two eggs beaten to a froth, and stirred in when the water is lukewarm, and half a tumbler of good lively yeast. Let it ferment three hours; then bottle, and tie the corks down.

883. *Imperial Pop.*—Three ounces of cream of tartar, an ounce of bruised ginger, a pound and a half of loaf sugar, half a tumbler of lemon juice, a gallon and a half of water, a wineglass of yeast. Shake well together; bottle, and cork well.

884. *Spruce Beer.*—Three gallons of boiling water poured upon one quart of West India molasses; mix well. When tepid, add one ounce of essence of spruce, one of essence of winter green, and a pint of yeast. Let it stand twelve hours; bottle, and cork. In half a day it will be fit for use.

885. *Ginger Beer.*—Boil together four gallons of water, one pint of hops, twenty races of ginger, beaten. Boil briskly half an hour; keep the vessel covered; strain; sweeten with good molasses. When tepid, add a pint of brisk yeast. Cover it closely with a thick cloth until morning; then bottle, and cork tight. Scald the corks, and drive them in, and tie down with twine. Keep in a cool place. It will be ready for use the third day. Less yeast may used if the taste is not liked.

886. *Cheap Beer.*—Two tablespoonfuls of pulverized ginger, one pint of hop yeast, one pint of molasses, six quarts of cold water; mix well, and bottle immediately; in twenty-four hours it may be used.

887. *Corn Beer.*—Boil a quart of corn until the grains crack. Put the grains into a jug, and pour in two gallons of boiling water; do not use the water it was boiled in; add a quart of molasses, a handful of dried apples, and a large tablespoonful of ginger. It will be ready for use in two or three days. If the weather is cold, set it by the fire. It may be kept up several weeks with the same corn, sweetening the water before pouring in the jug.

888. *Persimmon Beer.*—One bushel of sweet, ripe persimmons, mashed; half a bushel of wheat bran. Mix well, and bake in loaves of good size. Break the bread in a clean barrel; add twelve gallons of water; sweeten with molasses. As soon as the fermentation ceases it may be bottled. Make in a warm room.

Another way: Use the fresh fruit, putting on the bottom of a cask a layer of straw, then persimmons, dried apples, the honey locust broken up; a little wheat bran will assist fermentation; repeat this; fill the cask with warm water. Keep it in a warm room; when it ferments it is fit for use; draw from the cask. If the weather is very cold, fermentation may be hastened by putting hot rocks in the cask.

889. *Orange Syrup.*—Select sweet, thin-skinned oranges; squeeze the juice; add sugar enough to make a thick syrup. Boil and skim until clear. Pour off when clear, and when cool, bottle. A tablespoonful in a glass of water is delicious. Flavor with a little of the grated rind; put in before boiling; a little in pudding-sauce is good. Lemons may be prepared in the same way. Flavor the sugar by rubbing lumps upon the outside of the fruit, and then add it to the juice; this is better than adding the peel.

890. *Lemon Sponge.*—Dissolve one box of Cox's gelatine in enough boiling water to cover it; add the juice of three lemons when the water is nearly cold; rub lumps of sugar upon the outside of the lemons until they absorb the oil from the lemon peel; add this to the gelatine; stir well, and sweeten to taste. Stir in the whites of two eggs beaten to a froth. When it looks like sponge-cake batter, put in moulds. Eat with cream.

---

891. *To Make Vinegar.*—For a thirty-two gallon cask use two gallons of molasses, one quart of yeast, one quart of "*old mother*," three ounces of tartaric acid; fill the barrel with rain water. Insert a glass bottle in the bung-hole. Set in the sun.

---

892. *Another Way to Make Vinegar.*—One quart of molasses, three gallons of rain water, one pint of yeast. Let it ferment and stand four weeks. When grape or muscadine wine is made, pour water over the hulls; let it stand to ferment; strain it; add a tumbler of molasses to each gallon of liquor; put it in jugs, and after setting two weeks, drain the vinegar; wash the jugs, and return it. Dip coarse white paper in molasses; cut it in strips, and put a handful in the jug, unless a little of the "mother" can be obtained.

---

893. *Apple Vinegar*—Is made by adding a tumbler of molasses to two gallons of hard cider. Draw it once or twice. Good vinegar may be made by pouring water over honey-comb after the honey has been squeezed out, taking care not to make the water too sweet. Let it set several days; then strain it into jugs, and set in the sun. Never put it upon the ground; always elevate the jugs a little. Add paper if the "mother" cannot be obtained.

PICKLES.

894. *Higdon.*—Take equal quantities of cabbage, green tomatoes, and white onions, and half the quantity of green pepper; chop them fine, without bruising. Put them in an earthen vessel—a layer of the vegetables, a layer of salt. Let them remain half a day; squeeze them out, and pour over the mass weak vinegar. Let this remain twenty-four hours. Put into enough vinegar to cover them well, a seasoning of mustard seed washed and soaked half an hour; half a box of ground mustard to a gallon of vinegar. Tie in a thin muslin bag mixed spices to season high, and black pepper. Take the vegetables from the weak vinegar; put it in the jar in which it is to be kept; pour over the spices and vinegar; tie the jar; put it in a pot of water, and make the water around it boil an hour.

---

895. *Sweet Pickle.*—To three pounds of brown sugar put one gallon of vinegar; spice to your taste; boil all together a short time, and set off to cool. Fill a jar with the vegetables or fruits to be pickled; pour the vinegar over them when cool. If you discover a white scum on the surface, pour the vinegar from the pickle and boil again, adding a little more sugar. When cool, return to the jar. Peaches stuffed, after neatly removing the seed, are nice made in this way. Figs ripe, but not soft, are good; so are cherries.

---

896. *Another Sweet Pickle.*—To eight pounds of fruit put five of sugar, three pints of vinegar, two tablespoonfuls of allspice, two of cloves, and one of mace. Make the syrup; pour it over the fruit, boiling hot, three mornings in succession. The fourth morning put them on, and simmer them a little.

PICKLES.

897. *Tomato Pickle.*—Take tomatoes two-thirds ripe; prick them with a fork; put them in a strong brine, and let them remain eight days. Then put them in weak vinegar for twenty-four hours; remove them to a stone jar. To one gallon of the tomatoes, add half a pint of mustard seed, one bottle of mustard, on ounce of cloves, one ounce of black pepper ground, one dozen onions, peeled and cut into slices. Place them in layers; cover the whole with strong vinegar.

---

898. *Pickled Onions.*—Peel; boil in milk and water ten minutes; drain off the milk and water; pour over cold spiced vinegar.

---

899. *To Pickle Peppers.*—Take green peppers; remove the seed carefully, so as not to mangle the pepper. Soak twenty-four hours in salt and water. Stuff with Higdon, or chopped cabbage, highly seasoned. Put them in an unglazed jar; pour over weak vinegar boiling hot; pour it off, re-boiling three days in succession, and pouring hot over the peppers at the end of that time. Pour over cold vinegar to cover the pepper. Tie over oil-cloth or a bladder.

---

900. *To Pickle Cucumbers.*—Keep them in salt and water three days; then wipe them dry; put into a jar; put in spices, and a small lump of alum; pour over scalding vinegar. If a white scum rises, pour off the vinegar; scald, and pour over again. Always have plenty of vinegar to cover them well. Cucumbers can be kept in brine for a year; lay grape-leaves on top, and a weight to keep them under the brine.

---

901. *Mangoes.*—Young muskmelons, peaches, peppers, large cucumbers, are all nice mangoed. Cut a slit; carefully remove the insides, or stones, if peaches. Lay in salt and water three or four days. Then stuff with Higdon; put the edges together; tie with a string, or sew up separately in cloths. Lay in a stone jar, the cut side up. Boil sharp vinegar with a tablespoonful of alum to three gallons of vinegar; pour hot over the mangoes. The alum makes them firmer.

---

902. *Cabbage Pickle.*—Quarter the heads, and sprinkle pretty thickly with salt; let them remain about twelve hours. Take them from the salt; rinse in cold water, and wipe dry. If preferred, cut them fine. Put them in a jar, and pour over them cold spiced vinegar.

---

903. *Mustard Pickles.*—Four ounces of turmeric, one of mace, one of allspice, one of cloves, two bottles of English mustard (large size), two gallons of vinegar, one pint of mustard seed. Let all together just come to a boil. When cold, put into a jar, and keep them stirred. The older they are the better. To prepare cabbage for pickling: Put the cabbage in very strong salt and water for three days; take them out, and sun them for three days, turning them frequently. Then pour boiling water over them, and wring them out in a clean towel. They are then ready to be dropped in the above pickle. Spices should be pounded and put into a muslin bag.

---

904. *Green Tomato Pickle.*—One peck of green tomatoes sliced; one dozen onions sliced; sprinkle with salt, and let them stand until the next day; then drain them. Use the following as spices: one box of mustard, half an ounce of black pepper, one ounce of whole cloves, and one ounce of white mustard seed. Alternate layers of tomatoes, onions, and spices. Cover with vinegar. Wet the mustard before putting it in. Boil the whole twenty minutes.

---

905. *Mixed Pickle*—To each gallon of the strongest vinegar add four ounces of flour of mustard, three ounces bruised ginger, two of turmeric, half a pound of peeled eschalots *slightly* baked in an oven, two ounces of garlic prepared in the same manner, a

quarter of a pound of salt, and two drachms of Cayenne pepper Put these ingredients into a stone jar; crowd very closely; place near the fire for three days, shaking up occasionally. It will then be ready for the vegetables. Before putting the vegetables into the vinegar they must be kept in brine three days, and then dried in the sun—small cucumbers, button onions, cauliflower, beans, pepper, etc.

---

906. *Walnut Pickle.*—Take one hundred nuts when just soft enough to be pricked through the kernel with a needle, one ounce of cloves, one of allspice, one of nutmeg, one of black pepper (whole), one of ginger, the same of horseradish cut up fine, half a pint of mustard seed, and four heads of garlic tied in a bag. Wipe the nuts; prick them with a fork or coarse needle; pack them in a jar, sprinkling the spices between the layers. Add two tablespoonfuls of salt to vinegar enough to cover the walnuts. Boil it and pour hot over the nuts in the jar, and cover with an oil-cloth or something that will preserve the strength of the vinegar. Keep a year before using. The vinegar from it makes excellent catsup.

---

907. *Chow.*—Horseradish grated fine, two cups; one teaspoonful of turmeric, two tablespoonfuls of celery seeds, four tablespoonfuls of sugar, and two tablespoonfuls of white mustard seed; vinegar to cover it. Some persons use the horseradish without the addition of anything except loaf sugar and vinegar enough to acidulate it pleasantly. Packed in very small, wide-mouthed bottles and well corked, it keeps well. November is the proper month to make it. Then new beds may be set from the small roots that will not answer for grating. The tops cut closely, leaving a few eyes, will also answer for planting.

---

908. *Cabbage.*—Shred the cabbage, sprinkle with salt, and let it lie two or three hours; shake off all loose salt; put a layer of cabbage, one of grated horseradish, celery seed, a little green pep-

per, allspice, and, if liked, a little turmeric to give the pickle a yellow tinge. Add another layer of cabbage until all is disposed of. Cover with cold vinegar. Scald this if disposed to mould.

---

909. *Artichokes.*—Scrape well; soak a few hours in cold water (salted). Spice vinegar, adding coriander seed, mace, mustard seed, black pepper, allspice, and a few cloves. Pour this over the artichokes boiling hot. Cover well.

---

910. *Green Tomato Sauce.*—One quart of green tomatoes cut up fine, a small onion shred fine, a tumbler of good brown sugar, one of vinegar, pepper, salt, allspice, and cloves to taste. Boil to a jam, stirring frequently. It must not scorch. An excellent sauce for fresh meats. Keep in small jars.

COFFEE, TEA, ETC.

To have this popular beverage in perfection, several points require attention. First, the coffee must be of good quality, unadulterated. Nothing is better than old U. S. Java. Mocha is a superior coffee—dearer than any other. When a good article is found, it is best to buy by the quantity; age improves it if carefully kept. A box of seasoned wood answers the purpose. It should be elevated a few inches, that under it may be kept clean as well as around it. Coffee, before and after toasting, readily absorbs any disagreeable taste or odor with which it comes in contact. It is a good plan to wash, pick out all foreign substances, and dry well, several pounds at once. Keep in a well-covered jar. But in toasting it is different. Use a small quantity. It is best to toast only what is needed for the occasion. Very few persons like the trouble of doing this, but it certainly compensates. The grains must be of a uniform dark brown color from the surface to the centre. A roaster, such as is in very general use, answers the purpose much better than an open vessel. The grains should be constantly agitated to be of a uniform color. When the toasting is half accomplished, for a pound drop in an even teaspoonful of butter. When roasted sufficiently, glaze it; shut it up in a close, well-covered vessel (glass is best); keep it in a clean, cool place; grind as needed, neither too fine nor coarse. Coffee should not set after the boiling is completed. It loses every moment some of its delightful aroma. The coffee-boiler should always be kept clean, well-scalded, and sunned after each boiling. It is the practice of slovenly, careless cooks, to leave the grounds from time to time in the boiler, and when the vessel is needed, empty, and hastily rinse it, leaving much of the former contents adhering to the sides. The result of such management is, that the coffee, instead of being the deliciously exhilarating drink it may be, is flat, insipid, muddy, and absolutely pernicious. Even when the boiler is in perfect order for receiving the coffee it should be well-scalded. To make the coffee: Pour in boiling water, *exactly the quantity needed*, allowing a pint for every *two* heaped tablespoonfuls of fresh-ground coffee; add a teaspoonful of the white of an egg to this quantity (too much egg injures the coffee); use enough cold water to make the coffee into a paste; stir this into the boiling water. Never fill the boiler so full of water as to allow no room for the coffee to swell. As it swells it will be very apt to boil over, unless watched; remove the boiler a moment from the fire; scrape down on the inside. Boil very briskly a quarter of an hour. Take the boiler from the fire; pour in half a teacup of cold water; let the coffee settle five minutes. When the boiler is first put on the fire, fill the coffee-pot or urn in which it is to be served, with boiling water. When the coffee has settled, and is ready for the table, pour out the boiling water carefully, and immediately pour in the coffee on the grounds, being particular not to disturb them. Serve without delay, using good, rich cream, and good sugar. (Stir these together; pour in the coffee.) Where sweet cream cannot be procured, a slight acidity may be corrected by using a little soda; it should be used *very cautiously*, or the quality of the beverage will be affected. The next best to sweet rich cream is to boil fresh sweet milk, using it very hot.

A very good drink for children may be made by re-boiling the grounds with sufficient sweet milk.

---

911. *To Make Coffee by Filtering.*—Procure a percolator; take out all the inside machinery; scald it; allow four ounces of ground coffee to a quart of water; put this in the bottom of the vessel; add a small piece of isinglass or skin of cod fish (these answer for clarifying when eggs are scarce), half an inch square is sufficient for a quart of water; replace the strainers; pour in boiling water; set the percolator where it will keep hot without boiling until the water drips through; pour a little into a cup,

and, if not satisfactorily strong, pour the coffee out, and again pour into the vessel, and let it drip through the second time. Serve as soon as ready.

---

912. *Green Tea.*—There is no better way of extracting the 'spiritual part" of the essence of the leaves than this: Scald the pot in which the tea is to be drawn. Pour in as much boiling water as will be required; use for one teacup and a half of water a heaped teaspoonful of tea, this is a good proportion if the tea is strong and good. Sprinkle the dry tea leaves over the surface of the water; set it where it will keep hot; when the leaves fall to the bottom it is ready for the table. Use loaf sugar, and when cream is used, add it last. If to be served in a different pot, scald it *well.* It should be hot when the infusion is poured in. To replenish, keep a covered mug with one or two teaspoonfuls of tea, half filled with boiling water. When the first supply is exhausted, pour the tea from the mug into the tea-pot; add as much boiling water as is needed.

Another way: Scald the tea-pot; put in the tea; add a tumblerful of boiling water; set it where it will keep hot; after ten minutes, add as much water as will be required; this, of course, will depend upon the number of the tea-drinkers. Draw some in the covered mug as a reserve.

---

913. *Black Tea*—Is best boiled five or six minutes. Use a little larger quantity of leaves, as they are lighter than the green. Some persons prefer the two kinds mixed; it makes a pleasant beverage. Use only the best teas. Souchong is considered the best black; the Hysons are the best green teas; Pearl and Imperial Gunpowder are very fine. Good tea has an agreeable odor. Keep it well protected from the air.

---

914. *Chocolate.*—Grate it fine. Allow two heaped tablespoonfuls to a pint of fluid; this should be half milk, half water, but not mixed. Wet the grated chocolate to a smooth paste; boil it

five minutes in the water, then add the same quantity of sweet unskimmed milk; flavor with cinnamon or nutmeg. Serve very hot.

---

915. *German Chocolate.*—To a quart of unskimmed sweet milk use two heaped tablespoonfuls of grated chocolate. Mix to a smooth paste with a little cold water. Boil the milk. Just as it comes to the boiling point, add the chocolate paste, stirring it well with a wooden or silver spoon. Let this boil five minutes. Pour it off when it cools until only hot (not boiling); pour it gradually to two well-beaten eggs, stirring constantly. Return it to the fire until hot, and serve immediately. A stick of cinnamon may be boiled in the milk. Season to taste.

---

916. *To Mill Chocolate.*—A chocolate-mill somewhat resembles an ice-water pitcher. The handle of a round stick is passed up through the lid of the mill, fitting loosely. The bottom of the stick is wheel-shaped. Take the top of the stick, which should be several inches above the lid, between the hands, and turn it back and forth rapidly until there is a rich froth upon the chocolate. Serve hot.

THE DAIRY.

917. *To Milk.*—No animal better repays kind and generous treatment than the cow. In winter she should be well housed, and a sufficient quantity of dry straw provided for a litter, and this changed occasionally. Regular and proper feeding. She should be curried and rubbed with the same care bestowed upon the horse. How rarely anything of the kind is done! The miserable, half frozen condition of this valuable animal during the cold weather, without shelter of any kind, turned loose to pick up a precarious and scanty living, or only supplied with a few dry shucks thrown upon the ground, perchance a little dirty slop water, is a reproach to the master. The quality and quantity of milk and butter which would be yielded when well treated, is of itself (it would seem) an irresistible argument in favor of providing liberally for her comfort, to say nothing of her mute appeals to man's humanity.

---

918. *To Feed in Winter.*—There should be a boiler (the size depending upon the number of cows kept) fixed upon a furnace; a shelter over the furnace. Arrange the location so as to have it as near as may be to water, and the place where the animal is fed. It is better on account of convenience to put the furnace where a trough can be attached; the food, when cooked, put into the trough, and when cool it may be covered until the regular hour for feeding, and then drive the animal to the trough. Peas, pumpkins, corn meal, potatoes, beets, carrots, turnips, are all good articles of food for cows; add shucks stripped in small pieces (they are better for being soaked), a little salt. Boil in clear water. Any fragments of vegetables from the kitchen may be added *clean*. Turnips should be used sparingly; they impart a disagreeable taste to the milk. Green barley, late in the spring, should be provided. Rye gives a rich color to the milk and butter, but injures the taste of both. This may in part be corrected by salting the corn well. A patch of wheat should be ready to succeed the barley. By the time these are exhausted, the natural grasses appear, affording pasturage. Boiled food should not be discontinued, but may be given in reduced quantities. When cows are driven to and from their pastures, it should be done by a steady, careful person; racing them at the top of their speed, as is usually the case, injures the milk. They should be milked under shelter in bad weather. The milker should treat her charge kindly, gently, and soothingly, and perform the work as quickly as possible to do it thoroughly. Strip the teats closely; *there* lies the cream. Leave one or more teats for the calf, depending upon its age. When large enough, let it feed with its mother. Great care should be used to keep the milk clean. The milker should provide herself with plenty of water to wash the udder well, and then wipe clean and dry with a clean, coarse towel, kept for this purpose. Tie a thin cloth over the bucket into which the milk is poured as soon as it is milked. Use a smaller vessel for receiving the milk as it is drawn from the cow. When the milking is completed, take it to the dairy. Drive the cow and calf to their food. Have plenty of boiling water; scald the pans (which should be broad and shallow). When hot, pour out the water, and immediately strain the milk into them. Reserve in a small vessel sufficient to afford cream for coffee and tea. Into another vessel pour what is intended for the table. Stir it until all the animal heat is exhausted. In separate vessels put what is intended for the churn. The cream intended for the churn should never be touched until removed for that purpose.

---

919. *For Churning.*—In winter, the cream may stand two days. In summer, it should be churned every morning, as early as possible. In winter it is a good plan to reserve a part of the buttermilk from time to time, and add it to the fresh cream to turn it. The churn should be placed where it will have a sum-

mer temperature, or fifty-five degrees (Fahrenheit's thermometer). Greater heat than this gives the butter a white, spongy look. Scald the churn well in every case before putting in the cream. When the churn is prepared at night, add a portion of the night's milking to the cream; shake them well together. The buttermilk is better than when only cream is used. The cream, when taken from the pans, may be put in a covered jar, and slightly salted, where the buttermilk is not used as a drink. The cream will keep better, but the salt would injure the buttermilk. The churning should be done with a steady, regular motion. In very cold weather set the churn in a tub of warm water, which will keep the milk at the proper temperature; add more hot water if needed. In very warm weather set the churn in a vessel of cold water. The milk should be kept at an equable temperature. For a small churning a stone-ware jar is best, with a wooden cover, and a dasher—the handle running through the hole in the lid or cover. It should be unglazed. The stone-ware is much more easily cleansed than the wooden.

When the process of churning is complete, pour in a tumblerful of cold water; this hardens the butter, and makes it easier to collect. Have a pan or bowl of cold water ready; put the butter into it as it is taken from the churn. Work the buttermilk out; cover it again with cold water. Examine carefully for motes, and remove them. Work out all milk and water with a wooden paddle. *Never use the hand.* Add salt in the proportion of half a tablespoonful to a pound of butter. Make it into shapes. Keep in a cool, clean place. Nothing more need be done with butter intended for immediate use.

920. *For Packing Butter.*—Let it set in a cool place two or three days; work it well, and pour off the water; use more salt than for immediate use. Scald small unglazed jars with salt and water; when cool, pack the butter down *very close;* pour off the least water that rises; fill to within two inches of the top; then melt butter enough to fill the jar nearly full. Lay over this,

when cool, a quarter of an inch thick, this preparation: Three parts ground alum or solar salt (never use Liverpool salt), one of pulverized loaf sugar, one of saltpetre; cover with a tight-fitting cover; the air must be entirely excluded. Remove the top butter when used.

Another way: Pack the butter, free from milk, in jars scalded in salt and water. Pour over brine, and cover close.

Another way: Beat and sift four tablespoonfuls of alum or solar salt, two of loaf sugar, and one of saltpetre; add this quantity to every pound of butter; pack closely. Reserve a portion of the salt mixture; put it between a fold of muslin, and lay upon the top. Cover closely. Keep in a dry, cold place.

---

921. *To Freshen Salt Butter.*—Dissolve it in hot water. Let 't cool; skim it off the water, and churn it in sweet milk. A quart of milk is enough for a pound of butter. Only have the water hot enough to melt the butter.

---

922. *Patent Butter.*—A patent has been secured by a Mr. Clark, of London, for the following method of preserving butter: "Wash the butter, and press out the milk in the usual manner; then place it between two linen cloths, and submit it to severe pressure to remove the whey. Coat clean white paper on both sides with the whites of eggs, mixing fifteen grains of salt to each white; dry the paper. And just before wrapping it around the butter, iron it with a hot iron; use it heated. Keep in a cool, dry place."

---

923. *A Simple Plan to Keep Butter Cold in Summer.*—Procure a large new flower-pot to cover the plate of butter; a large saucer to hold the flower-pot when turned upside down. Put a small trivet or three muffin-rings on the bottom of the saucer. Set the plate of butter upon it; fill the saucer with water; turn the flower-pot over the butter so that the edge of the pot will be below the water. Put a cork in the hole in the bottom of the

flower-pot—the butter is now in an air-tight chamber. Occasionally drench the outside of the flower-pot with cold water.

924. *To Recover Rancid Butter or Lard.*—Use Darby's Prophylactic Fluid by the directions which accompany the bottles; cream it in thoroughly; then put the butter in a clean vessel.

The vessels used in the dairy should be kept scrupulously clean. First wash them, then scald well, and sun frequently. Keep white, well-washed sand for scouring the wooden vessels.

Cream, after it is skimmed from the milk, may be kept a day and night, by scalding it, and then slightly sweetening with loaf sugar. A thin cream may be raised from fresh milk by setting the vessel which contains it upon the fire; skim as the cream rises; repeat the skimming as long as there is any appearance of cream.

925. *To Preserve Milk for a Journey.*—Put the fresh sweet milk into bottles; put them into an oven of cold water; gradually raise it to the boiling point; take them out, and cork immediately; return the bottles to the water; raise it once more to the boiling point; let the bottles remain a minute. Take the oven from the fire, and let the bottles cool in it.

926. *Cheese.*—The articles used in making cheese are, a tub to hold the milk, a boiler to scald it, strainers of coarse linen, a cheese-basket for dripping, a cheese-press and hooks, cheese-board, and hoops. Strain fresh unskimmed milk into the boiler; warm it just blood-hot, and no more; pour it into the tub, and while warm, add rennet enough to turn it. About half a tumbler of strong rennet water to six quarts of milk will probably be sufficient, but it will very much depend upon the strength of the rennet water. Keep the tub covered with a blanket where the milk will be only blood-hot, and if in an hour the curd has not formed, add more rennet; use no more than is absolutely necessary, or the cheese will have a strong taste. As soon as the curd is formed, cut it gently into cakes, without moving them; this

will cause the whey to rise. Cut it across slowly and gently, pass the knife gently around between the tub and curd. Cut it again in checks an inch apart. Remove the whey as it rises, but do not disturb the curds. Cover the tub a quarter of an hour. The curds and whey must be separated very gently and slowly, or the milk will run off with the whey, and leave the cheese very poor. When the whey looks white, this is the case; when the whey looks green, the process is proceeding satisfactorily. After the tub has remained covered fifteen minutes, set the basket partly over the tub; spread the cloth (or strainer) over it, and dip the curds into it; shake the cloth to hasten the dripping. Gather the ends of the cloth up securely, and put a weight upon the curds for a quarter of an hour. Break up the curds again with the hand, and press again. Now salt it, using half a table-spoonful of salt to a pound of curd. Spread a thin cloth in and over the press; lay in the curds, a little heaped in the centre; pack it down tightly. The cloth should be large enough to allow the corners to cover the top of the cheese well; lay upon it a heavy weight. Let it remain two hours; cut up the curds; lay in the press a dry thin or gauzy cloth; put the curds again in press. Repeat this, without again breaking the curds, three or four times a day until the last cloth looks dry; then use a fine linen cloth wrung out of hot water; wrap this around and over the cheese, and let it remain a day. If firm enough (if not, let it remain another day), sprinkle the outside with flour; sew a cloth around it; put in a hoop. Keep it in a hoop until hard enough to handle; then put it on the cheese-board or shelf, and rub it with butter every day for a week. For six months grease it occasionally. For very rich cheese add to the morning's milk the cream of the over night's skimming. These rich cheeses do not need coloring, but for poorer ones use annotta, and a little ley added to the milk, along with the rennet; allow three drachms of annotta to ten pounds of curds; for green cheese use the juice of sage or spinach. To protect fresh cheese from flies, mix red pepper with the butter with which it is greased.

927. *Cream Cheese.*—One quart of cream; stir to it one teaspoonful of salt; let it stand covered two days. Lay in a sieve a cloth folded six times; sprinkle it with salt (the cloth should be much larger than the sieve, and hang considerably over the side of the sieve); pour in the cream; sprinkle a little salt on it. Change the cloth as soon as it gets moist. Repeat this; as the cheese dries, press it. This makes a good custard, washed before dry, and made into a batter, with eggs, milk, sugar, and a little butter. Season with lemon. Bake in a crust.

COOKING FOR INVALIDS.

"There is no creature on earth which has so many wants as man."

928. *Lemon Punch.*—Roll two large lemons under the hand well; cut them into thin slices; take out all the pulp, and throw away the seed. Put the pulp and yellow rind, and half a teaspoonful of good green tea, half a pound of loaf sugar, in a clean stew-pan lined with porcelain; pour over a tumbler of boiling water. Stir well, and add a pint of Champagne wine, or any preferred. Set it upon the fire until hot, and drink immediately. Excellent to promote perspiration in bad colds. The patient should drink it in bed. Half this receipt will be sufficient for one person.

---

929. *Mulled Wine.*—Boil together one tumbler of water, half a nutmeg, a small stick of cinnamon, a dozen cloves slightly bruised, the same of allspice; reduce it by boiling half; strain the spiced water into a pint of good Sherry or Madeira wine. Set it on the fire, and when it begins to bubble, take it off the fire; sweeten with loaf sugar, and serve. Cider may be mulled in the same way.

---

930. *Wine Whey.*—One pint of boiling milk, a tumblerful of good Madeira wine; boil until the curds form. Pour off the whey into a pitcher; sweeten, and serve. Cider may be used instead of wine.

---

931. *Drink for a Consumptive.*—Put into a tumbler a tablespoonful of strained honey, a wineglass of good brandy or whiskey; add milk just from the cow to fill the glass. Stir, and **drink** warm, before breakfast.

COOKERY FOR INVALIDS.

932. *Tamarind Whey.*—Boil one ounce of tamarinds in a pint of sweet milk; strain, and sweeten to taste.

---

933. *Apple-Water.*—Take dried apples; pour boiling water over them; let them set until cold. Or, bake green apples, and pour boiling water over. A pleasant drink in fevers. Sweeten if liked.

---

934. *Cranberry Tea.*—Mash ripe fruit; pour over boiling water. Strain, and sweeten to taste. Tamarinds may be used in this way, but without mashing the fruit.

---

935. *Corn Meal Gruel.*—Sift the finer part of the corn meal from the bran; boil the bran at least two hours in plenty of water. Keep the vessel covered, to prevent its being smoked. Be careful it does not scorch. Should the water boil down too much, replenish with boiling water. Strain the bran from the water. Season the water or gruel with sweet milk, a little fresh butter, and salt. Omit the butter if it would make the gruel too rich for the patient.

---

936. *Flour Gruel.*—Put a pint of fresh sweet milk to boil; mix to a paste an even tablespoonful of wheat flour, corn starch, or potato starch. Just as the milk boils, stir in the paste smoothly. Let it boil until the gruel is sufficiently thick. Season with loaf sugar and nutmeg; wine may be used if liked.

---

937. *Potato Starch Custard.*—Two heaped tablespoonfuls of potato starch, two eggs well beaten, with two tablespoonfuls of pulverized loaf sugar (more sugar may be used if liked); season to taste, with lemon, vanilla, or rose-water, and one pint of fresh sweet milk. Boil the milk; add the starch, wet up with cold milk; just as the milk begins to boil, stir constantly until as thick as very rich cream. Pour it out. When warm *only*, stir it to the eggs, mixing well. Return to the stew-pan, and boil until the eggs are cooked, which will require ten minutes. **Stir constantly.** Serve with or without sauce.

---

938. *Farina Custard.*—Put a pint of fresh sweet milk to boil with a stick of cinnamon. Wet up two tablespoonfuls of dry farina with cold milk; stir it to the boiling milk; let it boil ten minutes, stirring constantly. Remove it from the fire; beat the yolks of two eggs. Stir the farina to them when just warm; sweeten and season to taste. Pour into earthen cups; set the cups in a pan of hot water; put the pan in a moderate oven, and bake slowly until the custard is firm. Try one, by probing with the handle of a silver teaspoon. If baked in an oven too hot, the custards will be watery; if properly baked, they will cut firm, and have a beautiful solid look. These may be made of arrowroot, corn starch, or flour, and nothing of the kind can be more agreeable to an invalid. It is a nice dessert, baked in an earthen dish, the sugar in the custard omitted, and eaten with rich wine sauce. Grate nutmeg over the top.

---

939. *Corn Starch Custard.*—Beat the yolks of three eggs; boil a pint of fresh sweet milk; wet up a heaped teaspoonful of corn starch with cold milk; add it to the boiling milk; boil five or six minutes, stirring constantly. Set it aside to cool; then stir well into the milk. Return all to the boiler; stir well until as thick as liked. Pour into an earthen bowl; stir a few minutes, and when cool, season to taste with lemon, orange, rose, or vanilla. Whip the whites of two eggs to a strong froth;. add a few drops of the same flavoring used in the custard, and a tablespoonful of pulverized loaf sugar; pile this over the custard, and serve. These custards should be prepared in a double kettle, or in a tin bucket, set in an oven of boiling water.

---

940. *Arrowroot*—May be made of either milk or water. Mix an even tablespoonful of genuine arrowroot powder with water enough to make a smooth paste; mix in a bowl. Season with

sugar and wine; pour a tumblerful (very slowly, and stir rapidly) of boiling water. Put it into a stew-pan; scald well until transparent; pour out, and season to taste. Very little cooking is necessary. Fresh sweet milk may be used instead of water.

---

941. *Rice Gruel.*—Two tablespoonfuls of rice flour; wet it up with cold water. Boil twenty minutes in a pint of boiling water; then add one tumblerful of fresh sweet milk. Season to taste. Caudle is made by adding to this gruel, wine, and a little grated cracker.

---

942. *Corn Meal Pudding.*—One quart of sweet milk; add to this while boiling hot, sufficient fine corn meal to make a stiff mush. Let this get cold. Add four eggs, beaten separately; one tablespoonful of butter, one tablespoonful of yeast powders; add the whites, beaten very solidly, last. Bake quick. Eat with or without sauce. Tapioca boiled or baked is much relished by invalids. Receipts are already given for preparing these custards.

---

943. *Sago.*—Soak half a tumblerful an hour in cold water. Boil in a pint of hot water until soft. Stir it from the bottom; add a pint of sweet milk. Season to taste with wine, sugar, and nutmeg. Eggs may be added, and baked as a pudding.

---

944. *Panada.*—Mix three parts water, one of good Madeira wine. Put it into a stew-pan; add a large square cracker, grated, to a pint of the fluid. Let it become boiling hot; pour off into a bowl; season with sugar and lemon, or nutmeg. The water may be poured upon a well-beaten egg, if liked; stir briskly while pouring it on the egg.

---

945. *Cracker Toast.*—Put into a stew-pan a tumblerful of sweet milk, a teaspoonful of good fresh butter into which has been rubbed an even teaspoonful of flour. Set it on the fire until the butter and milk is boiling hot. Have ready a deep dish of boil-

ing water; dip the crackers in; put a layer upon the bottom of a hot covered dish. Just as the milk boils up, pour part of it over the crackers; put down another layer of crackers; so divide the sauce that some may be poured over each layer of crackers. Cover when the last is in, and serve immediately; if allowed to wait before being eaten, they become watery and sodden. With a soft boiled egg, a little grated ham or tongue, a good cup of tea, coffee, or chocolate, an invalid need not desire a better breakfast or lunch. Light bread or hard biscuit may be toasted and dressed in the same way.

---

946. *Toast and Water.*—Slice stale light oread, or toast the outside crust of corn bread. Immerse it while hot in a tumbler or pitcher of cold water; cover it for half an hour before drinking. Make it fresh once a day. The vessel may be refilled as the water is used.

---

947. *Rice Pudding.*—One small teacup of boiled rice, three well-beaten eggs, a pint of sweet milk, nutmeg and sugar to taste. Bake in a moderate oven until the custard sets. Boiled rice, seasoned with orange peel, milk and sugar, is a good dish for invalids. Use a little butter, if permitted; a little wine is also relished.

---

948. *Gelatine Blanc-Mange.*—Boil an ounce of gelatine in a pint of water until dissolved. Mix with a pint of sweet milk half a pound of loaf sugar; flavor with lemon or vanilla. Put upon a flat dish a quart of rich cream; beat to a stiff froth. Stir the milk and gelatine together; add the whipped cream; stir until it congeals.

---

949. *Beef Broth.*—Put half a pound of lean beef in a stew-pan, pour over it three tumblers of cold water. Set it over a slow fire where it will heat gradually. Remove the scum as it rises. After simmering half an hour, strain it through a thin cloth.

Season with salt and pepper. Very good broth may be made by pouring boiling water over cold steak. Scrape off the gravy first.

---

950. *Egg Nogg.*—To the yolk of each egg add a tablespoonful of loaf sugar; beat well together; add two tablespoonfuls of good brandy or three of Madeira wine. Beat the whites to a solid froth; put them to the yolks, and to every three eggs add a wineglass of thick rich cream. Stir lightly into the yolks. The cream may be omitted, if not liked. It injures the egg-nogg if not very thick and rich. This is excellent for persons suffering from bad colds and coughs.

---

951. *Drink for an Invalid.*—A new-laid egg, well-beaten, a cup of hot coffee, tea, or chocolate poured to it, stirring well, is a good drink for an invalid.

---

952. *Boullie.*—Boiled flour for persons suffering with weak bowels, and for infants teething. Boil half a pound of flour, tied loosely in a cloth, four hours. When cold, peel off the outer rind. To a pint of boiling sweet milk, add a tablespoonful of this boiled flour grated and wet into a paste with cold water; boil gently ten minutes. Season with salt and a little loaf sugar.

---

953. *Broiled Tomatoes.*—Slice large tomatoes, without skinning; put them upon a warm gridiron until thoroughly hot, turning them once. Season with butter, salt, and pepper. These are excellent for invalids suffering from constipation.

---

954. *Tomato Toast.*—Stew to a paste, after skinning them. Season to taste, and spread upon slices of toasted bread.

---

955. *Herb Teas.*—Make these by infusion, using green or dried leaves. Balm, catnip, pennyroyal, sage, are good drinks in fever to promote perspiration. Mint tea will sometimes relieve

nausea; use, if possible, the green leaves. Mullen and sassafras will purify the blood. Flaxseed and slippery elm are good for colds, influenza, etc. Tea of the uva ursi, with a piece of salt petre as large as a pea to a tumblerful, is good for strangury.

Herbs, intended for drying, should be gathered, just before they bloom, in dry weather, and dried in the shade. Put up in paper bags.

---

956. *Mutton Broth.*—Take half a pound from the scraggy neck part; cut off the skin and fat; put it in a stew-pan, and cover with cold water; a pint to half a pound will be a good proportion. Let it simmer gently (removing the scum as it rises) an hour, then strain it. Season to taste.

---

957. *Chicken Panada.*—Use the head, wings, neck, and giblets; cover them with cold water; stew until tender. Take out the chicken; add a little sweet milk and bread crumbs; salt to taste; stew five minutes; serve hot. Use the giblets with the rest of the chicken. Chicken tea is made by stewing the chicken as in the panada, using the same pieces; skim off all grease; season with salt to taste.

---

958. *Birds for Convalescents.*—Lay them upon the gridiron; broil until a light brown color; then put them in a stew-pan; pour over hot water enough to cover them. Let them stew until tender. Season with a little fresh butter, pepper, and salt. Chicken, birds, and squirrels, stewed in a double kettle, are very delicate for invalids. If permitted, stuff the fowls and birds with minced oysters.

---

959 *Oyster Soup.*—Pour off the liquor from the oysters. Put the oysters and a piece of butter (enough to make them sufficiently rich) into the stew-pan. Let the oysters stew until they lose their slimy appearance. To a quart of oysters, add a quart of their liquor, the same quantity of sweet milk, a teacup of

bread or cracker crumbs. Beat the yolks of two eggs, and add them just as the liquor boils up. Serve hot. This is a fine soup for a consumptive, or for one in a feeble state, where a generous diet is required.

---

960. *Mush.*—Wet up three tablespoonfuls of fine corn meal with cold water; stir it to three tumblerfuls of boiling water. Add salt to taste; stir frequently until the meal is thoroughly cooked, and the mush sufficiently thick. Eat cold or warm with sweet milk or syrup. Cut cold mush in slices, and fry.

961. *Hasty Pudding.*—Add to this quantity of mush two well-beaten eggs, a quarter of a pound of butter, sugar, and spice to taste. Bake in an earthen dish.

MEDICAL RECEIPTS.

"Safe guide to health: Keep the feet warm, the head cool, and the bowels open."

962. *For a Burn.*—Make half a tumbler of strong lime water; let it set a few minutes; then strain the water through a thin muslin to the same quantity of linseed or sweet oil (neat's or hog's foot will answer); mix it well, and spread over the burn; wrap over linen cloths. Do not remove the cloth for several days; saturate it frequently with the lime and oil until the inflammation is subdued. Should the odor become offensive, apply cold poultices of the flour of slippery elm; spread over with pulverized charcoal. A plaster of lard and soot is also good for a burn. Heal with any simple salve—a very good one is made by stewing together heart leaves, white lily root, agrimony, a few leaves of the Jamestown weed, and sweet gum. When the strength of the herbs is extracted, strain the water; throw away leaves, etc.; add fresh unsalted butter, and simmer gently until the water has evaporated. Keep this on hand for common sores, in a close-covered box.

---

963. *Healing Salve.*—Mutton tallow, four pounds; beeswax, one pound; rosin, half a pound; turpentine, three ounces. Melt the three first over a slow fire; then add the turpentine when they are nearly cold.

---

964. *Green Ointment.*—Boil the leaves of Jamestown weed in water until a very strong tea is obtained; add good hog's lard in the proportion of three pounds of lard to one gallon of the water. Stew until the water is evaporated. Strain, and to each pound add an ounce of turpentine; add it when the lard is nearly cold.

---

965. *Cure for Old Ulcers.*—Five grains of corrosive sublimate, the same of sugar of lead, fourteen grains of white precipitate, and two even tablespoonfuls of good lime; mix in a quart bottle of water. Boil tow in strong ley; dry, and card it; wet it, and apply to the sore. Keep the tow wet.

Another remedy: Mix half a teacup of sweet gum, pine gum (or rosin), beeswax, and tallow; melt them; add as much of the juice of green tobacco. Stew all together until it forms a salve. Poultice the ulcer the night before using the salve with a dough of corn meal and lard; then apply the salve. It is excellent for sores upon horses.

966. *Bone-Felon.*—Apply a salve of equal parts of soft soap and quicksilver. It is severe, but will relieve. To blister immediately with flies, is also good.

Another remedy: One yolk of an egg, a teaspoonful of fresh tar, the same of brown sugar, and fine salt; stir together; wrap in a cabbage leaf securely, and roast. Apply hot.

Another: One tablespoonful of red lead, the same of Castile soap, with as much weak ley as will make it into a salve. Apply it on the first appearance of the felon. It will cure it in ten hours.

For a run-round: Upon the appearance of the first symptoms, scald in hot ley.

When a nail is run into the foot apply grated beet: keep the foot still, and elevated. Or, bathe in a strong tea of wormwood, and then bind slices of fat bacon upon the wound.

967. *Quick Emetic.*—A teaspoonful of mustard in a tumblerful of warm water.

968. *Colic Mixture for Infants.*—Eighty drops of laudanum, fourteen of oil of anise, two tablespoonfuls of alcohol, and a piece asafœtida as large as a pea; put these in an eight-ounce phial, and fill with warm water. Sweeten with loaf sugar. D ;e from four to six drops to a child a few days old. Increase the dose as the child grows older.

---

969. *Chloroform Cough Drops.*—Sulph. morphine, three grains; two ounces each of syrup of squills and ipecac; chloroform, one drachm. A teaspoonful every two hours when the cough is very troublesome, longer time as the cough decreases.

---

970. *For Coughs and Colds.*—Equal parts of syrup of squills, Bateman's drops, and sweet spirits of nitre; make a tea of flaxseed; flavor it by boiling sufficient lemon in it; sweeten with loaf sugar if liked. Into a wineglass of this, put a tablespoonful of the mixture; take it upon going to bed. Paregoric may be used in the place of Bateman's drops. Give it at intervals of two or three hours until the cough is relieved.

---

971. *To Relieve a Cold.*—At the very first symptoms, have the feet bathed upon going to bed, and take three grains of quinine (five grains is sometimes given), twenty drops of laudanum, in a tablespoonful of ginger tea or water. If not relieved by the first dose, repeat the next night. Two doses will generally relieve an obstinate cold.

---

972. *Specific for a Cough.*—Take equal quantities of camomile flowers, elecampane, life-everlasting, mullen, a few races of ginger, and as much fat lightwood splinters as camomile. Boil to a strong tea; strain it, and add enough honey and sugar mixed in equal quantities; boil down to a syrup; add enough good apple vinegar to give a pleasant acid taste.

Pills made of fresh tar, brown sugar, and the yolk of an egg, are good for a cough. Pills of fresh rosin taken from the pine tree are also good.

An excellent remedy for a cough is: The root of the buttonwood boiled with comfrey to a strong tea; strain, sweeten with honey, and boil to a syrup; add to each pint a tablespoonful of paregoric. A tablespoonful is a dose; take as often as is necessary.

For bronchitis: Rub the throat daily with a drop of croton oil or tartar-emetic ointment until it is blistered.

---

973. *Plaster for Chest Affections.*—Dissolve together mutton suet and beeswax, the size of a hen's egg; a tablespoonful each of sweet oil, laudanum, turpentine, spirits of hartshorn; one ounce of gum camphor. Melt all together but the hartshorn; add that after the other things are melted and mixed. Spread upon a cloth.

---

974. *Putrid Sore Throat.*—Mix one gill of strong apple vinegar, one tablespoonful of common salt, tablespoonful of strained honey, half a pod of red pepper; boil them together; strain into half a pint of strong sage tea. In severe cases give half a teaspoonful for an adult every hour; decrease the dose as the disease is relieved. Use some as a gargle.

---

975. *Inflamed Sore Throat.*—Gargle with borax and alum, dissolved in water. Take equal parts of saltpetre and loaf sugar pulverized together; place upon the tongue, and let it trickle down slowly to the inflamed part. Use this two or three times a day. Rub the glands with a mixture of camphor, cantharides, myrrh, and turpentine. If this fails to reduce the inflammation, put a small blister within an inch of the ears. A gargle with red pepper tea is good. Give cooling medicines. Bathe the feet at night. Avoid taking cold.

---

976. *Whooping Cough.*—Bruise a tumbler of flaxseed, three ounces of liquorice, two ounces of loaf sugar, two of strained honey. Pour to these a quart of water; boil until reduced half. Give frequently. Hog's lard and molasses in equal quantities with a little laudanum is also good.

---

977. *Croup*.—A layer of onions sliced and brown sugar—a teaspoonful of the syrup is a dose. Put upon the chest a plaster of Scotch snuff. Grease a cloth three or four inches long, two or three wide; sprinkle over it the snuff. Remove the plaster as soon as the stomach becomes nauseated.

The premonitory symptoms of croup are a shrill, sonorous cough, cold hands, and flushed face. The patient is not always sick, and is often gayer than usual. Use without delay a plaster of mustard upon the throat, or apply to the throat a strip of flannel dipped in turpentine or spirits of hartshorn. Give nauseating doses of hive syrup or syrup of squills. When these remedies are used promptly, they usually give relief.

---

978. *Wash for Sore Throat and Mouth*.—One pennyweight of blue-stone, the same of alum; beat them fine, and add a tumbler of good apple vinegar. After it is dissolved, add a teaspoonful of quick-lime; strain it. Wash the throat with this every two or three hours until the white scabs are off. Gargle the throat frequently with ginger tea sweetened with honey. Occasionally gargle with the blue-stone and alum mixture, using half a teaspoonful at a time.

---

979. *Antidotes for Poisons*.—Eject them by vomiting, or neutralize them by antidotes.

For strychnine: Animal oil as much as can be gotten down.

Sugar of lead: An emetic first, then calcined magnesia.

Corrosive sublimate: Whites of eggs—add a little water; warm bath; drink freely of milk.

Prussic acid: Chloride of lime or bi-chloride of iron, chalk and water.

Arsenic: Hydrated oxide of iron in very large doses is a certain remedy. Should this not be on hand, use an active emetic of ipecac mixed with water, sweetened with sugar; then drink freely flaxseed tea and milk. Tobacco juice swallowed, is said to be a remedy.

Copper: Give large quantities of sweetened water; beat the whites of six eggs; add to them a pint of water; stir well; pour a half tumbler of this to the same quantity of sweet milk. Give every two minutes. Treat as for corrosive sublimate or any mercurial poison.

When copper vessels are used in the kitchen they should be laid aside and forbidden to be used when the inside tinning begins to wear off. The action of grease upon the copper produces a metallic poison, which will inevitably cause death unless very promptly relieved.

For belladonna or veratrum, etc.: Give an active emetic; then strong vinegar or lemon juice; then strong coffee.

Oxalic acid is sometimes mistaken for epsom salts. Give soap suds, or chalk and water, or calcined magnesia; then an active emetic.

For soda: Strong vinegar or lemon juice.

For an overdose of opium: Keep the patient in motion; use friction. Give strong vinegar, in which has been infused red pepper (a pod to a teacup of vinegar, or half a teaspoonful of the pulverized). Give a tablespoonful every five minutes to an adult until the danger is over. Then give strong hot coffee or a nourishing broth. This will relieve from the effects of taking any narcotic, if used in time.

Saltpetre: Vomit with mustard water; use sweet oil; apply onions to the stomach, soles of the feet, and wrists; slice them.

Poisoned mushrooms: Give an emetic. Then a dose of castor oil. After this operates, give strong coffee.

From foul air: Cold water dashed upon the head, and free exposure to the air.

---

980. *Convulsions.*— Give nauseating doses of ipecac. Rub spirits of turpentine on the stomach. If from constipation, give enemas of castor oil and warm water. If from teething, give paregoric and magnesia; cataplasms of mustard applied to the spine and extremities, may be used. Bathe the body in warm

water; put cold water on the head. It is sometimes best to dash it on violently.

---

981. *Dysentery.*—Make a strong tea of sweet gum bark; to a pint, add a gill of good brandy, half an ounce of laudanum, a little loaf sugar to make it palatable. Take a teaspoonful every hour until the effect of the laudanum is apparent, then at longer intervals, until the disease abates.

A very good and simple remedy, if used when the first symptoms appear, is: Give an adult five drops of spirits of turpentine in a teaspoonful of sweet milk. Repeat, if necessary. Give a child according to age.

Another remedy: A teacup half full of apple vinegar. Dissolve as much salt in it as it will hold, leaving a little at the bottom. Pour boiling water upon the solution until the cup is three-fourths full. Scald it, and remove the scum. Take a tablespoonful three times a day.

---

982. *Remedy for Diarrhea.*—Take a peck of the bark of green hickory. Clean an oven-lid; put the bark upon, and burn to ashes. Empty them carefully into an earthen bowl, and cover them well with warm water; stir well. Let them settle and remain until a moderately strong ley is made. Pour this into a jug, straining it by putting a piece of muslin cloth in the bottom of the funnel. The jug should be three parts full. Strip in very small pieces a handful of the inside bark of pine, for a gallon of the ley; put the pine bark in the jug; fill it with good whiskey or gin. A wineglassful is a dose for an adult. This is a valuable preparation for children teething. It will be a good plan to make a gallon the beginning of summer. Keep it in a cool, dry place.

Blackberry root is a fine astringent. A strong tea made of this and sweet gum bark, with a stick of cinnamon boiled with the root, is very good; a little paregoric may be added. Sweeten to taste.

A very good remedy is a dose of Dover's powders in a table spoonful of peach-leaf tea; if the case is severe, add ten drops of laudanum. Repeat in an hour if necessary.

---

983. *For Violent Pain in the Bowels*—Give an injection of a pint of starch, one tablespoonful of melted lard or sweet oil, one teaspoonful of laudanum; let it be warm. Quilt hops between a fold of cloth. Scald in hot vinegar, and apply as hot as can be borne. Lay dry flannel over the bag of hops. If hops cannot be obtained, use mullen or peach leaves. Apply bottles of hot water to the feet. Should violent inflammatory symptoms appear, add to the injection a teacup of hop yeast or hop tea.

---

984. *Colic.*—One or two heaped teaspoonfuls of common salt in cold water will sometimes relieve; repeat, if necessary. A teaspoonful of turpentine and twenty drops of peppermint is also good.

Another remedy: Half a teaspoonful of salts of tartar dissolved in a tumbler of warm water, and one teaspoonful of paregoric. Take a third of the tumblerful; in ten minutes, half of what remains; in ten minutes, the remainder. Cover up warm in bed, and lie still. Put a mustard plaster upon the chest.

Another remedy: One grain of opium and twenty grains of calomel. Make into four pills. Take two; in three hours, the other two. Abstain from liquids. Apply mustard to the extremities and stomach. Apply flannel wrung out of hot whiskey. Put bottles of hot water to the feet. If constipated, give enemas of castor oil and warm water. A prompt remedy in mild cases of colic is: A teaspoonful of paregoric, half the quantity of extract of ginger in a wineglass of water. Camphor, peppermint, and asafœtida, are all good remedies. Eat sparingly, and of nothing that will disagree with the stomach.

A remedy to prevent cholera, if given in the incipient stage (useful also in dysentery): Empty the bowels with oil and turpentine, or salts and red pepper. Use a mixture of sixty grains of super-carbonate of soda, fifty drops of laudanum, three drops of oil of sassafras, four ounces of water. Dose: Tablespoonful after each evacuation. If these are frequent, use enemas of red oak bark tea and laudanum—to a tumblerful of tea half a teaspoonful of laudanum. Rub the spine with a liniment composed of turpentine, camphor, laudanum, and No. 6. Eat sparingly and prudently. Drink slippery elm or sweet gum tea.

---

985. *Chills and Fever.*—Blue pill at night; oil in the morning. Before the paroxysms come on, at least two hours, begin taking a strong tea of boneset and red pepper. Keep the feet warm; cover up snugly. A tea of corn shucks, with a dose of morphine, will sometimes prevent an attack. Another way: Blue pill at night. Six or eight grains of quinine given in pills of two grains each; begin three hours before the chill comes on. This will sometimes prevent their return. Discontinue giving quinine before the fever comes on. Another: Pills of red pepper, pulverized; as much salt, four grains of quinine; divide in two pills; give one two hours before the chill is expected; repeat in an hour. Nothing is so reliable as quinine given in doses of six, eight, or even ten grains, but if used too long, may affect the hearing; hence, it is a good plan to discontinue it, and use boneset or one of the other remedies mentioned. One pint of sweet milk, a large tablespoonful of ground ginger; drink hot as the chill is coming on. Half a wineglass of green sage juice is also good.

---

986. *Congestive Chills.*—Give from ten to fifteen drops of spirits of turpentine in a wineglass of toddy. Make a liniment of equal quantities of turpentine and camphor. With this rub the spine, chest, and extremities well; but not enough to blister. Rub the extremities until reaction takes place. A cloth saturated with the mixture should be applied to the chest.

---

987. *To Give Tone to the Stomach of a Person Recovering from Chill and Fever.*—Half an ounce of rhubarb, the same of

aloes, half an ounce of bruised cloves, one quart of good whiskey. Tablespoonful night and morning.

Another cure for chills: One quart of gin, thirty grains of rhubarb, sixty grains of quinine. Dose: Tablespoonful two two hours before the chill comes on. Repeat in an hour.

---

988. *For Typhoid Fever.*—Ten drops of turpentine every two hours; increase the dose even to a teaspoonful until the right action is produced. Should strangury be produced, give spirits of nitre in flaxseed tea. A mild cathartic or enema as needed; give no strong medicines.

---

989. *Scarlet Fever.*—As soon as the nature of the disease is ascertained, rub the patient night and morning with fat bacon, rubbing every part of the body but the head slowly and carefully.

---

990. *To Prevent Scarlet Fever.*—Dissolve three grains of extract of belladonna in one ounce of cinnamon-water; triturate well in a mortar. Give three drops in a little sweetened water to a child one year old; increase the dose one drop for each additional year.

---

991. *Dropsy.*—A handful each of elder-buds, horehound, and rusty nails, five roots of black snakeroot, two tablespoonfuls of camomile flowers; boil in a gallon of good apple vinegar five hours, slowly; strain and bottle. Dose: A tablespoonful after each meal. Use light diet. Avoid cold and wet.

Another: One pint of hickory ashes, and one pint of good wine. Dose: A wineglassful three times a day.

---

992. *Jaundice.*—Equal parts of wild cherry-tree bark and sassafras root steeped in rum. A wineglassful every morning.

May apple root, dried and pulverized, given in molasses, is an excellent remedy for scrofula, chills and fevers, bilious fever, and all diseases of blood. It is an active cathartic, very much resembling jalap in its effects, and should be given prudently. As much as will lie upon the point of a case-knife is a dose for an adult. In scrofula it should be given in smaller doses, so that it may lie in the system. I have known it to cure very desperate cases. It may be necessary to use it a long time.

---

993. *To Rub on Swellings and Sores.*—Put two copper cents on a plate; pour on them two ounces of aqua fortis; let it remain twenty-four hours; add four ounces of strong vinegar. Put the cents and all in a glass bottle; keep it corked. Begin by putting two drops in a teaspoonful of rain water; apply to the sores three times a day with a soft brush or rag. If very painful, add more water.

In the spring of the year an excellent article of food for scrofulous persons is the poke-plant; boil it, and use as asparagus.

---

994. *Erysipelas.*—A poultice of cranberries, put on cold. Keep the patient cool, or wet the parts; cover well with wheat flour. Keep it covered until relieved. If the paste cracks, cover with more flour. Give a cooling cathartic. The latter may be used when cranberries cannot be had.

---

995. *Cure for Tetter.*—Boil together one pound of the bark of prickly ash, the same of dogwood, a quarter of a pound of walnut bark. Boil in three gallons of water until reduced to one gallon. Apply twice a day to the diseased part.

---

996. *Toothache.*—Powdered alum, two drachms; spirits of ether, seven drachms; mix, and apply to the tooth.

Another: Chloroform, one ounce; alum, five grains; morphine, three grains; mix, and apply with cotton.

If these fail, "*sun the roots*."

---

997. *Earache.*—Roast an onion; put a few drops of laudanum and sweet oil upon it while warm. Press the juice into the ear, and stop it with wool. Bind the warm onion to the ear.

998. *Cure for Thrush.*—One teaspoonful of burnt alum, one ditto of raw alum; beat them fine; add a tablespoonful of honey; warm it. First wash the mouth with sage tea; then apply the alum, etc.

Another remedy: Stir together the whites of two eggs, two tablespoonfuls of apple vinegar, two of good rum, a piece each of blue-stone and alum the size of a pea; beat these fine, and mix all well. Wash the sore places with a mop, using this mixture.

---

999. *Sore Mouth, or Tongue.*—Three drachms of borax, two of sugar of lead, half an ounce of alum, and one pint of strong sage tea. Use as a wash.

1000. *Sore Nipples from Nursing.*—Thirty grains of tannin, and one ounce of glycerine. This does not require to be washed off when the child nurses.

Another: Wash, after the child nurses, with six drops of the tincture of arnica in a small teacup of cold water.

1001. *To Prevent and Relieve Rising Breasts.*—Upon the very first symptoms, wrap the breast in linen cloth saturated with arnica. Keep the cloth wet until the soreness is relieved. After it has progressed, and the arnica is not used, apply Jamestown leaves, coddled, by boiling one or two minutes with a bacon rind. Apply the leaves thick; then lay over the rind, and envelop the whole in a dry cloth. I have this receipt from a lady who considers it infallible if persevered with. Apply warm.

1002. *Headache Pills.*—Aconite and hyerosramus, one grain each to a pill; take when the headache is coming on. Small doses of morphine and quinine are also good. For sick headache, an emetic should be taken; the feet kept warm; warm cloths applied to the head. Apply horseradish leaves scalded in vinegar, or brown paper saturated with pepper vinegar.

1003. *Neuralgia.*—Half a drachm of sal ammonia in an ounce of camphor-water; take a teaspoonful at a dose; repeat every five minutes. Apply chloroform externally to the pain. Pills of a quarter to half a grain of belladonna, three a day, before each meal, will sometimes give relief in this painful disease.

1004. *Asthma.*—Half an ounce of hydrate of potash put in a pint of water. Dose: A teaspoonful three times a day.

Another remedy: Saturate the dried leaves of the Jamestown weed (dry in the shade) with a strong solution of saltpetre; smoke it; fill the mouth with the smoke; then open the lips, and draw in the breath. Gather the leaves before they are injured by frost. For hay or rose asthma use quinine; two grains is a dose; repeat if necessary.

1005. *Diphtheria.*—In the early stages of the disease, accompanied by soreness and swelling of the throat, use a solution of salt and water, as a gargle, every ten minutes. Have a double piece of flannel; saturate it with hot salt and water, and sprinkle salt between the folds; bind this around the throat, putting a dry cloth upon the outside. If the patient is much prostrated, use a little stimulant. Lose no time, however, in calling in a doctor.

1006. *Cancer.*—Said to be infallible. Pulverized beech drops, twenty-nine grains; red puccoon root, three grains; pure arsenic, one grain and a quarter. Mix well, and keep in a dark place. Make an ointment of a handful of slippery elm bark and a handful of life-everlasting. Put them in a pot; cover with water, and boil slowly until reduced to one pint. Add a pound of rosin, and one of mutton suet. Continue to simmer until the water has all evaporated. Pour out the mixture, and stir while it is cooling.

To apply: If the cancer be not raw, scarify it. Spread this salve on a thin piece of cloth half an inch larger in diameter than the cancer. Apply it to the cancer at night; the next morning remove it, and spread over a good coat of the powdered beach drops, etc.; then lay over another cloth with the salve upon it. Let the powders remain thirty-six hours. Remove all, and repeat as at first. Do not wet the place with water. If the dead flesh does not all come off, cut it away. After the cancerous flesh is removed, use the salve until the place is cured. This is said to be the receipt used by the celebrated cancer doctor, January.

1007. *Cramp in the Legs.*—Stretch out the heel of the leg as far as possible, at the same time draw the toes as much as possible towards the leg. This is simple, but I have often known it to give immediate relief.

1008. *Bite of Insects.*—Use Darby's Prophylactic Fluid, or tobacco juice. Soda moistened with water is good; also hartshorn. Wrap the wound with a cloth, and keep it wet with arnica.

1009. *Bite of a Snake.*—Bind above the wound tight. Give whiskey or some kind of liquor, or give sweet oil, a wineglassful at once; repeat, and bathe the wound in sweet oil.

Another remedy: Beat an onion; as much tobacco cut up fine, the same quantity of salt; pour over a half tumblerful of boiling water; put it in a pot, and stew two or three minutes. Cord above the wound as soon as possible after the wound is inflicted; apply the poultice. Repeat until the danger is over. Give a wineglass of sweet oil. This is said to be efficacious in the bite of a mad dog.

1010. *Hydrophobia.*—Wash the wound immediately with warm vinegar. Dry it, and pour on a few drops of hydrochloric acid. Mineral acids will destroy the poison of saliva. Give pills, made by boiling the bark of black ash to a strong syrup. Three pills a day.

Another remedy: Burn to the bottom of the wound with lunar caustic, and drink large quantities of vinegar.

1011. *For a Fresh Cut.*—Draw the sides together; apply strips of adhesive plaster, and a cloth over this kept saturated with copal varnish or arnica tincture.

1012. *Lockjaw.*—If from a wound, wash it with arnica water; bind a grated beet upon it; rub around the wound, but not on it, with turpentine. Give ipecac in sufficient doses to nauseate; this will relax the nerves. If medicine cannot be swallowed, use an enema of ipecac and laudanum. Use twice as much as when taken by the mouth. Lose no time in procuring medical treatment.

1013. *Bleeding at the Nose.*—Snuff pulverized alum, or dried beef pounded or grated very fine, or beat sage to a powder, and snuff it. Put cold cloths upon the back of the neck. Put the feet in hot mustard or pepper water. Holding the arms up straight over the head is said to be a remedy.

1014. *To Prevent Discoloration from Bruises.*—Apply repeatedly cloths wrung out of hot water or the tincture of arnica.

1015. *Sprains.*—Bathe in strong mullen tea salted, or apply brown paper saturated with vinegar; keep the paper wet as long as necessary. Nothing is better than the tincture of arnica; wrap the place with a linen cloth, and keep the cloth saturated with arnica. This is also excellent to prevent risings and boils, and to relieve the pain and inflammation when advanced.

1016. *Scald Head.*—Apply pyroligneous acid to the diseased scalp. An ointment made by simmering in water until a strong tea is made, blood-root, green tobacco leaves, elder bark, in equal quantities. Add hog's lard until the water evaporates; strain, and while warm add to a pint a teaspoonful of fresh tar. Wash the head well with Castile soap, and wear a plaster of this; renew every day. The blood-root sliced and put in vinegar is good used as a wash. The black wash is also very good. Tobacco juice and vinegar are said to be good. This latter mixture will cure warts. The milk of fig leaves is also good applied after trimming the warts. Burning with lunar caustic is a sure remedy.

1017. *Corns and Bunions.*—Burn with caustic, after bathing; repeat, if necessary.

Another remedy: Apply the pulp of lemon until the hard part can be easily removed. Cotton greased with linseed oil or turpentine is very good; it softens the corn. Arnica is also good.

1018. *Chilblains.*—A turnip poultice is good. Bathe the feet in the water in which the turnips are boiled. When the skin is not broken, bathe in alum water. The soreness may be relieved by wrapping in cloths saturated with arnica; keep it wet.

1019. *Frost-bitten Limbs*—Should be immediately bathed in cold water, and rubbed until heat is restored. Avoid warming numbed hands and feet at the fire.

1020. *Dry Mortification.*—Blister the part. Keep the bowels open with castor oil. Give opiates at night.

1021. *Gangrene.*—Use poultices of red oak bark thickened with corn meal; sprinkle over thick powdered charcoal.

1022. *Cure for Ingrowing Nails.*—Heat a small piece of tallow in an iron spoon; drop two or three drops between the nail and outside flesh. It will not be necessary to repeat this if proper pains is taken to so apply this liquid cautery that it will insinuate itself in every interstice under the nail. Repeat, if necessary.

1023. *Itch.*—This disease is sometimes cured by washing in poke-root tea—not too strong, but sufficiently so to smart. An ointment of equal parts of brimstone and hog's lard is good. Give sulphur and cream of tartar to keep the bowels open.

1024. *To Stop the Bleeding from Leeches.*—Make a ball of cotton about the size of a pea; put this pellet of cotton or lint upon the wound; press it down firmly; keep up the pressure for a quarter of an hour. Remove the finger cautiously, taking care to let the pellet remain.

1025. *Gargle for Sore Mouth.*—Half a teacup of boneset tea; the same of tea made of the black haw. Use the bark of the root; a teacup of strong tea made of privet; a piece of alum the size of a nutmeg. Sweeten with honey.

1026. *Cholera Mixture.*—Two ounces of peppermint, two of spirits of camphor, two of laudanum, two of Hoffman's anodyne, one of extract of ginger, two of tincture of red pepper. Tablespoonful every thirty minutes.

1027. *Potato Poultice.*—Boil and mash the potatoes smooth, using warm water or sweet milk to give it the proper consistence. This is a soothing poultice, but may be made stimulating by using strong pepper tea instead of water. For foul ulcers use red oak bark tea, and sprinkle over it powdered charcoal.

In preparing poultices always make enough for two. Have two bags made of thin soft cloth; as one cools have the other ready to apply immediately, so that the heat and moisture may be kept up without interruption as long as necessary. When the last poultice is withdrawn, lay over the place a dry flannel or cloth of some kind. The poultice should be large enough to cover the place well, made smooth, and not too stiff. A hard, lumpy, heavy poultice should not be used. Never make them more than half an inch thick. Always lay a dry cloth over the poultice to prevent the person's clothing from becoming damp. When well prepared and managed they are very useful, but improperly made and carelessly used, they do more harm than good.

1028. *Charcoal Poultice.*—To a pint of potato, light bread or corn meal poultice, add a large tablespoonful of fresh burned pulverized charcoal. Good for foul ulcers.

1029. *Hop Poultice.*—Boil hops to a strong tea; thicken smoothly with potato, flour, or corn meal. Use when there is much pain and inflammation. Hop fomentation is excellent for swelled glands in scarlet fever, quinsy, etc. Rub the leaves between the hands; quilt them between a fold of muslin cloth; scald in strong vinegar. Apply as hot as can be borne. Make two bags, and have one cool; apply the other; use over it a dry cloth, and apply warm flannel when the last is removed. Peach leaves, mint, mullen, horehound, and tansy answer a good purpose, and are very good in all painful affections of the stomach and bowels.

1030. *Light Bread Poultice.*—Saturate the bread with sweet milk; put it on the fire until hot; grease over the top with a little sweet, linseed, or neat's oil. A very soothing poultice for simple sores. Never let a poultice remain long enough to become sour.

1031. *Slippery Elm Poultice*—Is best made of the ground elm. Druggists usually keep it in small packages. Take as much of the powdered elm as may be needed; stir cold water to it until it forms a jelly. Apply this, spread upon a soft cloth, immediately to the diseased part. This is excellent for sores from fire, or any inflamed sore. If there is any disagreeable odor, sprinkle charcoal over it. Change frequently.

1032. *Pepper Poultice.*—Make a strong tea of red pepper; thicken with wheat bran or corn meal.

1033. *Flaxseed Poultice.*—Grind or bruise the seed; boil in sweet milk or water until of the right consistence. Apply without putting a cloth between the flaxseed and the sore.

1034. *Cancer Poultice.*—Take equal parts of red oak bark, poplar root, dogwood root, and black sumac root; boil down in water to a strong tea; strain out the barks, and boil the tea to the consistence of syrup. Make a plaster of this; sprinkle over it pulverized bluestone. Apply the plaster to the cancer night and morning until the cancer is eaten out; then continue the plaster without the bluestone until the fever or inflammation is relieved; then use a healing salve.

1035. *Liniment for White Swelling and Palsy.*—Use the root and flower of the *bear foot* (any quantity); boil to a strong tea; strain it, and stew with hog's lard until the water has evaporated. Rub the part affected well, and wrap in flannel.

Another way of making this liniment is: A handful of the flowers of the bear's-foot, and one of the root; dry in the shade, and beat to a powder; mix with half a pound of fresh butter. Put it in a jar, and expose to the sun two days. Rub the part affected. This is also excellent for hard breasts, when there is danger of their rising.

1036. *A Good Healing Salve.*—A gill of soft turpentine from the pine tree, mutton suet the size of a hen's egg, three tablespoonfuls of linseed oil, the same of beef-foot oil, and three of wax; melt these together; mix well, and when just warm, work in a teaspoonful of laudanum, one of opedeldoc, and one of spirits of camphor.

1037. *To Dress a Blister.*—When the blister has drawn suffi ciently, prepare for dressing it, by trimming all the hard veins and stems from cabbage leaves; lay them in a deep vessel, and pour over boiling water; let them remain until ready to use. Remove the blister gently with a sharp-pointed pair of scissors; or clip them; hold a cloth doubled under to receive the water as it trickles from the blister. Apply the cabbage leaves putting them on three or four deep. Bind these on carefully with a cloth. Dress in this way for several days, three times a day, and once or twice during the night if painful; then use a wax cloth, made by melting together one part wax, and three parts tallow; spread upon a cloth.

1038. *A Good Styptic.*—Rub a little dry chloride of lime upon the wound.

1039. *Mustard Plaster.*—When required to act promptly, use only mustard mixed with water or vinegar; spread upon cloth, and apply immediately to the part; but if wished less stimulating, add a little meal or flour, and put a thin muslin over the plaster.

1040. *Mustard or Pepper Bath for the Feet.*—Have as much hot water as may be needed in a small tub; stir in mustard to make it sufficiently stimulating, or if pepper, boil a pod or two of pepper with the water. Put the patient's feet in the tub of water, and throw over the whole a blanket. Keep the water to the same temperature by adding a little warm water from time to time as may be needed. Rub dry with a coarse towel, and immediately cover up in bed.

1041. *Pepper Plaster.*—Beat the white of an egg with a tablespoonful of pulverized red pepper—a tablespoonful of spirits of turpentine is sometimes added. Spread upon cloth. Excellent for pains in the breast and sides, in severe cold, and influenzas.

1042. *Plaster for Boils.*—White of an egg, honey, and flour.

For a breast threatened to rise: Dip a cloth, cut to fit, in a mixture of equal parts of beeswax and tallow.

1043. *Rheumatic Liniment.*—Equal parts of sweet oil, spirits of camphor, hartshorn, and laudanum; or rub with No. 6, or Perry Davis' Pain-killer. For pains in the back, use the arnica plaster.

1044. *Piles.*—Castor oil on cotton is good. Also a salve made of Jamestown weed leaves, or the seed. Never allow the bowels to become constipated.

1045. *Fainting.*—Lay the person in a horizontal position; give plenty of fresh air. It is improper and thoughtless to crowd around a person in this condition. Bathe the face with cold water. Apply hartshorn or some stimulating smell to the nose. Loosen the clothing. If necessary, put mustard plasters upon the extremities.

1046 *For Nausea.*—Peppermint diluted is very good. A mint julip is also good. Make it in this way: Put a few sprigs of fresh mint in the bottom of a tumbler; if convenient, add a teaspoonful of ice broken into small pieces. In another tumbler dissolve a tablespoonful of loaf sugar in enough water to fill the tumbler half full; add a wineglass of good brandy; stir well, and pour it upon the mint. Give this in small quantities. Put a mustard plaster over the stomach.

1047. *To Extinguish Fire on a Person.*—When the clothes catch on fire, extinguish by smothering; wrap up in woolen if possible—a carpet, hearth rug, or anything within reach. I knew a case where a lady alone in her room, just in the act of retiring to bed, discovered her night clothes in a blaze; with admirable presence of mind, she leaped into bed, smothered the flame, and saved her life. Never rush into the air.

If the chimney catches, so as to endanger the house, throw salt upon the fire; spread a wet blanket before the fire-place.

1048. *Where a Person is Insensible from a Fall or Blow upon the Head.*—Put a mustard plaster on the back of the neck and extremities; rub briskly; then bathe the part with hot vinegar.

1049. *To Recover a Person Apparently Drowned.*—Strip the body; rub it dry; wrap it in warm blankets; use every means to heat the body by hot applications and friction. Wipe the mouth on the inside, should it be necessary; turn the head on the side, slightly elevated, to allow the water to run out of the mouth. Inflate the lungs, by introducing into one of the nostrils the pipe of a hand bellows; close the mouth and the other nostril; blow the bellows until the chest rises; then unstop the the mouth and nostril; press lightly on the chest to eject the air. Repeat this process. Never cease using remedies for at least six hours. When the patient is able to swallow, give small quantities of warm wine, or brandy and water.

1050. *From Freezing.*—Put the body in a cold bath for a quarter of an hour; rub briskly until warmth is restored; avoid the fire. Give, if the patient can swallow, a few drops of camphor; or if it cannot be swallowed, use camphor and water as an injection. As soon as possible give a cup of strong coffee.

1051. *Struck by Lightning.*—When a person is struck by lightning, dash cold water over the neck, face, and breast. As they recover, they should be kept quiet. If the feet are cold apply hot jugs of water.

1052. *From Hanging, Suffocation, etc.*—Rub with warm cloths. Apply hot bottles of water to the feet.

1053. *Apparent Death from Charcoal or other Noxious Vapors.*—Give the person plenty of fresh air. Dash over the face and neck cold water. When relieved, cover comfortably in bed;

keep quiet, and take some nourishing broth or a cup of strong hot coffee.

1054. *When Affected by Foul Air in Descending Wells*—Throw down unslacked lime, then several pails of water before venturing to go down.

1055. *The Severing of an Artery.*—When a person is in danger of bleeding to death from the severing of an artery, compress with the fingers the ends of the artery, as near as possible to the wound, or apply a piece of lint dipped in a tincture of arnica water; on this put a bit of sponge, and press this so as to stop the blood. Send for a surgeon without delay.

1056. *To Dress Wounds.*—Dress wounds loosely, so as to allow the secreted matter to escape easily in the lint; spread over the wound to exclude the air. Every day a suppurating wound should be cleansed, and bathed freely in lukewarm water. If a wound inflames, becomes hot, and swollen, put a warm bread and milk poultice over it.

1057. *For Bleeding at the Lungs*—Take strong salt and water; a teaspoonful every five minutes.

1058. *Worms—For Ascarides or Pin Worms.*—Give an injection every night until relieved, of a tablespoonful of sweet oil in half a pint of warm water. Use the homeopathic specifics for worms.

For other varieties of worms: Give a child a drop of turpentine upon sugar for each year old. For instance, if two years old, give two drops of turpentine before eating, and for nine successive mornings; then a dose of castor oil. When from the knotting of the worms violent pain is caused, rub with turpentine, using a little oil with it to prevent blistering. This treatment has been known to remove tape-worm. Tea of Jerusalem oak is efficacious in expelling worms.

1059. *Deafness.*—Fill a phial with house-leek leaves; stop it well; envelope it in corn meal dough, and bake slowly. Drop the juice in the ear three or four times a day. Wear a piece of wool in the ear.

Another remedy said to be good: Divide an onion, and from the centre take out a piece the size of a walnut; fill this cavity with a fresh quid of tobacco, and bind the onion in its usual shape. Wrap it in wet paper, and roast it. Trim it down to the part discolored by the tobacco; put it in a phial. Put three drops of this juice at one time in the ear. It may give some pain upon the first application.

1060. *Catarrh in the Head.*—Make a snuff of equal portions of bloodroot, gum Arabic, and gum myrrh. Use it as needed.

1061. *A Simple Febrifuge.*—One teaspoonful of saltpetre and five grains of ipecac. Mix well; divide into ten equal parts. Give one every hour in flaxseed tea, sage, balm, or catnip. If there is nausea, lengthen the time between the doses.

1062. *In Small-Pox to Prevent Pits.*—Saturate a cloth with sweet oil; cover the face with it, cutting holes for the eyes, nose, and mouth.

1063. *Measles.*—Very little medicine is necessary. Nearly everything depends upon good nursing. If there is much fever, give Dover's powders in a little ginger tea. If nausea, give a little soda or peppermint water. If the eruption suddenly disappears, give a sweat. Should there be great debility, use a little wine diluted. The patient should be kept within doors in a room comfortably warm. If in bed, the covering should not be oppressive. Diet light. The greatest danger from measles is the liability to relapse. Avoid taking cold. The patient must not leave the sick-room too soon. If the eyes are weak, darken the room.

1064. *Chronic Rheumatism.*—A good handful of the bark of white ash (the blooms are still better), it may be fresh or dry). Steep in a quart of gin. Dose: a tablespoonful three times a day. If it proves too active a cathartic, lessen the dose.

1065. *Acute Rheumatism.*—Take a tablespoonful of No. 6 three times a day before each meal, rubbing the part affected with the same.

1066. *Homeopathic Specifics.*—For rheumatisms, neuralgia, diseases of the nerves, particularly headache, pain in the eyes, restlessness, and inability to sleep, dyspepsia, etc., I have tried nothing equal to the *homeopathic specifics*.

1067. *To Cure Pimples on the Skin.*—Drink mullen tea, and anoint the skin (rubbing it in well) with milk mixed with as much sulphur as the milk will dissolve. Let it set an hour or two, and then rub it on. Make only a wineglassful at once. Use before washing.

1068. *Disinfectants.*—For a room where the disease has created a very unpleasant odor, nothing is so good as to burn green coffee. Have a small oven or pan half filled with good solid coals; throw upon them a handful of coffee; pass the vessel under the bed and around the room. Darby's Prophylactic poured in saucers, and set around the room, is good; so also is chloride of lime dissolved in water.

1069. *For Spinal Disease.*—Bathe spine in salt and water, or rub with tartar-emetic ointment until a good crop of pustules is produced. When these dry, repeat if not relieved.

1070. *For Excoriations upon the Flesh of Infants.*—Wash in tepid water. Dip a cloth in sweet oil and slightly grease the part. Sore navel of an infant: Grate over it very fine nutmeg, first cleansing with a suds of Castile soap.

1071. *Cholera Infantum.*—Pulverized rhubarb a teaspoonful, two-thirds full of saleratus or soda, a teacupful of peppermint leaves; pour over a tumbler of boiling water; sweeten with loaf sugar; from a teaspoonful to a tablespoonful for an infant every quarter or half hour, as the case requires. Should the stomach reject it, persevere and lessen the dose. An adult may take a wineglassful.

1072. *Remarks upon Medical Receipts.*—Emergencies occur in every family when the services of a physician cannot be procured promptly, and something should be done while "waiting for the doctor." Many of these "Medical Receipts" will, I hope, answer the valuable purpose of relieving suffering humanity. Many cases of sickness may be relieved by simple remedies, if used in time, without calling in a physician. Some useful directions will be found in these receipts. Judgment and discretion must be used in giving even " simple remedies."

1073. *Care of a Sick-Room.*—Avoid loud talking or whispering; either extreme is painful to a sick person. Make up the pillows, and turn them occasionally; arrange the bed-clothes quietly; assist the patients to change their position; anticipate their wants in giving drink, nourishment, etc., but avoid being "fussy." A nervous person would prefer neglect to being persecuted by unnecessary attentions and needless questions. Never take your seat upon a sick person's bed unless requested to do so. Avoid shaking the bed. Darken the room to a mellow, twilight light, and so ventilate the room that a draught of air will not blow directly upon the patient. If the patient is nervous, or laboring under great excitement, or wishes to sleep, *exclude all visitors.* Sensible, considerate people will never take offence at this course. Wear slippers or cloth shoes; tread lightly. Let every thing about the room be scrupulously neat. Bathe the face and hands of the patient upon awaking in the morning, and oftener if necessary. Change clothes and bed-clothing frequently, and be sure that they are perfectly dry. Follow the directions in giving medicine faithfully. Make the medicine, when preparing it to be taken, as palatable as possible. Give castor oil in hot coffee or toddy; hold a little vinegar in the mouth before taking the oil. Give salts in a little weak pepper tea, or add to it a few drops of extract of ginger, or No. 6. Use as little water as can be to dissolve the salts. Cover powders with roasted apples; this is better than syrup; though children may prefer the latter. Take pepper tea mixed with sweet milk, and, if liked, sweeten it. If taken too strong, the tender coats of the stomach will suffer. When food is offered to a sick person, cover the waiter with a clean, white napkin, with another napkin laid upon the waiter. The china, glass, knife, fork, every thing used, must be bright and clean, and a small quantity of food served and cooked, so as to be appetizing. Vary the dishes. The same things should not be offered every day. Never keep the patient waiting any length of time for nourishment; as far as possible anticipate their wants. When broth, soup, or meat is permitted, it is well to keep a tender chicken, steak, or birds killed, and in readiness. Use only part of the fowl at one time. Never serve broth or soup smoked or greasy. Black tea is best for invalids. Gruels should be boiled a long time, and be thoroughly done. Never tempt the appetite of sick persons by offering them unsuitable food. If milk is used, keep it in a cool place; the least acidity will injure the patient, unless in cases where buttermilk is prescribed. In making toast water, prepare it some time before it will be called for; toast the bread without burning. If sitting up at night is necessary, only permit such persons to assist who will have self-denial and benevolence enough to refrain from loud talking, and laughing, and reading newspapers; the rattling of the paper in turning sometimes gives exquisite torture. The rocking of chairs and other discordant noises must all be avoided. "Trifles," it has been said, "make up the sum of human happiness or misery." This is certainly true of a sick-room. Persons sitting up at night should be invited in another room if refreshments are furnished, one person remaining with the patient. A great deal of pain and suffering is inflicted upon the sick by a want of *consideration*, and not the wish or intention to be unkind. Never carry a sad, lugubrious face into a sick-room.

1074. *Hints to Housekeepers.*—Rise early in the morning, or you will not get a fair start with your business. Rise earlier on Sunday morning than any other day, that the children may be at Sunday-school in time; and domestics have time to so arrange their necessary business as to be able to attend Divine service. Do all the cooking for Sunday on Saturday, or, if it is absolutely necessary that some cooking be done, have it all completed at breakfast, and the fires extinguished for the day. Have the house cleaned and every thing put in order on Saturday. On Sunday only make the beds, and do such things as are *absolutely necessary*. On Monday it will be necessary to spend more than the usual time in cleaning and setting things to rights. On Monday evening look over the soiled clothes. Mend, and put on buttons and strings. Select out the white articles, and put them to soak. Have a separate basket or bag for keeping towels, napkins, and table-cloths. Put them to soak in a vessel to themselves. The soaking will soften the grease, and make it easier to wash out. Have the water drawn in barrels, if possible. Exposure to the air will soften the water, and will give time for the sediments to settle at the bottom. This will be found an excellent plan, particularly where there is limestone in the water. Have the wood cut and every thing in readiness, so that on Tuesday the washing may be carried through without interruption. Wash colored clothes first, and take them in as soon as they dry.

The practice of some washerwomen is to wet colored clothes too late to dry them, and then pack them away damp until morning. This is a severe and unnecessary trial to colors. Some colors fade from being long exposed to the sun. The ironing of course follows the washing, and should be done with as little delay as possible, and the cloths assorted and put away. Stockings and socks should be darned when brought in from the wash. System and order must be strictly observed in all household arrangements.

"A place for everything, and everything in its place." A time for certain duties, and the housekeeper must see that there is no infringement of the laws that are laid down. Children cannot too soon be taught the importance of order, neatness, and economy. A habit of system may be early formed, and prove a blessing through life. An ill-governed household, where there is neither system, order, neatness, nor frugality, is a bad school for children.

"Never leave things laying about—a shawl here, a pair of slippers there, a bonnet somewhere else, trusting to a servant to put them in place. No matter how many servants you have, it is a miserable habit. If you set an example of carelessness, do not blame your servants for following it. Children should be taught to put things back in their places as soon as they are old enough to use them, and if each member of a family were to observe this simple rule, the house would never get much out of order."

MISCELLANEOUS RECEIPTS.

1075. *Soap.*—The ashes should be strong (hickory is best), and kept dry. When put in the hopper, mix a bushel of unslacked lime with ten bushels of ashes; put in a layer of ashes; then one slight sprinkling of lime; wet each layer with water (rain water is best). A layer of straw should be put upon the bottom of the hopper before the ashes are put in. An opening in the side or bottom for the ley to drip through, and a trough or vessel under to receive the ley. When the ley is strong enough to bear up an egg, so as to show the size of a dime above the surface, it is ready for making soap; until it is, pour it back into the hopper, and let it drip through again. Add water to the ashes in such quantities as may be needed. Have the vessel very clean in which the soap is to be made. Rub the pot over with corn meal after washing it, and if it is at all discolored, rub it over with more until the vessel is perfectly clean. Melt three pounds of clean grease; add to it a gallon of weak ley, a piece of alum the size of a walnut. Let this stew until well mixed. If strong ley is put to the grease, at first it will not mix well with the grease. In an hour add three gallons of strong hot ley; boil briskly, and stir frequently; stir one way. After it has boiled several hours, cool a spoonful upon a plate; if it does not jelly, add a little water; if this causes it to jelly, then add water to the kettle. Stir quickly while the water is poured in until it ropes on the stick. As to the quantity of water required to make it jelly, judgment must be used; the quantity will depend upon circumstances. It will be well to take some in a bowl, and notice what proportion of water is used to produce this effect.

To harden it: Add a quart of salt to this quantity of soap; let it boil quick ten minutes; let it cool. Next day cut it out. This is now ready for washing purposes.

To prepare it for hand soap: Scrape off all sediment; shave it very thin; put it in a tin-pan, and hardly cover it with water. Set it on the fire; mash it to a jelly, and perfume with lavender, sassafras, or anything preferred. It will be nicer if it is melted in water and cooled two or three times before shaving it.

Soap will improve by age if kept well boxed in a cool, dry place.

1076. *Sal Soda Soap.*—Pour twelve quarts of soft boiling water on five pounds of sal soda. In another vessel pour the same quantity of soft or rain water upon five pounds of unslacked lime. Let them remain until the soda is dissolved; then pour the two mixtures together without disturbing the sediments. Let this remain twelve hours; then strain it off carefully. Heat three and a half pounds of clear grease; add to it three ounces of pulverized rosin. Warm the ley; pour it to the grease; boil an hour briskly. Turn it out to cool.

1077. *Potash Soap.*—Six pounds of potash, five pounds of grease, and a quarter of a pound of powdered rosin; mix all well in a pot, and, when warm, pour on ten gallons of boiling water. Boil until thick enough.

1078. *A Superior Receipt.*—To make a barrel of potash soap (or thirty-two gallons), twenty-five pounds of grease, two pounds of rosin pulverized, ten pounds of potash dissolved in twenty-eight gallons of hot water. Put the grease and rosin in a pot; add a gallon of hot water to it as the grease becomes hot; stir it well just as it begins to boil; add the hot potash water slowly, a few gallons at once, until all is in. Boil until thick enough. This receipt is reliable. I have used it over twenty years.

1079. *Brown Bar Soap.*—Take thirty gallons of soft soap, eight quarts of salt, and four pounds of rosin pulverized; mix, and boil half an hour. Turn it in tubs to cool.

MISCELLANEOUS RECEIPTS.

Another way: Put grease in a barrel; add strong ley to cover it; stir it in well. During the year, as the grease increases, add more ley, and stir it up frequently; keep a stick in it for this purpose. This will become soap by the time the barrel is full. To harden it: Add a quart of salt to three gallons of soft soap; boil half an hour. Turn it out to cool. Boiling longer will harden the soap, without the use of salt. The ley that remains in the bottom of the tubs after the soap becomes hard should be taken care of, and used for scouring.

1080. *To Make Starch.*—To make starch from wheat, send it to the mill and have it ground, but not bolted; put it to soak in plenty of water until it ferments. Squeeze all the milky fluid from the bran by pressing it between the hands, or by putting it in a thin bag; lay in tubs of cold water, and press as long as any white liquid runs. The bran may then soak a few hours, and be pressed again. Strain the water through a blanket. Let the starch settle to the bottom; pour off the water carefully; add fresh water every day; stir up the starch; let it settle again. Repeat the process until the starch is white; cut it in cakes, and dry upon dishes. It is best to have a platform made out-doors; upon this place the tubs.

1081. *Potato Starch.*—Grate the potatoes after peeling them; rub them through the hands until all the milky fluid has been pressed out. Strain out the hard part of the potato. Let the water set without being disturbed; the starch will settle at the bottom; pour off the water; add fresh water every day. Stir up the starch; let it settle again. Repeat as in the wheat starch until the starch is satisfactorily white; then dry. Keep in a dry place. Frozen potatoes yield more starch than those which have not been frozen, but must be used immediately.

1082. *To Prepare Starch for Use.*—Wet two tablespoonfuls of starch to a smooth paste with cold water; pour to it a pint of boiling water; put it on the fire; let it boil, stirring frequently, until it looks transparent; this will probably require half an hour. Add a piece of spermaceti as large as half a nutmeg, or as much salt, or loaf sugar—this will prevent the starch from sticking to the iron.

1083. *To Give a Gloss to Shirt Bosoms.*—Half an ounce of white wax, the same quantity each of gum Arabic and isinglass, and ten drops of alcohol; add half a tumbler of boiling water; mix well, and bottle it. To a quart of starch put a teaspoonful of this preparation. Starch while the article is wet; if dry, dip it in hot water, and wring dry; then starch. Rub the starch in well; then press in a towel to remove all on the outside. Spread it out; wipe over with a clean, dry cloth; then roll snugly; let it lie an hour or two, and iron.

Use for ironing shirts a bosom-board, made of seasoned wood, a foot wide, one and a half long, and an inch thick; cover it well by tacking over very tight two or three folds of flannel, according to the thickness of the flannel. Cover it lastly with Canton flannel; this must be drawn over very tight, and tacked well to prevent folds when in use. Make slips of fine white cotton cloth; put a clean one on every week. A skirt-board must be made in the same way for ironing dresses; five feet long, tapering from two feet at one end to a foot and a half at the other; the large end should be round. A clean slip should be upon it whenever used. A similar but smaller board should be kept for ironing gentlemen's summer pants. Keep fluting and crimping irons, a small iron for ruffles, and a polishing-iron.

1084. *To Starch Muslins, etc.*—Add to the starch for fine muslins a little white gum Arabic. Keep a bottle of it ready for use. Dissolve two ounces in a pint of hot water; bottle it; use as may be required, adding it to the starch. Muslins, calicoes, etc., should never be stiffer than when new. Rice-water and isinglass stiffen very thin muslins better than starch.

For black calicoes: Boil a strong tea of fig-leaves; mix the starch for stiffening with this. After washing the article through three warm waters, rinse it in the fig-leaf tea; when nearly dry fold; let it remain half an hour, and iron immediately. If starched articles are not soon ironed they become sour, and acquire a disagreeable smell. This is also the case if the starch is suffered to stand too long after being made. Cover starch after it is made to prevent its forming a useless skin. Spermaceti, salt, or loaf sugar will prevent its sticking to the irons.

1085. *To Remove Grease Spots from Calicoes, Muslins, etc.*—Cover the spots with the yolk of an egg; then wash off the egg after it has remained half an hour; use no soap on the spot, but wash in suds.

1086. *Where the Colors are Doubtful.*—Have two tubs of soap suds; throw a handful of salt into each. Prepare three rinsing waters; in the last, put to each gallon forty drops of elixir vitriol and a teaspoonful of the dissolved gum Arabic. Wash through the suds; then rinse; wring well, and dry in the shade, where the wind will dry it rapidly. All colored articles should be passed rapidly through the wash, dried, and ironed as expeditiously as possible. If colored goods fade, wash each article to itself, or the colors will mingle.

Ox-gall sets dark colors well; use a tablespoonful to a gallon of water. The smell is not pleasant, but exposure to the air will soon destroy it.

Iron muslins, needle-work, and fine embroidered handkerchiefs on the wrong side.

In washing delicate fabrics, do not rub them; gently squeeze and shake them out; pin them to the line, or to some large article, and take them in as soon as dry.

Bran-water is excellent to use in washing colored cottons or delaines, when the colors are not fast. Boil a peck of wheat bran and a pint of salt in five gallons of water, an hour; let it settle; strain the water; wash the articles through it, and rinse with water into which forty drops of elixir vitriol to the gallon is mixed. Wash all such articles on a clear, windy day, so that the air will dry them rapidly; take them in immediately.

1087. *To Wash Flannel.*—Never rub soap upon it; make a suds by dissolving the soap in warm water; rinse in warm water. Very cold or hot water will shrink flannel. Shake them out several minutes before hanging to dry. Blankets are washed in the same way.

1088. *To Wash Bombazine.*—Make a good soap suds; add ox-gall, a tablespoonful to a gallon of water. Press the cloth through the hands without rubbing. Rinse in tepid water, into which put a little dissolved gum Arabic. Shake the article, but do not wring it; press it carefully with a warm iron on the wrong side.

1089. *To Wash Ribbons.*—If there are grease spots, rub the yolk of an egg upon them, or French chalk on the wrong side; let it dry. Lay it upon a clean cloth, and wash upon each side with a sponge; press on the wrong side. If very much soiled, wash in bran-water; add to the water in which it is rinsed a little muriate of tin to set red, oil of vitriol for green, blue, maroon, and bright yellow.

1090. *To Bleach Clothes.*—Dissolve a handful of refined borax in ten gallons of water; boil the clothes in it.

Another way: One ounce of oxalic acid to a pint of water; a tumbler of this to three gallons of water. Put in the clothes; stir well; then rinse twice. To whiten brown cloth, boil in weak ley, and expose day and night to the sun and night air; keep the clothes well sprinkled.

1091. *Washing Mixture.*—A gallon of water, one pound of

sal soda, and one pound of soap; boil one hour; then add one tablespoonful of spirits of turpentine. Put the clothes to soak over night; next morning soap them well with the mixture. Boil well one hour; rinse in three waters; add a little bluing to the last water.

Save all old cotton and linen rags in bags for sickness.

1092. *To Remove Spermaceti.*—Scrape it off; put brown paper on the spot; upon that, a hot iron.

1093. *To Remove Grease from Silk or Worsted.*—Rub French chalk on the wrong side. Let it remain a day. Split a visiting card; lay the rough side upon the spot, and pass a warm iron over.

1094. *Grease Balls.*—Mix two ounces of fuller's-earth, a tea spoonful of pearl ash or saleratus, and strong vinegar to make a stiff paste; make it into balls; dry them. Use it by wetting the grease spot; scrape some of the ball on the place; dry it, and then wash in tepid water.

1095. *Stains from Acids*—Can be removed by spirits of hartshorn diluted. Repeat if necessary.

1096. *Tar and Pitch*—Can be removed by greasing the place with lard or sweet oil. Let it remain a day and night; then wash in suds. If silk or worsted, rub the stain with alcohol.

1097. *To Remove Oil from Carpets or Floors.*—Keep fuller's-earth upon it wet, renewing until the oil is removed. Add ox-gall to it to prevent the colors from fading.

1098. *For Rust and Ink Stains.*—Oxalic acid will remove iron rust and ink stains. Make a pint bottle full by mixing with that quantity of water half an ounce of the acid. Label it

"Poison." (This cleans brass beautifully.) Dip the stain in hot water, and apply the acid as often as necessary. Wash very soon, in half an hour at least, or the cloth will be injured by the acid.

1099. *To Remove Mildew.*—When the clothes are washed and ready to boil, pin Jamestown weed leaves upon the place. Put a handful of the leaves on the bottom of the kettle; lay the stained part next to them. Green tomatoes and salt, sour buttermilk, lemon juice, soap and chalk, are all good; expose to the sun.

Another way: Two ounces of chloride of lime; pour on it a quart of boiling water; add three quarts of cold water. Steep the cloth in it twelve hours.

1100. *To Take Ink Out of Linen.*—Scald in hot tallow. Let it cool; then wash in warm suds. Sometimes these stains can be removed by wetting the place in very sour buttermilk or lemon juice; rub salt over, and bleach in the sun.

1101. *For Fruit Stains on napkins, table-cloths, etc.*—Pour hot water on the spots; wet with hartshorn or oxalic acid—a teaspoonful to a teacup of water.

1102. *Stains from Scorched Goods.*—Boil scorched articles in milk and turpentine, half a pound of soap, half a gallon of milk. Lay in the sun.

1103. *Stains on Furniture.*—Rub stains on furniture with cold-drawn linseed oil; then rub with alcohol. Remove ink stains with oxalic acid and water; wash off with milk. A hot iron held *over* stains upon furniture will sometimes remove them.

1104. *Silver Soap—For Cleaning Silver and Britannia.*—One bar of turpentine soap, three tablespoonfuls of spirits of turpentine, half a tumbler of water. Let it boil ten minutes. Add six tablespoonfuls of spirits of hartshorn. Make a suds of this, and wash silver with it.

1105. *Furniture Polish.*—One pint of linseed oil, one wineglass of alcohol. Mix well together. Apply to the furniture with a linen rag. Rub dry with a soft cotton cloth, and polish with a silk cloth. Furniture is improved by washing it occasionally with soap-suds. Wipe dry, and rub over with very little linseed oil upon a clean sponge or flannel. Wipe polished furniture with silk. Separate dusting-cloths and brushes should be kept for highly polished furniture. When sweeping carpets and dusting walls always cover the furniture until the particles of dust floating in the air settle; then remove the covers, and wipe with a silk or soft cotton cloth.

1106. *Remarks upon House-Cleaning.*—There should be a general house-cleaning every year—in the spring and fall. Always begin up-stairs; clean and put everything to rights, and then descend. Whitewash once a year; it freshens and purifies.

1107. *Receipts for Whitewash.*—One pound of pulverized alum one pound of rice. Boil these in four gallons of water. Bury a barrel three parts in the ground; pack the dirt around it to prevent the escape of the steam; put into it half a bushel of unslacked rock lime. Pour over it the boiling rice water. Stir well, and cover for an hour; then add six gallons of cold water; stir well, and add a quart of alcohol; thin it if necessary.

Another: Put half a bushel of unslacked lime in a barrel; cover it with hot water; stir occasionally, and keep the vessel well covered. When slacked, strain into another barrel through a sieve. Put a pound of glue in a glue-pot; melt it over a slow fire until dissolved. Soak the glue in cold water before putting the pot over the fire. Dissolve a peck of salt in boiling water. Make a thin paste of three pounds of ground rice boiled half an hour. Stir to this half a pound of Spanish whiting. Now add the rice paste to the lime; stir it in well; then the glue; mix well; cover the barrel, and let it stand twenty-four hours. When ready to use, it should be put on hot. It makes a durable wash for outside walls, planks, etc., and may be colored. Spanish brown will make it red or pink, according to the quantity used. A delicate tinge of this is very pretty for inside walls. Lampblack in small quantities will make slate color. Finely pulverized clay mixed with Spanish brown, makes lilac. Yellow chrome or yellow ochre makes yellow. Green must not be used; lime destroys the color, and makes the whitewash peel.

1108. *A Good Whitewash.*—Dissolve two pounds of potash in five gallons of water; add two pounds of alum. When that dissolves, make a paste by stirring into this a little flour at a time until ten pounds of flour is added. Slack a bushel of lime. When cold, incorporate it with the first preparation.

1109. *A Cheap Paint.*—Two quarts of skimmed milk, two ounces of fresh lime, five pounds of whiting. Pour the milk upon the lime, stirring well; it will make a mixture resembling cream. Sprinkle the whiting over the top; mix well; apply with a paint brush. This may be colored.

1110. *A Cheap Passage or Kitchen Carpet.*—Whip together the edges of coarse, strong homespun; press the seam until it lies flat and smooth. Stretch it well, and keep it tacked; paste some pretty pattern of wall paper upon it as if papering a wall. When perfectly dry, varnish with two coats of varnish.

1111. *To Clean Carpets.*—Shake it well; tack it down, and wash it upon the floor; the floor should be very clean; use cold soap suds; to three gallons add half a tumbler of beef-gall; this will prevent the colors from fading. Should there be grease spots, apply a mixture of beef-gall, fuller's-earth, and water enough to form a paste; put this on before tacking the carpet down.

Use tacks inserted in small leather caps. In sweeping carpets use a soft brush. When it can be done, use straw matting (not straw) under the carpets; they last much better. Cover bricks with carpeting; put behind doors to prevent the knobs of locks striking against walls.

1112. *To Wash Matting.*—Use salt in the water, and wipe dry.

1113. *To Wash Oil-Cloth.*—Take equal parts of skimmed milk and water; wipe dry; never use soap. Varnish them once a year. After being varnished, they should be perfectly dry before being used.

1114. *To Make Stair Carpets.*—Make stair carpets longer than necessary, and change it so that it will not cover the steps in the same way each time of putting down. Moved about in this way, the carpet will last much longer. Clean the rods with camphene or oxalic acid. They should be kept bright.

1115. *To Clean Brass.*—If stained, rub over with oxalic acid or strong vinegar; polish with rotten-stone pulverized and whiskey or sweet oil, or turpentine; then rub with soft leather or buckskin. In the beginning of warm weather, when there is no farther use for andirons, wrap them carefully in tissue paper or old silk. I have seen them wrapped so tastily with the former as to make a handsome parlor ornament.

1116. *To Clean Papered Walls.*—Tie a pound of ginned cotton upon a long stick; brush the walls well with this. When soiled, turn it, or rub the walls with stale loaf bread. Split the loaf, and turn the soft part to the wall.

1117. *To Wash Paint and Hard Plastered Walls.*—Use strong soda water. Use the super-carbonate of soda. Soap gives a yellow tinge, and should not be used.

1118. *To Wash Windows.*—Wash well with soap suds; rinse with warm water; rub dry with linen, and finish by polishing with soft dry paper. A fine polish is given to window-glass by brushing it over with a paste of whiting. Let it dry; rub off with paper or cloth, and with a clean, dry brush remove every particle of the whiting from the corners. Once a year will be altogether sufficient for this.

1119. *To Wash Glass or China.*—Wash in plenty of hot soap suds; have two vessels, and in one rinse in hot water. Turn upon waiters, and let the articles drip before being wiped. Use linen towels for wiping.

1120. *To Clean Silver.*—Wash in hot soap suds (use the silver soap if convenient); then clean with a paste of whiting and water; or whiting and whiskey. Polish with buckskin, or clean with camphene. If silver was always washed in hot suds, rinsed well, and wiped dry, it would seldom need anything else.

1121. *To Remove Stains from Silver.*—Steep the silver in ley four hours; then cover thick with whiting wet with vinegar; let this dry; rub with dry whiting, and polish with dry wheat bran.

1122. *To Remove Egg Stains from Silver.*—Rub with table salt to remove egg stains.

1123. *Metal Dish Covers.*—Wash well every time they are used in hot soap-suds; wipe dry; occasionally rub them over with a paste of whiting or with pulverized rotten-stone and sweet oil. The oil should not be rubbed on the inside.

1124. *To Clean Knives.*—Cover a small heavy table or block by tacking over it very tight soft leather or buckskin; pour over half the leather melted suet.. Spread over this very fine pulverized bath brick or Tripoli; rub the knives (making rapid strokes) over this. Polish on the other side. Keep steel wrapped in buckskin. Knives should be cleaned every day they are used, and kept sharp.

1125. *To Clean Steel Forks.*—Have a small box filled with clean sand; mix with it a third the quantity of soft soap; clean the forks by sticking in the sand and withdrawing them rapidly, repeating the process until they are bright.

1126. *To Remove Rust from Polished Steel.*—Rub the spots with soft animal fat; lay the articles by; wrap in thick paper two days; clean off the grease with flannel; rub the spots well with fine rotten-stone and sweet oil; polish with powdered emery and soft leather, or with magnesia or fine chalk.

1127. *To Remove Grease from a Stone Hearth.*—Lay on plenty of hot ashes; wash off (after the grease is out) with strong soap suds.

1128. *To Prevent Flies from Settling upon Picture Frames.*—Brush them over with water in which onions have been boiled.

1129. *To Make an Ice Vault in a Cellar.*—Dig a pit eight or ten feet square, and as deep. Lay a double wall with brick; fill between with pulverized charcoal; cover the bottom also double with the same or tan-bark. If the pit is filled with ice, or nearly so, cover six inches with tan-bark; but if only a small quantity is in it, wrap well in a blanket, and over the opening in the pit lay a double bag of charcoal. Whitewash cellars often.

1130. *To Destroy Rats.*—Set traps and put a few drops of rhodium inside; they are fond of it. Cats are, however, the most reliable rat-traps. There is no difficulty in poisoning rats; but they often die in the walls, and create a dreadful effluvium, hard to get rid of. When poisoning is attempted, remove or cover all water vessels, even the well or cistern.

1131. *To Expel Fleas.*—Use penny-royal or walnut leaves; scatter them profusely in all infested places.

1132. *To Destroy Flies.*—Cream, sugar, and ground black pepper in equal quantities.

1133. *To Get Rid of Ants.*—Wash the shelves with salt and water; sprinkle salt in their paths. To keep them out of safes: Set the legs of the safe on tin cups; keep the cups filled with water.

1134. *To Prevent Moths from Getting into Carpets or Woolen Goods.*—Strew camphor under a carpet; pack with woolen goods. If moths are in a carpet, lay over it a cotton or linen cloth, and iron with a hot iron. Oil all cracks in store-rooms, closets, safes, with turpentine or a preparation of whiskey, and corrosive sublimate; this drives off vermin.

1135. *To Prevent Bed-Bugs.*—For bed-bugs nothing is so good as the white of eggs and quicksilver. A thimbleful of quicksilver to the white of each egg; beat until well mixed; apply with a feather.

1136. *To Make Beds.*—Never make up beds as soon as the occupants rise. Lay the cover back; admit the air upon the bed until the clothing is well aired. Sun feathers often; beat beds well every day they are used.

1137. *To Cleanse Feather-Beds without Emptying.*—On a hot, clear summer day lay the bed upon a scaffold; wash it well with soap-suds upon both sides, rubbing it hard with a stiff brush; pour several gallons of hot water upon the bed slowly, and let it drip through. Rinse with clear water; remove it to a dry part of the scaffold to dry; beat, and turn it two or three times during the day. Sun until perfectly dry. The feathers may be emptied in barrels, washed in soap-suds, and rinsed; then spread in an unoccupied room and dried, or put in bags made of thin sleazy cloth, and kept in the sun until dry. This kind of work should only be attempted in the long, hot days of June or July. The quality of feathers can be much improved by attention of this kind.

1138. *Beds, Table-Cloths, Towels, etc.*—Nothing does a housekeeper more credit than clean, sweet beds and mattresses, with the bed-clothing washed clean, and well ironed.

Table-cloths, towels and napkins should be kept faultlessly white; table-cloths and napkins starched; if the latter are fringed, whip the fringe until straight. After using a table-cloth, lay it in the same folds; put it in a close place where dust will not reach it, and lay a heavy weight upon it.

Napkins may be used the second time, if they are so marked that each person gets the napkin previously used.

Wipe all grease and spots from dishes, butter-stand, etc., all China, and glass, before sending to the table.

Lamps, casters, and salt-cellars should *always* be cleansed and filled after washing the breakfast dishes. Wash silver candlesticks in hot soap-suds. Clean brass ones with rotten-stone and whiskey, turpentine, or sweet oil. Have the knives and forks cleaned. Never defer attention to such things until they are needed. "Method is the soul of management."

1139. *To Remove Rust from Iron Utensils.*—Rub sweet oil upon them. Let it remain two days; cover with finely-powdered lime; rub this off with leather in a few hours. Repeat if necessary.

To prevent their rusting when not in use: Mix half a pound of lime with a quart of warm water; add sweet oil until it looks like cream. Rub the article with this; when dry, wrap in paper, or put over another coat.

1140. *Creaking Doors.*—Rub creaking doors with soft soap.

1141. *To Remove Putty from Glass, and Paint from Walls.*—Wet several times with strong soda-water.

1142. *To Clean Marble.*—Wash with soda, water, and beef-gall. Or mix together one part blue-stone, three parts whiting one part soda, and three parts soft soap; boil together ten minutes; stir constantly. Spread this over the marble; let it lie half an hour; wash it off with soap-suds; wipe dry with flannel. Repeat if necessary. Stains that cannot be removed in any other way, may be tried with oxalic acid water; but this should be used carefully, and not allowed to remain long at the time.

1143. *Cement for Stove-Pipes.*—Cracks in stoves and pipes may be closed with a paste made of equal parts of salt and ashes, wet up with water.

1144. *To Clean Stoves.*—Clean stoves when cold, with British lustre, mixed with strong alum-water.

1145. *To Clean Tainted Barrels.*—If large barrels, put a peck of charcoal and a tumbler of saleratus into each barrel; pour in boiling water until the barrel is full. Cover close, and let it remain until cold.

1146. *To Prevent Moths from Troubling Woolen Goods.*—Leaves of the China tree strewed among woolen garments prevent moths troubling them. They also prevent worms in dried fruit.

1247. *Safeguard against Insects.*—The common elder is a great safeguard against the devastations of insects. Scatter it amongst wheat, around cucumber and squash-vines. Place it on the branches of plum and other fruit trees subject to the ravages of insects.

1148. *To Keep Pea and Other Seed from Being Destroyed by*

Bugs.—Keep them in bottles, and put in a few drops of turpentine.

1149. *To Wash Hair Brushes.*—Wash in weak soda-water; dry with the bristles down.

1150. *To Clean Tin-Ware.*—Boil tin pie-plates in weak ley to cleanse them. Do this occasionally.

1141. *To Remove a Glass Stopper.*—Wrap around it a hot cloth.

1152. *To Preserve Apple Trees from the Depredations of Rabbits, etc., and the Ravages of Insects.*—Apply soft soap over the body and branches of the trees in March and September.

1153. *To Prevent Skippers in Bacon.*—One bushel of slacked ashes, and one pound of black pepper, ground; mix and rub on the meat before hanging to smoke.

1154. *To Correct Taint in Fresh Meat, Poultry, etc.*—Use Darby's Prophylactic Fluid. First wash the article; pour over the fluid. If bad, remove the bone. To boil a few lumps of charcoal with the meat is also good.

1155. *Cement for Bottles.*—Three-fourths rosin, one-fourth beeswax; melt. Or use half a pound of rosin, the same quantity of red sealing-wax, and a half an ounce of beeswax; melt, and as it froths up, stir it with a tallow candle. Use new corks; trim (after driving them in securely) even with the bottle, and dip the necks in this cement.

1156. *Label Bottles.*—Label and date all bottles, phials, and jars.

Keep medicines, poisons, etc., locked up.

1157. *Vulgar Hospitality*—To press people to eat more than they wish.

Excess of ceremony shows want of good breeding. That civility is best which excludes all superfluous ceremony.

When invited to partake of another's hospitality, and the invitation is accepted, be punctual in meeting the engagement. If unforeseen circumstances prevent the engagement being kept, immediately notify the person by sending an explanatory note.

"There is no social duty which the Supreme Lawgiver more strenuously urges than hospitality and kindness to strangers."

"The perfection of hospitable entertainment: Offer the best to visitors; show a polite regard to their wishes; give precedence in all matters of comfort and convenience."

1158. *Concluding Remarks.*—Before bringing this book to a close, I have one request to make of those who will honor my receipts by using them, viz., that they be *faithfully followed*. Few persons are aware how much mischief is done by even slight deviations. To illustrate: A friend weighed a cake in my presence; a small quantity of flour was left. She deliberated a moment, then tossed the flour into the cake, saying: "It is so much trouble to go back to the pantry with this, and JUST THAT LITTLE can do no harm." She destroyed the proportions by adding more than the specified quantity of flour, and spoiled her cake.

Receipts are often found fault with, and thrown aside as valueless, when the blame lies in the *unexact* manner in which they are tried.

It has been said that "an author has a *right* to demand that his book be read in the right place and at the right time." A stronger claim has the author of a book like this to " demand" that the directions be *correctly* carried out; *upon this depends success*. Much labor has been bestowed upon these *"Receipts."* No effort has been made to make it a *"flashy* work," but a *useful one*. The author has been influenced throughout by the maxim, "That nothing is *wise* that is not *practical*."

EXPLANATION OF CULINARY TERMS.

Baste—To dip or pour butter, lard, or some oleaginous substance upon meat during the process of cooking.

Blanch—To whiten. When applied to meat, it means that the article must be put in cold water, and this raised to the boiling point, then suddenly plunged in cold water.

To Blanch Almonds—Pour boiling water over them until the brown skin can be removed.

Bouilli—Boiled beef.

Bouillie—Thickened milk or pap.

Cuisine—Kitchen cookery.

Dredge—To sprinkle flour over meat, gravies, etc.

Dredging-box—A tin box; such as is used for holding mustard flour, with a perforated top.

Daube—Stewed meat. To prepare this for cooking: First bone; then spice it; roll it in good shape, and skewer or bind it with tape. It is usual (though not necessary where the meat is sufficiently fat) to pass thin strips of bacon through the meat by means of a larding-needle; hence this process is called "daubing."

Fricassée—To stew chicken.

Fricandeau—To stew veal.

Fillet—A thigh or upper part of the leg of an animal. This term is, however, applied to this mode of preparing large fish and other flesh: Raise the meat from the bone by running a sharp knife between the flesh and the bone; then take off the outside skin by passing the knife between the skin and the flesh; cut the pieces in good shape and size.

Glaze—Is to brush melted glazing over the meat once or twice; then let it cool.

Grill—To broil.

Haricot—To stew meat with turnips and other vegetables. It is also the name of a bean.

Larding—To insert strips of bacon *under the skin* of meat with a larding-needle.

Marinade—A highly-flavored broth used in stewing fish and meat. To make a marinade: Stew together any vegetables liked. Carrots, onions, parsley, and a little garlic are generally used; pepper, salt, spices. When the strength of these is extracted, strain, and add wine or catsup to taste. It may be bottled and kept several days in winter; less time in summer.

Ragout—To stew.

Soufflé—A puff; a breath. Is applied to a very light delicate way of preparing eggs.

Sautee—Used by Monsieur Soyer to mean semi-frying in very little lard or butter, and then immediately changing the appearance of the article cooked by giving it the seasoning proper for a grill or a broil, so that what seemed at first a fry is changed to a broil.

Truss—To bind fowls in good shape after being cleaned for cooking.

Vol-a-vent—This means pastry so light that (to appearance) a puff of wind might blow it away.

TABLE OF WEIGHTS AND MEASURES.

DRY MEASURE.

One quart of flour weighs................................one pound.
One quart of corn meal weighs.................one pound two ounces.
One quart of soft butter weighs.................one pound one ounce.
One quart of loaf sugar weighs............................one pound.
One quart of powdered sugar weighs............one pound one ounce.
One quart of brown sugar weighs..............one pound two ounces.
Ten eggs weigh..one pound.
One gallon is..half a peck.
Two gallons is..one peck.
Four gallons is..half a bushel.
Eight gallons is..one bushel.

LIQUID MEASURE.

Sixteen tablespoonfuls are...............half a pint or one tumblerful.
Eight tablespoonfuls are....................................one gill.
Four tablespoonfuls are...................................half a gill
A common-sized tumbler holds...........................half a pint.
A common-sized wineglass holds.........................half a gill.
A common-sized tablespoonful of salt is....................one ounce.

CONTENTS.

	PAGE.
Title Page	3
Introduction	5
Dedication	12
General Remarks	14
Kitchen utensils, etc.	14

SOUPS.

1. Brown soup ... 19
2. Mock turtle soup ... 19
3. Oyster soup ... 20
4. Gumbo ... 21
5. Vegetable soup—Gumbo ... 21
6. Asparagus soup ... 22
7. Corn soup ... 22
8. Green pea soup ... 22
9. Potato soup ... 22
10. Ochra soup ... 23
11. Tomato soup ... 23
12. Chicken soup ... 23
13. Curry soup ... 24
14. Pigeon soup ... 24
15. Rabbit soup ... 24
16. Chicken and oyster soup ... 25
17. Rich chicken soup ... 25
18. Mrs. H.'s receipt for making turtle soup ... 26
19. Another turtle soup, less complicated ... 27
20. Beef soup ... 27
21. Dried pea soup ... 28
22. Ox-tail soup ... 28
23. Portable soup ... 28
24. To clarify soup ... 29

FISH.

25. To fry fish ... 31
26. To fry shad ... 31
27. To fry fillets of fish ... 32
28. To broil fish ... 32
29. To broil salt mackerel ... 33
30. To broil fresh fish ... 33
31. Another method of broiling fresh fish ... 34
32. Mrs. Hale's receipt for broiling shad ... 34
33. Izak Walton's receipt for broiling fresh fish ... 35
34. To broil smoked fish ... 35
35. To boil fish ... 35
36. Another way to boil fish ... 36
37. A piece of boiled salmon ... 36
38. To stew fish ... 37
39. To stew catfish, eels, perch, etc. ... 37
40. Mrs. R.'s receipt for stewing fish ... 37
41. To bake fish ... 38
42. To cook salt cod ... 38
43. Codfish and potatoes ... 39
44. Cod sounds and tongues ... 39

45. Fish cutlets ... 39
46. To souse fish ... 40
47. To pot shad and other fish ... 40
48. Croquettes of fish ... 40
49. Salmon and lobster salad ... 41
50. Fricassee fish and tomatoes ... 41
51. To hash fish ... 41
52. Chowder ... 42
53. Eels — Dr. Kitchiner's receipt for stewing eels ... 42
54. To fry eels ... 43
55. To broil eels ... 43
56. Another way to broil eels ... 43
57. Lobsters ... 43
58. Mrs. K.'s receipts for cooking shrimps, crabs, and terrapins—shrimp patties ... 44
59. Shrimp pie ... 44
60. To pickle shrimps ... 45
61. Shrimp sauce ... 45
62. Terrapins ... 45
63. Crabs in the back ... 45
64. Saunderson's receipt for cooking terrapins ... 46
65. Clams ... 46
66. Oysters ... 46
67. To stew oysters ... 47
68. Oysters a-la-lloze ... 47
69. To fry oysters ... 47
70. To broil oysters ... 48
71. To scallop oysters ... 48
72. Oyster patties ... 49
73. Oyster chowder ... 49
74. To pickle oysters ... 49
75. To feed oysters ... 50
76. To keep fresh fish ... 50
77. To cook frogs ... 50
78. Mock oysters ... 50

MEATS.

79. Boiling meat ... 51
80. To boil a ham ... 53
81. Miss F.'s receipt for preparing whole hams for parties ... 55
82. To know when hams are sound ... 55
83. To glaze a ham ... 56
84. To boil a leg of pork ... 56
85. To boil a leg of mutton ... 56
86. To boil a loin of mutton ... 57
87. To boil a loin of veal ... 57
88. To boil a calf's head ... 57
89. Beef bouilli ... 58
90. To boil corn beef ... 58
91. To boil a salt tongue ... 59
92. To boil cow-heel ... 59
93. To boil tripe ... 60

CONTENTS.

NO.		PAGE.
94.	To boil a turkey	60
95.	To boil ducks or chickens	61
96.	A delicate way to cook fowls, rabbits, veal, or lamb	61
97.	To blanquette chicken	62
98.	Mrs. P.'s receipt for boiling chickens or ducks	62
99.	Another very excellent way to cook grown fowls	62
100.	Scraffle	63
101.	Souse	63
102.	Hog's head cheese	64
103.	Calf's head cheese	64
104.	Stewing meat	65
105.	Beef a-la-daube	65
106.	To stew a shin of beef—Dr. Kitchiner's way	66
107.	Veal or mutton stew	67
108.	Veal with curry powder	67
109.	Beef stewed, or steamed	67
110.	Delmonico stew	68
111.	Camp stew—Mr. B.'s receipt	68
112.	Mutton stew—Mrs. B.'s receipt	69
113.	Hotch potch	69
114.	Olio	69
115.	Pepper-pot	70
116.	To dress cold, underdone beef	70
117.	Minced veal, beef, or mutton	70
118.	Ragout of a breast of veal	71
119.	Stewed sweetbread (veal)	71
120.	To stew calf's head	71
121.	To stew pig's head, harslet, and feet	71
122.	To stew fresh pork with potatoes	72
123.	To make hash	72
124.	Irish potato hash	73
125.	Mrs. H.'s receipt for beef hash	73
126.	Mrs. J.'s receipt for Scotch hash	73
127.	Chicken oyster—Mrs. J	74
128.	Mrs. J.'s baked hash receipt	74
129.	Poultry or birds stewed with onions	74
130.	Chicken and oysters	75
131.	Stewed turkey—a French receipt	75
132.	To fricassee chickens (white)	75
133.	To ragout chicken	77
134.	Rice pillau	77
135.	Tomato pillau	78
136.	Sausage pillau	78
137.	To stew birds	78
138.	To semi-stew birds	79
139.	Beef tongue and mushrooms	79
140.	To stew cold fowls	79
141.	Roasting meat	80
142.	M. Soyer's time-table for roasting	82
143.	Roast beef	84
144.	Roast veal	84
145.	Roast fillet of veal	85
146.	Roast leg of mutton	85
147.	To roast a saddle of mutton	85
148.	Shoulder of mutton	86
149.	Lamb	87
150.	A haunch of venison	88
151.	Leg of pork	88
152.	Spare-rib	89
153.	Kid	89
154.	A roasted rabbit	89
155.	Roast turkey	90
156.	A goose	91
157.	A green goose	91
158.	Ducks	92
159.	Wild fowls	92
160.	To bake meat	92
161.	To bake a round of beef	93
162.	The round	94
163.	Dr. Kitchiner's receipt for baking a round of beef	95
164.	Beef a-la-mode	95
165.	A brisket of beef	96
166.	Mock goose	96
167.	A sirloin of beef	96
168.	Ribs of beef boned and stuffed	97
169.	Spiced beef	98
170.	Mrs. Randolph's receipt for hunter's beef	98
171.	Steak a-la-mode	99
172.	To bake a fillet of veal	99
173.	Veal a-la-mode	100
174.	To bake a calf's head	100
175.	To bake sweetbreads	101
176.	To bake fresh beef tongue	101
177.	Veal cake	101
178.	To bake mutton	102
179.	Mutton to imitate venison	102
180.	To bake lamb or kid	103
181.	To bake fresh venison ham	103
182.	Mock venison	104
183.	To bake a pig	104
184.	Baked pork and beans	106
185.	To bake turkey	106
186.	Goose	107
187.	Ducks	108
188.	Partridge	108
189.	Large fowls, chickens, guinea fowls, capons—how to fatten and bake	108
190.	Pompey's head—Mrs. B.'s receipt	110
191.	To fry meat	110
192.	M. Soyer's receipt for semi-frying round beef steak	111
193.	Beef steak	113
194.	Mrs. F.'s daubed beef	113
195.	Beef liver	114
196.	Beef Kidney	114
197.	Sweetbreads	114
198.	Fried tripe	115
199.	Cow-heel	115
200.	Veal cutlets	115
201.	Veal cutlets with oysters	116
202.	Veal cutlets with tomatoes	116
203.	Veal cutlets curried	116
204.	Another way to use the curry powders	117
205.	Mutton chops	117
206.	Mutton chops—another way	118
207.	Mutton collops	118
208.	A receipt for keeping collops	118
209.	Lamb steaks or cutlets	118
210.	Lamb's fry and pluck	119
211.	Venison steaks	119
212.	Pork chops	119
213.	Pork steaks	119
214.	Hog's or pig's feet	120
215.	Sausages	120
216.	To prepare sausage meat	121
217.	To clean the skins	122
218.	Chitterlings	122
219.	Liver pudding	123

CONTENTS.

NO.		PAGE.
220.	Cakes	123
221.	Mutton, beef, or veal sausages	123
222.	Soyer's meat fritter receipt modified	124
223.	To prepare chickens for frying	124
224.	To fry	125
225.	To fry chicken in butter	125
226.	To brown fricassee chicken	125
227.	To fricassee old chickens	126
228.	To turkey cutlets	126
229.	Croquets of poultry	126
230.	Rice croquets	127
231.	Brain croquets	127
232.	Force-meat balls	128
233.	To fry ham	128
234.	Ham fried in batter	128
235.	Broiling	129
236.	To broil beef steak—Mrs. H.'s receipt	130
237.	To broil beef steak, No. 2	130
238.	To broil steak another way	131
239.	Another way to broil steak	132
240.	To broil round steak	132
241.	Another way of cooking a pound or more of steak	133
242.	To cure beef for broiling	133
243.	Another way	133
244.	To broil dried or jerked beef	134
245.	Veal cutlets	134
246.	Broiling cutlets	134
247.	Veal steak (excellent)	135
248.	Steak "devilled"	135
249.	Mutton chops	136
250.	Mutton steaks	136
251.	Mutton cutlets	137
252.	To grill a shoulder blade of Lamb or pork	137
253.	Pork steaks	137
254.	Pork sparerib	137
255.	To broil ham	138
256.	Broiled sweetbreads	138
257.	To broil chickens	138
258.	To smother fowls	138
259.	To broil squabs, birds, etc	139
260.	To barbecue any kind of fresh meat	139
261.	Meat pies	140
262.	An oyster pie	140
263.	Veal and oyster pie	141
264.	Chicken pie	141
265.	Veal or mutton steak pie	142
266.	Rice chicken pie	143
267.	Pot pies ("so called")	143
268.	Calipash	144
269.	Irish potato pie	144
270.	Salmagundi	145
271.	Meat puffs	146
272.	Meat puddings	146
273.	Another style of pudding	147
274.	Virginia chicken pudding	147
275.	Potato pudding with meat	148
276.	Pease pudding	148
277.	Tomato meat pudding	148
278.	Beef	148
279.	To corn beef for winter use	150
280.	To pickle a hundred pounds of beef or pork	150
281.	Spiced beef	151
282.	To dry pickle beef or pork	151
283.	To cure beef hams for winter use	151
284.	To jerk beef	152
285.	To clarify suet	152
286.	To clarify and harden tallow	153
287.	Confederate candles	153
288.	To make a cheap sick room taper	153
289.	Veal	154
290.	To prepare rennet	154
291.	Mutton	155
292.	Lamb	155
293.	Venison	156
294.	Pork	156
295.	To fry the fat	157
296.	To cure bacon	158
297.	To cut up the hog	159
298.	To salt pork	159
299.	To cure hams	160
300.	To preserve hams by packing in ashes	161
301.	To pot meat	161
302.	To clarify butter for potting	161
303.	To pot calf's head	162
304.	To pot ham and tongue	162
305.	To pot beef, veal, lamb	163
306.	To collar meat	163
307.	To collar a leg of pork	164

SAUCES, STUFFINGS, AND GRAVIES.

309.	White sauces for boiled meats or poultry—Egg sauce	165
310.	Celery sauce	165
311.	Lemon sauce	166
312.	Oyster sauce	166
313.	Caper sauce	166
314.	Caper sauce, No. 2	166
315.	Onion sauce	167
316.	Mushroom sauce	167
317.	Parsley sauce	167
318.	To make parsley crisp	167
319.	Wine sauce for venison or game	167
320.	A French fish sauce	168
321.	Sauce for boiled fowls	168
322.	Bread sauce	168
323.	Dr. Kitchiner's receipt for wine sauce	168
324.	To make sauce to pour over boiled fowls or meat	169
325.	Brown sauces—Tomato sauce	169
326.	Lobster sauce	169
327.	Sauce for Lobster	170
328.	Sauce for anchovies, shrimps, or clams	170
329.	Mint sauce	170
330.	Apple sauce	170
331.	Horseradish sauce	170
332.	Mustard sauce	170
333.	Pickle sauce	171
334.	Curry sauce	171
335.	Sauce for barbecues	171
336.	Sauce for steaks, chops, and rice chicken	171
337.	Brown sauce	172
338.	Brown onion sauce	172
339.	Browning for sauces	172
340.	Plain gravy for roast meat	173
341.	Gravy, No. 2	173
342.	To make gravy for ham	173

CONTENTS.

NO.		PAGE.
343.	Beef steak gravy	174
344.	Gravy that will keep several days	174
345.	Gravy for baked fowls	174
346.	Gravy for baked pig	175
347.	Gravy for tripe, cow-heel or calf's head	175
348.	Stuffings—For a boiled fowl	175
349.	For baked or roast fowls	175
350.	Stuffing for pig	176
351.	Potato stuffing	176
352.	Stuffing for fish	177
353.	M. Soyer's receipt for stuffing for goose	177

VEGETABLES.

354.	Vegetables	178
355.	Asparagus	179
356.	Burr artichokes	179
357.	Jerusalem artichokes	179
358.	Beets	180
359.	Beans	180
360.	Lima, or butter beans	180
361.	Succotash	181
362.	Brocoli	181
363.	Cabbage	181
364.	To stuff cabbage	182
365.	Hot slaw	182
366.	Cold slaw	182
367.	Sauer Kraut	183
368.	Cauliflower	183
369.	Carrots	183
370.	Celery	183
371.	Cucumbers	184
372.	Corn	184
373.	Samp	184
374.	To stew corn	184
375.	Green corn fritters	185
376.	Green corn pudding	185
377.	Green corn pudding, No. 2—Mrs. C.'s receipt	185
378.	Green corn	185
379.	Eschalot	186
380.	Endive	186
381.	Egg-plant	186
382.	Egg-plant, No. 2	186
383.	Egg-plant, No. 3	186
384.	To fry egg-plant plain	187
385.	Greens	187
386.	Leeks	188
387.	Lettuce	188
388.	To make the sauce	188
389.	Winter salads	189
390.	Mushrooms	189
391.	Mushrooms, to stew	190
392.	Mushrooms, to bake	190
393.	Nasturtion	190
394.	Ochra	190
395.	To stew ochra	191
396.	To fry ochra	191
397.	To dry for winter use	191
398.	Onions	191
399.	Onion custard	191
400.	Onion stew	192
401.	Irish potatoes	192
402.	To boil potatoes fully grown	192
403.	To steam potatoes	193
404.	To boil old potatoes	193

405.	To stew potatoes	193
406.	To scollop potatoes	194
407.	Potato salad	194
408.	To fry potatoes	194
409.	To bake sweet potatoes	194
410.	To roast sweet potatoes	195
411.	To fry sweet potatoes	195
412.	To stew sweet potatoes	195
413.	Green peas	195
414.	Hoping John	196
415.	Dried peas	196
416.	Pumpkin	196
417.	Winter squash and cashaw	196
418.	Parsnips	196
419.	To fry them	197
420.	Parsnip fritters	197
421.	To fry them in batter	197
422.	Radishes	197
423.	Spinach	197
424.	Salsify	198
425.	Salsify fritters	198
426.	Squash	198
427.	Tomatoes	199
428.	To stew	199
429.	To bake Tomatoes	199
430.	To stuff	199
431.	Ochra and Tomatoes	200
432.	Tomato salad	200
433.	Tomato fritters	200
434.	Tomato leather	200
435.	Tomatoes	200
436.	Tomato paste	201
437.	Turnips	201
438.	Water cresses	201

STORE SAUCES.

439.	Tomato catsup	202
440.	Mrs. A.'s receipt for green tomato sauce	202
441.	Chetney sauce (imitation)	203
442.	Pepper catsup	203
443.	Imitation Worcester sauce	203
444.	Cucumber catsup	203
445.	Dr. Kitchiner's receipt for mushroom catsup	204
446.	Walnut catsup	204
447.	Lemon catsup	205
448.	Pudding catsup	205
449.	Noyau	205
450.	Capillaire	205
451.	Ratafia	205
452.	Orgeat	205
453.	To make curry powder	206
454.	Soy—To flavor vinegars for salads and sauces	206
455.	Sweet basil vinegar	206
456.	Pepper vinegar	206
457.	To prepare mustard for the casters	207
458.	Mustard that will keep good a month	207
459.	Brandy (good French) and wine	207
460.	To keep lemon juice	208
461.	Chicken salad	208
462.	Lobster salad	208
463.	Meat jelly	209
464.	To bone a turkey	209
465.	To make tough meat tender	210

CONTENTS.

466. To keep eggs during the winter...210
467. Rice flour cement.................210
468. Waterproof cement................211
469. To render water soft for washing..211

YEAST AND BREAD.

470. To make hop yeast.................212
471. Irish potato yeast................213
472. To make bread with Irish potato yeast..........................214
473. Sweet potato yeast................214
474. Milk yeast........................214
475. Corn meal yeast 215
476. Magic, or cold yeast..............215
477. To set a sponge for light rolls with yeast that requires to be kept warm...........................217
478. To know when the oven or stove is hot enough for baking........218
479. French rolls......................218
480. Secession biscuit 219
481. Potato bread......................219
482. Sally Lunn, No. 1.................220
483. Sally Lunn, No. 2.................220
484. Sally Lunn, No. 3.................221
485. Receipt for split rolls...........221
486. Rockbridge alum Sally Lunn.......221
487. Bread without yeast 221
488. Sponge biscuit...................221
489. Light bread......................222
490. Crumpets.........................222
491. Flannel cakes....................223
492. Raised waffles...................223
493. Rice waffles, No. 2..............224
494. Rice waffles, No. 3..............224
495. Rice flour, No. 4................224
496. Quick waffles, No. 5.............224
497. Sweet potato waffles, No. 6......224
498. Musk or hominy waffles, No. 7....225
499. Mrs. R. waffle receipt, No. 8....225
500. Muffins, No. 1...................225
501. Muffins, No. 2...................225
502. Muffins, No. 3...................226
503. Muffins, No. 4...................226
504. Muffins, No. 5...................226
505. Muffins without yeast, No. 6.....226
506. Corn meal muffins, No. 7........227
507. Mixed muffins, No. 8............227
508. Hominy muffins, No. 9—Mrs. W.'s receipt.........................227
509. Muffins, No. 10—Mrs. H.'s receipt.227
510. Batter-bread without eggs 227
511. Breakfast cakes..................228
512. Snow flakes—Mrs. R.'s receipt...228
513. Soda biscuit.....................228
514. Yeast powder biscuit.............228
515. Hard biscuit.....................229
516. Crackers, No. 1..................229
517. Crackers, No. 2..................229
518. Crackers, No. 3..................229
519. Crackers, No. 4..................229
520. Tea bread........................230
521. Mrs. W.'s Thomas-bread receipt..230
522. Clabber bread (excellent)........230
523. Rice flour loaf bread............230
524. Corn meal batter bread..........231
525. Rice bread......................231
526. Rice pan-bread...................231
527. Hominy bread 231
528. Egg bread........................231
529. Batter bread....................232
530. Rice corn bread..................232
531. Risen corn bread.................232
532. Cheese biscuit...................232
533. Buckwheat cakes..................232
534. Buckwheat cakes without yeast...233
535. Superior wheat flour batter cakes.233
536. Rice griddle cakes 233
537. Another way to make griddle cakes...........................233
538. Batter cake 234
539. Clabber cakes....................234
540. Soda batter cakes................234
541. Hominy cakes.....................234
542. Batter cakes without eggs.......234
543. Risen batter cakes...............234
544. Rye batter cakes.................235
545. Corn meal batter cakes...........235
546. Rice flour batter cakes..........235
547. Rye bread........................235
548. Rye drop cakes 235
549. Buttermilk cakes.................236
550. Short hoe cakes..................236
551. Johnny cake......................236
552. Corn meal Johnny cakes...........236
553. Plain corn bread.................237
554. Victoria wafers..................237
555. Corn meal wafers.................237
556. Wafers...........................237
557. Milk toast.......................238
558. Queen's toast....................238
559. Toast and cheese.................238
560. To make stale bread taste as if fresh..........................239
561. To boil grits....................239
562. Hominy cakes.....................239
563. Ley hominy.......................240
564. Macaroni.........................240
565. Dr. Kitchiner's macaroni pudding.241
566. To make vermicelli...............241
567. Cheese stewed....................242
568. Walsh rarebit (called rabbit) to be prepared on the table..........242
569. Eggs.............................242
570. To scramble eggs.................243
571. To poach eggs....................243
572. To fry eggs 243
573. To fricassee eggs................243
574. Another way to fricassee eggs....243
575. Pickled eggs.....................244
576. Omelette.........................244
577. Rice omelette—Mrs. B.'s receipt..245
578. To boil rice.....................245
579. Sandwich.........................246

PASTRY.

580. Puff paste, No. 1................247
581. A very light crisp paste, No. 2..248
582. A good, plain crust, No. 3.......248
583. A good crust for meat pies, No. 4.249
584. An easy way of making crust for plain family pies, No. 5........249
585. Potato paste for dumplings, No. 6.249
586. A plainer potato paste, No. 7....249

CONTENTS.

NO.		PAGE.
587.	A suet paste for boiled dumplings, No. 8	249
588.	A potato paste for meat stews, No. 9	249
589.	Risen paste, No. 10	250

PIES.

590.	Cranberry pie	251
591.	Blackberry pie	251
592.	Apple pie, No. 1	251
593.	Apple pie, No. 2	252
594.	Mock apple pie	252
595.	Peach pie	252
596.	Rhubarb pie	252
597.	Sliced potato pie	253
598.	Imitation of mince pie	253
599.	Pie-melon pie	253
600.	Mince meat pies	254
601.	Remarks upon pies and tarts	254
602.	Icing or meringue for tarts	255

PUDDINGS.

603.	Plain baked pudding	257
604.	Mrs. W.'s baked pudding	258
605.	Baked pudding (excellent)	258
606.	Bread pudding	258
607.	The queen of puddings—Mrs. C.'s receipt	258
608.	Cake pudding	259
609.	Bread and butter pudding	259
610.	Poor man's pudding	259
611.	Chambliss pudding	260
612.	Buttermilk pudding	260
613.	Molasses pudding	260
614.	French black pudding	260
615.	Taylor pudding	260
616.	Charleston pudding	261
617.	Corn meal pudding	261
618.	Corn meal pudding without eggs	261
619.	Apple pudding (excellent)	261
620.	Apple pudding, No. 2	262
621.	Tapioca pudding, No. 1	262
622.	Tapioca pudding, No. 2	262
623.	Rice flour pudding	263
624.	Grated potato pudding	263
625.	Sweet potato pudding	263
626.	Secession pudding (excellent)	264
627.	Sunderland pudding	264
628.	A superior bread pudding	264
629.	Rice pudding	264
630.	Vermicelli pudding	264
631.	A custard pudding	265
632.	A quick pudding	265
633.	California pudding	265
634.	A good cheap pudding	265
635.	Boiled puddings	266
636.	Currant pudding	266
637.	Quaking pudding	266
638.	Cracker pudding	266
639.	Boiled plum pudding	266
640.	Dr. Kitchiner's plum pudding	267
641.	A simple fruit pudding	267
642.	Mrs. P.'s plum pudding	268
643.	A cheap currant pudding	268
644.	Almond pudding	268
645.	A Charlotte	268

DUMPLINGS, ETC.

NO.		PAGE.
646.	Boiled apple dumplings	269
647.	Apple dumplings (stewed)	269
648.	Apple dumplings (baked)	269
649.	Snow balls	270
650.	Fritters	270
651.	Bell fritters	270
652.	Bread fritters	271
653.	Pancakes	271
654.	Puffs, No. 1	271
655.	Puffs, No. 2	272

CUSTARDS.

656.	Lemon custard, No. 1	273
657.	Lemon custard, No. 2	273
658.	Orange custard, No. 1	273
659.	Orange custard, No. 2	274
660.	Cocoanut custard, No. 1	274
661.	Cocoanut custard, No. 2	274
662.	Almond custard	274
663.	Citron custard	274
664.	Transparent custard	275
665.	Mock-lemon custard	275
666.	A delicious apple custard	275
667.	Apple custard	275
668.	Mush custard (excellent)	276
669.	Dried apple custard	276
670.	Breckenridge custard	276
671.	Potato custard	276
672.	Irish potato custard	276
673.	Pumpkin custard	276
674.	Rice custard	277
675.	Vanilla custard	277
676.	Barton custard	277
677.	Egg custard	277
678.	A simple egg custard	278
679.	Jelly custard	278
680.	Cracker custard	278
681.	Molasses custard	278

SAUCES.

682.	Transparent sauce	279
683.	Sponge cake pudding sauce	280
684.	Mrs. B.'s sponge cake sauce receipt	280
685.	Sauce for boiled pudding	280
686.	Arrowroot sauce	280
687.	Wine sauce for puddings	281
688.	A good sauce	281
689.	Cream sauce	281
690.	Mock cream sauce	281
691.	Syllabub sauce	282
692.	Sauce of any kind of jam	282
693.	Butter sauce	282
694.	Hard sauce	282
695.	Egg drawn butter	282
696.	Sauce for tarts	282

CAKES

697.	Fruit cake, No. 1	285
698.	Fruit cake, No. 2	285
699.	Black cake	285
700.	Confederate fruit cake	286
701.	A cheap fruit cake	286
702.	Currant cake	286
703.	Pound cake, No. 1	286

CONTENTS.

NO.		PAGE.
704.	Pound cake, No. 2	287
705.	Plain pound cake	287
706.	General Gordon cake	287
707.	Corn starch cake	287
708.	Cocoanut cake	287
709.	Almond cake	288
710.	Almond sponge cake	288
711.	Sponge cake, No. 1	288
712.	Sponge cake, No. 2	288
713.	Georgia sponge cake	288
714.	Croton sponge cake	288
715.	Indian pound cake	289
716.	Jelly cake, No. 1	289
717.	Jelly cake, No. 2	289
718.	Silver or bride's cake	290
719.	Golden cake	290
720.	Citron cake	290
721.	Spice cake	290
722.	White cup cake	290
723.	Cup cake	290
724.	Cocoanut tea cake	290
725.	Superior tea cake	291
726.	Plain tea cake	291
727.	Ristori cake	291
728.	Loaf cake	291
729.	Forrest cakes	291
730.	Doughnuts	292
731.	Doughnuts without yeast	292
732.	Jumbles, No. 1	292
733.	Jumbles, No. 2—Mrs. S.'s receipt	292
734.	Rusks	293
735.	Drop cake	293
736.	Sugar biscuit	293
737.	Sweet wafers	293
738.	Marmalade tea cakes	293
739.	Crullers	294
740.	Bunns and rusk	294
741.	Bunns	294
742.	Plain bunns	295
743.	Tip top cake	295
744.	Southern rights cake	295
745.	Railroad cake	295
746.	Nondescripts	295
747.	Shrewsbury cake	296
748.	Marvels	296
749.	Lady's fingers	296
750.	Soft ginger cake	296
751.	Soft ginger bread	296
752.	"Colquitt" ginger bread	297
753.	Mrs. H.'s soft ginger bread	297
754.	Fruit ginger cake	297
755.	Superior ginger cake	297
756.	Ginger crisps	298
757.	Ginger crisps, No. 2	298
758.	Ginger nuts	298
759.	Miss Matilda's ginger cakes	298
760.	Ginger cake—Mrs. S.'s receipt	298
761.	Spice ginger cake	298

ICINGS.

762.	Nonpareil icing	299
763.	Beautiful icing	299
764.	Almond icing	299
765.	Almond macaroons	300

FANCY DISHES.

766.	Meringues—Mr S.'s receipt	301

NO.		PAGE
767.	Prune meringues	301
768.	Lemon souffle	301
769.	Trifle	301
770.	Syllabub, No. 1	302
771.	Syllabub, No. 2	303
772.	Boiled custard	302
773.	Plain boiled custard	302
774.	White custard	303
775.	Tapioca boiled custard	304
776.	Floating island	304
777.	Gipsy squire	304
778.	Muffled cake	304
679.	Velvet cream	305
780.	Swiss cream	305
781.	Isabella cream	305
782.	Bohemian cream	305
783.	Apple souffle	305
784.	Egg souffle	306
785.	Apple float	306
786.	Apple snow	306
787.	Float	306
788.	Charlotte Russe	306
789.	Another Charlotte Russe	307
790.	Curds and cream	307
791.	Buttermilk curds	307
792.	Directions for freezing ice-creams and custards	308
793.	Milk sherbet	309
794.	Lemon-water ice	310
795.	Orange-water ice	310
796.	Sherbet	310
797.	Wine ices	310

FRUITS, ETC.

798.	To prepare the pineapple for the table	311
799.	Ambrosia	311
800.	Snow	311
801.	Oranges	311
802.	Bananas	312
803.	Peaches and cream	312
804.	Raspberries and strawberries	312
805.	A pretty dish	312
806.	Watermelons	313
807.	Breakfast fruits	313
808.	Calf or hog's foot jelly	313
809.	Gelatine jelly—Mrs. W.'s receipt	314
810.	Lemon jelly	314
811.	Wine jelly	314
812.	Blanc-mange	314
813.	Blanc-mange, No. 2	315
814.	Carrageen or Irish moss blanc-mange	315
815.	Corn starch blanc-mange	315
816.	Arrow-root blanc-mange	315
817.	Isinglass blanc-mange	316
818.	Ice pudding (a delicious dessert)	316
819.	Fruit jellies	316
820.	Apple jelly	317
821.	Crab apple jelly	317
822.	Orange jelly	317

PRESERVES, ETC.

823.	Oranges preserved whole	319
824.	Citron preserved	320
825.	Glass melon	320

CONTENTS.

NO.		PAGE.
826.	Pineapple preserved	320
827.	To preserve strawberries	321
828.	To preserve raspberries and blackberries	321
829.	To preserve cherries	322
830.	To preserve grapes	322
831.	To preserve plums	322
832.	To preserve muscadines	322
833.	Crab-apple preserves	322
834.	To preserve eggs	323
835.	Preserved peaches	323
836.	To preserve quinces	324
837.	Pear preserves	324

MARMALADES, JAMS, ETC.

838.	Orange marmalade	325
839.	Apple marmalade	325
840.	Quince and peach marmalade	325
841.	Strawberries, raspberries, blackberries and grapes	325
842.	Compote of apples	326
843.	Frosted fruit	326
844.	Apple or gooseberry fool	326
845.	To bake apples or quinces	326
846.	Stewed peaches	327
847.	Candied orange and lemon	327
848.	Peach chips	327
849.	Peach leather	327
850.	To dry figs	328
851.	Tomato figs	328
852.	To dry citron or watermelon rind	328
853.	To dry cherries	328
854.	To stew dried peaches and apples	329
855.	To save fruit without sugar	329

FOR MAKING CANDIES.

856.	Sugar candy	330
857.	To make ground pea candy	330
858.	Cocoanut candy	330
859.	Molasses candy	330
860.	Toffie	331
861.	To make almond macaroons	331

TO CAN FRUIT AND VEGETABLES.

862.	To brandy peaches	333

WINES, CORDIALS, ETC.

863.	Grape wine	335
864.	Muscadine wine	336
865.	Blackberry wine	336
866.	Cider wine	337
867.	Tomato wine	337
868.	Strawberry cordial	337
869.	Blackberry cordial	337
870.	Blackberry cordial No. 2	338
871.	Muscadine cordial	338
872.	Cherry bounce	338
873.	Crab apple beer	338
874.	To keep cider	338
875.	Cherry nectar	339
876.	Raspberry nectar	339
877.	Lemonade	339
878.	Sherry cobbler	340
879.	Lemonade au lait	340

NO.		PAGE.
880.	Cream beer	340
881.	Ginger beer (superior)	340
882.	Ginger beer, No. 2	341
883.	Imperial pop	341
884.	Spruce beer	341
885.	Ginger beer	341
886.	Cheap beer	342
887.	Corn beer	342
888.	Persimmon beer	342
889.	Orange syrup	342
890.	Lemon sponge	343
891.	To make vinegar	343
892.	Another way to make vinegar	343
893.	Apple vinegar	343

PICKLES.

894.	Higdon	344
895.	Sweet pickle	344
896.	Another sweet pickle	344
897.	Tomato pickle	345
898.	Pickled onions	345
899.	To pickle peppers	345
900.	To pickle cucumbers	345
901.	Mangoes	345
902.	Cabbage pickle	346
903.	Mustard pickles	346
904.	Green tomato pickle	346
905.	Mixed pickle	346
906.	Walnut pickle	347
907.	Chow	347
908.	Cabbage	347
909.	Artichokes	348
910.	Green tomato sauce	348

COFFEE, TEA, ETC.

911.	To make coffee by filtering	350
912.	Green teas	351
913.	Black teas	351
914.	Chocolate	351
915.	German chocolate	352
916.	To mill chocolate	352

THE DAIRY.

917.	To milk	353
918.	To feed in winter	353
919.	For churning	354
920.	For packing butter	355
921.	To freshen salt butter	356
922.	Patent butter	356
923.	A simple plan to keep butter cold in summer	356
924.	To recover rancid butter or lard	357
925.	To preserve milk for a journey	357
926.	Cheese	357
927.	Cream cheese	359

COOKING FOR INVALIDS.

928.	Lemon punch	360
929.	Mulled wine	360
930.	Wine whey	360
931.	Drink for a consumptive	360
932.	Tamarind whey	361
933.	Apple-water	361
934.	Cranberry tea	361

CONTENTS.

NO.		PAGE
935.	Corn meal gruel	361
936.	Flour gruel	361
937.	Potato starch custard	361
938.	Farina custard	362
939.	Corn starch custard	362
940.	Arrowroot	362
941.	Rice Gruel	363
942.	Corn meal pudding	363
943.	Sago	363
944.	Panada	363
945.	Cracker Toast	363
946.	Toast and water	364
947.	Rice pudding	364
948.	Gelatine blanc-mange	364
949.	Beef broth	364
950.	Egg nogg	365
951.	Drink for an invalid	365
952.	Boullie	365
953.	Broiled tomatoes	365
954.	Tomato toast	365
955.	Herb teas	365
956.	Mutton broth	366
957.	Chicken panada	366
958.	Birds for convalescents	366
959.	Oyster soup	366
960.	Mush	367
961.	Hasty pudding	367

MEDICAL RECEIPTS.

962.	For a burn	368
963.	Healing salve	368
964.	Green ointment	368
965.	Cure for old ulcers	369
966.	Bone-felon	369
967.	Quick emetic	369
968.	Colic mixture for infants	369
969.	Chloroform cough drops	370
970.	For coughs and colds	370
971.	To relieve a cold	370
972.	Specific for a cough	370
973.	Plaster for chest affections	371
974.	Putrid sore throat	371
975.	Inflamed sore throat	371
976.	Whooping cough	371
977.	Croup	372
978.	Wash for sore throat and mouth	372
979.	Antidotes for poisons	372
980.	Convulsions	373
981.	Dysentery	374
982.	Remedy for diarrhea	374
983.	For violent pain in the bowels	375
984.	Colic	375
985.	Chills and fever	376
986.	Congestive chills	376
987.	To give tone to the stomach of a person recovering from chills and fever	376
988.	For typhoid fever	377
989.	Scarlet fever	377
990.	To prevent scarlet fever	377
991.	Dropsy	377
992.	Jaundice	377
993.	Erysipelas	378
994.	Cure for tetter	378
995.	Toothache	378
996.	Earache	378

NO.		PAGE
997.	Cure for thrush	379
998.	Sore mouth or tongue	379
999.	Sore nipples from nursing	379
1000.	To prevent and relieve rising breasts	379
1001.	Headache pills	379
1002.	Neuralgia	380
1003.	Asthma	380
1004.	Diphtheria	380
1005.	Cancer	380
1006.	Cramp in the legs	381
1007.	Bite of insects	381
1008.	Bite of a snake	381
1009.	Hydrophobia	381
1010.	For a fresh cut	382
1011.	Lockjaw	382
1012.	Bleeding at the nose	382
1013.	To prevent discoloration from bruises	382
1014.	Sprains	382
1015.	Scald head	382
1016.	Corns and bunions	383
1017.	Chilblains	382
1018.	Frost-bitten limbs	383
1019.	Dry mortification	383
1020.	Gangrene	383
1021.	Cure for ingrowing nails	383
1022.	Itch	384
1023.	To stop the bleeding from leeches	384
1024.	Gargle for sore mouth	384
1025.	Cholera mixture	384
1026.	Potato poultice	384
1027.	Charcoal poultice	385
1028.	Hop poultice	385
1029.	Light bread poultice	385
1030.	Slippery elm poultice	385
1031.	Pepper poultice	386
1032.	Flaxseed poultice	386
1033.	Cancer poultice	386
1034.	Liniment for white swelling and palsy	386
1035.	A good healing salve	386
1036.	To dress a blister	386
1037.	A good styptic	387
1038.	Mustard plaster	387
1039.	Mustard or pepper bath for the feet	387
1040.	Pepper plaster	387
1041.	Plaster for boils	387
1043.	Rheumatic liniment	388
1044.	Piles	388
1045.	Fainting	388
1046.	For nausea	388
1047.	To extinguish fire on a person	388
1048.	Where a person is insensible from a fall or blow upon the head	389
1049.	To recover a person apparently drowned	389
1050.	From freezing	389
1051.	Struck by lightning	389
1052.	From hanging, suffocation etc.	389
1053.	Apparent death from charcoal or other noxious vapors	389
1054.	When affected by foul air in descending wells	390
1055.	The severing of an artery	390
1056.	To dress wounds	390
1057.	For bleeding at the lungs	390

CONTENTS.

NO.		PAGE
1058	Worms - For Ascarides or pin worms	390
1059	Deafness	391
1060	Catarrh in the head	391
1061	A simple febrifuge	391
1062	In small-pox to prevent pits	391
1063	Measles	391
1064	Chronic rheumatism	392
1065	Acute rheumatism	392
1066	Homeopathic specifics	392
1067	To cure pimples on the skin	392
1068	Disinfectants	392
1069	For spinal disease	392
1070	For excoriations upon the flesh of infants	393
1071	Cholera infantum	393
1072	Remarks upon medical receipts	393
1073	Care of a sick room	393
1074	Hints to housekeepers	395

MISCELLANEOUS RECEIPTS.

1075	Soap	397
1076	Sal soda soap	398
1077	Potash soap	398
1078	A superior receipt	398
1079	Brown bar soap	398
1080	To make starch	399
1081	Potato starch	399
1082	To prepare starch for use	399
1083	To give a gloss to shirt bosoms	400
1084	To starch muslins, etc	400
1085	To remove grease spots from calicoes, muslins, etc	401
1086	Where the colors are doubtful	401
1087	To wash flannel	402
1088	To wash bombazine	402
1089	To wash ribbons	402
1090	To bleach clothes	402
1091	Washing mixture	402
1092	To remove spermaceti	403
1093	To remove grease from silk or worsted	403
1094	Grease balls	403
1095	Stains from acids	403
1096	Tar and pitch	403
1097	To remove oil from carpets or floors	403
1098	For rust and ink stains	403
1099	To remove mildew	404
1100	To take ink out of linen	404
1101	For fruit stains on napkins, table-cloths, etc	404
1102	Stains from scorched goods	404
1103	Stains on furniture	404
1104	Silver soap, for cleaning silver and Britannia	404
1105	Furniture polish	405
1106	Remarks upon house-cleaning	405
1107	Receipts for whitewash	405
1108	A good whitewash	406
1109	A cheap paint	406

NO.		PAGE
1110	A cheap passage or kitchen carpet	406
1111	To clean carpets	406
1112	To wash matting	407
1113	To wash oil-cloth	407
1114	To make stair carpets	407
1115	To clean brass	407
1116	To clean papered walls	407
1117	To wash paint and hard-plastered walls	437
1118	To wash windows	408
1119	To wash glass or china	408
1120	To clean silver	408
1121	To remove stains from silver	408
1122	To remove egg stains	408
1123	Metal dish covers	408
1124	To clean knives	408
1125	To clean steel forks	409
1126	To remove rust from polished steel	409
1127	To remove grease from a stone hearth	409
1128	To prevent flies from settling upon picture frames	409
1129	To make an ice vault in a cellar	409
1130	To destroy rats	409
1131	To expel fleas	410
1132	To destroy flies	410
1133	To get rid of ants	410
1134	To prevent moths from getting into carpets or woolen goods	410
1135	To prevent bed-bugs	410
1136	To make beds	410
1137	To cleanse feather-beds without emptying	410
1138	Beds, table-cloths, towels, etc	411
1139	To remove rust from iron utensils	411
1140	Creaking doors	411
1141	To remove putty from glass and paint from walls	412
1142	To clean marble	412
1143	Cement for stove-pipes	412
1144	To clean stoves	412
1145	To clean tainted barrels	412
1146	To prevent moths from troubling woolen goods	412
1147	Safeguard against insects	412
1148	To keep pea and other seed from being destroyed by bugs	412
1149	To wash hair brushes	413
1150	To clean tin ware	413
1151	To remove a glass stopper	413
1152	To preserve apple trees from the depredations of rabbits, etc	413
1153	To prevent skippers in bacon	413
1154	To correct taint in fresh meat, poultry, etc	413
1155	Cement for bottles	413
1156	Label bottles	413
1157	Vulgar hospitality	414
1158	Concluding remarks	414
	Explanation of culinary terms	415
	Table of weights and measures	417

GLOSSARY

Those who are at all familiar with old cookery books know that words frequently change definitions over time or, depending on location, may have different nuances in meaning. Many early nineteenth-century terms and ingredients have been discussed in detail by Karen Hess in her excellent notes in the University of South Carolina Press facsimile edition of *The Virginia House-wife*. I have made no attempt to duplicate such a thorough glossary and include only such terms as are pertinent to an understanding of Mrs. Hill's text. For more on universal terms, or for details on specific ingredients, readers are referred to Mrs. Hess's glossary.

A few of Mrs. Hill's terms are no longer used in standard cooking parlance and warrant some explanation, but for the more frequently used culinary terms, I refer readers to Mrs. Hill's own glossary. Her definitions may not always align with either historical or modern understanding, but they are useful in illuminating her intentions.

A-la-daube and *a-la-mode*—These two terms get hopelessly tangled in American cooking. They, as well as the dishes they describe, are of French origin, but both were common in eighteenth-century English cookery, and it is from the English sources that most American recipes derive. Both terms describe a form of stew or pot roast. Though a modern French *daube* is usually eaten warm, in the South, meat *a-la-daube* is almost invariably associated with jelly and eaten cold, as *boeuf a la mode* is in France today. Mrs. Hill's distinction between the two is as fuzzy as that of most English and American writers. Usually, her *daubes* are stewed and almost always cold, her *a-la-modes* baked and served warm. But note that "Mrs. F.'s Daubed Beef" (no. 194, p. 113) is baked and meant to be served hot, and she almost always says that *a-la-mode* is excellent cold. Linguistic confusions aside, the recipes are wonderfully aromatic and excellent.

Barbeque—Today this word is most often associated with a sauce and, in some parts of the country, is indistinguishable from what Mrs. Hill would have called "broiling." However, for Mrs. Hill and most Southerners of the last three centuries, "barbeque" is not so much a sauce as a specific method of cooking. Her description is lucid and requires no elaboration. It is popular now to credit its invention to Native American cooks; early explorers' accounts of America do indeed relate that Indians were cooking meat by this method, and the word, at any rate, is American—from the Haitian Taino word *barbacoa* (the pit and wooden frame with which the cooking was accomplished). The method, however, is as old as civilization and has been known all around the Mediterranean basin for thousands of years.

Mrs. Hill's butter, vinegar, mustard, and cayenne basting sauce was the Georgia classic until well into this century, and it is still favored in some parts of the state. Its advantage over modern sweet tomato sauces is that it is less likely to burn.

Blackberries—The fruit of any of several native brambles of the genus *rubus*, related to roses. Blackberries are, of course, practically ubiquitous in America. They have long been used in Southern cooking in recipes such as jellies, wines, and cordials where black currants are usual in other cuisines. Blackberry wine (no. 865, p. 336) is still used in rural Georgia as a tonic.

Biscuit—Mrs. Hill's understanding of this word is completely modern American. Her biscuits are all small, cut or hand-molded, leavened rolls. European biscuits are what we know as crackers and cookies (the name originates from Latin *biscoctum*, "twice baked"). Early American cookbooks often used the name both ways, but by Mrs. Hill's day, American cooks used the word *biscuit* almost exclusively to mean leavened bread. Only our beaten biscuits (no. 515, p. 229) hearken back to older European useage.

GLOSSARY **431**

Burr artichoke—These are true artichokes, frequently called "burr" or "globe" to distinguish them from the then-popular Jerusalem artichoke, a tuber sunflower root (see below). Popular historians regularly promulgate the myth that Americans did not eat this vegetable until the end of the nineteenth century, but it was common in all early American cookbooks.

Cashaw (cushaw)—A native winter squash, common in the Deep South. Though shaped somewhat like yellow crooknecks, they are usually creamy-white with longitudinal green stripes. If left to mature, cushaws grow to be as large as pumpkins. *Webster's* indicates that the name is thought to be from an Algonquin language, probably from the word *escushaw*, "it is green."

Catsup—The name derives from a Southeast Asian name for a sauce made from the brine of pickled shellfish (either Amoy *ketsiap* or Malay *kechap*). Until the second quarter of the nineteenth century, catsups in England and America were made mostly from oysters or mushrooms. There was also a common catsup made from fermented green walnuts (no. 446, p. 204). Today, we are so accustomed to the tomato variety that we take for granted it is what a recipe means by "catsup," but tomato catsup did not come on the scene until the nineteenth century. Though already popular by Mrs. Hill's day (it is the first recipe in the "store sauce" chapter), it was not the only kind in her pantry. For many of her recipes, tomato catsup, especially the cloyingly sweet modern version, would not be appropriate. It would be far better to substitute a little Worcestershire sauce diluted with vinegar, or else oriental oyster sauce. Or make a batch of Dr. Kitchiner's mushroom catsup; it isn't difficult and keeps well in the refrigerator.

Charlotte russe—Charlottes are an old, simple dessert of stewed fruit (usually apple) baked in a casing made from slices of fried or toasted stale bread. Similarly, charlotte russe was originally a Bavarian cream in a casing of sliced sponge cake or, more common nowadays, lady fingers. Tradition attributes its invention to the great French chef Marie-Antoine Carême; however, it became popular in England and America during M. Carême's rather brief lifetime. Southern recipes appear to have come mostly from English sources. It was a popular standard "company" dessert in the South after the second quarter of the nineteenth century. Note that Mrs. Hill's charlotte russe has no cake casing; the cream is poured directly into a jelly mold as a blancmange, the common practice in western Georgia and eastern Alabama. She does mention the sponge cake in one recipe, but only in passing.

Chow—More commonly known today as chowchow. It is a completely Western interpretation of a Far Eastern mixed sweet-sour pickle. According to John Taylor, it originated in the East Indian region; Websters suggests Chinese (Pekingese language) as the origin of the name. Modern Southern chowchow almost invariably contains mustard, green tomatoes, sweet peppers, and at least one member of the cabbage family, but historical recipes varied wildly. In fact, Theresa Brown (*Modern Domestic Cookery*, 1871) indicated that it could properly be made from "almost anything fancied" and suggested cucumbers, muskmelons, green beans, and butter beans (limas).

Clabber—This is thick soured milk—for all intents and purposes, yoghurt. Use an all-natural, unsweetened, preferably nonhomogenized yoghurt.

Cobbler—This word denotes two distinctly different dishes in America. The older is as Mrs. Hill understood it, an alcoholic punch made with sherry or whiskey (see no. 878, p. 340). The other is the widely known deep-dish pie (see "*Cut and Come Again*," below). According to the *OED*, the origin for both uses is obscure, but both probably originate from the old English *cobble*, meaning "to piece together or patch roughly." By all early accounts, a cobbler pie was a rough, homey "patched together" dessert, too plain for company. The usual folk-etymological explanation for the name of the drink is that it was so-called because it was supposed to "patch up" the drinker.

Collop—An archaic name for a thin slice of meat. Usually, though not invariably, it meant the same cut as the French *escallope* or the Italian *scaloppine*—that is, a thin slice cut across the grain of the fillet of a round of veal, mutton, or beef. A scotched collop was scored with crisscross cuts to tenderize it (see *scotching*, below). Note that Mrs. Hill had a different understanding of a collop, to wit: "The difference between a chop and a collop is, that collops are partly fried and then stewed." That is, in fact, the way that they are usually prepared. Notice that her "Keeping Collops" are chopped meat (no. 208, p. 118). Such recipes were fairly common both in England and America. In fact, by the beginning of the twentieth century, most collop recipes (especially those called "scotch") were made with ground beef. The origins of the word "collop" are obscure. The *OED* suggests that it may derive from the German *klops* (beaten steak, from *klopfen*, "to beat"), or the Swedish *kollops* (stewed slices of beef).

"Cut and Come Again" Pie—This is an archaic, and apparently local, west-central Georgia name for peach cobbler. I have never seen or heard it used anywhere else. Mrs. Hill used "cobbler" in its older form, to name a drink (see above).

Fricassee and *fricandeau*—Mrs. Hill gives a definition of both these words in her own glossary, but they do not entirely explain things. Both words derive from French cookery. *Fricassee* is thought to have derived from *frire* ("to fry") + *casser* ("to break"). In the old recipes, the bones of the fowl or meat are cracked to release their marrow. The meat is first fried and then stewed. Mrs. Hill says that to *fricassee* means to stew chicken, but, at least in classic French cookery, it can be made with all kinds of meat. In fact she gives an excellent *fricassee* for fish and tomatoes which is true to the classic technique, as is her recipe "To Brown Fricassee Chicken" (no. 226, p. 125), though this one is not nearly as aromatic with herbs and spices as early fricassees. The white *fricassee* for chicken (no. 132, p. 75) and the one for "Old Chickens" (no. 227, p. 126) are less interesting, but more closely align with the definition in her glossary and with later American practice. Even though she defines *fricandeau* in her glossary, there is no recipe for it in her text. A classic French *fricandeau* is not the same technique as a *fricassee*, but in American cookbooks, the two are often indistinguishable from one another.

Green corn—Fresh corn—that is young, immature corn which has not been dried or preserved as hominy. The term is still common in west Georgia and Carolina. "Green" was also once commonly used to designate uncured pork hams and fresh shrimp, but such use is disappearing.

Ground peas—These, of course, are peanuts—variously known as "ground peas," "ground nuts," "goobers," and "goober peas" in the South. They are neither peas nor nuts, but actually a legume that grows below ground. Native to South America, they were introduced to Africa by the Portuguese and were quickly assimilated into the African diet. It is probably because of Africans that they have been so popular in the South. In fact, the name "goober" is thought to derive from an African language.

Higdon—A highly spiced, mixed pickle of finely chopped vegetables which was fairly popular in the mid-nineteenth century. Mrs. Hill's recipe was typical. Origins of the name are uncertain.

Hotch Potch (also *hodgepodge*)—A mixed stew of meat and vegetables (see *olio*). The apparent origin is French *hochepot*, from *hocher* ("to shake together") + *pot* ("pot"). I note an anachronism in Mrs. Hill's recipe: fresh corn, peas, asparagus, and squashes would never be in season at the same time, even in the mild climate of central Georgia. Early peas might overlap asparagus, late peas might still be available when the corn matured, and corn and squash would certainly be ripe at the same time, but asparagus would never still be around by the time corn was mature, and only rarely would it overlap early squash. Our appreciation of the seasonal aspect of vegetables is blunted by modern markets, whose coolers may contain all manner of produce year round.

Isinglass—An early form of gelatine made from sturgeon bladders. Commercially packaged gelatine eventually replaced it in America, though it is still available in Europe.

Jerusalem artichoke—The tuber root of a native American sunflower. The name is probably a corruption of the Italian *girasole*—literally, "to turn with the sun," which is, of course, what sunflowers do. The flavor of these tubers vaguely resembles that of artichokes, from whence comes the association. They were so popular in the South that in some areas they eclipsed the true artichoke. In Georgia, these tubers are nowadays used mostly for pickles (see no. 909, p. 348), but note that Mrs. Hill said that they were good (and popular) dressed as a salad. So they are.

Lobster—This crustacean is always a problem when it appears in an old Southern book. There is no way of knowing if it was merely a conceit or if Mrs. Hill could actually get lobster. Later on, it's clear that the lobster came out of a can, since the recipes invariably read "a can of lobster." But Mrs. Hill's heyday was before commercial canned fish was common, and she clearly tells us how to cook the critter. We can't dismiss the recipe as an anachronism: American lobsters were once found in the Atlantic off the coast of South Carolina. Also, LaGrange lies near the Chatahoochee River, which flows into the Gulf of Mexico. Mrs. Hill could have been using the large crayfish, so-called Florida lobsters common to the Gulf, though her notes on distinguishing gender are admittedly for cold-water lobsters.

Maigre and *au maigre*—The French literally translates "meager" and, in cooking, designates dishes that contain no meat.

The term is especially common in the cookery of New Orleans's largely Catholic French Creole community. *Au maigre* dishes are associated with Lent, Fridays, and other days of fasting, when meat is not allowed. A strict Lenten fast would not, of course, allow Mrs. Hill's butter. Notice that the essential structure of the vegetable soup *maigre* (no. 5, p. 21) is the same as a classic *minestrone alla romagna*.

Muscadine and *scuppernong*—The South's own native grapes. Muscadines usually have a deep, purple-black skin. Scuppernongs are actually a larger, cultivated strain of muscadine and are a pale greenish-tan color. The name probably derives from these grapes' distinctively musky flavor (*Webster's* points to French *muscat*, meaning "musky"). The word *scuppernong* is supposed to have come from a North Carolina river of that name. Unlike European grapes, muscadines do not have a natural "bloom" (the chalky coating of yeast on the skin of most grapes), and in order for them to properly ferment, yeast must be introduced to the mash. They have long been used to make wines, cordials, and sweet preserves.

Mushrooms—The mushrooms that Mrs. Hill so clearly describes are *agaricus campestris*, common field mushrooms. They are (or, at least, were) plentiful in open fields and pastures all over the southeastern portion of the country. They are also one of the most easily identified wild mushrooms. There are several other types available in Georgia, including *boletus edulis* (*cepes* or *porcini*), morels, sulfur shelf ("chicken mushroom"), and oyster mushrooms, but Mrs. Hill stuck to easily identified field mushrooms, saying shade-loving types were not wholesome.

Ochra—Of course, okra, the seed pods of the African *hibiscus esculentus*. The *OED* cites the West African word *nkru-ma* as the origin for this name. According to Karen Hess, okra was growing in Jamaica by the beginning of the eighteenth century. By the beginning of the nineteenth century, it was a defining characteristic of Southern cooking. Its other name, "gumbo," derives from Angolan *kingombo*. By Mrs. Hill's day, the word *gumbo* was most often used as it is today, that is, to name a stew made mucilagenous with either okra or *filé* (powdered sassafras leaves) or, as Mrs. Hill indicates, with both (see no. 4, "Gumbo," p. 21).

Olio—A stew whose name derives from the Latin *olla*, an earthenware stewpot. Both the pot and the name survive in Spain and Italy. In English, an olio is a hodgepodge or mixed stew of several meats and/or vegetables. Mrs. Hill's olio (no. 114, pp. 69–70) is true to form and is peculiarly Southern with its mixture of apples, tomatoes, squash, lima beans, fresh corn, and potatoes.

Pie melon—I take this to be an arcane name for certain tart melons such as citron or muskmelon, though it could be winter squash (such as acorn squash), which are related to melons and are still used for sweet pies in northern Georgia cookery today. Squash and melons are closely related botanically, and in the early days of the American colonies, both names were frequently used interchangeably. I must note here that some traditional Georgia and Carolina cooks favor the explanation that "pie melon" was actually a tart melon such as citron or muskmelon.

Pillau—All the various spellings—"perlow," "pilaff," "perloo," and so forth—derive from *pilau*, the ancient Persian rice dish from which all the variations (Turkish pilaf, Spanish paella, and classic lowcountry *pilaus*) are descended. For a detailed and excellent history of *pilau*, see *The Carolina Rice Kitchen* by Karen Hess. I cannot improve on Mrs. Hess's definition: "The classic pilau is not so much a receipt as a culinary concept"—that is, "long-grain rice that has been washed and presoaked is added to simmering aromatic broth, usually in the proportion of two parts of liquid to one of rice by volume, then covered and cooked until 'nearly dry.' " There must be a certain amount of fat in the broth to assure the requisite separateness of the grains, but in Carolina pilaus, at least, the rice is not sautéed in fat first but added directly to the broth. Mrs. Hill's pilaus reflect the classic technique, which was as widely used in Georgia as it was the Carolina lowcountry.

Pompey's Head—"Pompey's Head" (no. 190, p. 110.) is, as Mrs. Hill so clearly described it, a large, round meatloaf. Recipes for it were not uncommon, even as late as 1964. The origin of the name is obscure. One pop-etymological explanation is that the loaf is supposed to have resembled the broad head of the ancient Roman statesman Pompeius.

Pudding—Mrs. Hill, of course, meant the baked and boiled puddings of English tradition. What most Americans nowadays call "pudding," she called cornstarch "custard." For her understanding of them, I refer the reader to her introduction to the chapter.

Salamander—An iron disc attached to a long handle used for delicate browning and glazing. The disc was held to the fire until it was red hot, then passed over the top of the food to brown it. It became practically archaic with the advent of gas and electric oven broilers, though a similar iron is still made for melting the sugar topping of a *crème brulée*. The name derives from the salamander lizard's mythical imperviousness to fire.

Sally Lunn—A light tea bread, originally baked in small buns, essentially the same as French *brioche*. The name is English, and there are many convoluted legends about its origins; however, Elizabeth David, citing Dorothy Hartley's *Food in England*, offers the most plausible explanation--that it is, in fact, a corruption of *soleil lune*, "sun and moon," which the buns were called in France because that is what they were supposed to have resembled. Sally Lunn was very popular in the South, particularly Virginia, but was not limited to Southern kitchens. It was common in most American cookery books of the nineteenth century. At least as early as *The Carolina Housewife* (1847), the name was also applied to a sweet, baking-powder cake, but classic Sally Lunn is yeast-leavened and never sweetened. Mrs. Hill indicated that the dough could be sweetened and seasoned with spices, but she called the result a "cake."

Salmagundi—According to Karen Hess, who cites French lexicographer Paul Robert, this term appears in French by the mid-sixteenth century. The *OED*, citing eighteenth-century English lexicographer Thomas Blount, says its origins are Italian. Either way, the dish is generally a composed meat-salad of cold, roasted fowl—usually turkey. Peculiarly, Mrs. Hill's salmagundi is a rich and elaborate cold meat pie set with calf's foot jelly.

Sal volatile—An early form of chemical leaven based on ammonium carbonate. The name literally means "volatile salt."

Scraffle—Easily recognizable as "scrapple," a dish common from New England to New Orleans. Mrs. Hill's recipe is typical: cooked, chopped meat and cornmeal are highly seasoned, simmered together in broth until thick, and molded into a loaf. The dish is usually said to be of American origins, though it bears a certain resemblance to haggis and medieval pottages. The origin of the name is obscure; the usual explanation is that it derives from the fact that the dish is composed mostly of scrap meat.

Scotches, scotching—This is an old culinary term for tenderizing meat by scoring it in a crisscross with a knife. It has nothing to do with Scotland. By Mrs. Hill's day, it was rarely used and appears in the text within a quote from Izaak Walton, the famed seventeenth-century English writer on angling (see no. 33, p. 35). In the late nineteenth century, "scotch collops" came to mean chopped or ground meat. This was a foreshortening of "scotch mince collops," potted meat that was both scotched and chopped (see *collops*, above).

Souse—The usual explanation of the origin of this word is the medieval French *souz*, which meant "pickling." Effectively, the dish is jellied pork encased in fat and pickled in vinegar. In the eighteenth and early nineteenth century, souse was meant to be white, and the vinegar and seasonings were engineered to that end. Later, it became confused with head cheese, a similar dish, and fastidious instructions for preserving the color faded.

Squash—Any of a variety of edible native American gourds. The name is derived from an Algonquin Narragansett word. Mrs. Hill is not specific as to type, but she clearly means summer squash, probably cymlings (pattypans) or yellow crooknecks. One type she would probably not have known is our modern, ubiquitous zucchini, though vegetable marrows, which are similar, were advertised in American seed catalogs as early as mid-century.

Succotash—According to Webster's, the name derives from the Algonquin Narraganset word *msekwatas*, which referred to a mixture of corn and lima beans. The dish is certainly native to America, but by Mrs. Hill's day, recipes were usually adulterated with European touches—Mrs. Hill's wheat-flour thickening, for example, or butter, cream, and sometimes even tomatoes (which were not known to the upper regions of North America until after the European colonization). Notice that Mrs. Hill indicates it can be made from dried beans and corn.

Sugar—In Mrs. Hill's day, the finest cane sugar was still manufactured and sold in loaves, that is, in long, conical cakes. This is, of course, what was meant by "loaf" sugar. The cone was cut into lumps, which were then grated or broken up with a mortar and pestle. In all the recipes, granulated cane sugar is a fair one-to-one substitution.

Powdered sugar was loaf sugar ground fine with a mortar and pestle. Our modern confectioners' sugar will not answer as a substitute because it frequently contains cornstarch as an anti-caking and thickening agent. I suggest pulverizing granulated sugar with a mortar and pestle or food processor.

Mrs. Hill's brown sugar was actually only partially refined

and still contained some of the natural molasses. Modern brown sugar is actually fully refined white sugar with molasses added back to it. Demerara and turbinado sugar are closer to the type she used.

Sweetbreads—The thymus gland of young animals, the most common of which is veal. "Bread" here hearkens back to an ancient use of the word, meaning "morsel."

Sweet or *salad oil*—This meant olive oil. Surprisingly large quantities were imported into the South during the period. Often, it was called "Florence" oil in advertisements, but this was a generic name that meant the best quality oil. It did not mean that it was necessarily Tuscan (then considered the finest), though the inference was probably not lost on the vendors. Its expense prohibited its use in everyday cooking, and olive oil was reserved mainly for salads and apothecary uses. There were early attempts to grow olives in Carolina and Georgia, but the soil was too rich and the climate too severe. The experiment failed. Imagine what Southern cooking might have been like if those trees had survived and born fruit. Mrs. Hill seems to use more olive oil than other Southern writers, but her instinct when using it is invariably on the mark.

Syrup—For antebellum cooks, "syrup" was a clear, amber-colored cane syrup which was more refined and delicate than molasses. From the context, that was probably what Mrs. Hill intended. After the 1860s, however, "syrup" often meant a molasses-like substance made from sorghum, an African grass similar to sugarcane, though that type was usually specified as "sorghum syrup" or simply "sorghum." Sorghum and cane syrup are made the same way, but they are not at all the same. Sorghum became a popular and widely used substitute sweetener during the War Between the States, and it's possible that sorghum syrup was Mrs. Hill's intention, but given the context of the recipes where "syrup" is called for, that seems unlikely. Notice that she always makes a distinction between molasses and syrup, and, in at least one recipe, says that "syrup will not answer" for molasses.

Weights and measures—A perceptive and experienced cook will know better than to take Mrs. Hill's table of dry-measure/weight equivalents seriously. A pound of butter is two cups, half of what she indicates, as is a pound of modern granulated sugar. The table also points up the inconsistency of our American habit of measuring flour by volume instead of weight. Mrs. Randolph says that a quart of flour will weigh 1-¼ pounds (20 ounces); Mrs. Hill says it will weigh only a pound, because she sifts her flour before measuring it, whereas Mrs. Randolph did not. Unless you know this, the volume measure will lead to sure disaster. Interestingly, Mrs. Hill continued weighing her flour for cakes and was emphatic about the importance of doing so: "By all means be supplied with well-balanced scales, as in cake-making nothing can be done by guess-work, and *measuring is much less exact than weighing*" (p. 283; emphasis mine). For bread, it was a little less critical because, as Mrs. Hill (or any serious baker) knew, the final test for bread is the feel of the dough as it is kneaded.

Some historians claim that hen eggs are larger now than they once were, but notice that Mrs. Hill says that ten of them weigh a pound—no different from today. But the weight of eggs depends largely on their freshness. The same dozen eggs will weigh far less when they are a week old than they did when newly laid.

Gill, by the way, is pronounced with a soft "g," like the name "Jill."

For volume measures, the following notes are useful:

```
1 gallon  = 4 quarts (16 cups)
1 quart   = 2 pints (4 cups)
1 pint    = 16 fluid ounces (2 cups)
1 tumbler = ½ pint, 8 fluid ounces (1 standard cup)
1 gill    = ¼ pint, 4 fluid ounces (½ cup)
1 wineglass = 2 fluid ounces (¼ cup)
```

Notice that Mrs. Hill's tablespoon is identical to modern ones, and, in the text, three of her teaspoons work out to one tablespoon, just as they do now. Actually, spoon measures were more standard than popular historians would like us to believe and were essentially the same as modern ones, yet we regularly see Fanny Farmer given full credit for having standardized them.

Yeast—Mrs. Hill gives several recipes for making yeast, all of which would still work. For the less adventurous who prefer to use modern yeast, I recommend ¼ teaspoon of active dry yeast or a ½-ounce cake of compressed yeast, dissolved in the amount of tepid (room temperature) water indicated (e.g., a tumblerful of yeast would be ¼ teaspoon dissolved in a cup of water). Those measures are not printing mistakes; active dry yeast is very strong stuff, and ¼ teaspoon will answer for 2 tablespoons of Mrs. Hill's yeast. I also recommend the sponge method for all breadmaking, especially if you are using dry yeast.

In order to fully understand and use Mrs. Hill's bread recipes, start at the beginning and read the entire chapter. Many recipes are built on the methods of previous ones. This is also true for the cake chapter.

Yeast powder—In effect, baking powder. Mrs. Hill even gives the usual formula for single-acting baking powder (two parts cream of tartar to one part soda) as an alternative. Single doses of yeast powders were often sold wrapped in individual apothecary papers, much as were medicinal powders; hence recipes often read, "a paper of yeast powder." Notice that Mrs. Hill's dose is smaller than is usual today—a discretion we would do well to cultivate.

Though Mrs. Hill clearly made use of chemical leavens and obviously had nothing against them (see p. 283), for breads, she continued to prefer true yeast. She even suggested it for cornbread, which was by then very old-fashioned ("Risen Cornbread," no. 531, p. 232). Notice that chemical leaven isn't mentioned at all in the first twelve pages of the bread chapter; her recipe for bread "without Yeast" (no. 487, p. 221) is actually sourdough. The first recipe with baking powder is "Rice Flour Waffles, No. 4" (no. 495, p. 224), a breakfast bread. In most Southern households of the period, quick breads were for breakfast or tea and weren't generally thought suitable for proper dinner tables, where yeast bread continued to dominate.

APPENDIX I

Notes on the Edition Used

Mrs. Hill was first published by James O'Kane of New York in 1867 as *Housekeeping Made Easy: Mrs. Hill's New Family Receipt Book for the Kitchen*. The shortened—and more familiar title—*Mrs. Hill's New Cook Book* appeared on the cover and at the head of alternate pages. Some 1867 editions list James A. Gresham, New Orleans, as publisher in conjunction with O'Kane. The relationship between the two publishers is not clear.

Publication rights were later assumed by G. W. Carleton and Company, probably in 1870, when the copyright was renewed. With the Carleton editions, the lengthier title was dropped altogether. Carleton printed at least three subsequent editions* (1872, 1873, and 1875) before Mrs. Hill's death, and another appeared shortly after her death in 1878. The last known editions were printed by the G. W. Dillingham Company (1896 and 1898) with the slogan "The Great Southern Cook-Book!" above the title.

The introduction by the Rev. Ebenezer W. Warren suggests that Mrs. Hill may have originally had other intentions for the name of her book. The Rev. Warren refers to the book several times as *The Southern Practical Cookery and Receipt Book*. It was not unusual for book titles to change (sometimes the same book was unscrupulously reissued under a new title and advertised as a new work). For the present volume, we have elected to use that title.

Unfortunately, we were not able to find an 1867 O'Kane edition in good enough condition for reproduction. However, the

---

*The Carleton editions list a London publisher (S. Low, Son, and Co.), but I have not determined if this was merely an association or if there was, in fact, an English edition.

Carleton editions were printed using the same plates, and there were only minor changes in the text, all of which are obviously at Mrs. Hill's direction. This facsimile is taken from the 1872 printing.

Though I have not compared every recipe line for line, I have noted the following changes between the Carleton and the first O'Kane editions. "Hopping John" (no. 414, p. 196) was originally misspelled "Hoping John"—both in the text and in the index. Mrs. Hill corrected the spelling at the recipe, but overlooked the index (p. 421). I have found only one other place where the text is actually changed: the quantity of butter in the recipe for coconut cake (no. 708, p. 287) was changed from "one pound" to "½ pound." A defect in the printing of our copy accounts for the missing "to" a few lines later. It should read "Beat the butter and sugar *to* a cream."

There are a number of places where a single word or ingredient was removed from a recipe, leaving a blank in the plate. First, I note that the dark line in no. 113, "Hotch Potch," (p. 69) is not a change but a printing defect. It should read "tie together four or five sprigs. . . ." In recipe no. 190 (p. 110) "with half a tumbler of water" is deleted, leaving a gap in the text. Mrs. Hill knew what she wanted, and the recipe is all the better without the water. In no. 647, "Apple Dumplings (Stewed)" (p. 269), the sauce direction originally read "Make a sauce of nearly enough water to cover. . . ." In our edition, the word "nearly" has been removed. In no. 697, "Fruit Cake No. 1" (p. 285), the quantity of soda originally read "a light teaspoonful of soda." The word "light" was struck from our edition. In recipe no. 759, "Miss Matilda's Ginger Cakes" (p. 298), the words "the same of water" after "half a teacup of sour milk" were deleted. Again, Mrs. Hill knew what she wanted.

There may be other such minor changes. As I mentioned, I have not made a line-for-line comparison of the two editions, but these are the most obvious. Otherwise, the text is the same as the O'Kane edition, down to certain defects in the plates. There were, of course, no recipes added, and it is evident that Mrs. Hill did not fuss with the book very much after it was finished.

APPENDIX II

Notes on the Original Introduction and Its Author

The introduction to Mrs. Hill's book was written by the Rev. Ebenezer W. Warren, D.D. (1820–1893), a prominent Baptist minister who was then pastor of First Baptist Church, Macon. Dr. Warren and Mrs. Hill's brother, the Rev. John E. Dawson, D.D., were colleagues and had mutual interests. Both were involved, at various times, with Mercer University (a Baptist-operated school in Macon), and both had worked as editor of several Baptist publications. This is probably Dr. Warren's connection with Mrs. Hill, though I have not been able to verify it absolutely. Certainly they knew one another, but the acquaintance does not appear to have been an especially close one—at least, not until they were both living in Atlanta between 1871 and 1876, when Dr. Warren was pastor of First Baptist Church. Even so, that was well after the cookbook had been published.

The introduction is brief—just over six pages—and was probably not written until after the book had been sold to O'Kane. Certainly, it was written after the book itself and addresses cooking only peripherally. From the aspect of culinary history then, Dr. Warren's essay is, perhaps, of less value and interest than the recipes, with one exception, and that is his call for Southern men to bring their households' kitchens, well-pumps, and storehouses together under a common roof and attach them to the house.

These remarks point to a trend away from the old detached kitchens that was actually already beginning. The advent of the iron range helped hasten it along, since the range generated less direct heat than the open hearth and was certainly less of a fire hazard. Also, the drastic changes that were wrought on Southern households by the hardships of the War Between the States and by the Emancipation Proclamation made detached kitchens impractical. But impractical or not, for most Southerners such major renovations were not possible for many years after the war, especially in rural Georgia. Detached kitchens continued to be used and built. As late as the 1930s, many of them had survived virtually unchanged and were still in use.

It is important to remember that Dr. Warren and Mrs. Hill composed the foreword and "General Remarks" for the book when the war had literally just ended and the South was still under military rule. Though they had just emerged from four years of rationing, death, and innumerable hardships, they cannot have then known the hardships that Reconstruction and carpetbagger government were yet to impose. With the war and its terrific shortages more or less behind them, they clearly expected the economy to recover, but both recognized that their old way of life was gone forever and the world was not likely ever to be the same.

The young housewife to which these remarks were addressed faced a role very different from that of housewives in Mrs. Hill's heyday. Of course, the mythical opulence of the moonlight and magnolias South was, for most Southerners, just that—a myth, as Dr. Warren suggests in his remark that "the days of romance have passed, if they ever existed." In actual fact, only about 10 percent of the South's white population owned slaves at the onset of the War Between the States, and of that 10 percent, only a few could have been described as fabulously wealthy. Households without slaves were affected to some extent by emancipation and by postwar poverty, and not everyone in the South had lost everything. But the average housewife's role did change. The South's male population had literally been decimated, and by 1865, the majority of adult white women were either widows or aging spinsters with little prospect of marrying. A glance at the 1870 census tells a terrible story of the toll the war had taken. Not only were these women faced with expanded domestic duties; often they faced the burden of doing the work previously done by men.

Dr. Warren's comments about Mrs. Hill as author are interesting in several respects. In extolling Mrs. Hill's talent, he emphasizes her renown as a hostess and cook and extols her practical nature. He also indicates that everything relating to cookery in the book has been thoroughly tested by the author's own experience. Mrs. Hill bears this out herself in the recipes, which are full of asides as to her own findings, and preferences. When in a couple of instances she mentions a variation from another source that she has not tried, she states that fact frankly.

BIBLIOGRAPHY

A THOROUGH list of American cookbooks and books on American and English cookery would double the size of this volume. I have thus included only those works which I either quote or use directly in the notes and glossary. Some of the older books are available in facsimile, and I have noted those of which I was aware when this went to press.

Acton, Eliza. *Modern Cookery for Private Families.* London: Longman, Brown, Green and Longmans, 1845 and 1855. Miss Acton was a perceptive and excellent food writer, perhaps England's best until Elizabeth David. *Modern Cookery* was edited for American audiences by Mrs. Sarah J. Hale and published in Philadelphia in 1845. According to Karen Hess, there were nine American editions.

Aresty, Esther B. *The Delectable Past.* New York: Simon and Schuster, 1964. Mrs. Aresty's "translations" of the recipes are sometimes questionable, but her bibliography is instructive.

Atlanta and West End Directory for 1876. Atlanta: T. M. Haddock (Sunny South Steam Books), 1876.

Beard, James. *James Beard's American Cookery.* Boston: Little, Brown, 1972.

Beeton, Isabella. *Beeton's Book of Household Management.* London, 1861.

Bingham, Lillie, and Leana Bingham Castleberry. "Collected Recipes." Binghamwood, Talledega, Alabama. Unpublished, private collection. Binghamwood was the plantation homestead of a Pennsylvania family who settled in Talledega in the 1840s. No household notebook survives from the estate, though a collection of loose recipes has been preserved. Their mother's kitchen manual was Mrs. Hill's 1875 edition, which Mrs. Castleberry continued to use as a reference well into the 1960s.

Brown, Theresa C[lementine]. *Theresa C. Brown's Modern Domestic Cookery*. Charleston, S.C.: Edward Perry, Printer, 1871. Pendleton: Pendleton District Historical and Recreational Commission, 1985 (facsimile, paperback). An educated spinster from a prominent Anderson family, Miss Brown in many ways continued old-fashioned practice. Though she included recipes with chemical leavening, she protested vigorously against their overuse. Her yeast breads are classic and excellent. Both she and Mrs. Hill stood on the cusp of the technological revolution that so drastically changed American cookery during the latter part of the century. Also like Mrs. Hill, she was much influenced by Dr. Kitchiner and M. Soyer.

Bryan, Lettice. *The Kentucky Housewife*. Cincinnati: Shepard and Sterns, 1839. Columbia: University of South Carolina Press, 1991, facsimile, with introduction by Bill Neal. This excellent book is encyclopedic in its scope and provides a telling record of early nineteenth-century cookery. Unfortunately, nothing is known of Lettice Bryan beyond what appears to be her one effort at food writing.

Clark, Libby, Janet Cheatham Bell, and Jessica B. Harris. *The Black Family Reunion Cook Book: Recipes and Food Memories from the National Council of Negro Women* (Memphis: Tradery House, 1991.

Colquitt, Harriett Ross. *The Savannah Cook Book: A Collection of Old Fashioned Receipts from Colonial Kitchens*. New York: Farrar and Rinehart, 1933. Old-fashioned they certainly are, but one could hardly call them "colonial." Most of Mrs. Colquitt's sources are mid-nineteenth century and later. However, she does transcribe a number of the recipes verbatim.

Confederate Receipt Book. Richmond: West and Johnson, 1863. Athens: University of Georgia Press, 1960 (transcription). More interesting as a document of social rather than of culinary history, this book is primarily a collection of recipes for medicine, candles, beer, yeast, imitation coffee, and other goods in short supply during the War Between the States.

Couper, Frances. Collected Papers, ca. 1800–1820. Georgia Historical Society Collection, Savannah. Several very early recipes are scattered among the Frances Couper collection.

Crump, Nancy Carter. "Foodways of the Albermarle Region." *Journal of Early Southern Decorative Arts* 19, no. 1 (May 1993).

Darden, Norma Jean, and Carole Darden. *Spoonbread and Strawberry Wine*. New York: Fawcett Crest, 1978.

David, Elizabeth. *English Bread and Yeast Cookery*. Edited by Karen Hess. New York: Penguin, 1982. Worth having for Mrs. Hess's notes alone, this book is a lucid history of English baking.

———. *Spices, Salts and Aromatics in the English Kitchen: English Cooking Ancient and Modern*. Vol. 1. New York: Penguin, 1970.

Davidson, William H. *Pine Logs and Greek Revival*. Alexander City, Ala.: Outlook, 1964.

Dawson, Charles C. *A Collection of Family Records with Biographical Sketches and Other Memoranda of Various Families and Individuals Bearing the Name Dawson, or Allied to Families of That Name*. Albany, N.Y.: Joel Munsell, 1874.

DeBolt, Margaret Wayt, Emma Rylander Law, and Carter Olive. *Georgia Entertains*. Nashville: Rutledge Hill, 1988. Originally published as *Georgia Sampler Cookbook*. Norfolk, Va.: Donning, 1983.

Dull, Henrietta Stanley. *Southern Cooking*. Atlanta: Ruralist Press, 1928. Atlanta: Cherokee, 1989 (facsimile).

Egerton, John. *Southern Food*. New York: Alfred A. Knopf, 1987. One of the most comprehensive bibliographies of Southern cookbooks in print.

Evelyn, John. *Acetaria: A Discourse of Sallets*. London: B. Tooke, 1699. Brooklyn, N.Y.: Women's Auxiliary of the Brooklyn Botanic Gardens, 1937 (reprint of the first edition, not a facsimile).

The Ever Ready Cook Book. Savannah: Rector's Aid Society of St. John's Episcopal Church, n.d. (but before 1915).

Favorite Recipes from Savannah Homes, Many Before Unpublished: A Collection of Well Tested and Practical Recipes. Savannah: Ladies of the Bishop Beckwith Society, 1904.

Fox-Genovese, Elizabeth. *Within the Plantation Household: Black and White Women of the Old South*. Chapel Hill: University of North Carolina Press, 1988.

Garland, Sarah. *The Complete Book of Herbs and Spices*. New York: Viking, 1979.
Garmey, Jane. *Great British Cooking: A Well-Kept Secret*. New York: Random House, 1981.
Garrett, Franklin. *Atlanta and Environs: A Chronicle of Its People and Events*. Vol. 1. New York: Lewis Historical Publishing, 1954.
Gordon, Eleanor Kinzie (Mrs. William W.). Household Notebook, ca. 1858–1910. 2 vols. Collection of the Juliette Gordon Low Birthplace, Savannah, Ga. Mrs. Gordon, affectionately known as "Miss Nellie," was born and raised in Chicago. She married William Washington Gordon II of Savannah in 1858. The Gordons are better known as the parents of Juliette Gordon (Daisy) Low, the founder of the Girl Scouts of America. Mrs. Gordon recorded a number of her neighbors' and her black cook's recipes, and her book is one of the few records of the cooking of Leila (Mrs. Fred) Habersham, a Savannah matron who ran one of Georgia's first cooking schools.
Grover, Kathryn, ed. *Dining in America, 1850–1900*. Amherst: University of Massachusetts Press, 1987. A collection of essays from the Margaret Woodbury Strong Museum, Rochester, N.Y. The essays developed from a symposium that grew out of an exhibition on American dining, "Savory Suppers and Fashionable Feasts," conceived by Susan R. Williams, curator of the Strong Museum's collection of household accessories and tableware. Unfortunately, the South is practically ignored.
Grub, Alan. "House and Home in the Victorian South: The Cookbook as Guide," in *Joy and Sorrow: Women, Family, and Marriage in the Victorian South*, edited by Carol Blesser. New York: Oxford University Press, 1989.
Hanleiter's Atlanta City Directory for 1872. Atlanta: Plantation Publishing, 1872.
Hedrick, U. P., ed. *Sturtevant's Edible Plants of the World*. New York: Dover, 1972. Originally published as *Sturtevant's Notes on Edible Plants*. Albany: J. B. Lyon, 1919.
Hess, John L., and Karen Hess. *The Taste of America*. 3d ed. Co-

lumbia: University of South Carolina Press, 1989. Required reading for anyone who is serious about food.

Hess, Karen. "The American Loaf: A Historical View." *The Journal of Gastronomy* 3, no. 4 (Winter 1987/88).

———. *The Carolina Rice Kitchen: The African Connection*. Columbia: University of South Carolina Press, 1992. Includes in facsimile the *Carolina Rice Cook Book* (see Stoney, below). A thorough, beautifully written study of one of America's most distinctive cuisines.

———, ed. *Martha Washington's Booke of Cookery and Booke of Sweetmeats*. New York: Columbia University Press, 1981 (transcription with historical notes and "copious annotations"). The manuscript (ca. 1650–1690) was a Custis family heirloom which had belonged to Frances Parke Custis, mother of Daniel Custis, when it passed into Martha Washington's possession upon her marriage to that gentleman in 1749. Mrs. Washington gave it to her granddaughter, Eleanor Parke Custis Lewis, in 1799. The original author and transcription date are not known, but Mrs. Hess presents a persuasive argument for the theory that it predates Frances Parke Custis (who is popularly supposed to have written it) by two generations and may have been copied out in England. Required reading for any student of culinary history.

———, ed. *The Virginia House-wife*. Columbia, S.C.: University of South Carolina Press, 1984 (facsimile). See Randolph, below.

Hill, A[nnabella]. P[owell]. *The Life and Services of Rev. John E. Dawson, D.D.* Atlanta: J. J. Toon, 1872.

———. *Mrs. Hill's New Cook Book*. New York: James O'Kane, 1867. Some 1867 editions also list James A. Gresham, New Orleans, as publisher in conjunction with O'Kane. Editions after 1870 were done by Carleton Publishers, New York, which still held the publication rights when Mrs. Hill died in 1878. Posthumous editions put out by G. W. Dillingworth, Inc., turn up as late as 1898, "edited, expanded, and improved."

History of the Baptist Denomination in Georgia. Atlanta: Jas. P. Harrison for *The Christian Index*, 1881.

Johnson, Forrest Clark III. *Histories of LaGrange and Troup County, Georgia.* Vol. 3. LaGrange: Family Tree, 1987.

———. *Memories in Marble: Hill View and Hill View Annex Cemetaries, LaGrange, Georgia.* LaGrange: Southerland-St. Dunstan, 1993.

Kitchiner, William. *The Cook'e Oracle.* Edinburgh: Robert Cadell, 1831. Also referenced, 1855(?) edition. Originally published in London, 1817. There were a number of American editions of Dr. Kitchiner, beginning as early as 1822. *The Cook's Oracle* was widely used in the South and was very influential.

Krieger, Louis C. C. *The Mushroom Handbook.* New York: Dover, 1967.

Lane, Emma Rylander. *Some Good Things to Eat.* Clayton, Ala.: 1898. Clayton, Ala.: *The Clayton Record*, 1976 (transcription reprint, edited by Rebecca Parish Kelly). Mrs. Lane's little book is the one that gave the South its famous bourbon-laced Lane Cake, and it is largely on the reputation of this cake that the book survives.

Lane, Mills. *Savannah Revisited: A Pictorial History.* Athens: University of Georgia Press, 1969.

Leslie, Eliza. *Miss Leslie's New Cookery Book.* Philadelphia: T. B. Peterson and Brothers, 1857. Miss Leslie was one of the best and most prolific food writers of her day in America. Her books, especially *Directions for Cookery* (1837), were widely used and respected in the South, with good reason. *Miss Leslie's New Cookery Book* is the one Mrs. Hill is referring to in her gumbo recipe (no. 4, p. 21).

Lustig, Lillie S., ed., with S. Claire Sondheim and Sarah Russel. *The Southern Cook Book of Fine Old Recipes.* Asheville: Three Mountaineers, 1938.

Massey, Mary Elizabeth. *Ersatz in the Confederacy: Shortages and Substitutes on the Southern Homefront.* Columbia: University of South Carolina Press, 1952. Reprinted with introduction by Barbara L. Bellows, University of South Carolina Press, 1993.

McRee, Patsy. *The Kitchen and the Cotton Patch.* Anniston, Ala.: Higginbotham, 1982 (10th printing, originally published 1948).

Meldrim, Frances Casey (Mrs. Peter W.), and Sophie Meldrim

Shonnard. "Household Notebook." Savannah, Georgia, 1890–1915. Unpublished, private collection. Mrs. Meldrim's book was transcribed in the early 1970s, and the original manuscript was unfortunately lost. The wife of a prominent magistrate, Mrs. Meldrim was mistress of one of Savannah's most celebrated houses and a leader of society. Her notebook is an interesting look into the condition of Savannah cookery at the turn of the century.

Montagne, Prosper. *The New Larousse Gastronomique*. New York: Crown, 1977.

Neal, William F. *Bill Neal's Southern Cooking*. 2d ed. Chapel Hill: University of North Carolina Press, 1989.

———. *Biscuits, Spoonbread, and Sweet Potato Pie*. New York: Alfred A. Knopf, 1990.

Ortiz, Elizabeth Lambert. *The Complete Book of Caribbean Cooking*. New York: M. Evans, 1973. The parallels between Caribbean Creole cookery and Southern cooking are striking.

Parloa, Maria. *Miss Parloa's New Cook Book*. Boston: Estes and Lauriat, 1885 (1st edition, 1880). Principal of the Boston Cooking School, Miss Parloa was a prolific and popular food writer of the nineteenth century. Though not a Southerner, she produced books—among them, *The Appledore Cook Book* (1871)—that were widely used throughout America and were very influential in the second half of the nineteenth century.

The Picayune Creole Cook Book. 2d ed. New Orleans: Picayune, 1901. Also referenced, 5th (1928) edition. An interesting glimpse at *la cuisine Creole* at the turn of the century. The deterioration of cooking in general was slower in New Orleans than elsewhere. Mrs. Hill's influence can be felt, along with that of Mrs. Randolph, Sarah Rutledge, and others.

Ragsdale, B. D. *Story of Georgia Baptists*. Vol. 1. Atlanta: Foote and Davies Printers, 1932.

Randolph, Mary. *The Virginia House-wife*. Washington: Davis and Forth, 1824. Revised and enlarged editions, 1825 and 1828. Columbia: University of South Carolina Press, 1984 (facsimile, with historical and editorial notes by Karen Hess). The edition includes transcriptions of the recipes added by Mrs. Randolph in 1825 and 1828—the South's first and still best food writer.

Renwick, Ethel H. *Let's Try Real Food*. Grand Rapids: Zondervan, 1976. A devastating indictment of America's "agri-business" and the much-adulterated food produced by that industry.

Rudisill, Marie. *Sook's Cookbook*. Atlanta: Longstreet, 1989.

Rutledge, Sarah. *The Carolina Housewife, or House and Home*. Charleston, S.C.: W. R. Babcock, 1847. Also referenced, 2d (1851) and 3d (1855) editions; John Russel, publisher. Columbia: University of South Carolina Press, 1979 (facsimile, with introduction and historical notes by Anna Welles Rutledge). This book was very influential throughout the Southeast. Miss Rutledge was an excellent editor, and her eye for characteristic lowcountry cookery makes this book an invaluable record.

The Savannah Cook Book. Savannah: Ladies of Westminster Presbyterian Church, 1909. Not to be confused with the Colquitt book of 1933.

Shapiro, Laura. *Perfection Salad*. New York: Farrar, Straus and Giroux, 1986.

Sholes' Directory of the City of Atlanta, for 1877. Atlanta: A. E. Sholes, Sunny South Publishing House, 1877.

Simmons, Amelia. *American Cookery*. Hartford: Hudson and Goodwin, 1796. New York: Oxford University Press, 1958 (facsimile, with foreword by Mary Tolford Wilson). Reprinted as *The First American Cookbook*. New York: Dover, 1984. Though other English cookery books had been published in America during the eighteenth century, Miss Simmons's book is widely believed to be the first penned by an American. It is especially valuable in demonstrating the common Englishness of most early American cooking.

Smith, Clifford L. *History of Troup County*. Atlanta: Foote and Davies, 1933.

Smith, E[liza ?]. *The Compleat Housewife: or, Accomplsh'd Gentlewoman's Companion*. London: R. Ware, 1753. Originally published 1727. This book was circulated in colonial America and eventually printed in Williamsburg by William Parks (1742), the first known printing of a cookbook in America (essentially a reprint of the 5th London edition). It was very influential in the eighteenth century.

Stoney, Louisa Cheves Smythe, ed. *Carolina Rice Cook Book.* Charleston: Lucas-Richardson, 1901. Published in facsimile by the University of South Carolina Press as part of *The Carolina Rice Kitchen*, 1992 (see Hess, Karen).

Taylor, John Martin. *Hoppin' John's Lowcountry Cooking.* New York: Bantam, 1993. One of the best recent regional American cookbooks and *the* best lowcountry book since that of Miss Rutledge.

Telfair, Sarah Gibbons, and Mary Telfair. Household Notebook, ca. 1820–1875. Georgia Historical Society Collection, Savannah. The Telfairs were one of Savannah's oldest and most influential families. They were well-known for their philanthropic work, which included funding for the Georgia Historical Society headquarters building, a hospital for women, and Savannah's Telfair Academy for the Arts and Sciences. The manuscripts are full of typical antebellum recipes, and Mary Telfair provided an interesting and exhaustive list of "Nostrums that are used at fashionable entertainments."

Texas Cook Book. Houston: Ladies Association of First Presbyterian Church, 1883. *The First Texas Cook Book.* Austin: Eakin, 1986 (facsimile, with introduction by David Wade and Mary Faulk Kooch). Reportedly the first cookbook published in Texas, it contains little that one would recognize today as Texas cookery. There is a distinct eastern influence, and recipes from Mrs. Randolph, Mrs. Hill, and others appear.

Thornton, P[hineas]. *The Southern Gardener and Receipt-Book.* 2d ed. Newark: A. L. Dennis, 1845. (First published privately in Columbia, S.C., 1840.) Birmingham: Oxmoor House, 1984 (facsimile of the 1845 edition). The book was published under the name of a Georgia matron, Mary L. Edgeworth, in 1859, but according to Karen Hess, it was Thornton's book.

Townsend, Abbie (Mrs. Charles B. Lansing). "Recipe Book." Unpublished manuscript, signed "Miss Abbie Townsend" and dated July 28, 1849, Albany, New York.

Townsend, Abigail Spencer (Mrs. John). "Receipts." Unpublished manuscript, undated, but possibly as early as 1810. Mrs. Townsend died in 1849. The caligraphy is clearly an older style. These mother/daughter manuscripts are especially valuable in demonstrating how little American baking varied between North and South.

Tucker, Martha Goode. "Household Notebook." Rose Hill, Milledgeville, Georgia, ca, 1855–1868. *Housekeeping Diary of an Antebellum Lady*. Milledgeville: Milledgeville Town Committee of the National Society of the Colonial Dames of America in the State of Georgia, 1990 (transcription).

Tyree, Marion Cabell, ed. *Housekeeping in Old Virginia*. Louisville, Ky.: John P. Morton, 1879. Louisville, Ky.: Favorite Recipes Press, 1965 (facsimile). This was an early recipe collection-for-charity book, edited by a Virginia matron. Both Mrs. Randolph's and Mrs. Hill's recipes make an appearance.

Waring, Mary Joseph. *The Centennial Receipt Book*. Anonymously published as "by a Southern Lady" (in Charleston?), 1876. Copies are extremely rare. True roasting lingers here. There are recipes for rice breads, oysters, fish, and such local specialties as "atzjaar" pickle, but oddly enough, no pilaus.

Webster, Mrs. A. L. *The Improved Housewife*. 20th ed. Hartford: Ira Webster, 1854. Originally published 1838. Dozens of Mary Randolph's recipes appear verbatim. An interesting aspect is that the baking chapters differ little from Southern ones.

Williams, Susan R. *Savory Suppers and Fashionable Feasts: Dining in Victorian America*. New York: Pantheon, 1985. Ms. Williams—curator of the collection of household accessories and tableware at the Margaret Woodbury Strong Museum, Rochester, N.Y.—also launched a major exhibition under the same title as this volume (see Grover, above). Unfortunately, Southern cookbooks are completely ignored, but Ms. Williams is nonetheless informative.

Wilson, Mrs. Henry Lumpkin, ed. *Tested Recipe Cook Book*. Atlanta: Foote and Davies, 1895. *The Atlanta Exposition Cookbook*. Athens: University of Georgia Press, 1984 (facsimile, with introduction by Darlene R. Roth). A souvenir book from the Cotton States and International Exposition of 1895, compiled by the Board of Women Managers. The deterioration of Georgia cooking since Mrs. Hill is alarming.

Ye Old Time Salzburger Cook Book. Ebenezer, Ga.: Georgia Salzburger Society, n.d.

www.ingramcontent.com/pod-product-compliance
Lightning Source LLC
Chambersburg PA
CBHW021138160426
43194CB00007B/615